New Brethren in Flanders

New Brethren in Flanders

The Origins and Development of the
Evangelische Christengemeenten Vlaanderen,
1971–2008

THOMAS J. MARINELLO

☙PICKWICK *Publications* · Eugene, Oregon

NEW BRETHREN IN FLANDERS
The Origins and Development of the *Evangelische Christengemeenten Vlaanderen*, 1971–2008

Copyright © 2013 Thomas J. Marinello. All rights reserved. Except for brief quotations in critical publications or reviews, no part of this book may be reproduced in any manner without prior written permission from the publisher. Write: Permissions, Wipf and Stock Publishers, 199 W. 8th Ave., Suite 3, Eugene, OR 97401.

Unless otherwise indicated, all Scripture quotations are from The Holy Bible, English Standard Version® (ESV®), copyright © 2001 by Crossway, a publishing ministry of Good News Publishers. Used by permission. All rights reserved.

Pickwick Publications
An Imprint of Wipf and Stock Publishers
199 W. 8th Ave., Suite 3
Eugene, OR 97401

www.wipfandstock.com

ISBN 13: 978-1-62032-189-8

Cataloguing-in-Publication data:

Marinello, Thomas J.

New Brethren in Flanders : The origins and development of the *Evangelische Christengemeenten Vlaanderen*, 1971–2008 / Thomas J. Marinello.

xii + 290 pp. ; 23 cm. Includes bibliographical references and indexes.

ISBN 13: 978-1-62032-189-8

1. Evangelicalism—Belgium—History. 2. Christianity—Belgium—Flanders—20th century. 3. Christianity—Belgium—Flanders—21st century. I. Title.

BV2920 M27 2013

Manufactured in the U.S.A.

Contents

Acknowledgments | vii
Preface | ix
Abbreviations | x

1. Introduction | 1
2. Backgrounds to the Forming of the *Evangelische Christengemeenten Vlaanderen* | 14
3. Workers and Works of the *Evangelische Christengemeenten Vlaanderen* | 58
4. Ecclesiology of the *Evangelische Christengemeenten Vlaanderen* | 143
5. Conclusions | 228

Appendices

1. *Thirteen Essential Qualities for a Church Planter* | 253
2. *Fulltime Workers of the* Evangelische Christengemeenten Vlaanderen | 258
3. *Assemblies of the* Evangelische Christengemeenten Vlaanderen | 259
4. *Locations of the Assemblies of the* Evangelische Christengemeenten Vlaanderen | 261

Bibliography | 263
Index of Names | 287
Index of Places | 289

Acknowledgments

I EXPRESS MY SPECIAL gratitude to three women who prayed for me, stood beside me, and listened to me while this project unfolded itself: my wife, Patti; my mother, Helen; and my daughter, Laura.

I also express special gratitude to the two men whose insights and expertise were vital for the successful completion of this book: Professor Dr. Donald G. Tinder and Professor Dr. Patrick Nullens.

Finally, I gratefully acknowledge the one Triune God. He is the giver of life and all that we have, and the guarantor of all that we hope for. As the Apostle Paul wrote in his Epistle to the Ephesians 3:20–21 (ESV):

> [20]Now to him who is able to do far more abundantly than all that we ask or think, according to the power at work within us, [21]to him be glory in the church and in Christ Jesus throughout all generations, forever and ever. Amen.

Preface

The *Evangelische Christengemeenten Vlaanderen* (ECV) began in the early 1970s as a result of evangelistic church-planting efforts led by a group of Canadian, Christian Brethren missionaries. What began in Flanders as a series of evangelistic home Bible studies grew into a fully recognized denomination within a few decades of the first study. This result was surprising at a number of levels. First, the speed was remarkable at which the churches were planted. In just under twenty years, the ECV grew from one evangelistic home Bible study to over thirty local churches in Flanders, the Netherlands, and Germany. These local churches were composed almost entirely of newly converted, evangelical Christians. Second, the suddenness of the ECV's growth was matched by the equal suddenness of its cessation of growth. New converts became infrequent and new churches were not planted after the early 1990s. Third, none of the founders envisioned the move from an informal movement to a denominational organization recognized by the Belgian government. Their purpose was to form home Bible studies with the goal of planting autonomous, independent churches throughout Flanders or in southern Holland.

The story begins with the socio-religious setting into which the new churches were planted. This overview includes the secular socio-political milieu as well as the religious setting. Both the predominant religious setting and the historical Brethren setting are presented. Following this is a recounting of the history of the backgrounds and works of founders and shapers of the ECV. Once recounted, the origins and development of the ECV from 1971 to 2008 are recorded. After this rehearsal of the history of the ECV, an analysis is presented of the functional ecclesiology of the ECV as well as an evaluation of its essential ecclesiology. The concluding chapter explores some of the possible reasons for the sudden growth and equally sudden cessation of growth. Additionally, the final chapter suggests avenues for further research.

Abbreviations

ARPEE	*Administratieve Raad van de Protestants-Evangelische Eredienst*
BEZ	*Belgische Evangelische Zending*
BIB	*Bijbelinstituut België*
CEF	Child Evangelism Fellowship
CMML	Christian Missions in Many Lands
DAWN	Discipling a Whole Nation
EVSF	European Values Study Foundation
EAV	*Evangelische Alliantie Vlaanderen*
ECV	*Evangelische Christengemeenten Vlaanderen*
ETF	*Evangelische Theologische Faculteit*
EJV	*Evangelisch Jeugdverbond*
EOS	Echoes of Service
FS	*Federale Synode van Protestantse en Evangelische kerken in België*
GLO	Global Literature Outreach
IT	International Teams
LST	*Limburgse Studiedag Toerusting*
OM	Operation Mobilization
TCV	*Toerustingscentrum Christengemeenten Vlaanderen*
VEG	*Vrije Evangelische Gemeenten*

Abbreviations

VMC	Vision Ministries Canada
VPKB	*Verenigde Protestantse Kerken van België*
VVP	*Verbond van Vlaamse Pinkstergemeenten*
v.z.w.	*verenigingen zonder winstoogmerk*

1

Introduction

OVERVIEW OF THE STUDY AND ITS SETTING

The *Evangelische Christengemeenten Vlaanderen* (ECV) began as a result of evangelistic church-planting efforts led by a group of Canadian missionaries in the early 1970s. These missionaries were from one of the many distinct, historically Protestant, evangelical movements known as Brethren.[1] What began as a series of home-based, evangelistic Bible studies grew into a fully recognized denomination within a few decades of the first study. However, these simple introductory remarks present a challenge, as the question of defining this particular Brethren movement first must be addressed.

To study the history of people and churches associated with these Brethren is to grapple with a group that, though identifiable to insiders as well as outsiders, often makes the claim of being without either a linking structure or a distinctive name. Accordingly, one of the challenges of any work about this group is what to call this movement. These Brethren have been known in the English-speaking world under several different titles, including "Plymouth Brethren," "Christian Brethren," "Brethren," or simply "brethren" (lower case "b").[2] Further complicating this naming is the need to determine which part of

---

1. For a listing and summary of the various groups that have been called Brethren except for the *Unitas Fratrum*, cf. "Brethren," in *Religions of the World*, eds. Melton and Bauman, 1:168–69. For information on the *Unitas Fratrum*, cf. Norman, "Moravian Brethren," 676.

2. Lowercase "b" Brethren adherents usually are those who most strongly oppose any attempt to see the Brethren as an identifiable group within the larger body of Christ. Nonetheless, they usually are the most adamant as to which local church practices must

the movement one is discussing. The more conservative within this movement strongly would refuse any title, since to accept one is considered divisive and sectarian in nature. As one historian explained, "The refusal has a theological base in 1 Corinthians 3:3–6 where the Corinthian church was rebuked for manifesting a party spirit and dividing the body of Christ with each group taking a different name."[3] Accordingly, more conservative Brethren refer to themselves merely as Christians and to their gatherings as "assemblies of believers" or "the meetings."[4] To press further for some type of distinction is to be greeted with statements such as:

> I think he would be unwilling to identify himself in any way other than as a believer in the Lord Jesus Christ. I suspect that the term Plymouth Brethren would be just as offensive to him as it is to me and to most of us who simply want to be Christians, to follow the New Testament as best we can understand it, and to reject any denominational labels.[5]

In light of all the preceding, this book normally will use the title of Brethren.[6]

The central focus of this group, however named, traditionally has been the celebration of the Lord's Supper. It is the very heart of the Brethren gatherings. Indeed, to call one's gathering a part of this Brethren movement without the centrality of the Lord's Supper is to deny the history and practice of the Brethren since their inception in the early nineteenth century.[7] While the Brethren in the nineteenth and most of the twentieth century were noted for their biblically based preaching and their prodigious quan-

---

be kept in order to be considered in fellowship with the other "brethren" churches.

3. McLaren, "Triple Tradition: The Origin and Development of the Open Brethren in North America," vii.

4. Even the traditional Dutch and Flemish Brethren often use terms which translate the same: *vergadering van gelovigen*. Cf. http://www.vergadering.nu/ and associated links to local Brethren assemblies throughout the Netherlands and Flanders. Almost all the local assemblies will refer to themselves as *Vergadering van gelovigen te* (city name).

5. Stahr, personal letter to Ross McLaren, quoted in McLaren, "Triple Tradition," vii.

6. For a further summary history and definition of this particular group of Brethren, cf. Tinder, "Christian Brethren," 1:268–69.

7. Contrary to common Brethren thought in many circles, this movement cannot legitimately trace its roots back to the Apostolic church in an unbroken, non-Roman Catholic line. This idea of an unbroken line outside of Roman Catholicism is exemplified in Broadbent, *The Pilgrim Church*; cf. Beattie, *Brethren: The Story of a Great Recovery*. Instead, the movement should be understood as one of restoration, recovery, and/or renewal. Cf. Bruce, *In Retrospect: Remembrance of Things Past*; Coad, *A History of the Brethren Movement: Its Origins, its Worldwide Development and its Significance for the Present Day*; Neatby, *A History of the Plymouth Brethren*; Noel, *The History of the Brethren*, 2 vols.; Rowdon, *The Origins of the Brethren: 1825–1850*.

tity of written works related to the study of the Bible, the central meeting of the local church was that in which the celebration of the Lord's Supper took place. Although one author has argued that early in the history of the movement the "Bible reading" or Bible study was the "characteristic religious activity," nearly two hundred years of history and countless other studies aptly have demonstrated that people inside the movement and others observing from the outside see the celebration of the Lord's Supper and not the form of Bible study as the characteristic meeting.[8] In practice, this means that most Brethren assemblies historically have had a separate meeting during which the Lord's Supper is celebrated. This has been done as a corrective to what the Brethren see as a de-emphasis on the Lord's Supper which characterizes most Protestant churches, either through the shortness of time spent in its celebration or the infrequency of its celebration.[9]

An additional terminological matter is that the common Brethren designation for a local church congregation is "assembly." Brethren argue that this is a better translation of ἐκκλησία. This book, however, will use the terms "local church" and "assembly" interchangeably. Also, the term "the assemblies" is used to refer to a group of these local Brethren churches.[10]

A final area of definition is necessary for terms used throughout this book. As with many evangelical churches, a person who has undergone evangelical conversion is said to have been "saved" or "born again." Those who have not are "unsaved." The Brethren commonly identify a person who has been saved as a "believer." A person who has not undergone evangelical conversion would be called an "unbeliever." A fellow believer would be called a "brother" or a "sister." Note that the terms *believer*, *unbeliever*, *brother*, and *sister* are not unique to the Brethren, but are common among any number of evangelical, free church movements. Nonetheless, they note a clear demarcation concerning the relation of the person to the evangelical faith, as well as the family sense of those who have undergone evangelical conversion, whether or not the converted are part of a Brethren assembly.

The purpose of this study, then, is to examine one of the groups associated with this nineteenth-century movement as it exploded on the scene in the Dutch-speaking part of Belgium at the end of the twentieth century and the beginning of the twenty-first. As noted at the beginning, the ECV began as a result of evangelistic church-planting efforts led by a group of Canadian

---

8. Rowdon, *Who are the Brethren and Does It Matter?*, 33.

9. Fish, "Brethren Tradition or New Testament Truth?," 141.

10. When Pentecostal churches using similar terminology is meant, the full title for these types of churches will be used, such as Assemblies of God. Also, "Church" is used to refer to the universal body of Christ, and lower case "church" is used to refer to a local manifestation of the universal Church.

Brethren missionaries in the early 1970s. What began as a series of home-based, evangelistic Bible studies grew into a government-recognized denominational organization within a few decades of the first study. This result was surprising at a number of levels. First, the speed at which the churches were planted was remarkable. After decades of little or no growth among the Brethren in Flanders, twenty-six churches were planted in a nineteen year period.[11] Further, these churches were composed almost exclusively of new believers as opposed to the transfer growth of believers from other Protestant churches. Second, the suddenness of the growth of the ECV was matched with the equal suddenness of the cessation of growth. After a certain point, no new churches were planted and a few even ceased their operations. Third, while the purpose of the founders of what would become the ECV was to plant Bible studies "all over Belgium or in southern Holland in homes" with the goal of planting churches, none envisioned the move from an informal movement to a governmentally recognized denominational organization, even having some of its workers paid by the Belgian government.[12]

With these three points in mind, the task of this work is to record the origins and development of the *Evangelische Christengemeenten Vlaanderen* as it grew surprisingly rapidly, but then leveled off and developed in ways that its founders might not have expected. This book will offer some suggestions as to why these events happened as they did as it traces the history of this movement.

OVERVIEW OF THE PREVIOUS AND PRESENT RESEARCH OF THE ECV

As of this writing, no scholarly research has been done in any language which addresses the history of the *Evangelische Christengemeenten Vlaanderen* (ECV). In fact, no scholarly research of any kind has been done which considers the history of the Brethren in Flanders from its arrival in the late nineteenth century until modern times. That said, a number of short, popular-level pieces have been written which specifically treat the history of the ECV, though none have investigated the events behind the surprising, sudden growth and equally surprising and sudden stop of growth which has been associated with this part of the Brethren in Flanders nor its change into a regularly recognized denomination. These pieces include only a handful

---

11. One additional church was planted in the Netherlands, and "three" more in Germany. Cf. chapter 3, "Planting of the ECV," and its subsections for a more complete explanation.

12. R. Haverkamp, interview, 25 April 2003.

Introduction

of articles in Brethren missions magazines[13] at the popular level as well as a part of a chapter in a popular level, multivolume work as commissioned and published by the Brethren missions service agency in the United Kingdom, Echoes of Service.[14] While of some use, this multivolume work is noted more perhaps for its readability and somewhat hagiographical approach rather than its precision in historical matters.

Only one known study is available in which the ECV plays a significant role. This work was a Dutch-language master's thesis.[15] Additionally, the work of the ECV is mentioned, or at least its existence is noted in a few other MA theses as well.[16] No other scholarly studies at any level or in any language are known. At the popular level, a series of articles tracing the history of the ECV and its workers have been published in Dutch. Entitled, "Handelingen," these very short pieces appeared in *De Werkerskrant*, a magazine printed by the ECV themselves.

The timing of this study is significant as the principal figures in the founding of the ECV are aging, and some are in poor health. As will be noted below, oral history is a major part of this research since written records are scarce in some areas. Consequently, in another decade or less, much of the material will be beyond research as the people with the firsthand information die. Even during the time of this research, one of the early founders died.

SOURCES AND METHODS OF THE STUDY

Primary sources have been sought as the leading avenue of research. Interviews were conducted with the central participants in the founding and shaping of the ECV, as well as those outside the ECV who had close contact with these churches or their leadership. Those interviewed included the principal missionary church planters, the Flemish leadership, and people who had contact with the ECV but were never a part of the group. Interviews were conducted with appropriate people scattered across five countries on two continents to include friends, family, former co-workers, and elders in the Brethren assemblies in Canada who sent out the missionaries

---

13. *Missions*, the monthly news magazine of Christian Missions in Many Lands, the North American Brethren mission service agency; and *Echoes*, the monthly news magazine of Echoes of Service, the British Brethren service agency.

14. Tatford, *West European Evangel*.

15. van der Laan, "Gemeentestichtende Evangelisatie in Vlaanderen."

16. E.g.: Demaerel, "Tachtig jaar pinksterbeweging in Vlaanderen (1909–1989): Een historische onderzoek met korte theologische en sociologische analyse."

5

as "commended to the Lord's work" in Belgium.[17] In addition to these interviews, the personal journals, popular publications, newsletters, and Bible courses created by leaders and teachers inside the ECV were examined for pertinent information related to the origins and development of the ECV. Material was found beginning in 1990 which includes the official minutes of meetings, as well as long-range planning documents and statements of faith. All of the above were examined with an eye on the chronological and geographical spread of the ECV, as well as a comparison and contrast of these factors among the various churches within the ECV. Moreover, a comparison and contrast was noted between the groups which were either organically or theologically related to the ECV during these same years. For this comparative aspect, interviews with principal players in other groups as well as archival research was done. Particularly useful in the comparative aspects of this project, as well as providing insight into the relationship of the ECV with other evangelical groups, was the use of the archives of the *Belgische Evangelische Zending* (BEZ) and *Vrij Evangelische Gemeenten* (VEG) at the BEZ headquarters in Brussels.[18]

For describing the Brethren setting as well as the early years of the ECV, archival and family record research was done in Canada, England, the Netherlands, and Belgium. Archival material was used from *Uitgeverij Medema* in the Netherlands to help establish the earliest instances of Brethren assemblies in Flanders. This information was supported and enhanced through research in written family records of the founder of the first Brethren church in Flanders, Aloysius Van Der Smissen, as well as records from the French families whose Brethren church inspired the man who planted that first Brethren assembly in Flanders. Archival material also was used from the British Brethren missionary service agency, Echoes of Service, to establish the founding of one branch of the Brethren in Flanders in the early twentieth century. Finally, archival material was used from the Canadian Brethren missionary service agency, MSC Canada, especially with regard to the work of the two living founders of the ECV, as well as a third Canadian missionary whose work has played a critical part in the shaping of the ECV.[19]

The challenges inherent to this study relate to the relationship of the author to the subject, the methods of gathering much of the material,

---

17. Commendation is the commissioning or recognition of someone for full time Christian service by the local assembly. This can include service in the worker's home country or service as a missionary. Cf. Barlow, "Commendation by the Local Church," 28–37.

18. The BEZ and VEG archives now are part of the *Protestants-Evangelisch Archief- en Documentatiecentrum* (EVADOC). Cf. http://www.evadoc.be.

19. "MSC Canada" was called "Missionary Service Committee, Inc.," at the time of the arrival of the first Canadian Brethren missionaries. Cf. "How Did MSC Canada Begin?"

Introduction

and the recentness of the history under consideration. This author comes from the same church background as the founders of the ECV, and this has both advantages and challenges. The chief advantage is that the peculiarities and emphases of the Brethren which may not be understood by an outsider are known from personal experience, in addition to that which can be ascertained through normal academic study. This familiarity also has its challenges, however, as too much familiarity can cloud a researcher's perceptions. This author is served by a sister Brethren service organization to that which serves the two remaining founders of the ECV such that the author used to see them in social contexts about once a year or so at an annual conference. Also, given the likeable nature of the principal subjects, the challenge was to maintain an academic objectivity.

Hopefully, balance was provided by the many years of church life outside the Brethren due to geographical distance to the nearest Brethren assembly, as well as years of living and working around the world, such that Christian fellowship was sought and enjoyed with many different groups. Further, the study and professional teaching of Church history in a multicultural, multidenominational setting continually provides the author opportunities to observe and interact with many different church groupings. Thus, a clinical approach has been attempted here such as is commonly applied to any Christian work in history.

The challenges intrinsic to tracing a history through oral means are well known. Different people often have divergent perceptions of the same event, especially concerning an event's factual composition or importance. This is the same phenomenon encountered by any discipline which depends upon eyewitness accounts, such as trial law. Second, memories are not necessarily the most accurate way to record a history, especially a history about which the interviewed subject has a vested interest. Human nature can tend to gild what is remembered and discard what was unpleasant. Additionally, the tendency of wanting to speak well of others can cause the interviewee to relate all information in only the best light. This tendency is especially prevalent among committed, mature Christians such as made up most of the pool of those interviewed.

To try to ameliorate these challenges, multiple subjects were interviewed who were inside and outside the ECV, including those outside the Brethren altogether. In addition, factual recollections were checked as far as possible through the examination and analysis of personal journals, correspondence, popularly written magazine articles, and any sorts of official records which may be available. Some work was done as well with those who have left the ECV in less than happy circumstances.

This leads to the third area of challenge. The founders, shapers, and workers of the ECV had no idea that any academic research would be done about their work, either in their lifetime or after they died. As with many tightly focused, pragmatic Christian works, history is beyond the scope of the day-to-day needs of the ministry. While letters were written to supporters, systematic written records of the "hows" and "whys" of the work were not a prime consideration, especially in the first two decades. In later years, however, more strategizing was evident and is seen in the neatly typed minutes now kept of the gatherings of the ECV leadership, as well as in the multiyear plans and goals documents.

The challenges related to the recentness of the history under consideration are twofold. First, the a number of the principal members of the ministry under consideration still are living and active in the ECV. One of the serious challenges was how to do proper research without harming an ongoing work or creating a tension among those who have been interviewed. Thus, appraisals of the work can be a delicate matter, especially when the observations of the principals of their coworker or others concerning the principals' work is less than favorable. To have free access to people and material while not being a possible source of strife in an ongoing Christian work, this study uses anonymous sources in places. The material or person quoted or referenced is well known to the author and a careful record kept of the material, but the identity of the source sometimes is not listed.

This was done for a number of reasons. Some interviewees would not talk "on the record" about matters important to this research. When such a request was made, every effort was taken to verify the information. Further, the character and relationship of the source to the matter or person under discussion was examined closely to check for issues of bias. Also, while this book is a scholarly study, this author still is bound by New Testament commands for harmony. The requirements of this study do not negate this teaching, but neither do the New Testament commands need necessarily to lower the standards of research. Overall, anonymous sourcing has been kept to a minimum and should be considered an "exceptional event."[20] Thankfully, the founders and shapers of the ECV are as interested as this writer as to the reasons behind the way in which the ECV grew and stopped growing, so the main figures have been quite open. That said, this author erred on the side of caution

---

20. For a good discussion on guidelines for anonymous sources, cf. Thompkins, "Guidelines for Interviewing Confidential Sources: Who, When, and Why?" While this article is not a guideline for scholarly research, the ethical issues are the same.

Introduction

if a potential for trouble was perceived.[21] As one interviewee poignantly noted, "You are a man who walks around with a bag full of heads."[22]

Related to the challenge of not causing strife in an ongoing work has been the reluctance or refusal of some former members of the ECV to talk about their time working within this group. Especially difficult was the refusal of one of the Dutch men who was key to the early history. To work around this challenge, family members, coworkers, and friends were interviewed and written information was sought. Further, before this man disassociated himself from the ECV, he gave an interview for the previously noted Dutch master's thesis in which some of the issues pertinent to this study were addressed, as well as an interview for an informal article written for those inside the ECV.

The second challenge related to the recentness of the history under consideration is the long term and, in some instances, close relationship of the other evangelical organizations in Flanders with the ministries and members of the ECV. The challenge is that many Flemish readers already may have settled opinions on areas related to the matters at hand. This makes the presentation of the research somewhat of a daunting task, as this study's conclusions may be different than the perceptions of the readers whose opinions were formed through personal interaction at various places along the history of the ECV. Attempts have been made to include these important perceptions and experiences in the research by interviewing key people from *Evangelische Theologische Faculteit* (ETF) and the BEZ, for example, who had extensive firsthand knowledge of the ECV or its chief figures. Additionally, written studies, letters, and other material was considered.

Within the ECV itself, an important research emphasis was in the area of ecclesiology as a possible key to understanding the history of the ECV. An early challenge was to find a widely accepted model which compares the churches of the ECV with other similar works, as well as the early years of the ECV with the latter. A widely used model of the Church comes from its earliest days in the four traditional marks of the Church. The use of "one, holy, catholic, and apostolic" is something which can be applied across denominational boundaries as well as churches within a specific grouping over a select time frame. This is a new concept to apply to any group of Brethren churches since their inception in the early nineteenth century.

---

21. As with almost all interviews conducted by this author, audio recordings were made and have been archived. When a recording was not made of a short interview, such as a telephone conversation or remark over a meal, etc., notes were made as soon after the conversation as was possible. Most often, what was recorded in the notes was written mere minutes after hearing what was said.

22. Vleugels, interview, 14 August 2007.

While using the traditional four marks of the Church for the overall comparative aspects of the essential ecclesiology, the leadership style and common practices of the local church were examined more specifically in conjunction with the functional ecclesiology. In the areas of leadership style, a record of the training and methods of producing new leaders was considered. Common practices included an examination of the meetings before an assembly was formed, as well as the actual meetings of the local church. Additionally, the structural change was traced from a loose association of churches to what functioned as a government-recognized, formal denomination. While this has happened with other groups of Brethren assemblies throughout the world, the rapidity of this change in Flanders was especially noteworthy.

Methodologically, this work primarily is a historical piece. Thus, while it necessarily has some sociological elements, the purpose of this writing is not to exhaustively answer or even address all of the various sociological questions which could have been explored. That said, a number of scholars from various backgrounds have noted the close connection between a historical study and a sociological one. As one observed,

> History relates what men did at a certain time and place and under certain specific circumstances, however extensive the period and theatre of operations. Sociology takes up where history leaves off. Proceeding from the results of historical research, it seeks to find in them and through them the inner connections and causal laws of the actual historical process. Considerable historical data had to be amassed before sociology became possible.[23]

Another writer from a different perspective wrote,

> The sociologist of religion has the obligation to know doctrine, practice, and religious history—or to avail himself of the expertise of those who do have this knowledge and collaborate with them—before proceeding to applications of concepts leading to "explanations."[24]

Thus, the historical material uncovered and presented here is part of the information which the sociologist can use as he pursues his studies and makes his explanations. General sociological comments and observations are included in this study, and suggestions for further study are provided at the end.

---

23. Novak, "Sociology and Historical Materialism."

24. Swatos, "The Comparative Method and the Special Vocation of the Sociology of Religion," 109.

Introduction

The structure of this book is first to record the general setting of Flanders in the 1970s by noting the socio-economic, cultural, and general religious milieu. This is followed by an overview of the Brethren, and then by a specific accounting of the origins and early development of the various groups of Brethren present in Flanders when the founders arrived. Included in this overview is a record of the three ways in which the Lord's Supper was viewed by the various Brethren groups. These three ways were explained since the meeting devoted to the practice of this ordinance almost always has been the central focus of local churches associated with the Brethren throughout its history in any part of the world. The overview continues with a description and definition of the various types of local church leadership models found among the Brethren. This section ends with a definition and use of the four traditional marks of the Church as the means by which the Brethren in Flanders before the 1970s are evaluated. This model will be applied subsequently to the work of the ECV.

The narrative of the founding of the ECV begins with consideration of its most crucial actors, namely, the founders and the shapers. Extensive historical background and analysis of the traits and actions of the founders is presented first, as almost all the significant leaders and those who would fundamentally shape the ECV were converts of the founders. The backgrounds of two crucial shapers of the ECV then follows. Once the main personalities are presented, then the historical material is recorded chronologically according to the particular province in which the ECV assemblies were planted.

In the next section, the functional ecclesiology of the ECV is presented and explored. The four functional emphases are identified; the process of going from loose association to organized association, to organized denomination is rehearsed; the interaction of the ECV with other Christian groups is described; and then the four traditional marks of the Church are applied to the results.

The last section contains the reasons for the results of the work of the founders and shapers of the ECV as well as suggested areas for future research.

ACCOUNT OF PRESUPPOSITIONS HELD

A number of presuppositions are pertinent to this study. First, the work of the ECV has been seen by its participants and numerous other observers as an example of what revival scholars label as "the outpouring of God's grace" upon Flanders, especially in the early years of the movement. Within the Brethren in Flanders, and indeed within the evangelical churches in Flanders, little to no growth had been experienced in many decades. The only exception was some growth within the Pentecostal churches beginning about ten years before the first ECV Bible studies were formed. Even within the Pentecostal churches, however, their greater growth occurred within the same period as that of the ECV. Thus, this sudden growth by the ECV as measured by the numbers of conversions/baptisms and the ensuing church plants was most likely only part of a greater revival which occurred during the same period in Flanders. Beyond the scope of this study is the comparison of similar growth in other European countries. Accordingly, the working definition of revival for this study is best described as "not the employment of unusual or special means but rather the extraordinary degree of blessing attending the normal means of grace."[25] While certainly new methods were tried during the boom years of growth, these same methods or other attempted changes in approach had little effect across the evangelical spectrum in Flanders after the early 1990s. Further, the same men who were instrumental in the presentation of the evangelical faith, as well as the facilitators of the subsequent conversions of many Flemish to that faith, continued their work while seeing the new converts go from a flood in the 1970s and 1980s to a trickle in the 1990s and beyond. Thus, a specific acknowledgement of the work of the Holy Spirit in the boom years is indicated. That said, evangelical revival scholars note that the Holy Spirit uses men and their methods. This study, accordingly, will examine the men and their methods. These men began with nothing and subsequently oversaw the creation of a thriving denomination in Flanders in a very short period of time.[26]

Second, the planting of the ECV happened during a time of great change within Flanders. Religious, political, and economic forces created a time of great instability within the fabric of society during almost the first two decades of the work of the founders of the ECV. In the years ahead, when greater historical perspective is possible due to distance of time, future studies should consider whether an equally significant philosophical shift occurred such as is commonly associated with what is called postmodernism.

GENERAL INFORMATION

Research for this project came from a variety of types of sources in a number of languages. Material was gleaned not only in English, but also Dutch, French, German, and Italian. Unless otherwise indicated, all quotations from the non-English sources were translated by the writer.

25. Murray, *Revival and Revivalism*, 129.

26. For a general discussion of the challenges of the Christian historian's task, cf. Pelikan, "The Predicament of the Christian Historian."

Introduction

    The Dutch-language material included written sources from the nineteenth through the twenty-first centuries, a time period during which the Dutch language underwent significant changes. As a result, the Dutch used in quotations and in the titles of sources was recorded as it appeared in the sources, not necessarily in modern Dutch. Part of the reason for this is to assist other researchers, especially as more of these resources are digitized and made available for research via Internet portals, computerized records in archives, and other similar means of electronic retrieval which require exact search parameters.

2

Backgrounds to the Forming of the *Evangelische Christengemeenten Vlaanderen*

THE FLEMISH SITUATION IN THE 1970S

NO PROPER HISTORY OF the origins and development of the ECV can be done without a consideration of the locale. Studies which fail to take into account the canvas on which the history is painted may fail to provide important indicators as to the challenges facing the founders and shapers of the ECV, as well as its identity within the flow of history. To help provide this information, a summary follows of the milieu into which the ECV was planted. Both the socio-economic and cultural milieu and the general and specific religious milieu will be reviewed.

Socio-Economic and Cultural Milieu

Flanders was a very prosperous locale during the *Ancien Régime*, especially in areas such as Antwerp.[1] After the Napoleonic conquest, however, Flanders faced an uneven economic footing, one made even more unstable by

---

1. "The period before 1789, known as the '*Ancien Régime*,' was essentially different from the years which followed. This was not just a question of detail. It encompassed the whole structure of the state and society" (Carson, *Fair Face of Flanders*, 205). Such a monumental shift took place during the French Revolution that Belgium's history is divided starkly into pre-1789 and after.

Backgrounds to the Forming of the Evangelische Christengemeenten Vlaanderen

the linguistic burden and prejudice which came with the ascendancy of the French language throughout Belgium. Thus, a lasting result of the time of Belgium as a Napoleonic Consulate

> was the encouragement of a middle class strongly attached to French ideas and French culture, and not only in the parts . . . which had always been French speaking, but in Flanders as well . . . Anyone who wanted to get on in the new regime had to speak French. This was unfortunate in Flanders for it meant that there was no extensive Dutch speaking middle class.[2]

Language groups were created which were to comprise the upper and lower classes of Belgium; those who spoke only Dutch became associated with the lower classes. By the time the men who planted what would become the ECV came to Flanders in the early 1970s, Belgium as a whole had more Flemish than any other group; nevertheless, 84 percent of the officials in Brussels spoke French, as opposed to 16 percent who spoke Dutch. This is especially significant given that over 50 percent of the Belgian population spoke Dutch as its first language, as opposed to only a little over 33 percent who spoke French as their first language.[3] Discontent with this unequal state of affairs, a number of Flemish nationalistic political parties and cultural organizations were increasingly vocal as a general part of the unrest seen throughout Western Europe beginning in the 1960s; these nationalistic parties have continued to the present day. From 1968 onwards, the political parties of Belgium split into Dutch-speaking and French-speaking ones, thus ending nationwide political parties. Additionally, more radical political parties formed, parties committed to separating Flanders from Belgium. The formation of such parties included the *Vlaams Blok* in 1977.[4] To gain a sense of this vocal part of the political milieu, one only needs to read the response of *Vlaams Blok* Party Leader Frank Vanhecke, MEP, as he reacted to the Belgian Supreme Court's decision of 9 November 2004 which outlawed his party:

> Belgium, established in 1830 by French revolutionaries, is an artificial construct dominated by the Socialist Francophone minority in Wallonia. Our party's main objective is the secession of Flanders from Belgium.

---

2. Carson, *Fair Face of Flanders*, 209.

3. Petrovic, "Balkanization, bilingualism, and comparisons of language situations at home and abroad," 239; Johnstone, *Operation World*, 102.

4. "A party unlike any other."

> Today, our party has been killed, not by the electorate but by the judges. We will establish a new party. This one Belgium will not be able to bury; it will bury Belgium.[5]

As predicted, the *Vlaams Blok* was replaced by the *Vlaams Belang* and continues to aim at the voter who

> strives for the secession of Flanders from the artificial Belgian state. Our aim is to dissolve Belgium and establish an independent Flemish state. This state will be sovereign over the Dutch-speaking territory of Belgium and will include Brussels, which is the capital of Flanders but will have a separate linguistic status.[6]

The politics of Flanders was not the only thing changing during the time of the planting of the initial ECV churches. After the Second World War and until approximately 1973, Belgium as a whole experienced "a time of unprecedented national prosperity."[7] Flanders especially benefited from this time of explosive economic growth, though they still had a greater number of unemployed than those who lived in Wallonia until closer to the end of the twentieth century.[8] During this era after the Second World War, Flanders changed from a rural to an industrial economic base. The Organization of the Petroleum Exporting Countries (OPEC) oil embargo of 1973 ended this economic boom and brought to the fore underlying social and economic differences between Flanders and Wallonia. One of the results was that Belgium's traditionally open door to foreign workers was closed. Nevertheless, some of these foreign workers will be seen as part of those reached by the work of the ECV. Perhaps more pertinent to the study of the ECV is sociologist Renee C. Fox's observation:

> The economic crisis moved the public from a sense of abundance and open opportunities to a psychology of "blocked horizons," penury, and restrictions. Individualism and privatization seemed to gain momentum in Belgian life, while the cardinal Belgian value of "solidarity (solidariteit/solidarité)—with its shared Catholic, socialist, and humanist conceptions of common good, community, social welfare, and mutual aid—appeared to recede.[9]

---

5. Vanhecke, "Today we were executed, but we rise."
6. "The Manifesto of the Vlaams Belang."
7. Fox, *In the Belgian Château*, 11.
8. Carson, *Fair Face of Flanders*, 246, 250.
9. Fox, *In the Belgian Château*, 18.

Backgrounds to the Forming of the Evangelische Christengemeenten Vlaanderen

Could this monumental sociological shift and economic disruption have made the Flemish listeners more open to a Christianity outside the Roman Catholic Church? Historians have recorded in the American context the phenomenon of the rise of new religious groupings and "revivals" during a time of national unsettledness, noting that "it was a time of rapidly shifting social standards and institutional life."[10] Writing about the revivals of the Second Great Awakening in America, one such historian records, "Religion not only gave meaning to their lives and was a consolation in distress, it was the only relief from the daily hardship of work."[11] Another has suggested that

> the Awakening in its social aspects was an organizing process that helped to give meaning and direction to people suffering in various degrees from the social strains of a nation on the move into new political, economic and geographic areas.[12]

While the geographical expansion is missing in the Flemish context, certainly new political and economic realities were unfolding. Politically, the era of the founding of the ECV was the time when both Flemish and Wallonian nationalistic political parties became a very vocal, permanent part of the political landscape in Belgium. Thus, the same kinds of disruptions experienced in the early nineteenth century in Britain and the US concurrent with religious change were a part of the European context, specifically in Flanders during the 1970s and 1980s. These changes with the accompanying social and economic stresses left the Flemish more open to a fresh presentation of their Christianity.

General Religious Milieu

One faces an impossible situation trying to describe the cultural and religious setting which the founders of the ECV encountered without considering the Roman Catholic milieu into which these churches were planted, even though Belgium officially is a country with no state religion, According to generally accepted statistics, 89 percent of the Belgian population was of the Christian religion around the time that the founders of the ECV came to Belgium. Of this group of Christians, 85.8 percent were Roman Catholic (though only 30 percent were practicing), and a mere 1 percent were

---

10. Ahlstrom, *A Religious History of the American People*, 474ff. Cf. Hannah, "The Church in America," 32; Johnson, *A History of the American People*, 283–307.

11. Johnson, *A History of the American People*, 297.

12. Matthews, "The Second Great Awakening as an Organizing Process," 203.

Protestants.[13] Certainly during the early years of the ECV, the influence of the Roman Catholic church in Flemish society was waning, as was the Christian religion throughout Europe.[14] This de-Christianization of Europe during and after the 1960s cannot be noted too strongly, especially with respect to the Roman Catholic Church since this is of greatest importance to this study. In Flanders, for example, the level of traditional Roman Catholic observance had declined steeply. Those such as Flemish Jesuit Van Isacker understood this decline as a result of the pronouncements of the Second Vatican Council. He observed,

> In a half generation priests have succeeded in people unlearning kneeling. The kneelers have disappeared. In their place came the pew of emancipation . . . The church is a gathering hall where proper worship has been forgotten: in God's presence people should fall to the ground, speechless for the mystery.[15]

One prominent sociologist records "the 'massive exodus' of the faithful in the Western world, as well as the similar 'desertion of the priests,'" also noting the same phenomenon in other predominantly Roman Catholic areas, such as Quebec.[16] Others note a more general secularization among the Flemish populace.[17] Historically, social mobility in Flanders had been tied to both the speaking of French and attending church services of the Roman Catholic Church. Writing about the period from 1967–1973, the years just prior to the coming of the ECV's founding missionaries from Canada, an article in *SA. Sociological Analysis* stated,

> Studies done in the late 1970s and early 1980s revealed that church involvement . . . was statistically no longer significantly related to social class . . . In this very short period the Catholic Church lost a relatively large part of the upper and upper-middle classes, resulting in low attendance in all social classes . . . And although in 1973 relatively more Flemings were still attending church on weekends than the Walloons and inhabitants of the

---

13. Dobbelaere and Voyé, "From Pillar to Postmodernity," S3; Johnstone, *Operation World*, 102.

14. For a thoughtful description and appraisal of this Europe-wide move to "post-Christendom" (as opposed to post-Christian or postmodern), especially in an Anglican context in England, cf. S. Murray, *Post-Christendom: Church and Mission in a Strange New World*.

15. van Isacker, *Ontwijding*, 9.

16. Dobbelaere, "Trends," 26–27.

17. Ibid., 23ff.

Backgrounds to the Forming of the Evangelische Christengemeenten Vlaanderen

> Brussels region . . . , in those six years the decline was twice as dramatic in Flanders as it was in the two other Belgian regions.[18]

These trends might reflect the effects of the Second Vatican Council's pronouncements, or the change in requirements for social mobility, or other causes, but what is undisputed is the decline in Roman Catholic practices in Flanders beginning just before and accelerating during the time of the planting and forming of the ECV. From 1970 to 2000, baptisms of Roman Catholic children dropped from 95 percent to 65 percent, and Roman Catholic marriages dropped from 90 percent to 50 percent. The decline in both of these rituals not only increased, but was accelerating.[19] In addition, anticlericalism became more vocal, and the younger population was uneasy about ecclesiastical authority. These younger Roman Catholics especially were openly rebellious against the Roman Catholic Church's positions on the status and role of women, birth control, abortion, and sexuality in general. Additionally, there was a steep rise in divorce and a growing cultural acceptance of cohabitation without marriage.[20] While the Roman Catholic Church had experienced a "religious revival" after the Second World War, the Roman Catholic Church's numbers waned in Belgium and throughout Europe from the early 1960s onward. As Episcopal Bishop John Shelby Spong noted during a visit to Belgium at the beginning of the twenty-first century,

> The future of Christianity in Belgium looks grim.
>
> When I enquired who were the young rising theological stars, I received only blank stares. The Bultmanns, Barths, Brunners, Pannebergs, Tillichs, and Bonhoeffers of the previous century are no more. Even the troublers of Rome like Küng and Schillebeekx, now in their 70s and 80s, appear to have no successors.
>
> Belgium as my window onto the continent did not present me with a pretty vision of Christianity's future. The choice between conservative xenophobic religion on one side and fearful liberal paralysis on the other side is sterile. Neither side shows signs of life.[21]

---

18. Dobbelaere and Voyé, "From Pillar to Postmodernity," S3.

19. Dobbelaere, "Trends," 13ff. Funerals of Roman Catholic nature declined only slightly from 1970 to 2000, but this is to be expected if the sweeping changes were generational in nature as statistics record. Even the decline in these types of funerals accelerated, however, as the older generations passed away.

20. Fox, *In the Belgian Château*, 15.

21. Spong, "A Bishop Speaks."

New Brethren in Flanders

Earlier, Spong had noted the steady decline of candidates for the priesthood in Belgium which began in the 1960s and 70s. Additionally, he noted the accusations and counter accusations of the conservative and liberal parts of the Roman Catholic Church in Belgium as they tried to diagnose the reasons for the steady decline of candidate priests and practicing Roman Catholics. The conservatives blamed liberal faithlessness as the cause of the decline, and the liberals blamed the conservatives' failure to adapt to "new knowledge, new insights, [and] new truth."[22] The founding years of the ECV were not as bleak as the very late twentieth and early twenty-first centuries for the Belgium Roman Catholic Church; nevertheless, the unquestioning hold of this church over society was weakening. Even so, the waning but still strong hold of the traditions of the Roman Catholic Church clearly was observed and encountered by the founders of the ECV among the population as a whole. Writing about the early times of the era under consideration, respected sociologist Renée Fox wrote:

> A majority of Belgians still baptize their infants, send their children to Catholic schools, belong to Catholic sick funds and trade unions, and are both married and buried in the church . . . Belgium has no state religion . . . [b]ut it is the metaculture of Belgium—its ethos—that makes it a Catholic society . . . Many of the symbols and images, values and beliefs that pervade the economic and political, domestic and everyday life of the country, as well as its art and literature, have deep roots in the cultural traditions and cosmic outlook of Belgian Catholicism.[23]

She goes on to note that even institutionalized and supposedly ideologically antithetical organizations such as Belgian Free Thought and Free Masonry were shaped by the Roman Catholic Church in their manner of organization and practices![24] During her sabbatical of 1977–78 in the midst of her thirty years of study of Belgium's culture and society, her fellow academics and various societal elites tried to impress upon this sociologist that religion was no longer important in Belgium. In marked contrast, this religious and national outsider found that indeed Roman Catholicism was still an integral part of the culture and society, though in an increasingly complex relationship.[25] While society may have been experiencing a de-Christianization as a whole, the symbols of the past were very much in evidence and had their influence on many day-to-day customs. Alternatives to Roman Catholicism

22. Spong, "A Bishop Speaks."
23. Fox, *In the Belgian Château*, 16.
24. Ibid.
25. Ibid., 132.

Backgrounds to the Forming of the Evangelische Christengemeenten Vlaanderen

were shunned in the early years of the work of the founders of the ECV, even as local priests and the bishops did all they could to try to keep their flock faithful to the Roman Catholic Church. Still, a very small Protestant presence existed in Flanders in the early 1970s, some of which dated back to the previous century.

In the early 1970s, the Protestant churches represented in Flanders were various mainline, free, and Pentecostal gatherings. The mainline churches primarily included branches of the historic Reformed church and the Methodist church under three groupings. These three groupings would unite in 1978 to form the *Verenigde Protestantse Kerk in België* (VPKB).[26] Non-Pentecostal free church groupings in Flanders included sixteen churches which were a result of the work of the *Belgische Evangelische Zending* (BEZ), planted from 1919 until 1944, as well as an even smaller number of Plymouth Brethren assemblies.[27] Twenty-one Pentecostal churches existed in Flanders when the founders of the ECV arrived. Note that the Pentecostal churches doubled in numbers from the late 1950s until 1970.[28] These churches included indigenous works and those resulting from the missions efforts of both American and Scandinavian Pentecostal denominations, as well as descendants of immigrant churches which had served the Italian, Chinese, and various African peoples.[29]

In spite of all the previously mentioned Protestant groupings, when the founders of the ECV arrived in the early 1970s, a weakening but still predominant Roman Catholic Church characterized Christianity in Flanders. Into this strongly Roman Catholic setting came the founders of the ECV. Thus, for the Flemish to make the choice to become part of the churches planted by the founders of the ECV meant that the participants had to leave behind various communities, such as their social groups, in addition to their church.[30] Since the founders of the ECV came from a traditionally Protestant grouping, these new churches immediately began as ones which were part of one percent of the overall population. Within this small group of Protestants, the Plymouth Brethren are catalogued. The extant Brethren assemblies in 1972 were split into two groups commonly known as Exclusive

---

26. *Verenigde Protestantse Kerk in België* in Flanders and *l'Église Protestante Unie de Belgique* in Wallonia. Dhooghe, "Het Belgische Protestantisme," 344ff.

27. "Chronologische indeling van het Gemeentestichtend werk van de B.E.Z.," 1. A similar number of BEZ churches existed in Wallonia, with only a few more planted from 1944 until the founders of the ECV arrived in Flanders in 1972.

28. Demaerel, "Tachtig jaar pinksterbeweging in Vlaanderen (1909–1989)," 374.

29. For a complete history of these churches and their locations, cf. Demaerel, "Tachtig jaar pinksterbeweging in Vlaanderen (1909–1989)."

30. Boersema, "De Evangelische Beweging in de Samenleving," 309.

and Open Brethren assemblies, as will be explained below. From where did these Brethren churches come, and how did this handful come to have three identifiable groupings within the major divisions of Exclusive and Open?

GENERAL BRETHREN BACKGROUNDS AND THE BRETHREN IN FLANDERS UP TO THE 1970S

A premise of this book is that the churches of the ECV were a new type of Brethren previously unknown in Flanders. Accordingly, who are the Brethren, and what characterized the type of Brethren which preceded the coming of the founders of the ECV?

The immediate cause of the formation of the gatherings which would become the Brethren came as the result of reactions to the prevailing ecclesial attitudes and practices in the early nineteenth century United Kingdom. At the beginnings of the Brethren movement in Britain and Ireland, the walls between various denominations were quite high. While certainly ecumenical works of charity were engaged in during the week, this ecumenicism stopped on Sunday morning when corporate services were scheduled.[31] Not only were the usual ecclesiastical barriers present between the Roman Catholic Church, the various Eastern Orthodox churches, and the masses of churches from a Protestant background, but within Protestantism each denomination kept its distance from other Protestant churches, both locally and nationally. In fact, most Protestant communicants were prohibited from partaking of communion in other than their own local church and, in some cases, even from attending another's local church once a measure of residency had been established.[32] One of the early Brethren was excommunicated for his refusal to have "special membership with one particular congregation" and his conviction from Scripture that he need not have a "special membership" to partake of the Lord's Supper since "all true believers are members of the body of Christ."[33]

Even tougher to accept was the realization that if those headed out to missionary work were not ordained, they could not even celebrate the Lord's Supper with those whom they led to Christ.[34] Thus, this divisive factionalism and denominationalism caused considerable consternation among those who would later be identified as the early Brethren. This is not to say that they believed that no restrictions for fellowship should exist; the creeping

31. Rowdon, *Origins*, 7ff.
32. Ibid., 37.
33. Beattie, *Brethren: The Story of a Great Recovery*, 12.
34. West, "Worship and the Lord's Supper," 53.

Backgrounds to the Forming of the Evangelische Christengemeenten Vlaanderen

universalism of the Church of England was rejected by the early Brethren. In point of fact, the Brethren believed that "the Church of England was too broad in its basis and the dissenting churches too narrow."[35]

Further complicating issues and adding to their burden was the stark division between the clergy and the laity. Welcome participation and a thoughtful, questioning review by those in the pew such as is common in many churches in the present age was most unwelcome by those in the pulpits of the early nineteenth century United Kingdom. The public teaching of the Bible, pastoral care, and most assuredly administration of the ordinances all were the sole domain of the ordained ministers. Thus, only the ordained minister could administer the ordinances of baptism and the Lord's Supper.

Facing this dilemma, a number of men from both clerical and nonclerical backgrounds came to the conclusion that to gather in groups other than in a nonsectarian gathering in the name of the Lord Jesus Christ alone was to deny the teaching of Scripture.[36] To them, names such as Baptist, Anglican, Lutheran, and even Brethren or Plymouth Brethren emphasized what made the members of the body of Christ stand apart from one another. One of the earliest leaders and men of noteworthy theological acumen was John Nelson Darby. As Darby's modern biographer, Max S. Weremchuk, notes of Darby's early convictions and that of other Brethren,

> Believers should simply gather to the Lord's name alone (not around a teacher or creed) on the basis of the unity of the body of Christ (1 Corinthians 10:17) with those who call upon the Lord out of a pure heart (2 Timothy 2:22).[37]

In their thinking, the Bible's doctrine of the Church's unity was based upon the believer's identity as "in Christ." This belief had as one of its practical results the unhindered association of believers in local churches such that any and all believers who were not "living in sin" were welcome to attend and remember the death, burial, resurrection, and imminent return of the Lord Jesus in the celebration of the Lord's Supper. Further, the Brethren maintained and still practice a Lord's Supper at which no official of the church needs to be present in order "to remember the Lord," their term for the celebration of the Lord's Supper.[38] Titles for this gathered body of believers were couched in terms found in Scripture. One of the early noteworthy Brethren wrote,

---

35. Reid, *F. W. Grant*, 3.

36. The Brethren were not the only group in the early 19th century to come to this understanding. For a summary of this impetus, cf. Callahan, *Primitivist Piety*, 67–68.

37. Weremchuk, *John Nelson Darby*, 82.

38. Tinder, "The Brethren Movement in the World Today," 14.

> The titles given to the Church in Scripture bespeak heavenly unity, such as the body, the vine, the temple of God, a holy nation, a chosen generation, a royal priesthood . . . but the names which have been invented by men are names of sects and declare our shame.[39]

Over a century later, another well-known Brethren author wrote,

> We shall search our Bibles in vain to discover the "Baptist" denomination, or the "Presbyterian" or the "Episcopal" or the "Congregational" or the "Methodist," or a host of others we might name. . . .
>
> When we open the pages of the New Testament, we find the people of God are called "Christians," "disciples," "saints," "believers," "brethren," etc.[40]

With this background and understanding, the Brethren before the ECV came to Flanders mainly as two somewhat distinct groups. Without a great deal of elaboration, the two groups generally can be categorized as those which resulted from the split within the Brethren in 1848.[41] As with many ecclesiological issues within the Brethren, this split ultimately centered on practices related to who should be allowed to take part in the Lord's Supper, the central meeting of the Brethren. One modern Brethren author has well noted that a subtle but profound shift in the thinking of some happened such that local gathering of Brethren assembled themselves around "the 'truth of remembering the Lord' rather than around the person and worth of the Lord Jesus."[42] Some twelve years before the split of 1848, the first Brethren missionary, Anthony Norris Groves, wrote in a letter to Darby, "I feel some little flocks are fast tending, if they have not already attained it, making *light* not *life* the measure of communion."[43] This *light* versus *life* argument provides a very useful distinction between the two Brethren groups, though even these lines can blur in Brethren history.

The first group in Flanders would have come from the Exclusive Brethren, those who valued certain understandings above all else—the *light* grouping—and the second would have come from the Open Brethren, those who were more inclined to value salvation alone above certain cherished

---

39. Quoted in Peterson and Strauch, *Agape Leadership*, 32.

40. Gibbs, *Scriptural Principles of Gathering*, 12.

41. For a concise review of this matter and the ensuing results, cf. Shuff, "Open to Closed," 10–23.

42. Smith, *Roots, Renewal, and the Brethren*, 88.

43. Anthony Norris Groves, letter to John Nelson Darby, 10 March 1836, in Coad, *A History of the Brethren Movement*, 288.

Backgrounds to the Forming of the Evangelische Christengemeenten Vlaanderen

practices and traditions—the *life* grouping. Eventually, a worldwide disruption within the Exclusive category came to be known among the Exclusives in Flanders such that two groups of Exclusives were present. These were the Continental Brethren, known as the Lowes in England and Ireland, and another group called the Tunbridge Wells, so named after the location of a Brethren dispute in England.[44] William F. Knapp explains some of the overall picture by his 1936 sketch, *A Chart of the Seven Sections of the Brethren*, in volume 2 of Napoleon Noel's work tracing the history of the Exclusive Brethren. The titling of the sections of this chart is very instructive as to the view of the Exclusive Brethren versus others who were not of their camp.[45]

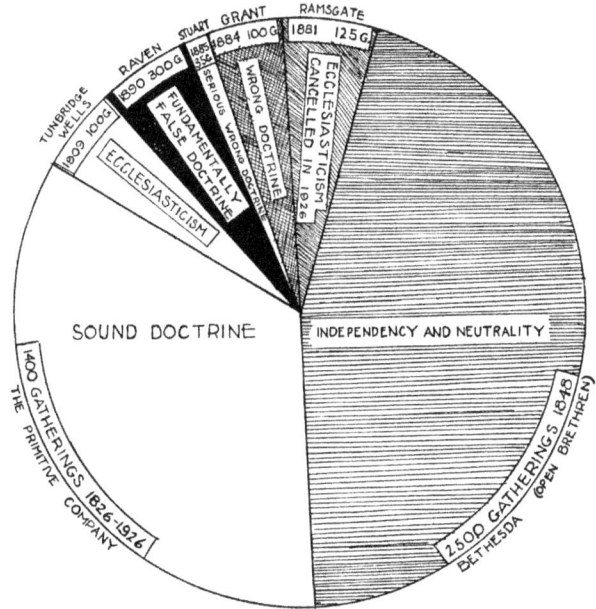

In summary, the common beginnings of both groups are such that the same two ingredients, broadly speaking, could be noted as characterizing their beliefs: "their negative characterization of contemporary Christianity

---

44. "Brethren III, called the 'Continental Brethren' because of the relative numerical strength of their European counterparts, came into being when the Brethren who had rejected Grant divided among themselves in 1890 over the ministry of a British leader, F. E. Raven (died 1905). Brethren III rejected Raven." Piepkorn, "Plymouth Brethren (Christian Brethren)," 165–71. The Continental Brethren also are called Kelly-Continental in the English-speaking world. For more information on the history of this grouping, cf. Coad, *A History of the Brethren Movement*; Neatby, *A History of the Plymouth Brethren*; Noel, *The History of the Brethren*; Rowdon, *The Origins of the Brethren*; Ouweneel, *Het verhaal van de "Broeders."*

45. Knapp, "A Chart of the Seven Sections of the Brethren," in Noel, *The History of the Brethren*, 2:734.

in all its forms, and their positive affirmation of apostolic or New Testament Christianity."[46] Further, one study accurately noted,

> The positive factors which united the early Brethren can be arranged into five general categories: the norm of the apostolic church; the soteriological principle of unity; divine initiative in reviving concern for primitive ecclesial practices; advocacy of primitive simplicity in meetings of worship; and the authority of spiritual rather than academic or ecclesial qualifications for ministry in the church.[47]

This general negative and positive characterization of the identity of the early Brethren also was seen in the work done by the founders of the ECV.

Exclusive Brethren in Flanders

The roots of the Exclusive Brethren throughout Belgium can be traced to Darbyist workers from the United Kingdom, Germany, the Netherlands, and France. Within the specific region of Flanders, groundwork for the planting of Brethren assemblies was accomplished by Dutch evangelist Hermanus Cornelius (H. C.) Voorhoeve (1837–1901), the man who was to be the editor of a Brethren devotional magazine, *Bode des Heils Christus*, for forty-five years.[48] Voorhoeve's work in Belgium was conducted sometime after 1858, but certainly some of this work was conducted after the first Pentecost Weekend Conference (*pinksterconferentie*) held in Steinseifersdorf (Germany) in 1861 when he was only twenty-four.[49]

While a number of efforts for evangelism are recorded, as will be enumerated below, no record is found of a lasting local church as a direct result of Voorhoeve's work. Nevertheless, a family history records that the first Dutch-speaking congregation established in Belgium was a result of contact with an unnamed Exclusive Brethren colporteur from the Netherlands. The assembly was established sometime between 1870 and 1875 in the region of Brussels.[50] This is the same assembly mentioned in an announcement of newly listed assemblies dated 1876 in the Dutch magazine published by Voorhoeve which told of Christian work outside the Netherlands.[51] Guil-

---

46. Callahan, *Primitivist Piety*, 33.
47. Ibid.
48. Ouweneel, *Het verhaal van de "Broeders,"* 135.
49. Ouweneel, *"Gij zijt allen broeders,"* 213.
50. Hanssens, 13 December 2005.
51. *Mededeelingen omtrent het werk Gods in onze dagen*, vol 13. Cf. also Hanssens, 24 June 2006.

laume and Jean-Baptiste Hanssens received a Gospel tract from this colporteur while they were working their fields in Zaventem. They subsequently were converted after hearing gospel messages preached by Dutch Brethren in Duden Park in Saint-Gilles.[52]

At first, this assembly met in the back room of a café in the town square of Brussels, but objections from the Dutch Brethren to the Flemish practice of drinking a courtesy glass of beer after the meeting caused the assembly to find a new place of meeting where this practice was not necessary.[53] As has been a common routine among the Brethren, the assembly relocated into the house of one of the "leading brothers," Guillaume Hanssens.[54] This assembly in Brussels initially was Dutch-speaking, but became bilingual Dutch and French, and finally only French-speaking as a result of the demographic changes in this part of Belgium in the late nineteenth century. Swiss and French nationals became part of this meeting, as well as people from Wallonia. Specifically, the arrival of the Wallonian Brethren in the 1890s, and the arrival of a Swiss wholesaler of clocks from Paris named Marc Tapernoux (1868–1937) around the same time, furthered the transition to a French-speaking assembly.

Tapernoux's family was originally of French Huguenot origin in the Rhone Valley. Persecution forced them to emigrate to Switzerland at the end of the seventeenth century. While living in Vevey, a city on Lake Geneva, they were converted as a result of the evangelistic efforts of the early Brethren sometime between 1830–1840.[55] From this time onward, the family was among the Brethren.

Marc Tapernoux was in fellowship at the Paris-Faubourg-Saint-Honoré assembly where he started this assembly's first Sunday School prior to moving to Brussels.[56] Tapernoux became one of the main leaders of this assembly in Brussels, and a specially remodeled part of his house became the permanent location of the congregation in 1907. His daughter, Gabrielle, eventually married Jacques Hanssens, Guillaume's son. By not later than

52. Laügt, *Région de Bruxelles*.

53. While the exact reason for this objection is unknown, most likely the Dutch brothers objected to commerce of any kind on a Sunday given that the Dutch were not abstainers from alcohol. The opposition by many Dutchmen to Sunday commerce continues into the twenty-first century. Cf. den Tek, "Dutch Sunday shopping—the debate continues."

54. Laügt, *Région de Bruxelles*.

55. Tatford notes the presence of both J. N. Darby and Anthony Norris Groves in this region during this timeframe. Tatford, *Western Europe Evangel*, 456. Cf. Groves, *Memoir*, 253.

56. Hanssens, "Re: Brussels assembly," 24 June 2006.

1907, all the main meetings of the assembly were conducted in French.[57] Nevertheless, at least a Thursday evening Dutch-language Bible study continued until the 1950s.[58] Connections between this assembly in Brussels and the other Exclusive assemblies in Flanders would be maintained until at least the 1950s via the annual two-day Bible conference each November.[59]

This initially Dutch-speaking assembly in Brussels had a direct effect on the planting of Brethren churches in Flanders. The record of this connection is supported in part by correspondence from a Flemish man in fellowship at one of the modern Continental Brethren assemblies in Flanders who had hoped to write a complete history of the Brethren in Flanders. He states that the first Dutch-speaking church started in about 1880 as a result of the work of Brethren from Brussels in the province of East Flanders in Ninove, a small, ancient city twenty-five kilometers west of Brussels. The formation of the assembly coincided with the rapid increase in Ninove's population at the end of the nineteenth and beginning of the twentieth centuries.[60] He thinks that they probably gathered in a small room behind a bar. This assertion seems to be a conflation of the record with the aforementioned assembly in Brussels, since the meeting place of the assembly in Ninove seems fairly well established as outlined below. Aloysius (Louis or Lodewijk) Van Der Smissen (1856–1943) was one of the "fathers" of this assembly. Confusingly, the writer then goes on to state,

> The first really "flemish" [sic] assembly started in Gent in 1919, as a result of the preaching of Br. Hengeveld in Harderwijk. In this camp in Holland many Belgian refugiees [sic] were gathered (Bontinck, Martens, Berth, De Groot) who heard the preaching of Br. Hengeveld.[61]

This correspondent's original assertion concerning Ninove as the earliest Dutch-speaking Brethren assembly in Flanders was noted clearly in the history of this Brethren assembly as presented at its 105th-year celebration in 1988.[62] This event was a joint celebration of the anniversary of the assembly as well as the work of a Brethren worker named Piérre Van Der Smissen. Pierre would leave a profitable profession in 1934 to become a fulltime

---

57. Hanssens, email, 13 December 2005
58. Laügt, *Région de Bruxelles*.
59. Hanssens, email, 13 December 2005.
60. de Clerq, "Ninove: de oudste, de stoutste en de wijste van de steden."
61. Liagre, email, 31 July 2003.
62. Taffijn, "Geschiedenis van het ontstaan en verdere ontwikkeling van de vergadering van gelovigen te Ninove," 1.

Backgrounds to the Forming of the Evangelische Christengemeenten Vlaanderen

Christian worker with the Brethren and took over from Louis upon the latter's death in 1943.

According to family-commissioned genealogical studies in both Dutch and French and confirmed with present descendants, Louis Van Der Smissen was the father of Pierre via a second marriage after the death of this first wife.[63] Although Louis was raised as a devout Roman Catholic,[64] the Van Der Smissen family name also was well known throughout Germany and parts of the Netherlands as part of the German pietistic movement, as well noted in *Van Der Smissen: Eine mennonitische Familie vor dem Hintergrund der Geschichte Altonas und Schleswig-Holsteins: Texte und Dokumente*.[65] He became a believer through the efforts of a Belgian believer by the name of Van Cauwenbergh (Cauwenberghe). While investigating various evangelical meetings after his salvation, Louis first witnessed a Brethren meeting in Brussels, and upon seeing it declared, "Here I found my place."[66] He returned to Ninove and began a similar meeting there in 1883. Not later than 1886, he married Johanna Hanssens—the niece of Guillaume Hanssens—thus creating an important and long-lasting link between two prominent families among the Flemish Brethren in Belgium, one in Brussels and the other in Flanders.[67]

As is common with many newly formed Brethren assemblies, this one met in a home for a number of years—first in the home of Louis' parents, and then in Louis' own home.[68] Even meeting in a home was difficult in the early days, as the local residents opposed the rental of any building to the Van Der Smissen family, as it might be used by the Brethren for their meetings.[69] Eventually, the assembly met in a specially built annex to the Van Der Smissen drug store and home at Brusselstraat 17.[70]

---

63. Cf. P. Van Der Smissen, *Genealogie de la Famille Van Der Smissen, 1570–1970*; S. Van Der Smissen, *Genealogie Van Der Smissen, 1600–1983*; Family Van Der Smissen, Ninove, to Samuel Van Der Smissen, Kwaremont, 12 February 1943, Printed death notice for Lodewijk Van Der Smissen; S. Van Der Smisse-Wackenier, "Re: Family Studies," 29 June 2005.

64. Taffijn, "Geschiedenis van het ontstaan en verdere ontwikkeling van de vergadering van gelovigen te Ninove," 1.

65. For more information, cf. Rauert and Kümpers-Greve, *Van Der Smissen: Eine mennonitische Familie*."

66. Taffijn, "Geschiedenis van het ontstaan en verdere ontwikkeling van de vergadering van gelovigen te Ninove," 1.

67. P. Van Der Smissen, *Genealogie*, 22. Laügt has the marriage in 1888, but this is highly unlikely since the first child of this marriage was born on 13 January 1887, and each subsequent year another was born, until Jeanne died in childbirth on 26 July 1889.

68. Ibid.

69. *Mededeelingen omtrent het werk Gods in onze dagen*, vol. 58.

70. Van Der Elst, letter, 20 August 2005; Taffijn, "Geschiedenis van het ontstaan en

New Brethren in Flanders

As also is common in many Brethren meetings, the Van Der Smissen family became a major influence in this assembly and in Flanders for a number of years due to their many offspring and intermarriages within the movement.[71] An interesting precedent to the effect of meeting in Louis Van Der Smissen's home is outlined in *House Church and Mission: the Importance of Household Structures in Early Christianity*, the English translation of the exhaustive work of Roger W. Gehring's 2000 German PhD dissertation. Gehring raises pertinent questions about the tight relationship between leadership recognized in the local church and ownership of the structure in which the local church met. The final chapter summarizes the function and significance of the house for the mission of the Church in relation to its architectural, socioeconomic, and ecclesiological significance.[72] While this study concerned only the time of the early Church, Gehring also notes its potential significance for the modern house church model. This is what would have been at the heart of the Brethren assembly in Ninove as well as many other Flemish assemblies up to and including the last Brethren grouping which would become the ECV.

Other early work by the Brethren in Flanders is recorded in the Dutch-language magazine which reported on Exclusive Brethren work by believers of many nationalities. This magazine also was edited by H. C. Voorhoeve and later by his son Johannes Nicolaas (J. N.) Voorhoeve (1873–1948). Entitled in old Dutch, *Mededeelingen Omtrent Het Werk Gods in Onze Dagen* (hereafter just *Mededeelingen*), it began publication in 1874.[73] When the Exclusive Brethren splintered, this magazine became the chief Dutch magazine of the Continental Brethren, the largest faction in the Netherlands. *Mededeelingen* contains a series of letters reporting on Exclusive Brethren missionary work worldwide, including Belgium, and demonstrates a clear connection between the Brethren in the Netherlands and those in Flanders as well as Belgium as a whole. Further, many of the reports are of evangelistic efforts by Dutch Brethren in Flanders as well as other parts of Belgium.

The earliest efforts are contained in a report penned by H. C. Voorhoeve relating the evangelistic work of a "br. Sergant" in Brussels during the

---

verdere ontwikkeling van de vergadering van gelovigen te Ninove," 2. Cf. P. Van Der Smissen, *Genealogie*, 22.

71. Van Der Elst, letter, 20 August 2005.

72. Cf. Gehring, *House Church and Mission*, esp. 288–311.

73. The consulted book of the bound volumes of the *Mededeelingen* (1874–1902) is mistitled as containing volumes 2–126. The book's bound volumes begin on page 9, hand-labeled as "N 2." Volume No. 1, pages 1–8, follow at the end of "N 2," page 12. Volume 4 is missing, pages 17–21.

Backgrounds to the Forming of the Evangelische Christengemeenten Vlaanderen

summer of 1875.[74] The next mention of a Brethren assembly in Brussels is dated spring of 1876. This announcement said that a new meeting was to be added to the address list of approved Brethren assemblies.[75]

Another early Dutch-language effort was made in the city of Antwerp at the Exporter's Exhibition in 1885 by H. C. Voorhoeve and others. Since the organizers had assured Voorhoeve that Christian literature could be sold at the exhibition, almost four hundred guilders were spent printing six thousand small booklets and tracts, as well as a number of Bibles. As the time drew near for the exhibition, however, the organizers contacted the Brethren and told them that no "religious propaganda" would be allowed inside the exhibition hall. Thus, this evangelistic effort in Antwerp was limited to handing out free literature at the exits and entrances to the exhibition. Nevertheless, the Brethren were encouraged as they reported that "thousands received the Word who had never heard before."[76]

Other than this one assembly in Ninove, certainly much important work within the Continental Brethren also was done by missionary Gerard-Jan Hengeveld. His initial coming to Flanders from the Netherlands as a young man was declared an answer to prayer by an unknown Brethren writer in 1919 in a letter published in the *Mededeelingen* by J. N. Voorhoeve.[77] Many other letters were published from and about Hengeveld which reported his work from just after the end of WW1 right up until his death in 1939.

Finally, another influence on the development of the Flemish Continental Exclusive assemblies should be noted. A German Brethren evangelist and preacher named Carl Brockhaus (1822–1899) would have had a significant, though somewhat more indirect, effect on the character of the Flemish assemblies. Eylenstein's 1927 journal article, *Carl Brockhaus: Ein Beitrag zur Geschichte der Entstehung des Darbysmus in Deutschland,* summarizes Brockhaus' role as one of the "leading brothers" in the German Exclusives who often preached at regional conferences. Brockhaus had a very active ministry among the Dutch assemblies out of which came the men who evangelized and planted churches in Flanders.[78] Brockhaus also was known to have had personal correspondence and a warm relationship with J. N. Darby, the man whose ideas were most prominent in the Exclusive branch of the Brethren worldwide.[79] Further, Brockhaus was the author of many of

---

74. "België," *Mededeelingen omtrent het werk Gods in onze dagen*, vol. 6.
75. *Mededeelingen omtrent het werk Gods in onze dagen*, vol. 13.
76. *Mededeelingen omtrent het werk Gods in onze dagen*, vol. 53.
77. J. N. Voorhoeve, ed., *Mededeelingen omtrent het werk Gods in onze dagen*, vol. 186.
78. Eylenstein, *Carl Brockhaus*, 7–8.
79. Ibid.,14ff.

the hymns used at the central meeting of the Dutch-speaking Brethren in the Netherlands and Flanders, the weekly celebration of the Lord's Supper.[80] Accordingly, Carl Brockhaus would have left quite a mark in the Dutch-speaking Exclusives of both the Netherlands and Flanders.

The other Exclusive group represented in Flanders was a Tunbridge Wells assembly founded in Menen.[81] This assembly was formed in 1952–53 as a result of "one brother from the Netherlands" bringing to light the issue of this worldwide split among the Continentals who, in England, were known as Lowe Brethren. This 1909 split among the Lowes was over a case of church discipline in which the assembly at Tunbridge Wells insisted that "a local assembly's decisions must be regarded as binding on all others and not open to investigation."[82] Two families initially departed from the Continental meeting in Menen. As one older man in the Continentals wrote in a letter at the beginning of the twenty-first century, "they let themselves be influenced by a man who was 'a good talker' rather than examining for themselves like those in Berea 'to see if these things were so.'"[83] Over time, some who joined this Tunbridge Wells meeting returned to the Continentals, but this Tunbridge Wells meeting still meets at the time of this writing.

Hence, when the founders of the ECV arrived in Flanders, six Exclusive meetings were extant: Gent, Antwerp, Ninove, Menen, Nieuwpoort, and Veldegem (near Brugge). Later, another assembly was formed in Woesten (near Ieper), and the small assembly in Veldegem dissolved during the 1980s.[84] While the ECV did not have direct or continuous contact with the Continentals due to the Exclusives' practice of separation, they still were part of the religious milieu into which the ECV was planted, and particularly that of the Brethren milieu.[85]

---

80. Cf. any edition of *Geestelijke Liederen*. The current edition is the 18th edition published in Vaassen: Uitgeverij Medema, 2003. Brockhaus was author of 39 of the 236 listed hymns in the 17th edition.

81. Ver Gouwe, "Re: Vergadering in Woesten," email, 30 July 2005.

82. Grass, *Gathering to His Name*, 205.

83. Van Der Elst, letter, 20 August 2005.

84. van der Bijl, "Re: Vergadering in Vlaanderen," email, 23 June 2007.

85. The most widely known branch of Exclusive Brethren and the one often mentioned in popular publications is the Raven-Taylor Brethren. This group was not present in Flanders when the founders of the ECV arrived. For a summary of this branch of the Brethren, cf. Barrett, *The New Believers*, 162–65.

Backgrounds to the Forming of the Evangelische Christengemeenten Vlaanderen

Open Brethren in Flanders

The Exclusive Brethren were not the only Brethren group active in Flanders. Antwerp again was a site of evangelistic activity at the end of the nineteenth century through the efforts of William J. (d. 1930) and Mary J. E. Nock of the United Kingdom. This couple was not part of the Continental Brethren, but would have come from the Open Brethren; they were listed with the UK Open Brethren missionary service organization, *Echoes of Service*. While the Nocks had gone to Belgium on evangelistic holidays in years past, in 1896 they committed themselves to be Brethren workers in Belgium on a full-time basis. Initially, they lived near the center of Antwerp and used door-to-door efforts to reach its inhabitants. Central to Mr. Nock's work was the sale of Christian literature as a colporteur. Interestingly, he notes that the city's Scandinavian residents were particularly receptive to the message of the evangelical gospel, just as the Italian immigrant community would be receptive to the efforts of the founders of the ECV some eighty years later. Mr. Nock wrote a report of his arrival in Antwerp and his plans saying, "I purpose trying meetings in French (and in Flemish as soon as I am a little proficient in the latter) in our house to begin with, and to invite the people living around, who are nearly all Flemish."[86] In 1897, he moved to the Wallonian part of Belgium. There he assisted another evangelist who already had established a Brethren work.[87] Nevertheless, he did gain proficiency in Dutch in a short period of time and was able to preach in Dutch, as he records in his letter of 5 January 1898.[88]

During his years of missionary activity in Flanders and Wallonia, he composed a number of letters reporting of his work among the Flemish population. In a letter dated 30 October 1897, Nock wrote that part of his work in Dampremy was a planned preaching once a week in Dutch with the help of a "poor shoemaker" who could speak Dutch in addition to his normal French. This was part of a new work in the neighboring village of La Docherie. Nock wrote,

> The shoemaker is a very earnest fellow, and as he can speak Flemish [Dutch] we hope to preach once a week in that tongue as there are a good many Flemish people around *utterly neglected* and in the greatest ignorance. Being an Englishman I am unfettered by racial differences which are strong in Belgium.[89]

---

86. Nock, letter dated 20 August 1896, *Echoes*.
87. Tatford, *Western Europe Evangel*, 44.
88. Nock, letter dated 5 January 1898, *Echoes*.
89. Nock, letter dated 20 August 1896, *Echoes*.

New Brethren in Flanders

Nock returned repeatedly to Berchem, a district in the southern part of Antwerp, and worked diligently among the Flemish people. His coworker, Frenchman Georges F. Gaudibert (1857–1934), wrote of Nock's work saying, "Our brother Mr. Nock paid us a flying visit last week. The work at Berchem is very difficult, and I am not surprised that such is the case. The Flemings are hard to evangelize, more so than the Walloons."[90] Several of Nock's letters also mention work done among the prisoners where he preached in both French and Dutch.[91] His Dutch-language ministry was not limited to Belgium, however. His letter of 16 January 1900 reports going to Amsterdam to prevent "the danger of Irvingism" leading astray young believers located there.[92] Nock also went to the Netherlands as a colporteur, in addition to his work to encourage the Brethren assemblies there as he records in 1902. He hints at tensions within the Dutch assemblies, as these assemblies were composed of "people with different ideas."[93] Nock later tells of printing tracts which have French on one side and Dutch on the other for use in Brussels. His desire for specifically Dutch-language tracts was because

> these people are rather neglected, and not being great readers, they need simple things that they can understand. This is a contrast between now and ten years ago, in that Christian young men are beginning to be active in the gospel, and doors are open in a good many places.[94]

Another worker, Ghislain Piérard, was a native of Brussels who was converted in London in 1902.[95] He returned to Belgium in 1906. In 1912, he went to an unnamed Flemish village where a young girl underwent evangelical conversion. While a number of gospel outreaches were attempted over the years in the Flemish areas, not until 1913 did the Open Brethren have a

---

90. Gaudibert, letter dated 27 March 1898, *Echoes*.

91. Nock, letter dated 27 February 1899, *Echoes*.

92. Irvingism was a doctrinal heresy promulgated by Edward Irving in the 1820s, a Scot who moved to London where he became a prominent preacher. Irving claimed that Jesus came in sinful and fallen flesh like ours and was perfectly subdued by the Holy Spirit. In addition, Irvingites came to believe that twelve apostles were always necessary. By 1875, three of these apostles lived in Amsterdam. Further, contemporary critics saw that Irving used the miraculous gifts to confirm this doctrinal error. Cf. Stallard's paper presented at the annual Pre-Trib Study group on 8–9 January 1997 at Tyndale Theological Seminary of Ft. Worth, TX, from which much of this information was drawn. Cf. also Grass, *Edward Irving: The Lord's Watchman*, 175; T. Kolde, "Catholic Apostolic Church."

93. Nock, letter dated 12 September 1902, *Echoes*.

94. Nock, letter dated 23 October 1906, *Echoes*.

95. Tatford, *Western Europe Evangel*, 46.

work which saw real potential for permanence, a work in a village nearby Brussels. In an undated letter sometime in 1913, British evangelist Ransome W. Cooper wrote,

> An interesting work was begun several months ago in a Flemish village not far from Brussels. This was the first effort of its kind among the Flemings, and at first great interest was aroused. People came in considerable numbers, and from eighty to one hundred unsaved attended regularly for some months, which is unusual for Belgium.[96]

Nonetheless, to date no record is found that a Brethren assembly resulted from these efforts.

The First World War caused the departure of the Nocks to the UK. Letters which do record the work of assemblies again demonstrate that these churches were both French- speaking and behind German lines. In the "Brief Notes" section of the *Echoes of Service* magazine, the list of Brethren assemblies in Belgium records eight locations. All were in the French-speaking portion of Belgium, with the exception of the one in Brussels. Earlier letters, however, made quite clear that this, too, was a French-language gathering.[97] Other obstacles presented themselves; one of the French workers who could speak Dutch, Ghislain Piérard, was killed in an accident. For some unknown or unmentioned reason, he had brought home two grenades from the scene of an explosion of 150 wagons of munitions which he passed while returning from preaching. He then used a knitting needle to tinker with one of the grenades—with not surprising but deadly results.[98]

After the war, the Nocks returned to Belgium and continued their work, but mainly in the Wallonian areas. In June of 1920, Nock writes of Brussels, "There is now a breaking-of-bread meeting in Flemish, as well as French. I am thankful for this, because thus far little headway, relatively speaking, has been made among the Flemings."[99] Nonetheless, Mr. Nock's desire continued for the evangelical conversion of the Flemish, and he conducted successful evangelistic efforts in the open air and in private homes, as well as the sale of Bibles in "one of the most fanatical villages in Flemish-speaking Belgium," the village of Heist-op-den-Berg.[100] In addition

---

96. Cooper, letter dated 1913, *Echoes*.
97. Gaudibert, letter dated 25 March 1919, *Echoes*.
98. Ibid.
99. Nock, letter dated 21 June 1920 from Ghent, *Echoes*; later evidence is absent of this meeting continuing.
100. Nock, letter dated 6 August 1920, *Echoes*. Nock's letter used the French name of "Heyst-op-deu-Berg," rather than the old Dutch name of "Heyst-op-den-Berg."

to one young man converted, Nock's letter of 6 August 1920 notes that he found several believers in a few Flemish villages who had been converted while interned in Netherlands during the First World War. As always, the local priests bitterly opposed their work, though the people readily took the gospel tracts that he offered to them.[101] In another letter, Ghislain Piérard's widow records Nock's report of "the zeal of the Flemish brethren." They purposed to have a gospel literature outreach among the Roman Catholic pilgrims who gathered on public holidays. This type of approach is seen again and again in reports in *Echoes of Service Magazine* for the next several years. Still, no mention of the regular meeting of a Dutch-speaking assembly is noted from these efforts.[102] In fact, the next mention of the Brussels meetings has a clearly French-speaking nature about it with no mention of the Flemish one.[103] She, however, does mention in 1922, "a little work is commencing among the Flemings" in Tienen (Tirlemont).[104] This saw some measure of success; she later reports that she helped to carry bricks and to make mortar for a meeting hall attached to her home in Tienen.[105] Other letters refer to this meeting as late as 1924, when Mme. Piérard ceased her work as a missionary.[106] Still, this work was not an easy one; she also records the beating of her children by the neighbors until an uneasy peace was established between the believers and the Roman Catholic families of the town.[107] Finally in 1926, the Nocks returned to the United Kingdom because Mr. Nock's health did not allow his work any longer. In his last report to *Echoes of Service Magazine*, he notes the continued, severe opposition to the evangelistic efforts in Malines (Mechelen).

Ultimately, Dutch-speaking Open Brethren assemblies were planted in at least Brussels, Mechelen, Tienen, Waregem, and Menen, for these five continued until the arrival of the missionaries who would plant the ECV in the mid-1970s. Tienen actually became part of the ECV. At this writing, only Mechelen and Menen remain outside of either the ECV or the Continentals.[108]

101. Ibid.
102. Piérard, letter of Easter, 1921, *Echoes*.
103. H. Bain, undated report in "Notes and Comments," *Echoes*.
104. Mme. Piérard, letter of 1922," *Echoes*.
105. Ibid.
106. Ibid.; Tatford, *Western Europe Evangel*, 529.
107. Mme. Piérard, letter of 1924, *Echoes*.
108. R. Haverkamp, interview, 29 July 2005.

Backgrounds to the Forming of the Evangelische Christengemeenten Vlaanderen

ECCLESIOLOGICAL SUMMARY OF THE BRETHREN GENERALLY AND IN FLANDERS PRIOR TO THE ECV

Given this history of the planting of the Brethren churches in Flanders, what was the nature of the ecclesiology which animated these gatherings? What was (and remains) the most noteworthy feature of Brethren ecclesiology? Additionally, what other aspects of ecclesiology were important during the years in which the ECV was planted and formed?

As with any Brethren church in any part of the world, the most noteworthy feature of Flemish Brethren ecclesiology was both the importance of the Lord's Supper and the manner of its celebration. Of the four commonly held categories of the Lord's Supper, the Brethren held a memorial view.[109] Within that part of Christendom which holds to a memorial view of the Lord's Supper, the Brethren have a somewhat unique view and resultant practice in at least two areas: the Lord's Supper as the central mark of identity of the Church and, inseparably, the Lord's Supper as a mark of unity. Further, among the more conservative Brethren groups, the Lord's Supper also is viewed as a mark of purity. The nature of the uniqueness is that these views are held and practiced in a non-sacrificial, non-sacramental, and non-sacerdotal manner.[110]

In addition to the importance to this study of various Brethren views of the Lord's Supper are its views toward leadership. The various leadership options within Brethren thinking will be of significance as the founders of the ECV planted their churches.

The Lord's Supper as the Central Mark of the Brethren

The Brethren hold at least two, and some hold three beliefs concerning the Lord's Supper. All understand the Lord's Supper as the mark of identity and unity within the Brethren. Some also understand the Lord's Supper as a mark of purity.

---

109. Commonly held views are generally categorized according to the presence of the Lord within the elements, the bread and cup. These views are: literal sacrificial presence (transubstantiation); literal non-sacrificial presence (consubstantiation); spiritual presence (virtualism); and no presence other than what is usually ascribed to the Lord in any other place or setting (memorial).

110. "Non-sacramental" specifically means that the taking of the elements does not provide the recipient with grace, salvific or otherwise. That said, some see a near-sacramental presence, though not in the bread and wine, because of an overemphasis on Christ's presence at the celebration of the Lord's Supper based upon Matthew 18:20. Cf. Dickson, review of "The Lord's Supper in Brethren Ecclesiology: the Mark of Identity, Unity, and for some, Purity," 98–100.

The Lord's Supper as the Mark of Identity Within the Brethren

Each of the many particular movements and denominations which comprise the religion of Christianity can be identified both by what it says about itself and by what others say about it. This is especially true with respect to the practices they hold most dear or to which they give prominence in their gatherings. For example, Roman Catholicism may be identified at its core by the celebration of the Mass, the Southern Baptists by the evangelistic message and accompanying altar call, the Reformed churches by the preaching of the Word, the modern Charismatic churches perhaps by praise songs which have spread throughout much of the rest of Christendom, etc.[111] Without a doubt, the identifying mark of the Brethren movement and that by which it often is identified by outside observers is the importance given to the communion service and its method of practice.

While the actual ceremony or practice accompanying the taking of the elements varies from place to place and has changed somewhat over time, "the centrality of the *Breaking of Bread* has been significant."[112] This priority is based upon their centrality of the person of Christ in the Church and the priority of worship as characterized at the communion service.[113] J. N. Darby writes, "The 'occupation' of the church ought to be constant, incessant reference to its Head . . . This is its grand occupation."[114] On another occasion, he describes worship as "the employment of heaven."[115] In his typically verbose and somewhat dense style, Darby says that worship is not the sermon, nor prayers of supplication, nor the work of God towards man. Ultimately, he understands the Lord's Supper "as representing that which forms the basis of all worship, is the center of its exercise," for worship is "the remembrance of the sacrifice of Christ, which is commemorated in the [Lord's] Supper."[116] Darby is far from alone in his thinking among the Brethren writers. For example, another well-known Brethren author expresses much the same view when he writes,

> Worship is the first thing realized by Christians who have understood what the Assembly is, for it supposes persons united in

---

111. Bloesch, *Life, Ministry, and Hope*, 88–89.
112. Liefeld, "Suggestions for Defining Some Identifying Characteristics of the Brethren," 291.
113. Ibid.
114. Darby, "The Church—What is It?" 382.
115. Darby, "On Worship," 88.
116. Ibid., 110–14.

> one body by one Spirit. Worship takes place in the presence of God the Father and around the Lamb....
>
> We find a second feature of worship in 1 Corinthians 10 and 1 Corinthians 11. The Lord's Supper is presented there as *the visible centre of the Assembly* gathered at *the table of the Lord, the Lord Himself being the invisible centre.*[117]

Commonly found in Brethren writings is the reference to Matthew 18:20 as the description of and support for a gathering of local believers. The principle of "where two or three have gathered together in My name, there I am in their midst" demonstrates the centrality of the Lord Jesus in Brethren gatherings, and in turn the celebration which remembers His death, burial, resurrection, and imminent return. For example, noted Brethren writer William Kelly writes,

> Also the Lord instituted His Supper, to which He invites all that are His. His name is their passport and guarantee. His Supper is the constant feast for the family of God: they break the bread, they drink the cup, in remembrance of Christ. Before inaugurating this feast, Jesus had already in His view the dangers His own must meet, the difficulties they have to surmount, the decline and the fall of Christian profession; and He had consoled the disciples with those words of love, "Where two or three are gathered together unto My name, there am I in the midst of them" (Matt. 18: 20). This is His real presence; it is our need, and His assurance. His word ever abides, His love never fails.
>
> The Supper then is the common privilege conferred by Christ on all His members.[118]

Even the common objection that this passage from Matthew 18:20 is in the context of church discipline is turned aside with statements such as,

> If the church can rely on the promise of Christ that He is in their midst when they gather to judge one who is unrepentant, how much more can the church count on the presence of the Christ when it is gathered to worship, and pray, and fellowship, and teach?"[119]

---

117. Rossier, "What is a Meeting of the Assembly?"
118. Kelly, "Letters on the Lord's Supper."
119. Fish, "Brethren Tradition or New Testament Truth?" 120.

For those inside the movement, this communion service goes by the various English-language titles of "the Breaking of Bread," the "worship service," the "morning meeting," or simply "the meeting." This last, seemingly off-hand title in reality is pregnant with meaning. Even today, this communion service is such an integral part of the identity of the local Brethren churches that no one inside the movement—or certainly not those associated with its more conservative elements—would ask, "Which meeting?" when asked, "Are you coming to the meeting Sunday?" Additionally, it is common practice among the more conservative parts of the movement for people to delay holidays, outings, or even business meetings so that this one most central meeting can be attended.[120] Even a departure delay of simply one hour beyond the Lord's Supper meeting often is not practiced if the preaching service follows the Lord's Supper, since the Lord's Supper service is considered as the only gathering which "really counts." One well-known itinerant Brethren preacher and writer questioned the wisdom of accepting even an opportunity to "preach the Gospel" or "open the Word" at "some denominational group" if it should cause the speaker to miss the celebration of the Lord's Supper at his home assembly, since then "he is missing from the trysting place of his Lord and Savior, and thus fails to respond to the request: 'This do in remembrance of Me.'"[121]

The early Brethren had great appreciation for the study of and public exposition of the Bible, but they uniformly decried the relegation of the "remembrance feast" to a place of secondary importance. One well-known modern theologian properly describes this change of priorities throughout historically Protestant churches. He notes that the sermon went from equal footing to a place where preaching overwhelmed the celebration of the Lord's Supper due to cultural changes in the aftermath of the Reformation.[122] While certainly not subscribing to a salvific mass as had become the practice of the Roman Catholic Church early in Church history, the Brethren did want to return to what they understood was the emphasis placed upon the Lord's Supper as found in the Book of Acts as well as in the writings of the Church fathers. Thus, although the Reformers of the sixteenth century had recovered the importance of the preaching of the Word, they failed to recover the importance of "the remembrance feast" in all its simplicity, in the view of the Brethren. Contrary to this movement, the centrality of the Lord's Supper is what the Brethren have believed since their beginnings. In fact, this concern

---

120. The author has witnessed this practice or priority repeatedly in Brethren meetings throughout North America, in the United Kingdom, and in the Netherlands over at least a thirty-year period.

121. Gibbs, *The Lord's Supper*, 191.

122. H. Berkhof, *Christian Faith*," 363.

Backgrounds to the Forming of the Evangelische Christengemeenten Vlaanderen

of not relegating the Lord's Supper to a place of secondary importance within the Brethren was raised with respect to all the practices of the local church. One distinguished nineteenth century Brethren author writes,

> If we abandon the supper for the sermon, or for large congregation, or for any other religious scene or service, we have given up the house of God in its due characteristic and divinely appointed business and worship . . . And were we right hearted we would say, "What sermon would be more profitable to us? What singing of a full congregation more sweet to our ears than the voice of the ordinance which tells us so clearly and with such rich harmony of all kinds of music, of the forgiveness of our sins, of the acceptance of our persons, and of our waiting for the Lord from heaven, and all this in blessed and wondrous fellowship with the brightest display of the name and glory of God?"[123]

Although the Lord's Supper certainly is listed among the four common practices of the early Church in Acts 2:42, in Brethren thinking it occupies the chief place. A well-known twentieth century Brethren author and preacher wrote,

> An examination of the practice of the early Church, as seen in the book of Acts, seems to indicate that brethren of a given community came together *each Lord's day* to show forth the Lord's death in the breaking of bread (Acts 20:7). They came primarily, not to hear preaching, but to break the bread, symbolic of the body of their Lord and Savior; and drink the cup, symbolic of His precious blood.[124]

This same centrality of the Lord's Supper is found widely among the hymnody of the Brethren, especially those hymns written or composed throughout the nineteenth century. These same hymns are used actively up through today. Brethren historians have noted that the central themes of Brethren hymnody have prevented it from finding wide usage outside the movement for at least two reasons. One is the "too self-conscious renunciation of the world and its ways," and the other is that "many of the really original and choice pieces are written with the distinctive communion service in view."[125] This second theme is evident in a variety of Brethren hymnbooks in any number of languages.[126] Even some of the most modern collections are

---

123. Bellett, "The Lord's Supper."
124. Gibbs, *Scriptural Principles*, 31.
125. Coad, *A History of the Brethren Movement*, 231.
126. Cf. *A Few Hymns and Some Spiritual Songs, selected 1856 for the Little Flock*;

compiled with an eye towards the meeting in which the Lord's Supper is celebrated. Writes one group of compilers at the end of the twentieth century,

> *Worship* is a compilation of hymns, songs and choruses chosen specifically for the Remembrance service . . . More than fifteen different hymn books were searched and from these, two hundred and twenty-seven hymns and choruses were selected. A balanced combination of traditional and contemporary songs, with emphasis on Christ and His redeeming work at Calvary, was the criterion used.[127]

Scholarly studies of Brethren hymnody have noted the sharp distinction between "worship hymns" and "gospel hymns" such that the books which are used in the Lord's Supper service are composed mainly, though not exclusively, of hymns by Brethren authors. Nevertheless, as one person wrote of the composers contained in one Brethren hymnbook used for well over a hundred years, "The writers represent all walks of life, centuries of time, and various religious backgrounds. These men and women placed great value upon the Person, Work and Offices of the Lord Jesus Christ."[128] Overwhelmingly, the theme of these collections centers on the Brethren's identifying mark of the Lord's Supper in its celebration of the death, burial, resurrection, and return of the Lord Jesus.[129]

Why would the Brethren see such a central role of the celebration of the Lord's Supper? Fundamentally, because of the importance they understand that the Lord placed upon this remembrance as He instituted it on the night He was betrayed. They often cite the intensity of expression used by the Lord at His last supper in Luke 22. If He was earnest in His desire that He institute this celebration on the night before His death, we too, it is reasoned, should be equally earnest in our desire to remember Him.[130] Following this observation in the writings of many Brethren authors are references to Old Testament worship as support for the importance of remembering the Lord in this way. When one begins to read these writings, a distinct and common hermeneutic surfaces. One well-known writer characteristically notes that the sons of Zadok in Ezekiel 44 were to minister to the Lord Himself, not to His house. He goes on to see this distinction of ministering to God versus His house as a separation of the roles of the Holy priesthood and

---

Hymns of Worship and Remembrance; *Cantini Cristiani*; *Célébrons sa Mémoire: Cantiques pour le Repas du Seigneur*; *Geestelijke Liederen*, 17th ed.

127. *Worship*, preface.
128. Paisley, *The Believers Hymn Book Companion*, 5.
129. Andrews, "Brethren Hymnology," 208.
130. Darby, "On Worship," 110ff.

the Royal priesthood in 1 Peter 2. He then reasons that the New Testament believer in his priestly role, a role which all believers have, is thus to bring the spiritual sacrifices of worship to the Lord when the believers gather for the Lord's Supper.[131] Referring to another Old Testament passage, the same author typically and typologically says,

> Worship is beautifully pictured for us in Leviticus 16. On the Day of Atonement, when the high priest was to enter the holiest of all, he was to take *his hands full of the sweet incense beaten small* into the Holy of Holies, place it upon the burning coals of the censer that the cloud might fill the place. Without that, no further service was to take place. The sweet incense speaks of the fragrance of the Person of Christ. This is to be presented to the Father as we enter in as holy priests.[132]

This sort of Old Testament usage is seen throughout the writings of Brethren authors and heard in conversation with Brethren preachers to the current day, even among many of those trained in seminaries and who have committed themselves to a historical-literal-grammatical interpretation of the text.[133]

Second, the Brethren point to the attitude of the early Church toward the Lord's Supper as recorded in Acts. The centrality of the remembrance was noted by Cullmann in his work, *Christ and Time*, where he wrote, "In the earliest times an assembly of the congregation without the celebration of the Lord's Supper was unthinkable."[134] The early Church celebrated this remembrance daily as a "constant source of joy and fellowship," as recorded in Acts 2:46: "And day by day, attending the temple together and breaking bread in their homes, they received their food with glad and generous hearts." The Brethren writers almost uniformly understand this breaking of bread not merely as a common meal, but as the remembrance spoken of in

---

131. Nicholson, "Divine Ordinances," 64–65.

132. Nicholson, "Divine Ordinances," 70.

133. This author had an extended conversation with a colleague at Emmaus Bible College (the flagship, four-year college associated with the Brethren in North America) concerning issues dealing with this typological interpretation found among the Brethren. This man, then a PhD candidate at Dallas Theological Seminary, staunchly but quite cordially defended a typological view of Song of Solomon as legitimate. This type of "legitimate" interpretation often is seen in the writings of Brethren authors when referring to various attributes of Christ in connection with the Lord's Supper, and is often used by the men who share a thought concerning the person or work of Jesus Christ at the Lord's Supper meetings. Particularly instructive about this theologically educated man's defense of this hermeneutic was the fact that he did not come among the Brethren until the last year of his undergraduate Bible education. Thus, he made a conscious decision to interpret the Bible in this very Brethren manner.

134. Quoted in Inrig, *Life in His Body*, 70.

verse 42 of the same chapter. Later on, whenever the local church gathered, the Lord's Supper was at the center of the purpose, as seen in Acts 20:7 (ESV): "On the first day of the week, when we were gathered together to break bread, Paul talked with them, intending to depart on the next day, and he prolonged his speech until midnight." They often note that the previous verse says that Paul and his companions stayed seven days in Troas for the express purpose of celebrating the Lord's Supper, even as they note that Paul's teaching was not the purpose of the gathering, according to verse 7. Further evidence for the centrality of this remembrance is seen in 1 Corinthians 11:17f, as again it is understood as the purpose of the gathering.[135]

The Lord's Supper as a Mark of Unity Within the Brethren

Identity alone, however, is not all that the Lord's Supper means to the Brethren. Equally important is the unity that it represents since this is "the zenith of assembly fellowship."[136] In keeping with their historical conviction from Scripture, the Brethren believe in only one unified body of believers, not a divided body. The chief witness to this unified body is the Lord's Supper. This is in contradistinction to the Roman Catholic view which says that taking the Eucharist *causes* the unity.[137] As one Brethren writer and preacher noted,

> It is the Lord's Supper that is the symbol of this unity and the scriptural observance of this memorial feast is really the expression of Christian unity. Thus, the Lord's people gather together and bear witness of their oneness in life in Christ and in the Body of which He is the Head. It is in this way that every evidenced believer is welcome to enjoy Christian privilege and fellowship according to scriptural simplicity and order.[138]

Another oft-quoted statement is, "The chief aim was to exhibit, in a Scriptural way, the common brotherhood of all believers."[139] Some call this remembrance an act of "personal identification." By partaking of the Lord's Supper, the individual believer identifies himself with the risen Lord and acknowledges the presence of his fellow believers, all of whom are making the same statement of identity. Thus, the Brethren hold that the celebration of the supper cannot be accomplished by individual believers in isolation from

---

135. Inrig, *Life in His Body*, 80.
136. Nicholson, "Divine Ordinances," 64.
137. Abbott, ed., *The Documents of Vatican II*, 16.
138. Reid, *The Chief Meeting of the Church*, 12.
139. Reid, *Grant*, 3.

one another, even though the act of identification is personal. This breaking of bread is to be accomplished as a joint activity of the local church.[140] Further, "[w]orship so generated expresses the corporate nature of the church as a free association of individual members bound together by a common bond with their head and upbuilding themselves in common life."[141] In a public presentation later printed and widely distributed, one modern Brethren writer found himself trying to describe the Brethren. After rejecting the usual titles of Plymouth Brethren or Christian Brethren, and finally settling for New Fellowship, he notes that a believer can live in isolation, but the concept of church carries with it a sense of community. That community is "pre-eminently expressed in the only *collective* ordinance of the Church revealed in Holy Scripture—the Breaking of Bread," a strong statement of both identity and unity.[142]

One of the best known Brethren authors, J. N. Darby, also writes concerning the Lord's Supper as something which should not be used to divide the body of Christ. He lamented in a letter to Halle theologian Friedrich A. G. Tholuck,

> The Lord's supper, symbol of the unity of the body, had become a symbol of the union of this latter with the world, that is to say, exactly the contrary of what Christ had established.[143]

Elsewhere in response to an inquiry from an unnamed person, Darby clearly admonished the questioner not to create a divisive tool from the fact that a non-Brethren person had partaken of the Lord's Supper, lest "the unity of the body is denied by the assembly which refuses him," and lest the "principle of Brethren's meeting is gone, and another sect is made—say with more light, and that is all."[144] Further, if somehow the Breaking of Bread is used as a means of division, such was the case in 1 Corinthians, "it is but sectarianism; the Lord Himself has lost His place."[145] This unity should be palpable since, in Brethren thinking, the Holy Spirit makes believers conscious of this unity and is its author, the same Spirit whose indwelling from the time of salvation is what joins believers to the body of Christ.[146] Thus, this visible representation of the unity of the body is tightly bound up to

---

140. Borland, "The Lord's Supper," 76.
141. West, "Worship and the Lord's Supper," 60.
142. Mudditt, *The New Fellowship*, 10.
143. Darby, letter to Prof. Tholuck dated [1855], 301.
144. Darby, "Principles of Gathering," 381.
145. Mackintosh, "Thoughts on the Lord's Supper," 14.
146. Darby, "On Worship," 112.

the central identity of the local church, the celebration of the Lord's Supper. Brethren hold that nothing should be allowed to disband this celebration and the unity it represents.

Supporting this view, one early twentieth century Brethren writer noted when commenting on 1 Chronicles 13 and 15 and thereby drawing analogies to Acts 20:6–12,

The fall and death of Eutychus interrupted, but did not dissolve that meeting. This we learn from verse 11: "When he therefore was come up again, and had broken bread, and eaten, and talked a long while, even till break of day, he departed." The unity of the whole Assembly, as we have seen already, is expressed in the breaking of bread, and it was that which gathered the saints at Troas—not to hear Paul speak, though he did speak, and speak twice.[147]

How far would this observation be pushed in modern times? This writer was told a story by an eyewitness of a man who suddenly died at the Lord's Supper while addressing the gathered believers. Four of the brothers (including the eyewitness) merely carried out the man, the meeting continued, and details such as notifying the authorities were left until after the passing of the elements was complete![148]

Why the strong statements and commitment to the unity expressed in the Lord's Supper? Because of a continual theme throughout Brethren writings of an oft-repeated consciousness that the Lord Himself instituted this memorial as is recorded in the Gospels, and it is around the Lord Himself that the Church gathers. "[T]he person of Christ is God's center of union."[149] For many of the Brethren, the unity symbolized is not merely that of the local church, but refers to the unity of all believers–the universal, invisible Church of God.[150] This drive for unity is so strong that the individual believer has a responsibility to be sure that the table at which he partakes of the Lord's Supper does not act as a barrier to the unity of the Church.[151] Unity has its limits in Brethren thinking, however, for in some Brethren circles, equally strong is the admonition that this unity must not be at the expense of purity.

---

147. Wolston, "King David's New Cart."

148. Meschkat, conversation with author. Meschkat served as an elder at South Plains Bible Chapel for many years. Another eyewitness told a similar story concerning a Brethren meeting in Scotland.

149. Mackintosh, "Thoughts on the Lord's Supper," 27.

150. Ibid., 18.

151. Ibid., 22.

Backgrounds to the Forming of the Evangelische Christengemeenten Vlaanderen

The Lord's Supper as a Mark of Purity Within the Brethren

Although beginning with biblical statements of identity and unity, within a few decades the Lord's Supper also was viewed as a symbol of purity among the most conservative elements of the movement. The desire to avoid the broadness of the Church of England became a campaign to maintain the purity of the Lord's Table. Even the unity symbolized in the Lord's Supper came to be couched in terms of purity. As J. N. Darby wrote,

> Of this unity and fellowship, I may add, the Lord's supper is the symbol and expression . . . [T]he church's unity was based upon the power of the Holy Ghost come down from heaven, separating a peculiar people out of the world to Christ . . . He establishes the holiness of the church and its unity in its separation to God.[152]

The Brethren understand the Bible to teach that "the unity of the church is God-given; it is the work of the Holy Spirit and is therefore indestructible."[153] Nevertheless, the visible expression of this unity has been destroyed by men because they did not follow the direction of the Holy Spirit. Thus, men such as Darby, initially, and more and more of his followers preached a need for separation from the various denominational bodies who failed to keep this visible unity by gathering themselves according to some "man-made name." They taught that only men who separated themselves from evil, such as exampled in 1 Kings 19:18, and worshipped with a pure heart, such as in 1 Timothy 2:22, should be allowed to partake of the Lord's Supper lest one partakes of a table of demons and not the Lord's table.[154] Consequently, the Lord's Supper became more a symbol of purity than unity. A subtle but profound shift in the thinking of some has been noted by a number of Brethren writers, such that local gatherings of believers assembled themselves around "the 'truth of remembering the Lord' rather than around the person and worth of the Lord Jesus."[155] The result was that unity became not defined by a believer's identity in Christ, but upon conformity to the right doctrine. "It also meant everyone had to be scrutinized carefully for 'a little leaven leavens the whole lump.'(1 Cor. 5:6)."[156]

---

152. Darby, "God's Principle of Unity," 361–62.
153. Weremchuk, *John Nelson Darby*, 81.
154. Ibid., 82.
155. Smith, *Roots, Renewal, and the Brethren*, 88.
156. Ibid., 89.

The scriptural basis for this type of unity is found in 1 Corinthians 10:17 (ESV), "Because there is one bread, we who are many are one body, for we all partake of the one bread." One of many Brethren writers said,

> The very reason for which He "hath tempered the body together, having given more abundant honour to that part which lacked," is "that there should be no schism in the body" (1 Cor. 12: 18–25). In the Lord's supper, the touching memorial left behind Him by Christ of His dying love, the same oneness is beautifully set forth.[157]

He ends by quoting 1 Corinthians 10:17.

The one loaf in particular repeatedly is emphasized as the noteworthy symbol of the unity in keeping with Scripture since the Lord used up to four cups at the institution of the remembrance.[158] As the wheat was merged into one loaf by the baking, so too are all the believers merged into one body through the work of Christ on the cross and the baptism of the Spirit into one body.[159] So strongly held is this one-loaf identification and the symbol that it represents that the Brethren commonly reject the prepared individual wafers often used by many churches, since this clearly suggests the broken condition of what should be one—namely, the Church. The symbol of individual wafers is thus one of shame, not unity.[160]

The same strongly typological hermeneutic noted earlier also supports the symbolism of the one loaf. One author compares the Old Testament sacrificial system to New Testament practices, and notes in his lesson concerning the Day of Pentecost in Acts 2:

> The wave sheaf, then, has been presented before the Lord—Christ risen from the dead—and accepted; and the two loaves "baken with leaven," I have no doubt, figuratively represent the Church, accepted in all the value of Christ's acceptance. There are two component parts of the Church—the Jew and the Gentile . . . but when we come further on in the New Testament narrative we find, not two loaves, but one loaf (1 Cor. 10: 17), expressive of the unity of the Church.[161]

---

157. Baines, *The Lord's Coming, Israel, and the Church*.

158. Fraser, *The Lord's Supper*, 2/5.

159. This baptism of the Holy Spirit does not refer to a subsequent work of God after justification, but happens at the time of justification ever since the coming of the Spirit on the day of Pentecost in Acts 2. Cf. 1 Corinthians 12:13.

160. McClure, *The Tabernacle: Its Types and Teachings*, 97–98.

161. Wolston, *"Another Comforter."*

Backgrounds to the Forming of the Evangelische Christengemeenten Vlaanderen

Models of Brethren Leadership

Leadership styles within the Brethren have been associated closely with the two major divisions within the Brethren, the Exclusives and the Opens. While the pattern has been fairly uniform within the Exclusives, leadership within the Open Brethren has shown a variety somewhat similar to that of other free churches within Protestantism, with the exception of a formally ordained minister—though even the title of "Pastor" has been seen in some locales. Part of the variance between the Exclusive and Open models of church leadership is associated with their overall view of the Church. Exclusive Brethren view the Church as a "Church in ruins," such that New Testament models of leadership cannot be recovered.[162] Thus, the Church is considered to be a remnant of faithful believers who remember the Lord at the weekly celebration of the Lord's Supper, and then go out and spread the evangelical faith while they wait for the return of the Lord. The more conservative elements of the Open Brethren would hold a similar view. The majority of Open Brethren, however, would see themselves as a restorationist group such that the New Testament model of leadership can be recovered and applied in spite of the failures of the past.

Exclusive Brethren Leadership

The basis of the Exclusive Brethren type of leadership is a belief that the Early Church apostatized from the biblical pattern early on. This process of apostatizing is seen in the institutionalization of the Church as it moved from independent local bodies to a top-down structure which eventually had the Bishop of Rome as its head. Combined with this observation is a strong commitment to a dispensational approach to Scripture. As with any of the seven normally recognized dispensations, the people of God are given a test in each era.[163] In each dispensation, the test is failed so that man stands guilty before God irrespective of the circumstances. Thus, the gift of God's grace by faith is each man's only hope. In the particular dispensation which commenced with founding of the Church at Pentecost (Acts 2:1ff), the test was to stay true to the New Testament principles of gathering. According to the Exclusives, Church history records a spectacular failure to keep to these patterns and principles, and thus man failed once again. Nevertheless,

---

162. Cf. Darby, "Scriptural Views Upon the Subject of Elders." Cf. also Darby, "The Apostasy of the Successive Dispensations."

163. For a standard description of the teachings of dispensationalism, cf. Ryrie, *Dispensationalism Today*.

a remnant of faithful believers held themselves outside this institutionalization and were thus the ancestors of the group of believers now "gathered in the name of Jesus alone," the "so-called Plymouth brethren," or simply "the brethren" with a lower-case b.

Since the Church failed the test, the New Testament model of leadership cannot be recovered, nor should the Church attempt to do so. Accordingly, recognized leadership in the local Brethren churches is viewed as wrong. Obstacles are listed, such as the methods of appointing or recognizing the elders, as well as the classification of the people over whom the elders exercise authority as a sect, especially if others disagree with the choice of leadership.[164] After working his way through both 1 Timothy 3 and Titus 1 to support his rejection of elders, Darby strongly rejects the idea of recognized elders:

> Neither in the Epistles to the churches nor in those addressed to Christians in general is there anywhere found the smallest word relative to the choice or establishment of elders, nor to the necessity of choosing or establishing them, whilst one finds in them that there were leaders that the faithful were exhorted to recognize and respect by very different motives to that of an official establishment.[165]

In a similar vein, twentieth century Canadian Brethren preacher, hymnwriter, and author Leslie M. Grant goes on to say,

> It was necessary to have apostles as the connecting link between the dispensation of law and that of the grace of God, necessary that such men of devoted character should be used to lay the foundation of Christianity (1 Cor. 3: 10–11; Eph. 2: 20), that is, to lay down the truth of God concerning Christ in all His relationships. Apostles themselves passed away, but they have left their writings, scriptures that are authoritative, and by which the Church of God may be guided and preserved in all her subsequent history. While they were living, apostles did appoint elders in various assemblies, and Paul instructed Titus to appoint elders in each assembly in Crete (Titus 1: 5). Assemblies never did appoint elders, and there are no apostles living to do so now, nor delegates of the apostles.
>
> However, once the Church has been established, there is no reason why believers should not be unitedly guided by the Spirit of God, who remains as a living power in the Church,

---

164. Darby, "Scriptural Views Upon the Subject of Elders," 226.
165. Ibid., 213.

Backgrounds to the Forming of the Evangelische Christengemeenten Vlaanderen

> as was not true under the dispensation of law. Are there no elders therefore? By all means elders are still in the Church, but not as appointed by men. There are those who can do the work without any appointment, for God has fitted them for the work. We should certainly pray for such, and appreciate their wise counsel and help.[166]

Thus, as with other foundational events in the establishment of the Church, recognized elders are no more, according to the view of the Exclusive Brethren. In its place is a gathering of the men of the assembly who are in fellowship, namely, those who have been allowed to partake of the Lord's Supper and to participate in the public ministries of the local church. This can mean that all decisions are made at this "men's meeting," or that certain men are named responsible for certain areas, such as distributing the money collected at the weekly celebration of the Lord's Supper or overseeing the children's work.

In practice, the oldest brother or brothers in the local church often are given the loudest voice in every decision. Further complicating the leadership structure is the common practice of allowing traveling preachers to have a say in the affairs of the local churches to whom they preach on occasion. For example, areas such as the Netherlands and Flanders ended up with perhaps five "leading brothers" whose pronouncements were the "final" word in disputes or discussions within or between local assemblies. Thus, these leading brothers or traveling preachers acted much like bishops, though that term would be met with very strong denial and revulsion.

Open Brethren Leadership

Types of Open Brethren leadership were succinctly and accurately catalogued by veteran missionary and practical missiologist Kenneth C. Fleming in his presentation at the Second International Brethren Conference for Mission which was held in Rome during the summer of 1996. His lecture was entitled "Leadership in Open Brethren Assemblies of North America."[167] Significantly, this author heard Fleming's model used in the aftermath of the presentation by a number of the conference delegates from around the world to describe their own country's leadership forms. The four styles of leadership posited by Fleming are the "Gospel Hall" type, as led by itinerant preachers; the "New Jersey Chapel" type, as led by elders and itinerant workers; the "Piedmont Chapel" type, as led by

166. Leslie, "Is the Church of God an Organization or an Organism?"
167. The paper also can be found in Fleming, "Leadership," 57–66.

elders and itinerant workers but with the addition of a resident worker or pastor; and the "Progressive" type, as led by the ministry team.[168] Fleming is clear to note that these types are not rigid categories. He further notes that the geographical descriptions given some of the types of leadership do not mean that they are found only in these regions of North America. Accordingly, these four types provide a helpful description under which Open Brethren leadership worldwide can be catalogued.

The Brethren assemblies within the Gospel Hall types are a tight circle of closed fellowship gatherings. Only those within this particularly recognized circle of churches are allowed the privileges of fellowship at the Lord's Supper. In many ways, these meetings listed among the Open Brethren function more like the Exclusive Brethren in their beliefs and practices than the Open Brethren of whom they claim they are a part.[169] The day-to-day leadership in this type is left to the "men's meeting," much as it is in the Exclusive Brethren. However, itinerant preachers are allowed to "effectually define the issues and control the direction of the strictly defined assemblies."[170] While the itinerant preachers strongly would deny their characterization as bishops, they function very much as bishops would function in hierarchical denominations with respect to authority. They also function as bishops with respect to a defined geographical region of influence, though overlapping geographical regions can cause dissention when two itinerants disagree.

New Jersey Chapel type leadership is characterized by the rule of a local board of recognized elders for each individual church. These recognized elders would exhibit the traits listed in 1 Timothy 3 and Titus 1.[171] That said, select itinerant preachers would have a large say in the overall practices of these churches and teaching emphases so as to maintain "Brethren distinctives" generally, as well as particular Open Brethren distinctives of a quite conservative nature. These itinerant preachers usually would be men self-taught in the Scriptures, and many would be suspicious of formal Bible education. These itinerants would not have as much authority as would those who are itinerant among the Gospel Hall type assemblies.

---

168. Ibid., 63–65.

169. These "Open Brethren" churches are listed alongside other, more open gatherings in the annual publication which, for many years, has listed Open Brethren meetings in the US, Canada, and the Caribbean. For an example of this publication, cf. *2006 Address Book of Some Assemblies of Christians in the United States, Canada, and Other Countries*.

170. Fleming, "Leadership," 63.

171. For a very comprehensive biblical and practical discussion of these traits, as well as the responsibilities of elders from an Open Brethren perspective, cf. Strauch, *Biblical Eldership*.

Backgrounds to the Forming of the Evangelische Christengemeenten Vlaanderen

Leadership among the Piedmont Chapel types would be similar to the New Jersey Chapel type, but they would include a resident worker or pastor among the recognized leadership. This resident worker may or may not be part of the board of elders, but he typically would be charged with much of "the administration, counseling, visitation, and preaching as arranged with the elders."[172] Fleming notes that the worker's role is normally quite visible, but he still may not be the dominant decision maker. Many of these resident workers would have some level of formal theological training, ranging from a Bible institute all the way through a seminary education, including a doctorate in some cases.[173] Resident workers who do not have a formal Bible education usually are men drawn from the business world after demonstrating successful managerial skills. The particular needs of the local Brethren church and the desires of the elders dictate the type of man asked to come as the resident worker. This type of leadership, and especially the title of "pastor," constitutes a significant step away from traditional structures of leadership among the Open Brethren in many parts of the world. As one worker stated, "When I first came here, if anyone used the word 'pastor,' he might have been struck down by lightning."[174]

The fourth category of Open Brethren leadership is the Progressive type, characterized by a ministry team whose members usually are highly trained and paid for their efforts. When Fleming spoke, he knew of no women who functioned as part of this team-leadership model, but women can be found among both the elders and paid staff at this writing, more than a decade later. Significantly, Fleming notes that the spontaneous, participatory manner of celebrating the Lord's Supper which has characterized the Brethren since its inception is seen as "non-user friendly, and so would be given a lower priority."[175] Also significant is that many within these assemblies would not be cognizant of their identity as part of the Brethren, thinking rather that they merely are members of an independent, conservative evangelical church.[176]

---

172. Fleming, "Leadership," 64.

173. While a doctorate is rare, it is not unknown, especially in Brethren assemblies whose common worshipper is highly educated. Bethany Bible Chapel in Wheaton, IL, USA, is an example of such a local church.

174. Krayenhoff, "Changing of the Guard at Oaklands Chapel."

175. Fleming, "Leadership," 65.

176. Prime example of this type of non-identification with the Brethren (even though listed in successive editions of *Address Book of Some Assemblies of Christians*) would include Plano Bible Chapel, TX, USA. Their extensive website makes no mention of their association or roots in the Brethren as they describe their ministries, history, or beliefs. Further, joint youth activities with other self-identified Brethren assemblies nearby were discouraged by the staff, as witnessed by this writer in the mid-1980s. The

Ecclesiological Modeling of the Exclusive and Open Brethren Prior to the ECV

While the Lord's Supper is certainly the central ecclesiological mark of all the Brethren, and certainly styles of leadership within and between the Exclusive and Open Brethren are pertinent to this study, a starting point for a further evaluation of the ecclesiology of the Exclusive Brethren in Flanders perhaps is seen best in *The Four Point Statement* agreed to by the vast majority of Exclusive Brethren worldwide in the aftermath of a series of meetings which came to be known as the Reunion of 1926. From this time forward, the Exclusive Brethren in Flanders would be noted most accurately as Continental Exclusives. Napoleon Noels' two-volume work, *The History of the Brethren*, contains this four-point statement. This statement is worth quoting in its entirety to set the stage for the Exclusive ecclesiology from this point until nearly the end of the twentieth century.

> Association—As to reception and discipline, we refuse to seek such principles as leave the door open to evil; thus seeking to preserve the sanctity of *God's House*.
>
> Congregationalism—Which makes assemblies independent of each other, we refuse, as it practically denies the *Unity* of the Body of Christ; reducing the corporate responsibility and testimony to that of mere local assembly, or even that of the individual.
>
> Ecclesiasticism—Which unduly exalts assembly action, we should guard against. We acknowledge the Lord's authority by *His Word*, to which the assembly, as well as the individual, is to be subject.
>
> Liberty of Ministry—We recognize, both within and without the assembly, while fellowship and *counsel* as to it should be regarded, since we are members of one another.[177]

Both the Continental and the Open Brethren in Flanders particularly were concerned that the purity of the Lord's Supper be maintained, though certainly the Continentals and the one Tunbridge Wells assembly would have

---

reason given for this lack of joint activity was the desire not to be too closely identified with the Brethren. Cf. "Plano Bible Chapel." Another example would be Countryside Bible Chapel in Lexington, MA, USA. Again, no mention is made of the Brethren, and on the home page of their website they self-identify as "an independent Bible church." Cf. "Countryside Bible Chapel."

177. Noel, *The History of the Brethren*, 2:777.

Backgrounds to the Forming of the Evangelische Christengemeenten Vlaanderen

been even more restrictive, as seen in the above point "Association."[178] This purity emphasis in the Open assemblies of Great Britain came about as a result of a "tightening process" beginning in 1870.[179] Not until years after the arrival of the founders of the ECV would the Open Brethren and Continental Exclusives in Flanders have a closer connection. This connection came in the aftermath of a change of thinking as well as of a number of difficulties in the Netherlands which caused most of the formerly Exclusive meetings to break with their Continental Brethren connection. This final break came as a result of problems in an assembly in North Holland at Den Helder.[180] Brethren historian Donald Tinder notes that, within much of the worldwide communion of Exclusive assemblies, the resulting move toward an Open Brethren position would be (and still is) referred to as "Dutch disease."

So how might one compare and contrast the Brethren groups found in Flanders when the founders of the ECV arrived, as well as the ECV churches themselves which were later to come? Given the transcontinental nature of the Brethren and the often vague or contradictory self-identification of groups within the Brethren, this is a relevant question. Part of the challenge in categorizing these Flemish assemblies lies in the perspective of the one who is doing the categorization. From a North American perspective, which is that of the founders of the ECV, one might label the Open Brethren churches "tight opens" because they functioned in many ways like Exclusive assemblies. Still, this nomenclature would not be common in Flanders.

One way to compare the various Brethren in Flanders in light of these challenges is by using the historical four marks of the Church: one, holy, catholic, and apostolic. Because the definitions of these four marks have been interpreted widely throughout the ages—a challenge commonly noted by theologians such as G. C. Berkouwer—a succinct set of definitions follows, definitions in line with what many free church groupings would understand.[181]

One refers to the unity of the Church, as seen in the role of the Holy Spirit making the many one in 1 Corinthians 12:13, as well as in 1 Corinthians 3:16, where the plural "you" indicates that the Holy Spirit dwells in the

---

178. Mead, *Handbook of Denominations in the United States*, 66–67.

179. Conard, *Family Matters*, 95.

180. "'Keiner kann mir Vorwürfe machen, dass ich mich geändert habe': Interview mit Willem J. Ouweneel," 21.

181. Berkouwer, *The Church*, 12. For comparison of the four marks of the Church from a more high order church, such as a Roman Catholic perspective, cf. Dulles, "The True Church," 114–29; "The Hierarchical Structure of the Church with Special Reference to the Episcopate," in Abbott, ed., *The Documents of Vatican II*, 37–56; Küng, "The Dimensions of the Church: The Church is Catholic," 296–318.

corporate body of believers. The oneness based upon the work of the Holy Spirit does not require sameness. To require sameness, as did some of the Brethren groups discussed, would be to practice a less-than-biblical unity.

Holy is based upon the positional or declared holiness of believers, as evidenced by their title "saints" in Ephesians 1:1, as well as a practical outworking of this status in Ephesians 4:1. A holy Church is one which recognizes the positional holiness of the believer and does not over-exaggerate holiness by adding a legalistic framework of manmade expectations, as did some of the Flemish Brethren groups. Conversely, a holy Church would not simply accept positional holiness and ignore the practice which should follow position.

Catholic is merely all who are in Christ in line with Ephesians 2:12–19. This depicts the Church of Christ as neither broader nor narrower than those who are part of the body through the crosswork of Christ. As Miroslav Volf has noted simply, "to be catholic means to be comprehensive and complete."[182]

Apostolic is to practice and promulgate the doctrine of the Apostles. The debate within the Brethren comes with the form of local church government actually taught by the apostles, versus what is allowed now due to "failures" as seen through a dispensational grid mentioned earlier. Thus, the understandings can differ of what exactly *apostolic* entails, especially when the Exclusive and Open Brethren assemblies are compared and contrasted.

Using the four traditional marks of the Church, the Exclusive Brethren can be described as a group whose oneness is limited due to their practice of the Lord's Supper being closed to those believers who do not believe the same way they do, whose understanding of holiness is exaggerated due to legalism, and whose catholicity is narrower than those who are part of the body of Christ. As one well known, late nineteenth century Exclusive Brethren author wrote,

> Even suppose we could see a man's name written in the book of life, that would not be the ground of receiving him into the assembly on earth, or retaining him there. That which the Church is held responsible for, is to keep herself pure in doctrine, pure in practice, and pure in association, and all this on the ground of being God's house . . . We have not only to maintain the *grace* of the Lord's table, but the *holiness* of it also.[183]

Most other Christian bodies thus would be considered those with whom the Exclusive Brethren could not cooperate or fellowship because of their

---

182. Volf, *After Our Likeness*, 261.

183. Mackintosh, "Thoughts on the Lord's Supper," 13, 17.

Backgrounds to the Forming of the Evangelische Christengemeenten Vlaanderen

failure to follow the example and practices of the Exclusive Brethren. This truncated sense of oneness and overstated holiness is witnessed in an even more exaggerated form in the one Tunbridge Wells assembly which was planted in Menen in the early 1950s.[184] Amazingly, the Flemish Exclusives' drive for holiness as defined by "purity of the Lord's Table" superseded even current events and cultures. During the Second World War, occupying German soldiers from the "proper" Brethren assemblies in Germany were allowed to fellowship at the Exclusive Brethren assembly in Gent, even though Flemish believers from other Christian groups were not![185]

In slight contrast, the Flemish Open assemblies planted by the Nocks and later missionaries would have had a similar, though a bit less exaggerated, concept of holiness due to the tightening process in the United Kingdom begun in 1870, as mentioned earlier. In practical terms, this would have barred partaking of and public participation in the Lord's Supper to any who did not agree with the traditional practices of the Brethren with respect to type of Church government, role of women, perhaps even acceptable music, dress, etc. This created a great obstacle and ultimately lay behind the reasoning of the founders of the ECV to start new assemblies rather than to work within the existing Open Brethren gatherings.[186]

Irrespective of the historical-theological evidence, the Flemish Continental assemblies which the early founders of the ECV encountered probably would not have considered themselves "Exclusives" since they were not of the decidedly more restrictive and radical grouping known as the Taylorites.[187] Still, both the Flemish Open Brethren and certainly the Continental Brethren held to many of the same practices in their meetings and had a very restrictive view of the communion table. This was in line with most of the assemblies in the Netherlands and much of the continent of Europe at that time. The Continental Brethren certainly could have been labeled Exclusives given their clearly drawn "circles of fellowship." Accordingly, a similar outworking of the four traditional marks of the Church would characterize both the Continental and Open Brethren which were present when the founders of the ECV arrived in the 1970s.

---

184. Ver Gouwe, "Re: Vergadering in Woesten," email, 30 July 2005.

185. Van Der Elst, letter, 20 August 2005.

186. R. Haverkamp, interview, 29 July 2005.

187. For more information, cf. the same resources listed in chapter 1, n7. Cf. some of the information contained in Barrett, *The New Believers*, 162ff.

"# 3

Workers and Works of the *Evangelische Christengemeenten Vlaanderen*

FOUNDERS OF THE ECV: CONVERSION AND BACKGROUND

THE EXISTENCE OF THE ECV primarily can be traced back to the work of a number of Canadian and US missionaries in the early 1970s and 1980s.[1] These missionaries were from the movement commonly called the Plymouth Brethren or Christian Brethren. Accordingly, these Christian workers were sent out from local Brethren congregations in North America, but serviced by the "missionary service organization" known as Missionary Service Committee (MSC) in Canada and Christian Missions in Many Lands (CMML) in the United States.[2] Founded in 1940, MSC officially

---

1. These workers also would have been known as commended workers. A commended worker is someone from the Brethren who has been recognized by an assembly for full-time Christian service. A letter of commendation is the instrument used to designate such a worker. For a more complete description, cf. Yuille, "Commendation," 37–48; Porter, *Commendation*; A. Pulleng, *"Go Ye Therefore . . .",* 16–20.

2. These agencies were and are dedicated to the overseas, cross-cultural activities of the Brethren movement from primarily English-speaking North America, but have very little or no control over the workers or the direction of their work. For more information, including a very brief history on MSC, cf. http://www.msc.on.ca/ For more information on CMML, cf. http://www.cmmlusa.org/

changed its name to MSC Canada on 28 January 1993.[3] Subsequent to the work of both nations' missionary service organizations, and as a result of their work, a considerable number of indigenous workers became an active part of the ECV, including several who played a key part in the growth and success of the movement.

Canadian Founders of the ECV

Who were the men that founded the ECV, and what was their background and character? While one figure from the Netherlands will be included as a founder due to gifting and work, the three main founders of the ECV were Canadian missionaries—namely, Herb Shindelka, Richard Haverkamp, and Henk Gelling. The order below is according the chronology of their arrival in Belgium.[4]

Herb Shindelka, 1971–1976[5]

The earliest worker in Flanders associated with what would become the ECV was Herb Shindelka. While he had neither formal Bible training nor even a university education, Shindelka had been very active in the Brethren assemblies in the province of Alberta before coming over to Belgium. He had spent a good number of years leading Bible studies as well doing personal evangelism and personal discipleship before coming to Europe.[6] In 1966, he and two other men planted an assembly in Sherwood Park, a thriving bedroom community just to the southeast of Edmonton. Shindelka came from Belmont Gospel Chapel, a mid-1940s hive-off from another Edmonton Brethren assembly, Bethel Gospel Chapel. The other two men came from Bethel Gospel Chapel itself.[7] This new assembly was called Sherwood Park Bible Chapel until 1976 when the name became Wycliff Bible Chapel.[8] While committed to "traditional Christian Brethren teach-

---

3. Masuello, email, 13 August 2007.

4. While Haverkamp arrived in Europe before Shindelka, Shindelka was the first of the three Canadian founders to settle in Belgium.

5. Dates given in the titles for key people in this chapter refer to the years of their active service with the ECV, not to dates of birth or death.

6. R. Haverkamp, interview, 30 April 2003.

7. Peterson, "A History of Some Assemblies of Christians in the United States and Canada." Cf. S. Tordoff, email, 13 February 2008.

8. Elders of Sherwood Park Bible Chapel, "Letter of Commendation," 26 May 1971. Signatories were Dr. Gerald L. Higgins, Stanley H. King, Ronald A. Reyburn,

ing," this assembly was more progressive in attitude given the very close proximity to Edmonton, the capital city of Alberta.[9] Wyecliff would go on to commend three overseas workers and three local workers.[10] Of all the Canadian workers who were instrumental in founding what would become the ECV, Shindelka was the only one from a Roman Catholic background. He experienced evangelical conversion in his mid-twenties in 1964 through the witness of friends who took him to an evangelistic outreach.[11]

Shindelka was known as an attentive listener, a careful note-taker during sermons. He also was one with whom the elders of his local assembly spent a great deal of time. This attentive listening to sermons and mentoring by the elders would comprise his "formal" teaching.[12] His ministry involvement chiefly was in the areas of personal evangelism and youth work, though he also did some pulpit ministry. Very notably, he encouraged people to commit themselves to "foreign missions," and he is credited with Winston Roan's lifelong commitment to Thailand working with New Tribes Missions.[13] A very close family friend noted, "Herb's zeal for the Lord was infectious, while his people skills were noteworthy, both in the secular and in the Spiritual. He truly loved the Lord and wanted to serve Him first and foremost."[14]

Additionally, Shindelka's wife, Lillian, was involved in the ministries of the local assembly where they were members. Like Shindelka, Lillian was converted from a Roman Catholic background.[15] As well as working with the youth alongside her husband, Lillian and another woman distributed evangelistic literature to nearly every home in Sherwood Park. This likely was a distribution of well over five thousand tracts.[16]

Gordon S. Buzzacott, Sidney Tordoff, and Joseph Clark. A Letter of Commendation is the means by which a person is identified to other Brethren assemblies as one who is engaged in vocational Christian work. Normally these letters are signed by either the leadership of a particular local church or other designated persons on behalf of the entire local body. The concept and wording reflects the ideas of Acts 14:26.

9. S. Tordoff, letter, undated (postmarked 01 February 2008).

10. Peterson, "A History of Some Assemblies of Christians in the United States and Canada."

11. S. Tordoff, letter, undated (postmarked 01 February 2008).

12. Ibid.

13. S. Tordoff, email, 13 February 2008, and "Letter of Commendation," 26 May 1971.

14. B. Tordoff, letter, undated (postmarked 01 February 2008).

15. S. Tordoff, letter, undated (postmarked 01 February 2008).

16. B. Tordoff, letter, undated (postmarked 01 February 2008). While B. Tordoff's letter mentions no exact numbers, official government statistics record that Sherwood Park had 5,885 private dwellings in 1970, the year before the Shindelkas moved to Belgium. Cf. BC Stats, "2006 Census: Edmonton-Sherwood Park-FED," 6. Sherwood

Workers and Works of the Evangelische Christengemeenten Vlaanderen

Outside the local church, Shindelka was a highly successful businessman. He was a top seller of modular housing units before going into fulltime Christian work.[17] Initially, he worked as a sales manager for Alberta-based Nelson Homes, a manufacturer of modular home components, and later he set up dealers for pre-built homes manufactured by Atco, Ltd., a company headquartered in Calgary, AB.[18] Atco had such confidence in his work and character that Shindelka was issued a blank purchase order. Such was Shindelka's prowess as a salesman that a close friend noted, "he could sell refrigerators to the Eskimos."[19] The same family friend commented that this skill was not always a welcome trait since some viewed Shindelka as "over-aggressive, probably due to his personality and sales ability."[20] Nevertheless, Shindelka left this very successful and lucrative career to plant churches in Belgium.

Shindelka's move to Belgium was not without its obstacles, however. His move to Flanders was delayed for a full year because his wife was not yet convinced of his desire to live as commended workers in Belgium.[21] Once Shindelka's wife accepted the idea, Shindelka and his family arrived in Europe in August 1971, having been "commended to the Lord's care for His work in Europe" by the Wyecliff Bible Chapel.[22] His first target was in and around the city of Antwerp since his wife had relatives in Belgium, the country of her birth. Richard Haverkamp was already in Europe in the Netherlands, so Haverkamp was the one to meet Shindelka and his family at the airport and drive them to Antwerp. Haverkamp knew the Shindelkas quite well from their days in Canada, and even had stayed in their home in Edmonton when Haverkamp had special meetings at their assembly in Sherwood Park.[23]

Shindelka's background, gifts, and abilities were particularly well suited to planting new churches. First, as mentioned earlier, Shindelka had

---

Park's official census population lists a steady 6,339 from 1966 to 1970. This number jumped to 14,282 in 1971. Cf. "Alberta Population Profile: Sherwood Park."

17. H. Gelling, interview, 25 April 2003, says Northwest Territories; Haverkamp, interview, 30 April 2003, says Yukon Territory.

18. For information on Nelson Homes, cf. http://www.nlc.ca/index.php?page_id=aboutus. For information on Atco, Ltd., cf. http://www.ucalgary.ca/applied_history/tutor/calgary/atco.html.

19. S. Tordoff, letter, undated (postmarked 01 February 2008).

20. Ibid.

21. Ibid.

22. Hampton, email, 24 January 2008 with a forward from S.Tordoff, email message to Ron Hampton, 24 January 2008. Cf. R. Haverkamp, interview, 25 April 2003; R. and M. Haverkamp, newsletter to supporters, May 1972.

23. R. Haverkamp, interview, 25 April 2003.

been active in his home assembly. He merely was continuing what he had been doing for many years, but now in a Belgian context. This vital background of previous, proven ministry was evident among all the Canadian workers who would come to Belgium to help with the ECV in the early years. So important was this concept of having proven oneself before going out to a cross-cultural work, that even the minimal and optional Missionary Orientation Program offered by the American and Canadian missionary service agencies of the Brethren repeatedly stated this idea during their five day course for newly commended missionaries or for those who are considering missionary work.[24] Many other mission organizations and veteran missionaries treated this as axiomatic as well.

Second, personal or "one-on-one" evangelism was considered Shindelka's chief gift by those who worked with him. For example, Richard Haverkamp would teach at a Bible study or a youth meeting, and Shindelka would sit in the corner and watch people. When Haverkamp was finished, Shindelka would go over and engage in conversation with those who seemed to be responding. While Shindelka was also a very able Bible teacher, he especially was well-known for this type of personal work.[25]

Another of Shindelka's gifts was that "he was a real people person . . . a jolly old fellow," and people were attracted to him.[26] He always was talking to people, whether in the home Bible studies or out in the community. Shindelka would talk to people at bus stops lines at the store, etc., to make a new contact for an evangelistic Bible study or to share the message of the evangelical gospel on the spot. One of his early coworkers in Belgium noted, "Herb was the kind of person that took twenty minutes to shake hands with everyone in the room." This worker went on to note that during the time Shindelka was talking to someone, that person had his undivided attention, not the feeling that he merely was going through the motions before moving on to the next person.[27] Another part of his personable nature was that Shindelka was not afraid to use what little he knew of the Dutch language (or French or German as the occasion arose). This linguistic boldness amazed even one as outgoing as Haverkamp since Haverkamp also knew a few words of French and German; Haverkamp would not speak either language when he was among people who spoke those languages. Shindelka's willingness to engage people in conversation in Flanders was particularly

24. Missionary Orientation Program, CMML and MSC Canada, Greenwood Hills, PA. The author heard this emphasis repeatedly while attending part of one of these programs in June 2000.

25. R. Haverkamp, interview, 30 April 2003.

26. Ibid.

27. H. Gelling, interview, 01 May 2003.

noteworthy among the founders of the ECV as he had no hereditary language exposure in Dutch, unlike Haverkamp and Gelling.[28]

Finally, Shindelka had a very good knowledge of the Bible. Nevertheless, he initially used his Bible in a way which was not tolerated in Flanders. For example, Haverkamp notes that Shindelka used to quote Proverbs 16:27 against smoking since the verse had something about "fire between the lips."[29] This was a common practice among the Brethren in Canada, to take a verse out of context and use it for a point that the speaker wished to prove. In Flanders, however, people would ask what else might be in the passage. Consequently, Shindelka had to change his method of using the Bible as that which he had practiced among the Brethren in Canada was rejected.[30] All the same, Shindelka led Bible studies quite successfully in Belgium, and he would leave a time after the study to answer all questions posed. The man who would take over Shindelka's position when Shindelka left Christian work noted that Shindelka would provide a "beautiful answer" even though the question may have been completely unrelated to that evening's study. This same worker was certain that the task of planting churches in Flanders would have gone faster had Shindelka not "lost focus" and left the work since he was a "tremendous personal worker and a tremendous teacher."[31]

Sadly, Shindelka's commendation necessarily was withdrawn by his home assembly in July 1976.[32] After leaving Christian work "for family reasons," he returned to the business world.[33] He initially lived in Flanders, though his work with the building products industry caused him to travel mainly throughout the Netherlands. When he eventually returned to Canada, Shindelka went into ranching. He ran a very profitable specialty horse business just north of Vernon, BC.[34] He died in 2006. A thoughtful observer noted about the Shindelkas, "Their lesson to us and the church: 'How much we need to pray for one another, especially for those in the forefront of Satan's attack.'"[35]

---

28. R. Haverkamp, interview, 30 April 2003.

29. Proverbs 16:27 (KJV): "An ungodly man diggeth up evil: and in his lips there is as a burning fire."

30. R. Haverkamp, interview, 30 April 2003.

31. H. Gelling, interview, 25 April 2003.

32. S. Tordoff, letter to Missionary Service Committee, 10 July 1976.

33. R. Haverkamp, "Wie der Herr Jesus Christus Gemeinden baut," session 1. The sessions are numbered in order of occurrence: 7 lectures, 1 question and answer period, and 1 lecture.

34. S. Tordoff, letter, undated (01 February 2008).

35. B. Tordoff, letter, undated (01 February 2008).

New Brethren in Flanders

Richard Haverkamp, 1971–2009

GENERAL BACKGROUND

Richard Haverkamp was born on 18 May 1940 in the Netherlands in Vorden, a small village near Zutphen in the province of Gelderland, though he also lived in Limburg in the city of Heerlen for a number of years. He was in the midst of completing his secondary education at a *Hogere Burger School* when his health forced him to stop. Instead, he completed this segment of his education at a school of agriculture.[36] Haverkamp was catechized and confirmed in the *Nederlandse Hervormde Kerk*, but he recalled that his experiences there were not good ones.[37] "The ministers there never smiled. That's what turned me against the church. I enjoy life and a good laugh . . . I grew up with the thought that if you believe in God you cannot enjoy things."[38] He emigrated to Canada at the age of eighteen. During the first two years in Canada, Haverkamp worked on some large farms as well as in house construction.

Haverkamp's evangelical conversion was rather dramatic. Far from his parents, Haverkamp was glad to be free. Though he went to church occasionally with Dutch friends of his parents, he knew something was not right, and he began to become very despondent. During this time of despondency, he met a Bible school graduate who read the Bible to him. Haverkamp mocked this young man as "the Bible was for small children and grandmothers."[39] Irrespective of this, Haverkamp was prayed for by this young man as well as another young man and two female classmates, including Marina Funk—the woman who later would become Haverkamp's wife.[40]

As Haverkamp continued to search for relief from his despair, he heard at a local restaurant the words in a song sung by blues singer Chuck Willis, "What am I living for?"[41] These words haunted Haverkamp that day and into the night. Finally, he took out the Bible that his mother had given him as a small boy and began to read. As he read, he says that he remembers that

36. R. Haverkamp, written response to questions from Koen Schelstraete, n.d. (file dated 06 November 2000).

37. R. Haverkamp, interview, 02 September 1988.

38. R. Haverkamp, "Wie der Herr Jesus Christus Gemeinden baut," session 2.

39. R. Haverkamp, written response to questions from Koen Schelstraete, n.d. (file dated 06 November 2000).

40. M. Haverkamp, interview, 25 April 2003.

41. Willis, *What Am I Living For?* Haverkamp notes that the overall message of the song was not the reason, as the song has to do with a broken relationship with a woman, but rather the simple repeated phrase listed above. R. Haverkamp, "RE: Song Ttile [sic], please?" email, 16 July 2007.

Workers and Works of the Evangelische Christengemeenten Vlaanderen

"a violent fight began in my heart. This fight continued until I thought, 'I've tried everything else, and nothing has brought me any luck. I surrender.'"[42] Haverkamp wept for a very long time after this surrender, but when he stopped crying, he says he looked at the world through new eyes. Even those around him noticed the immediate difference when he saw them the next day. Immediately, Haverkamp was filled with the desire to tell others about what had happened to him. He even went so far as to look for and pick up a hitchhiker so he could share what had happened to him. This fervent desire to speak about the evangelical faith would characterize him from that point forward.[43] As he looked back on his conversion many years later, Haverkamp would say, "When I was converted . . . I did not understand this 'salvation' and 'born again.' There was only one thing I understood: God wanted everything or nothing at all."[44]

In the September following his July conversion, Haverkamp enrolled in a four year program at the non-denominational Millar Memorial Bible Institute in Pambrun, Saskatchewan, the same school at which his future wife was enrolled.[45] This Bible institute was the follow-on to the Moose Jaw Bible Institute founded in 1928 by the Scottish Baptist pastor, William J. Millar, who was "one of the fathers of the Canadian Bible School movement."[46] Millar had been converted under the ministry of D. L. Moody in Scotland, and after years of ministry in Africa and Scotland, came to Canada where he ministered until his death in 1932.[47] Millar was noted for his uncompromising commitment to dispensationalism, as were the teachers at his school.[48] This dispensational emphasis would be part of the training received by the Haverkamps during their years at Millar Memorial Bible Institute. This school also was noted for its commitment to the clear teaching of the Bible as well as to practical ministry experience in areas such

42. R. Haverkamp, written response to questions from Koen Schelstraete, n.d. (file dated 06 November 2000).

43. Ibid.

44. R. Haverkamp, "Wie der Herr Jesus Christus Gemeinden baut," session 1.

45. R. Haverkamp, interview, 02 September 1988.

46. Holthaus, "Die Gründer der Bibelschule: A. John Parschauer."

47. Bredin, "NBBI's Beginnings: An Early History of the New Brunswick Bible Institute."

48. Hindmarsh, "The Winnipeg Fundamentalist Network, 1910–1940: The Roots of Transdenominational Evangelicalism in Manitoba and Saskatchewan." Cf. James Opp's MA thesis, "Culture of the Soul," for Millar's break with well-known Canadian fundamentalist T.T. Shields over matters related to the issue of dispensationalism. An email received by the author from Dr. Opp records, "Shields was an unusual fundamentalist in that he was essentially 'amillennial' in eschatology, and decidedly hostile to dispensationalism" (Opp, "Fwd: Attn: Dr. James Opp," email, 29 July 2003).

as evangelistic meetings and campaigns, short-term missions trips, and a variety of children's work in five-day clubs, vacation Bible school, and Bible camps.[49] Both Richard and Marina Haverkamp would make these emphases a part of their philosophy of ministry.

Marina Elizabeth Funk was born on 26 February 1937 in Saskatchewan, Canada. She was the child of Russian immigrants who fled the Bolsheviks because her grandfather was a preacher in the Evangelical German Mennonite Church. As a result, she grew up in a home where the Bible and the evangelical gospel was well known. Mrs. Haverkamp was committed to cross-cultural Christian work at the age of six, even before she was converted at the age of nine.[50] She says that her childhood commitment led her even to "sometimes eat weeds and grass to prepare me" for whatever strange things she might be called upon to eat in overseas service.[51] Since Mrs. Haverkamp understood her calling to be work among the children of Africa, she became associated with Child Evangelism Fellowship (CEF). Her geographical direction was changed, however, when she was shocked to hear a Belgian CEF worker's statement: for every 200 Christians in the Belgian Congo, one was in the country of Belgium itself. As a result, she shifted her focus to serving in Belgium one day.

About a year later, she met Richard Haverkamp while they were both students at Millar. She was manning a sign-up sheet at a table to help organize children's meetings, when a "tall, dark, handsome man" signed up to be a part of the team. When she looked to see the name, she was shocked. This young man was the one for whose conversion she had prayed years earlier, "the wild guy," Richard Haverkamp. Although he had only recently experienced evangelical conversion, Mrs. Haverkamp says that Haverkamp wanted to be involved in anything and everything to do with "the Lord's work." Haverkamp was immediately appreciated by Marina as he took charge.[52] She was used to having to lead the youth work. Normally, she had to ask the young men to step out and talk with the teens standing around on the street or to take care of the details of a particular outreach. She also was uncomfortable in leadership as she understood that to be a man's role. As a result, she was quite happy when Haverkamp took control. Together,

---

49. "Millar College of the Bible." "A motto that could be seen on the walls of the quonset during conferences was 'Where the Bible is Wholly Taught' which reflected the desire of Millar's leaders at the very beginning of the school's history and is still the focal point of the teaching today."

50. M. Haverkamp, written response to questions from Koen Schelstraete, n.d. (file dated 09 September 1999).

51. Ibid.

52. M. Haverkamp, interview, 25 April 2003.

she and Haverkamp organized a series of children's meetings that eventually led to the formation of young adult Bible studies as well. A good number of people were converted as a result of Haverkamp's work in these meetings.[53] The following year, Richard Haverkamp and Marina Funk were married on 15 September 1962.

In the six years which followed Richard Haverkamp's graduation from Millar, he was involved in a variety of different types of Christian work, including evangelistic meetings and pastoring a Baptist church while it looked for a permanent pastor. Also during this period, Haverkamp lived for a short time at a home run by the New Testament Missionary Union before he and Marina were married. During his stay, he carefully read a book by Alexander R. Hay, the organization's founder, entitled, *The New Testament Order for Church and Missionary*.[54] Haverkamp later would say that this book was the only training he received about church planting.[55] While Alexander Hay was not from the Brethren, his work so closely parallels their teaching that many have mistakenly included it among Brethren writings.[56] One published essay well notes, "The usefulness of this book is its thorough attention to the biblical data, which is then cast into a programmatic scheme for church planting. Its weakness is that it assumes all churches to be organized in the same manner without regard to cultural milieu."[57] Especially the idea of a close biblical patterning without a strict adherence to a traditional Brethren way of doing things would indeed characterize Haverkamp's approach to church planting in Belgium.

Haverkamp's involvement with the Open Brethren came about almost by accident since after he was converted he regularly attended a Baptist church. He even had stated that he would never have anything to do with the Brethren as his first contact had been with men from the Canadian Exclusives.[58] While pastoring or simply attending the Baptist church, he continued his habit of conducting evangelistic meetings in a number of locales. These meetings caused him to be known among the Brethren in his area as he conducted a series of meetings from one week to three weeks between 1965 and 1970.[59] His long term contact with people from the assembly which would send him to Belgium came as a result of

---

53. Ibid.
54. Hay, *The New Testament Order for Church and Missionary*.
55. R. Haverkamp, interview, 25 April 2003.
56. See Stanford, "Plymouth Brethren Emulators."
57. Kopp and Zerbe, "Bibliographic Essay on Church Leadership."
58. R. Haverkamp, interview, 25 April 2003
59. Ibid.

evangelistic meetings which he conducted in 1969 in Moorefield, a Canadian town located in the center of a Dutch immigrant region. The elders of this assembly noted a number of things about Haverkamp. First, he was a dynamic speaker, filled with enthusiasm. This attracted listeners; they would come to hear someone who was "awake, alive, and well-spoken."[60] Second, he was a self-starter. Haverkamp had been converted from a very ungodly lifestyle with only a nominal affiliation with the Dutch Reformed Church. Because of the content of his evangelical gospel message, however, he would not have been well received in many corners of his childhood denomination since long ago these had become theologically liberal. Accordingly, Haverkamp organized evangelistic meetings on his own. One of the most significant and prolific church planting pioneers in Ontario among the Brethren noted of Haverkamp,

> We offered him a lot of opportunity for preaching, so he did a lot of that. Not only would he be satisfied sitting down and preaching every Sunday. So he would be visiting people and contacting people and out on the move trying to contact people making them acquainted with the Gospel.[61]

Third, he largely was unknown to the elders of Wallenstein Bible Chapel, the Open Brethren assembly which would become his main point of contact within the Brethren. After Haverkamp spoke at the series of evangelistic meetings in nearby Moorefield, the elders quickly came to believe he was a worthwhile man who would need a supporting group if he were to go anywhere.[62] One Sunday morning, he and his wife finally attended Wallenstein Bible Chapel and witnessed the Brethren celebration of the Lord's Supper. Haverkamp described this experience as "marvelous" as he never "felt right" when he was the pastor of the Baptist church. He was especially uncomfortable with his role as "the pastor" because as a result, none of the men who could preach and teach would do so at the church.

The Sunday evening of his first visit to the Brethren assembly, he and his wife came to a service to witness a baptism and to listen to well-known Canadian Brethren itinerant preacher Arnot McIntee. For some reason, McIntee never arrived. Faced with a roomful of people and no speaker, one of the elders, John Martin, went to Haverkamp and asked if he would preach that night since he had heard Haverkamp during other evangelistic meetings. Haverkamp agreed to speak and asked them to sing for another

---

60. Former elders of Wallenstein Bible Chapel, interview, 01 September 2006.
61. John and Melissa Martin, interview, 01 September 2006.
62. Former elders of Wallenstein Bible Chapel, interview, 01 September 2006.

Workers and Works of the Evangelische Christengemeenten Vlaanderen

five minutes while he prayed in a back room and gathered his thoughts. Haverkamp viewed these circumstances as "of the Lord" since his preaching went well.

From that evening onward, he and Mrs. Haverkamp "fellowshipped" among the Brethren; they were active in the ministry of and committed to the local Brethren assembly as well ministry in the surrounding assemblies. Interestingly, Martin had earlier declared to Haverkamp at one of the evangelistic meetings, "You are one of us."[63] This was quite an endorsement, especially given that Martin had ministered full time among the assemblies since 1935 and was responsible for the planting of quite a number of Brethren assemblies throughout southwestern Ontario.[64] Both Martin and another Wallenstein elder, Israel Hoffman, informally discipled Haverkamp until his departure for Europe because "he was a very good Gospel preacher, but he was not instructed in what we called New Testament principles."[65] Nevertheless, Haverkamp says he never really was taught by any of the Brethren *per se*. He says that he became interested in "assembly principles" from Hay's book.[66] "I'm not really Brethren with a big 'B.' It's the principles I like. I love the breaking of bread and the plurality of elders."[67] This belief would become apparent during his years of work in Belgium as he successfully, and of necessity, distanced the churches that he planted from the sometimes poor reputation of the long-established Exclusive and Open Brethren assemblies in Flanders.

HAVERKAMP'S CALL TO BELGIUM

While Mrs. Haverkamp's initial decision to go to Belgium mainly was through circumstances, Haverkamp's initial decision was associated with a vision from God or a really strong impression during his "quiet time," a daily time of personal prayer and Bible reading.[68] Haverkamp recounted the vision as the Lord saying, "One day, you are going to have Bible studies

---

63. R. Haverkamp, interview, 25 April 2003.

64. Martin, *Saved to Serve*, 27–28. Unlike the normal Brethren pattern, Martin was an elder at three different assemblies at the same time. All three assemblies were among those which he had started. See Martin, *Saved to Serve*, 53.

65. John and Melissa Martin, interview, 01 September 2006. NB: Israel Hoffman was the cousin of Melissa Martin.

66. R. Haverkamp, interview, 25 April 2003.

67. Ibid.

68. R. Haverkamp, "Wie der Herr Jesus Christus Gemeinden baut," session 8, "Fragen und Antworten."

all over Belgium or in southern Holland in the homes." Haverkamp's initial response was, "Go away. I'll never go back to Holland."[69]

Two points are noteworthy about this guidance. First, Haverkamp was not from a Pentecostal or charismatic background. He would have been somewhat more open in his beliefs concerning the working of the Holy Spirit as compared to the churches which sent him to Belgium, yet he did not believe that a special baptism of the Holy Spirit as evidenced by speaking in tongues occurred subsequent to justification. Instead, he believed that the baptism of the Holy Spirit happened to every believer at the time of his justification.[70] Second, he did not blindly follow this vision, but says that he "waited on the Lord" to lead through circumstances. He sought the advice of older Christians as well. Haverkamp understood that vision as merely a foretaste of what the Lord eventually would lead him to do.[71] Accordingly, Richard and Marina Haverkamp took steps to prove the veracity of this vision.

First, the Haverkamps committed the matter to prayer. They prayed diligently about the matter, and over a period of years they repeatedly asked the believers at Wallenstein Bible Chapel to pray about their future ministry at the weekly prayer meeting. Many of Richard and Marina Haverkamp's classmates from Millar had followed the pattern of committing themselves to a missionary agency in the third year of studies. After two years of raising support following graduation, the graduates would go out into the field. The Haverkamps did not follow this pattern, though they were very active in evangelism and other local church work in Canada as they prayed about going to Europe. The milieu among the Canadian Christians from whom the Haverkamps had received their training was such that their active Canadian ministry really was not good enough. "We felt very bad as people looked at us as sort of backslidden because we were not on the mission field."[72] Part of the necessity for this prayer for specific direction was that they also had a desire to work among the native Indians in northern Canada. Mrs. Haverkamp's brother was married to a woman who was part Indian. The need among these peoples for evangelical conversion certainly was evident to the Haverkamps, and commitment to spreading the evangelical faith among these peoples would have satisfied those who were wondering about the sincerity of the Haverkamps.

Second, the Haverkamps sought the active advice and consent of the elders at Wallenstein Bible Chapel concerning their move to Europe. If even

---

69. R. Haverkamp, interview, 25 April 2003.
70. R. Haverkamp, interview, 02 September 1988.
71. R. Haverkamp, interview, 25 April 2003.
72. R. Haverkamp, interview, 30 April 2003.

Workers and Works of the Evangelische Christengemeenten Vlaanderen

one of the eleven or so elders had not been supportive, the Haverkamps said they would not have gone to Europe. Many of the Haverkamps' classmates had gone out as missionaries throughout the world. After six years or so of ministry, however, these classmates had nothing to show for their efforts. Many returned home and never attempted another cross-cultural work. Haverkamp believed that the main problem was that they went into cross-cultural Christian work too soon. "Often God will give you the call well ahead, but before His right time comes you often have to wait a while. We had to wait ten years before we came over."[73] The Haverkamps avoided this pitfall by seeking and listening to the advice of their local church elders. When they finally announced to the elders that they thought the Lord had directed them to Europe, the elders smiled and said, "We've been waiting for a long time, and have known you'd be going. We are all in agreement."[74]

Third, the Haverkamps waited until all the circumstances came together in such a way as to unmistakably confirm their call from God. They even took time to visit the Netherlands as they tried to sort out God's direction for their future work.[75] In September of 1970, the Haverkamps spent a week fasting and praying about their future. During this week, they composed a two-column list as to why they should go to Europe versus the Indians of northern Canada. Haverkamp remembered that the list was three for staying in Canada and twenty-three for going to Europe. Later in that same week during their family quiet time, they read Hebrews 11:8: "By faith Abraham, when he was called to go out into a place which he should after receive for an inheritance, obeyed; and he went out, not knowing whither he went." Richard and Marina Haverkamp said their eyes met as they both understood God to be confirming their call through this verse. Both note that as they went to the assembly that following Sunday to make their announcement, they had a freak accident with their car which should have caused serious damage or death. Instead, they merely departed the road after spinning around between oncoming cars and the Mennonite buggies which were all over the road. They interpreted this event as part of God's confirmation of their call to Europe. Haverkamp said, "This was an absolute miracle. We felt as if the devil was trying to say, 'If you want to announce this, I am going to give you something.'" Both the accident and their preservation from harm were understood as God's confirmation of their call to Europe.[76]

73. Ibid.
74. Ibid.
75. H. Gelling, interview, 25 April 2003.
76. R. Haverkamp, interview, 30 April 2003.

New Brethren in Flanders

On 12 September 1970, the Haverkamps were "commended to the grace of God" as missionaries, even though they had only been at Wallenstein for just over a year. Nonetheless, "their Christian character and their zeal to spread the gospel of Christ" during that time had been exemplary.[77] In their letter of commendation, the elders of Wallenstein Bible Chapel said:

> Since coming into fellowship with us here at Wallenstein we have come to appreciate Richard as a devoted and zealous servant of the Lord with a special gift for evangelism... We believe it is their sincere desire to preach the gospel of Christ and to build up believers in strong, scripturally gathered assembles according to the New Testament pattern and teaching. It is with this confident conviction that we send them forth to serve the Lord in Holland and Western Europe.[78]

In the subsequent months until they departed in mid-1971, Haverkamp had an unwavering understanding that the time was finally right for them to depart. Looking back, he said,

> People worry about the Lord's will. But people need not worry for as someone has said, "The Lord's will is a series of God-given impressions that lead to a God-given conviction." It is a number of things that add up, and then you say, "Ah yes."[79]

He also noted about another time in his work,

> We said we'd wait for the Lord's time, but when the Lord's time comes, things really move, and they did. Things moved so fast that I said, "Lord, please slow down a bit because it's going too fast and we can't keep up."[80]

Even before the Haverkamps left for Europe, however, they began to try to recruit Henk and Beryl Gelling to come and join them in Europe.[81]

---

77. Elders of Wallenstein Bible Chapel, Haverkamps' Letter of Commendation, 12 September 1970.

78. Ibid.

79. R. Haverkamp, interview, 25 April 2003; Haverkamp, "Wie der Herr Jesus Christus Gemeinden baut," session 8, Fragen und Antworten.

80. R. Haverkamp, interview, 30 April 2003.

81. H. Gelling, interview, 25 April 2003. Cf. "Gelling's Call to Belgium" for details of this recruitment.

Workers and Works of the Evangelische Christengemeenten Vlaanderen

HAVERKAMP'S ARRIVAL IN EUROPE

Richard and Marina Haverkamp and their three young children arrived in the Netherlands on 7 June 1971.[82] The Haverkamps first tried to go to the Netherlands as missionaries, rather than to Belgium, because of the historical animosity between the Netherlands and Belgium, and because they were given an apartment in which they could stay.[83] They spent about six months in the Netherlands in the home of a missionary in Koudekerk aan de Rijn, Zuid-Holland, while that missionary was on furlough back in Canada. They came to Zuid-Holland with the idea of "waiting on the Lord for further direction as to whether to move to southern Holland or northern Belgium" because this part of the Netherlands was not their intended location for ministry.[84] Haverkamp referenced this in a letter to MSC when he wrote,

> We have for years been burdened for Southern Holland and Northern Belgium which are 90% R. Catholic. There are no open assemblies in that part of Holland and very few if any in that part of Belgium. We will be engaged in pioneer evangelism, visitation and much literature work.[85]

As they waited, Haverkamp stayed busy, nonetheless. He went back and forth throughout the Netherlands looking for an opportunity to start an assembly or to associate with an ongoing work, but "no doors were opened." Although he also was active at the Brethren assembly nearby, he said, "I never had any feeling toward that assembly. I did it because I was there. It was never a burden on my heart."[86] His reaction was similar regarding a very successful contact he made through his niece in the eastern part of the Netherlands. There he found a group of young people aged sixteen to twenty-five who were "hungry for the Word." In response to this need, he scheduled and led a weekend conference of three Bible studies a day for the three days. "That was far too heavy and negative. The next time we did it totally different."[87] Even after the Haverkamps moved to Belgium, they kept contact with these young people, and at least

---

82. Christian Missions in Many Lands (Canada) Inc., "Pertinent Information, Necessary to Complete our Records."

83. Affordable housing was notoriously difficult to find in the Netherlands and Belgium. Supply of a place to stay provided what Haverkamp viewed as "the leading of the Lord" as the Haverkamps took their initial step into Europe.

84. R. Haverkamp, letter to John H. McKechnie, Secretary of MSC, 26 August 1971.

85. R. Haverkamp, letter to MSC, 08 September 1970.

86. R. Haverkamp, interview, 30 April 2003.

87. Ibid.

once scheduled a week of youth meetings, allowing the twenty-five young people to stay in their "tiny home."

Still, both of the Haverkamps were convinced that the Lord did not want them in the Netherlands in the area in which they had been living. "I felt like we were supposed to be in the Catholic south. The Catholics were the open field then. So I knew it had to be somewhere in southern Holland or Belgium."[88] They often had gone to visit the Shindelkas since first transporting them to Belgium, and by August 1971, the Haverkamps were convinced that they should accept an invitation from Shindelka to come help him in Antwerpen. Burdened with the need in Belgium and excited about the possibilities, Haverkamp wrote in a letter to the Secretary of MSC, "What a mission field. There are only 5 open assemblies among the 5 million Flemish speaking people. And very little other Evangelical work too."[89] On 23 December 1971, the Haverkamps and their three young children moved to Edegem, Antwerpen.[90] He looked back at that time in this way:

> So, we had no experience, no books to guide us, no tapes to listen to, and no older missionary with years of experience to help us. We were all on our own! But one thing we did have and of one thing we were sure. That is what kept us going and pulled us through. We knew why we were in Belgium; we knew that God had sent us there. We knew what our mission was—planting churches all over Flemish Belgium as quickly as possible. This we set out to do, with youthful enthusiasm and with faith in God![91]

Henk Gelling, 1975–Present

General Background

Henk Gelling[92] was born on 20 May 1942 in the ancient farming town of Onstwedde, Groningen, near the border of the Netherlands with Germa-

---

88. Ibid.

89. R. Haverkamp, letter to John H. McKechnie of MSC, 30 August 1971. McKechnie had been associated with MSC since 27 February 1962 and became its vice president on 14 April 1969. He subsequently is noted as Secretary in the corporate minutes of 6 May 1972, a position he held until 22 April 1983. He resigned from the oversight of MSC before the annual meeting held on 20 March 1986. Cf. *Form 122-62, Schedule C*, "Resolution of the Board of Directors of Missionary Service Committee, Inc.," 17 July 1963; also Schakelaar, email, 13 May 2008.

90. R. Haverkamp, newsletter, May 1972.

91. R. Haverkamp, "God is at Work in Belgium," 3.

92. "Hank" Gelling in English. Both Henk and Hank will be found in the reference

Workers and Works of the Evangelische Christengemeenten Vlaanderen

ny.[93] For some period of time before emigrating to Canada with his parents at the age of eleven, Gelling's family also lived in Deventer, Overijssel, a village bordering the province of Gelderland near the city of Apeldoorn. While in the Netherlands, Gelling was a member of the *Christelijke Gereformeerde Kerk*. He was educated at a Christian school, and he had committed believers within his extended family. Among these three influences, he learned at least the stories of the Bible and some basic theology.

> I received good training in the Reformed Church. I just wasn't saved. My grandfather was born again. My grandfather used to read the Bible at every meal and accompany that with long prayers. The meals had *bidden voor de maaltijd* and *danken na de maaltijd* [prayer before the meal and thanksgiving after the meal].[94]

When his family arrived in Canada, they affiliated themselves with the Christian Reformed Church, and Gelling stayed an active member of it until he was twenty-seven.[95] Still, a close observer noted that he was a "rough Dutchman" with an "Elvis Presley look."[96] His wife, Beryl Stevens, was a child of parents who had immigrated from the United Kingdom in 1954, ten years after she was born. Beryl was born on 23 December 1944 in Hetton-le-Hole, County Durham, England.[97] She was raised in the Anglican Church.[98] She was confirmed as child during her family's four-year stay in Metz, France.[99] Her mother was converted at a Billy Graham crusade in London in 1953, and her father was converted after an accident left him paralyzed a few years before the Gellings were married on 23 April 1966. He was from a Christian background in Devon, England.[100]

After his conversion, Beryl Gelling's father used to say to Gelling, "Don't worry about me when I die. I am going to heaven."[101] Gelling said

---

notations according to the manner in which Gelling referred to himself. Throughout the text of the book, however, Henk will be used.

93. Onstwedde has been part of the town of Wildervank since 1969. Cf. "Onstwedde."

94. H. Gelling, interview, 25 April 2003. To be saved is to undergo evangelical conversion. Cf. chapter 1.

95. H. Gelling, interview, 16 May 1989.

96. Bruce and Diane Lobb, interview, 02 September 2006.

97. J. Gelling, "RE: Beryl's birthplace?" email to author, 05 July 2008.

98. H. Gelling, interview, 16 May 1989.

99. B. Gelling, interview, 15 August 2007.

100. H. Gelling, interview, 25 April 2003.

101. Ibid.

that he was scared to death of dying, even though he and Mrs. Gelling were very active in the Christian Reformed Church, were participating in all the ceremonies of the church, and had learned doctrines of the church "like the TULIP."[102] From 1966 until their conversion in 1970, Gelling remembers that both wanted to be saved, but did not know how. During that period, they began to watch American evangelist Rex Humbard on the television. They even attended some of his evangelistic meetings in person. Finally in 1970, a friend, Keith Koetsier, asked them to go to a religious service on a Tuesday night to hear a guest speaker—Richard Haverkamp. Mrs. Gelling recalled Koetsier saying, "You've got to come. This guy is terrific."[103] Though Gelling thought this was "crazy" to go to a church service in the middle of the week, he went and listened, and then went back every evening until the week of meetings was ended. Mrs. Gelling was converted on Wednesday of that week, although she did not tell her husband until after he, too, was converted. Gelling was converted the following Sunday at the Rex Humbard Easter pageant. It was not until that point, Gelling says, that he realized that Christ had died for him as well. Before that point, Gelling thought of himself as "too great a sinner to be saved." This would have been in accordance with the teaching of the Christian Reformed Church as he understood it. Nonetheless, he said, "I was glad for the teaching I had, because until a man knows he is a sinner, he doesn't need a Savior."[104]

The effect on Gelling's life was immediate. One of the elders at the assembly he would begin to attend in the near future noted that his "new life was a radical change."[105] Gelling recalled that from that day forward, he never had the urge to curse, "a terrible habit" that he had been trying unsuccessfully to stop for four years. In addition to the change of speech, he and his wife had a strong desire to know all they could about what the Bible taught. On Sundays, they would go to the Christian Reformed Church since that was where their friends were, but the rest of the time they would go to hear teachers like Haverkamp.

Soon, Haverkamp challenged Gelling to be baptized as an adult "according to the Scripture," something that seemed "bizarre" to Gelling at that point since he had been baptized as a baby. Shortly thereafter, he watched his mother-in-law and her new husband (the first husband had died) be

---

102. TULIP refers to the commonly used acronym which enumerates the type of Calvinistic doctrine taught by the Christian Reformed Church in Canada at that time: Total Depravity, Unconditional Election, Limited Atonement, Irresistible Grace, Perseverance of the Saints.

103. B. Gelling, interview, 15 August 2007.

104. H. Gelling, interview, 25 April 2003.

105. Fred and Hilda Munnings, interview, 02 September 2006.

baptized by immersion, and Gelling was very upset by what they had done. About a month later, Mrs. Gelling came home and said that she wanted to be baptized. This was a major problem as Gelling thought life was great; he was going to the Christian Reformed Church, witnessing to his friends, and going to the Brethren chapel on Tuesday evenings "to be fed." If he were baptized, he knew that he would be forced out of the Christian Reformed Church. He did not want to deny his wife her conviction (which he said was really also his as well), but he knew this would upset his plans. "I had it all worked out." They hoped to have a third child, but when that baby was born, they would not get him baptized. The elders would challenge him; he would tell them that infant baptism was unbiblical; and then they would tell him to leave. This plan would give Gelling a couple of more years since that baby was only planned and not even beginning to form yet. Despite his misgivings, Gelling called the minister and asked him to meet on a Monday evening in the summer of 1970.[106]

That evening, Gelling asked the minister to show him from the Bible proof for infant baptism. Gelling said that he would not accept proof merely from the three forms of unity—the Belgic Confession, the Heidelberg Confession, and the Canons of Dort.[107] If the minister had been able to show Gelling from the Bible, he happily would have stayed in the Christian Reformed Church since "that's where my whole life was." The minister's response was, "You will be visited." For Gelling, this response was fine because he thought the minister would have to get his notes together. The minister then prayed with him, and in this prayer Gelling unexpectedly realized that the minister was saying goodbye to the Gellings. Later that night, the minister had a meeting with the elders from the Christian Reformed Church where the Gellings were members since they were worried about "this neo-Pentecostalism" which was coming around. That was the only way they could describe the Gellings' expression of their faith, even though this was a mischaracterization of it. Gelling said he learned a lesson from that event: sometimes leaders get ahead of themselves. "They should have just talked with us to find out what it was all about."[108] This would be an important lesson when the Gellings moved to Belgium.

On Tuesday evening after prayer meeting at the assembly, Gelling was visited by two elders from the Christian Reformed Church. The minister did not return. As with the minister the previous evening, Gelling merely wanted the elders to open the Bible and show him about infant baptism.

---

106. H. Gelling, interview, 25 April 2003.
107. "Beliefs," Christian Reformed Church.
108. H. Gelling, interview, 25 April 2003.

Had they done this, then Gelling would have been satisfied. When Gelling asked to open the Bible together to search out the issue, the elders said that would not be necessary. He was amazed that neither the minister nor the elders would open the Bible with him. This was the second great lesson that Gelling said was learned from this event. When he began to plant churches in Belgium, Gelling tried to find biblical justification for the practices and beliefs of these churches. Even statements of belief constructed in the later years of the ECV made Gelling uneasy.[109] He said that he liked it before the formal statement of faith was adopted since when people asked what the ECV believed, he could just hold up his Bible. That night, the elders pulled out a paper and told the Gellings that, if they were baptized the following Sunday, they no longer would be members of the Christian Reformed Church. Gelling then blurted out, "This is great!" The elders were shocked, one saying that this was not a good thing because "there won't be a dove come on your head."[110]

Looking back at that event, Gelling said, "I was saved from my sin, but now I was saved from 'you must not do this and you must not do that' and 'what would the minister say about this.'"[111] Henk and Beryl Gelling were baptized by immersion at the assembly the following Sunday and dismissed from the Christian Reformed Church as a result. Subsequently, they "came into fellowship" in the Brethren assemblies. They associated themselves with the Brethren assembly in Clinton, Ontario, an assembly which had been founded at the beginning of the twentieth century.[112] One of the men there, Neil Lowey, was an informal but important mentor to the Gellings during their years at the Clinton assembly.[113] When they became members of the assembly in Clinton, they had no idea that five years later they would be in Belgium.

As soon as the Gellings started attending Fellowship Bible Chapel, they started a boys and girls club in their home. To start the kids' club, the Gellings just went to a store in London, Ontario, and asked for material to start a club. "We were very creative; we used 'multimedia'—flannel graph! So here I was with rough hands from farming and running a milk transport.

---

109. Cf. "Identiteit en Werking van de Evangelische Christengemeenten."

110. The statement refers to the work of the Holy Spirit, and the man was warning Gelling that he would not get his "Pentecostal" experience if he left the Christian Reformed Church.

111. H. Gelling, 25 April 2003.

112. H. Munnings, compiler, *A History of Fellowship Bible Chapel*, 1. Perhaps two different home meetings are the "forbearers" of Fellowship Bible Chapel.

113. B. Gelling, interview, 15 August 2007; F. and H. Munnings, interview, 02 September 2006.

The flannel graph stuck to my hands." Beryl taught forty girls upstairs, while Henk taught forty boys downstairs. Gelling later observed, "You can't do that, but we didn't know any better so we just did it. Beryl taught the life of Christ and the Gospels, and I taught the Patriarchs."[114]

Their next creative project was to help another couple, Bob and Carole Stephenson, bring over a double-decker bus from England.[115] They painted it up and drove it to caravan parks for kids' clubs.[116] Shortly thereafter, they had the idea to start a drive-in church because of a similar evangelistic outreach they had heard about in Wallenstein, a city about 75 miles from where they lived. Wallenstein had a gospel caboose; the Gellings had a great location on the highway with a large meadow. So Gelling built a building on stilts with a stage. He remembers that

> on Sunday nights there was an ad in the paper stating, "Come as you are in the Car." People would come from the beach, etc. We would show movies. I have pictures of forty or fifty cars watching the movie. We were a small assembly. There's no way these people would have come to the assembly, but they would come to the drive-in.[117]

In 1972, Gelling rented a bus and put an advertisement in the paper saying he would take young people to hear Nicky Cruz in London, Ontario. Cruz was a powerful speaker who had been the leader of Harlem, New York's, infamous Mau Mau street gang back in the 1950s. He was dramatically converted through the ministry of David Wilkerson.[118] While at this meeting, Gelling came in contact with people from Youth for Christ who told him about a coffee bar ministry they had. When Gelling returned to Clinton, he secured a location and opened up a coffee bar ministry. He then got the young people involved remodeling some decommissioned Canadian Air Force apartments and opened the "One for All" Coffee Bar.[119]

During the years from 1970 until the Gellings departed for Belgium in 1975, Gelling worked from twelve to fourteen hours per day on a very successful chicken farm he had built from nothing, as well as with his equally successful milk transport business. While working all these hours, he still was very active in evangelistic and teaching ministries: Tuesday prayer

---

114. H. Gelling, interview, 25 April 2003.

115. H. Munnings, A History of Fellowship Bible Chapel, 8.

116. H. Gelling, interview, 16 May 1989.

117. H. Gelling, interview, 25 April 2003.

118. For the complete story of Nicky Cruz's dramatic conversion, cf. Wilkerson, *The Cross and the Switchblade*.

119. H. Gelling, interview, 25 April 2003.

meeting, Wednesday night boys and girls club, Friday night Young Couples Club, and the Saturday night coffee bar. Nevertheless, he was careful not to slight his family in the midst of all this activity.

> Beryl and I did all this activity together. The kids were small so they were home with a babysitter. Whether Beryl stayed at home or we had a babysitter would have made no difference since they were in bed by the time we left for the evening activities.[120]

Gelling's Call to Belgium

In 1970, very soon after the Gellings began attending the assembly in Clinton, Ontario, Haverkamp began asking them to join him in Europe. Though the Haverkamps had not yet left for Europe, Haverkamp wanted the Gellings to join him and his wife. Gelling surmised that the main item that caught Haverkamp's attention was the way in which they had started so many evangelistic works immediately after beginning to attend the Clinton assembly.[121] Gelling's initial reaction to the conversations before the Haverkamps left for Europe, and to continual letters after he was in Europe, was one of stark disbelief. Gelling had a very successful chicken farm and an equally successful milk transport business. Neither one of these could be "left on a whim." As Gelling would say, "you can't just leave 30,000 chickens and run off to Belgium."[122]

In 1972, however, the long days of delivering milk were about to get much longer. Gelling's partner had decided to open another unrelated business. As a result, Gelling would have to work sixteen hour days to cover for his partner's absence; Gelling was quite concerned about how little time he would have to spend with his children.[123] Still, he struggled with this decision. About two weeks before he sold the milk transport, his wife suggested that he sell the business. Gelling reacted by saying,

> I thought she was not okay. After all, this is something I had built up. We had started with cans, and now we were into bulk. We had this shiny truck. Our names were on it: "Elliot and Gelling." I was proud as punch driving through Clinton. I mean this was me![124]

120. H. Gelling, interview, 01 May 2003.
121. H. Gelling, interview, 25 April 2003.
122. Ibid.
123. Ibid.
124. Ibid.

Workers and Works of the Evangelische Christengemeenten Vlaanderen

Two weeks later, Gelling sold the milk business to his partner. This still left the issue of the chicken farm. The following year, Mrs. Gelling's sister and her husband were converted during a visit to their home by John Martin, the elder who had asked Richard Haverkamp to speak at the baptism mentioned earlier. A little while later, these in-laws offered to run the farm while the Gellings went to be with the Haverkamps in Belgium.

In the spring of 1974, the Gellings went for a visit to explore the work that the Haverkamps and Shindelkas were doing. At this point, the first church of what would become the ECV had been established in Berchem, a part of Antwerpen. Beginning in 1972 with a contact of the Haverkamps and the Shindelkas, two couples, and a teenager, this group had developed into seventy adults plus the children within a year.[125] This remarkable growth, however, was not what caught Gelling's attention. During a midweek prayer meeting of Shindelka, Haverkamp, Gelling, and about six Belgian brothers, Gelling was astounded to hear these men pray for ten more churches in ten years. Gelling remembers

> that this "church" was just a handful of people meeting in a room filled with cast-off kitchen chairs, an old pew, etc.—a truly sad-looking sight. I'm good with figures; this church was going for two years and could hardly be called a church. How could they pray for ten churches?! This meant they had to start nine churches in the eight years which remained.[126]

Nonetheless, the Gellings thought the Lord was calling them to this work.

When the Gellings returned to Canada, Gelling says that the doubts began. His wife spoke no Dutch, and Gelling could not understand the Flemish version of Dutch. Gelling also knew he had no education which would have prepared him for the missionary work in Belgium. How could they do this work given that they had three children? Who was going to look after the farm long-term? As a result, to every visiting speaker who would come to the assembly, Gelling would pose the question, "How do you know the will of the Lord?" Gelling says he was asking the Lord to show him what He wanted, and then Gelling would say "yes" or "no." As a result, Gelling noted that he heard nothing. He said that a very important lesson for life was learned during this time. "Until you are willing to say, 'Lord whatever you say, I'm willing to do that,' you will hear nothing. I did not know that at the time."[127]

In September 1974, Haverkamp came back to Canada for a visit of six weeks. During this time, he visited Fellowship Bible Chapel in

125. van der Laan, "Gemeentestichtende Evangelisatie in Vlaanderen," 34.
126. H. Gelling, interview, 25 April 2003.
127. Ibid.

Clinton. Gelling finally seemed ready to join Haverkamp, but when he told Haverkamp that he was ready to come, Haverkamp shocked him by saying, "You need to get serious with the Lord."[128] Gelling said that he was going through the most awful six months of his Christian life. In retrospect, he was convinced that this was the Lord trying to get him to go to Belgium. At the time, he wanted to do what the Lord wanted, but he said that really did not include going to Belgium. In contrast, Mrs. Gelling believed that the Lord wanted them to go, but patiently waited until her husband also was convinced. One Sunday night, Gelling decided that he would "get serious with the Lord." Instead of sleeping, he got on his knees, opened a Bible, and sought the Lord's will. Still, he said, he avoided *Acts*, as he was sure that reading there would make him go to Belgium. So he decided to go to *Mark*. The passage that made the difference was Mark 1:36–38 (KJV):

> 36 And in the morning, rising up a great while before day, [Jesus] went out, and departed into a solitary place, and there prayed. And Simon and they that were with him followed after him. 37 And when they had found him, they said unto him, All men seek for thee. 38 And he said unto them, Let us go into the next towns, that I may preach there also: for therefore came I forth.

Gelling realized that this was completely out of context. "Somebody theologically would say, 'This is crazy.' But it was just like the Lord said, 'I want you to go.'" Gelling both understood and was thankful that the Lord gave him an answer early in his time of reading and prayer as he had to work the next day. He agreed with "what the Lord told him" and never looked back again. On 28 October 1974, the Gellings were "commended to the Lord's care for His work in Europe." The letter of commendation reads in typical Brethren fashion, in that both the nature of the work and the qualification or character of the Christian worker is included.

> To the Lord's People;
> We commend to your loving fellowship, our brother and sister, Mr. and Mrs. Hank Gelling, who have felt the Lord's call to serve Him in Europe and particularly Belgium.
> Mr. and Mrs. Gelling have proved themselves over the past four years as earnest, faithful witnesses to the Lord and we are happy to commend them to this work.
> Please accept them in the Lord as fellow-believers and as fellow workers in His harvest field.[129]

---

128. Schelstraete, "Handelingen (3)," 3.

129. Fellowship Bible Chapel, Clinton, ON, "Letter of Commendation," 28 October 1974. Fellowship Bible Chapel did not have elders at that time.

Workers and Works of the Evangelische Christengemeenten Vlaanderen

This letter was signed on behalf of the Fellowship Bible Chapel by Menno Martin, Wallace G. Avery, Brant Bylsma, Neal Lowey, Irvin Martin, and Wilfred A. Munning. On 20 June 1975, the Gellings arrived in Belgium.[130] While they initially had come "for a three year stay," their work in Belgium was to last much longer.[131] Gelling later remembered with amusement that though he had come to Belgium to be a "fisher of men," his "first important work" was to dig a hole for a septic tank for the mill which housed the assembly that met in Beerse.[132] The Gellings' final business ties to Canada would come to an end when they returned to Canada for a time in 1980–81 to sell the chicken farm as well as to help their young children learn English well.[133]

The Other "Founder" of the ECV: John den Boer, 1976–1996

The first person living in Flanders to associate with the ECV as a fulltime worker was John den Boer. Den Boer was born in the Netherlands on 17 August 1954 in Rotterdam. He was raised in the *Nederlandse Hervormde Kerk*.[134] He was baptized as an infant, but never attended church as this was not a priority with his parents.[135] At age seventeen, events began to coalesce which would result in den Boer's evangelical conversion. His brother, Loek, was "walking on a bad path" which caused the family a great deal of sorrow and concern.[136] After a time, Loek returned home. During this return, the family home was visited by representatives of the Jehovah's Witnesses, and Loek began to meet with them to study the Bible. When asked by den Boer what was happening, Loek replied, "God lives in my heart," though den Boer later noted that his brother was not truly a biblical Christian at this point.[137] Still, Loek's interest in the Bible also piqued den Boer's interest. Over time, Loek's contact with the Bible convinced him that the teachings of the Jehovah's Witnesses were not correct, and he relayed his doubts to den Boer. After a time, den Boer witnessed a remarkable change in the life of his formerly wicked brother after he underwent evangelical conversion.

130. Schelstraete, "Handelingen (3)," 3.
131. H. Gelling, interview, 25 April 2003.
132. Schelstraete, "Handelingen (4)," 3.
133. H. Gelling, letter to MSC, 17 November 1980.
134. This denomination joined with two others to form *De Protestantse Kerk in Nederland* (PKN) on 01 May 2004. "Welkom bij de Protestantse Kerk in Nederland."
135. den Boer, interview, 26 June 1989.
136. Valkenburg, *België: kent u het zo . . . ?*, 120.
137. Ibid., 121.

Through the testimony of his brother and through a concerted effort to read the Bible at the suggestion of his brother, den Boer also underwent evangelical conversion in 1972. The change in his life was dramatic as his discouragements vanished, and he said that he was able to work with dedication and love even at the pet shop where he was employed.[138] Initially, he attended the *Pinkstergemeente van Rothuizen* which met in Doelen.[139]

At age nineteen, den Boer came in contact with Johan Lukasse, later the head of *Belgische Evangelische Zending* (BEZ). This contact was during an evangelistic campaign of the BEZ in Genk, a campaign at which Erich Hutchkins also ministered. Den Boer then spent a week in Belgium in the city of Bilzen, Limburg, where he saw the work of the BEZ firsthand. In the fall of 1973, den Boer became part of a similar evangelistic team which worked in Turnhout under the leadership of BEZ missionary Leslie Message.[140] For the next two years, den Boer would learn "how to pray, teach Bible lessons, freely witness, and live a life of trust and dependence upon God."[141] Still, the opposition was so great that he became discouraged at the end of this first year in Turnhout, and he considered ending his service with the team. The turning point in his decision to continue was his understanding of Isaiah 42 and 43 as well as encouragement from Joshua 1:8–9. From Isaiah, he finally understood that the work he did was God's work and not his work. From Joshua, he understood that all would go well if he would only "be strong and courageous." Lukasse and the director of the *Bijbelinstituut België* (BIB), George Winston, also encouraged him greatly in his work as he made the decision to stay for a second year.[142]

In this second year, den Boer's faith became such that he asked the Lord for fifty new believers. This was considered an outrageously high number by most on his team, but fifty new converts were gained nonetheless. Den Boer said that he was very young and lacked experience, but the difficulties which he endured, and great acts of God in response to prayer during those two years, became the firm foundation of his life of Christian service. During these two terms of service, he would meet and "lead many to Christ," including an eighteen year old man named Gie Vleugels. Vleugels would go on to become a New Testament scholar and professor at BIB as well as one of den Boer's closest friends. Vleugels said that den Boer was

---

138. Ibid., 122.

139. den Boer, interview, 26 June 1989.

140. Ibid.

141. Schelstraete, "Handelingen (7)," 3.

142. For a summary history of the BIB, cf. Campbell, *Light for the Night in Europe*, 226–40.

Workers and Works of the Evangelische Christengemeenten Vlaanderen

the first one ever to explain to him that the work of Christ was personal, not merely general.[143]

This time period also was when den Boer met the woman whom he would marry on 20 September 1975, Marga van de Riet.[144] Marga was born in 1953 and grew up in Emmen, the Netherlands. She was raised in a traditional Protestant family. She underwent evangelical conversion in the late 1960s, probably through the efforts of a Billy Graham Crusade or its related activities.[145] Finally, during this same two-year time frame, den Boer committed himself to full time Christian work. He subsequently followed his brother to BIB where den Boer completed his bachelor's degree in Bible. Before committing to study there, he went to the BIB to tell his brother of his decisions. John surprised him when he said, "I have been praying much that you, too, would become a minister of the Gospel."[146]

Den Boer was characterized by his BIB classmates as a pious man who took his Christianity very seriously. At that time of his life, he read through the entire Bible every year and challenged others to do the same. Though he gained much from his academic study, he also developed a dislike for the type of academic theology whose truths were not put into practice. Further, he wanted his convictions to be based clearly on what he found in the Bible rather than what a particular man might teach. For example, although den Boer held a high opinion of the school's director, Winston, he disagreed with Winston's support of an expansive role for women in the local church. Den Boer was convinced of a less expansive role from passages such as 1 Corinthians 14 and 1 Timothy 2, a conviction that he would keep throughout his life of ministry. He had a similar hesitation about some of the views of Haverkamp (in areas unrelated to the role of women), though he held Haverkamp in high esteem.[147] His school years also were a time when he came into contact with Brethren-type teachings, initially through reading the biography of Georg Müller and studying the works of Watchman Nee such as *The Normal Christian Life*. He absorbed as many of these ideas as he found consistent with his understanding of the Bible.[148]

Den Boer came to be known to the Canadian missionaries of the ECV when he appeared on Gelling's doorstep in the mid-1970s. He had become

143. Vleugels, interview, 14 August 2007.

144. Christel van Nes (*née* den Boer), email, 26 October 2007.

145. Perhaps the London Crusade of 1967? See Billy Graham Crusade Statistics: Chronological dated June 2005, Facts like the year of conversion have been difficult to ascertain because John den Boer declined to be interviewed for this book.

146. Valkenberg, *België: kent u het zo . . . ?*, 122.

147. Vleugels, interview, 14 August 2007.

148. Ibid.

aware of this ongoing work through a classmate of his, Eric Rutten.[149] At that time den Boer was only a student at the BIB, but he already had a successful history as a Christian worker with BEZ. Gelling noted that den Boer was very enthusiastic about the vision and methods of the ECV and asked to be a part of the work.[150] In the fall of 1976, den Boer left the BEZ and became part of the work of what would become the ECV.[151] He would remain as part of the ECV until his decision to leave and return to the BEZ in 1996.[152] The assemblies in Ham and Leopoldsburg had a reception on the den Boers' final day, Sunday, 29 December 1996. They wished them well and noted that they would be missed.[153] Though he did not leave the ECV on the happiest of terms, den Boer was asked in future years to come and preach in the assemblies in Limburg, and Gelling kept an open door to him for fellowship and ministry. Years later, Gelling reported on a church that den Boer later started in Lummen, Limburg, "It is good to see the Lord go on and work."[154]

Analysis of the Founders of the ECV

Missionaries and founders of significant Christian works are prepared for their work in a number of ways. What were the common and unique gifts and abilities that Shindelka, Haverkamp, Gelling, and den Boer possessed and demonstrated before coming to Belgium to found or become involved with the work of the ECV? How well did their life and ministry experiences demonstrate the characteristics of a church planter before coming to Belgium or associating with the ECV? These necessary characteristics can be described best, perhaps, by the measure used extensively in the West by training groups, mission organizations, and seminary classes as described by Charles R. Ridley's list of thirteen traits.[155] While the initial study in 1984 was done mostly on a male, North American Caucasian population, Ridley

---

149. Gielen and Symons, interview, 14 August 2007.

150. H. Gelling, interview, 15 August 2007.

151. "Jaarsverslag Vlaams Evangelisatie-Komitee vor de BEZ Konferentie van 19 November 1977."

152. 29 October 1996 BEZ "Aan de leden van de Vlaamse raad."

153. Vandereyken, "Afschied en intrede," 6.

154. H. Gelling, "52nd Belgium," email to MSC, 17 October 2004.

155. Ridley, *How to Select Church Planters*, 7–11, 101–3. Ridley's traits are found in print at multiple websites, for multiple denominations, and in multiple languages such as, http://www.churchplanting4me.org/ridleyfactors.htm, and the site for "www.Mehr-und-bessere-Gemeinden" found at http://ncdnet.blogs.com/mbg/. This work is referenced in numerous church planting ministries since the time of its publication, and seemingly is referenced in every church planting study published since 1984.

Workers and Works of the Evangelische Christengemeenten Vlaanderen

understood that "the identified performance dimensions" have relevance across gender and ethnic lines.[156] Ridley's basic idea, as used by many diverse groups, is that past performance is an indicator of future success. Each of these traits now will be considered, and examples noted in the lives of the founders before involvement in the work in Belgium.[157]

The basic questions would be two. First, would a local church have sent these men if the church had followed this commonly used rubric of evaluation? Second, would these men have had a reasonable expectation of success as church planters? This evaluation is particularly instructive as the extent of initial planning was merely a sincere belief and impression from God that they were to go to Belgium and plant churches.

Visionising Capacity

All three Canadian missionaries showed evidence of this trait before going to Belgium, though certainly it was seen more readily after they arrived there. For example, Haverkamp and Gelling believed in God's capacity to do great things such that they could express their burden effectively to others. Haverkamp's stream of letters to the Gellings were a vivid example of this. This is particularly pertinent when one realizes that Gelling initially saw no need to evangelize and plant churches where the Haverkamps were going because it was "already Christianized." Further evidence was witnessed in the Antwerpen prayer meeting led by Shindelka and Haverkamp which amazed Gelling. This struggling new church in a decidedly Roman Catholic culture was led by Shindelka and Haverkamp to ask God for a seemingly impossible multiplication of churches.[158] Part of this transmitted vision was an unspoken but certain identity as to the type of churches which the ECV would become.[159]

All three men faced cultural and linguistic barriers which could have been used as reasons not to go. Shindelka knew nothing of the language of Belgium even though his wife had been born there. Both Haverkamp and Gelling spoke a dialect of Dutch which was unknown in Flanders. Gelling's initial visit to Belgium almost caused him not to return since, contrary to his expectations, he could not understand the local dialect. He later was

156. Ridley, *How to Select Church Planters*, 11.

157. To preclude a lengthy rehearsal of the definition of each trait, the list of Ridley's traits and their bulleted explanations is attached as "Appendix 1: Thirteen Essential Qualities for a Church Planter."

158. Cf. above, this chapter, "Gelling's Call to Belgium."

159. den Boer, interview, 26 June 1989.

surprised to learn that he was not understood when he spoke as well.[160] Further, neither Mrs. Haverkamp nor Mrs. Gelling spoke a word of Dutch before going to Belgium. Also, since Haverkamp and Gelling were native Dutchmen, they likely would face hostility if they went to Belgium due to the historical tensions between the Flemish and the Dutch. This Dutch connection was even a potentially greater obstacle for den Boer as he came to Flanders directly from the Netherlands. Finally, neither the Haverkamps nor the Gellings had done any work among a Roman Catholic audience, nor had they any special training for the planting of evangelical churches among Roman Catholics. Haverkamp says that he has no recollection of ever explaining the evangelical gospel to a Roman Catholic before going to Belgium.[161] Nonetheless, all these potential negatives were treated as challenges rather than obstacles by all four men.

Intrinsically Motivated

All three of the Canadian founders of the ECV evidenced this trait strongly before going to Belgium. All three men were obvious self-starters and willing to build from nothing. For example, Shindelka and Gelling had shown this trait by starting very successful businesses. In Shindelka's case, one does not become the top salesman in a major portion of Canada unless one is a self-starter. Additionally, Haverkamp and Gelling had started a number of successful evangelistic outreaches in Canada. While aware of the reality, lack of formal Bible training was not considered an obstacle, nor were the difficult circumstances in which they began. For example, when the Gellings first came into the assembly in Clinton, ON, only five couples and two men comprised the total group.[162] Instead of leaving this church or avoiding it altogether, the Gellings immediately started the boys and girls club. Even after Gelling says they found out that the "saints" there were common sinners "just like us," they continued to attend and work hard "for the kingdom of God." Certainly the many who were converted under the ministry of Haverkamp in Canada, and the assemblies which were rejuvenated under his teaching, give evidence of his intrinsic motivation before going to Belgium.

The outgoing natures of both Haverkamp and Shindelka, though appreciated by most, were a bit too much for some. Shindelka's aggressiveness as a salesman was seen in some cases as a liability in Christian work by those who knew him best. Nevertheless, a far greater majority saw this trait as a

---

160. H. Gelling, interview, 25 April 2003.
161. R. Haverkamp, interview, 30 April 2003.
162. H. Gelling, interview, 25 April 2003.

Workers and Works of the Evangelische Christengemeenten Vlaanderen

helpful fearlessness which opened doors for the presentation of the evangelical faith. "[Shindelka's] zeal for the Lord was infectious . . . He truly loved the Lord and wanted to serve Him first and foremost."[163]

Creates Ownership of Ministry

This trait was seen clearly only in Gelling before he went to Belgium, though it was very evident in both Gelling and Haverkamp once they went there. Perhaps the best early example of this trait in Gelling was his goal to have the young people help with the remodeling of the Canadian Air Force barracks for the "One for All" coffee bar. His decision to involve the young people was calculated to give the teens a sense of ownership, not done merely because he had a need for construction workers. Certainly the need for people in Canada to take ownership of all three men's ministry in Belgium was seen in their commendation from their local assemblies as well as by the financial support which the men received for their work. Unless the needs of the particular mission field are convincing, no commendation to missionary service will be forthcoming irrespective of the quality of the worker.[164]

Relates to the Unchurched

Shindelka's gifts as a "people person" have been noted by both Haverkamp and Gelling. Haverkamp's "wild days" in Canada before he was converted as a young adult certainly meant that he knew what it was to live as an unbeliever. His struggles in the months just before he was converted were as fresh in his memory many years after the fact as if they had happened just a few weeks or days previous. He would speak with emotion about that time, an emotion which seemed bred of compassion, especially in juxtaposition with the need of others to be converted. For example, the elders from his commending assembly saw his burden to take the gospel to "his people," his gift of teaching, and his heart for "lost people" even after knowing him for only a short period of time. Further, they note that his cheery, outgoing nature drew people to him and allowed him to make very strong, confrontational statements from the pulpit without causing offense. "Richard loves people," his elders stated, "he knows they are lost, and that's his focus."[165]

163. S. Tordoff, letter, 01 February 2008.

164. For a more complete picture of commendation, cf. A. Pulleng, *Go Ye Therefore . . . : Missionary Service in a Changing World*; *Global Strategy: the Biblical Plan of Mission*.

165. Wallenstein elders, interview, 01 September 2006.

Interviews with Gelling demonstrate his knowledge of the outlook of one who is at least "without Christ" if not completely unchurched. For example, he clearly remembered how he viewed common church practices as "bizarre" or "absolutely crazy" before he was converted, such as in the example in the scheduling of a Tuesday meeting where he first heard Haverkamp preach, or the ordinance of adult water baptism by immersion. Theologically, as a part of his conversion, he noted the need for the unconverted to realize their sinfulness before they would understand their need for a Savior. Additionally, Shindelka's and Gelling's years of experience as successful businessmen meant they had spent many years interacting with the unchurched. Overall, Gelling was not the stereotypical missionary or church-planter who spoke in "stained-glass" tones. Both his manner and vocabulary readily gave evidence of the demeanor of a "regular guy." Thus, as a believer, he certainly was different from the unchurched and the unconverted, but evidence before leaving for Belgium and in interviews since would not have characterized him as a man who had lost touch with the world around him.

Spousal Cooperation

Marina Haverkamp and Beryl Gelling were solidly behind the work of their husbands in Canada and the ensuing move to Belgium. The Haverkamps' relationship began as co-workers in children's work while both were students at Millar Memorial Bible Institute. Additionally, Mrs. Haverkamp spoke of her respect for and appreciation of Haverkamp's character and goals. Both Richard and Marina Haverkamp relate the same story as clearly understanding the will of God that they move to Belgium during their week of fasting and the family Bible reading in Hebrews 11. Gelling noted that his wife led girls' Bible studies upstairs in their home for forty young people, while he was downstairs with forty boys. Additionally, he noted that they went to all their outreach activities together after their children were in bed. Finally, he related that Mrs. Gelling was convinced of their call to Belgium before he was.

In contrast, Mrs. Shindelka initially did not support their family's move to Belgium. One of the elders from Shindelka's commending assembly later said, "At the time Herb requested commendation to the work in Belgium, we advised them not to do so then, because Lillian was not one with him in this step. It was almost a year after that they had come to agree. Therefore we felt comfortable to issue their commendation."[166]

---

166. S. Tordoff, letter, undated (01 February 2008).

Workers and Works of the Evangelische Christengemeenten Vlaanderen

Effectively Builds Relationships

Both Shindelka and Haverkamp were natural salesmen, and Gelling made his milk business grow through sales to new clients. As noted earlier, Shindelka was a premier salesman in the companies for which he worked. While Haverkamp was never in the business world, he had the same traits in this area as Shindelka and Gelling. Haverkamp said he probably would have become a salesman had he not become a Christian worker.[167] Nonetheless, neither Shindelka's nor Haverkamp's motivation for going to Belgium was for the purpose of making a "sale" to the listeners. Still, a "natural salesman" is interested in people primarily, since a person who is interested only in sales will be discovered over time merely as a user of people.

The elders of Haverkamp's commending assembly note that he always was open to them in all areas; he made himself known to them personally. This openness began in Canada and remained this way as Haverkamp went to Belgium.[168] Reviewing the open, thirty-plus year relationship with Haverkamp, one of Wallenstein's elders said, "I don't sense any area that was 'don't touch.'" Further, Haverkamp was noted for his infectious, enthusiastic manner, a manner well attested by those who knew him before his departure for Belgium as well as after he arrived.[169]

Committed to Church Growth

Haverkamp and Gelling certainly understood the local church as having a central role in God's work in the world with the establishment of the Church by the coming of the Holy Spirit at Pentecost as recorded in Acts 2. For example, while Haverkamp did some independent evangelistic outreaches while in Canada, the vast majority of his evangelistic meetings were conducted as special meetings associated with a local church. The purpose of these meetings was to see people converted, which in turn would cause the local church and the Church to grow. Similarly, when the Gellings witnessed the small size of the assembly in Clinton, their reaction was not criticism or departure, but finding a way to help the assembly to grow. This was partially their motivation for all the creative evangelistic efforts in which they were involved. Like Haverkamp, they wanted to see people converted, and through conversion the church would grow.

167. R. Haverkamp, interview, 30 April 2003.
168. Wallenstein elders, interview, 01 September 2006.
169. Ibid.

New Brethren in Flanders

They both would have rejected McGavran's principle of the "homogeneous unit" as a tenet of Church growth.[170] Although they targeted a Roman Catholic part of Europe, they did not focus on a particular educational or social class. In a Canadian example, Gelling used to advertise widely for the various evangelistic ministries with which he was involved. A particular people group was not the target, but rather any who might read the paper, see a flyer, or hear about the particular outreach from a friend. The same pattern of contact via word of mouth was continued by all three men once they arrived in Belgium. The itinerancy of Haverkamp's evangelistic work in Canada, as well as the nature of the pointedly evangelistic creative outreaches of Gelling, both support Ridley's qualifier in this criteria which speaks of not falling prematurely into a ministry of maintenance. Their goal was never to become pastors of a church in Canada or anywhere else; their work in Belgium would demonstrate this.

Responsive to Community

No evidence was found that indicates that any of the three Canadian founders of the ECV were involved in a process of identifying a particular community's needs. The only "community" identified by Haverkamp and Gelling was that of people who were unconverted. In Belgium, this would become a bit more particular as their primary efforts were toward Roman Catholics. Since this entailed nearly 86 percent of the population, however, no real targeting was necessary other than to be physically in the country.

Utilizes Giftedness of Others

Haverkamp's recognition of the Gellings' gifts and abilities caused him to ask the Gellings to join the work in Belgium.[171] Haverkamp began to encourage the Gellings to come even when they were but a few months converted. For the Gellings' part, Gelling recognized his limited maturity in the faith as he had only been converted for a short time when he began actively evangelizing in Canada in a number of creative ways. These creative methods were often a modification of the ideas of others; he recognized their ability to create similar ministries which might prove effective in his area. Gelling recognized the gifts and abilities which he and Mrs. Gelling his wife had and acted according to those gifts and abilities as they designed

170. Cf. Wagner, "Homogenous Unit Principle," 455.
171. Cf. above, this chapter, "Gelling's Call to Belgium.".

the evangelistic outreaches. These gifts would become very obvious once the work in Belgium proper was commenced, and prayer newsletters and newspapers of the ECV make this creative edge evident as will be recounted.

Flexible and Adaptable

Clues of this trait as characterized by Ridley are evident in the work of both the Gellings and the Haverkamps before arriving in Belgium. Creativity and flexibility were the hallmarks of the wide variety of evangelistic ministries the Gellings either started or in which they became involved. They would do whatever was required to see their evangelistic efforts "be used of God." This does not mean that they were guilty of being "gospel hucksters," but rather that they adapted their methods and tried all manner of new ones.

For example, a major adaptation of their schedule happened when founding the boys and girls club. Given all the other Christian activities in which they were involved, Wednesday evening was the only available night for the clubs. However, the Gellings played badminton on Wednesday evenings, and Gelling was president of the club. So they initially decided to have the club meetings from 7 to 9 p.m. and play badminton from 9 to 11 p.m. Once the club started, though, they never again played badminton as they had to drive kids home, talk to the parents, and so forth. Gelling also said that they really never had any second thoughts given the needs of the children's work and given the contacts for sharing the gospel with the parents.[172] Haverkamp's flexibility is seen in his frank admission of error with respect to the heavy Bible study schedule that he planned and executed during his first youth conference weekend in the Netherlands. As noted earlier, he consciously changed the schedule of the next youth conference weekend that he planned and executed.

Builds Group Cohesiveness

Perhaps the clearest evidence of the ability to build group cohesiveness before leaving Canada was seen in the string of successful works in which all three men were involved. The best example would be the manner in which Haverkamp recruited Gelling, as he later would do with others, to develop a "nucleus group . . . as a foundation."[173] Another example would be the church which Shindelka planted. The assumption here is that unless group

---

172. H. Gelling, interview, 25 April 2003.
173. Ridley, *How to Select Church Planters*, 10.

cohesiveness is maintained, this type of work quickly founders. The history of this assembly is quite the opposite as it thrived and became a church which had an effect not only on the surrounding area of its location, but throughout the world with the sending out of a number of missionaries. It also supported other missionaries as well.

Resilience

Although this was very apparent in the work once Haverkamp and Gelling reached Belgium, there was little evidence prior to their departure from Canada. After arriving in Belgium, the list of workers who came and went would show the comparative resilience of Haverkamp and Gelling as well as the manner in which they would confront many struggles as they planted churches and tried to nurture them to a mature state. With one possible exception, the other foreign worker's departures would be due to the toughness of the work, rather than personalities or differences in ministry goals and methods. Particularly noteworthy will be the manner in which Haverkamp and Gelling responded in the aftermath of Shindelka's departure.

Exercises Faith

Of all of the traits put forward by Ridley, the exercise of faith by the Canadian founders of the ECV was the strongest. Haverkamp and Gelling seemed to be remarkable in this area. Accordingly, each of the subcategories will be enumerated and examples will be provided.

Possessing a Conviction Regarding One's Call to Church Planting Ministry.

From almost the beginning of his conversion, Haverkamp had his call from God via the vision he had of one day planting churches all over Belgium or the southern Netherlands. More remarkable, however, was the series of "proofs" which have been related above. These ranged from circumstances to people to what he read in the Bible. The Haverkamps went to Europe with no doubts of their call to plant churches, and Haverkamp noted that this was what kept him and his wife at the work and helped them through the difficult times.

The case was similar with the Gellings. The Gellings took a significant financial risk by divesting themselves of two very successful businesses. In

Workers and Works of the Evangelische Christengemeenten Vlaanderen

addition, not only was the milk transport business successful, but Gelling noted that the strong bonds that go with pride of ownership were present to a high degree. This type of methodical divestment and accompanying financial risk normally was not done in Brethren circles unless one was absolutely certain of God's call; the divestments were done slowly and with much forethought and prayer. The final time of prayer as a result of the challenge from Haverkamp also confirmed the call of the Gellings. Notably, neither man had any lingering doubts once he arrived in Belgium and commenced his missionary work.

Believing in God's Action

Neither Haverkamp nor Gelling would have gone to Belgium unless he was certain of God's blessing. The financial, logistical, educational, cultural, and linguistic obstacles were far too big. Gelling particularly was amazed to see how quickly God acted once he was willing to go. For example, paperwork from the Canadian government which should have taken many months to process was accomplished within days or weeks at the most.[174] Haverkamp also noted that none of the three of them had any real training for the task of church-planting cross-culturally—just the conviction that God would act.[175]

Having Expectation and Hope

The best example for the Gellings before they went to Belgium was their expectation that the "outrageous goal" of ten churches Gelling heard Shindelka and Haverkamp pray about in the Berchem prayer meeting was something of which he wanted to be a part. Unless the Gellings had the qualities of expectation and hope, they never could have joined together with people who had such seemingly unattainable goals. While this prayer was made after both Shindelka and Haverkamp were in Belgium, it speaks well of their character in this area also.

Having a Willingness to Wait for Specific Answers to Specific Prayer Requests

The greatest example of this in the life of the Haverkamps prior to going to Europe happened in the months before they asked for the permission of

---

174. H. Gelling, interview, 25 April 2003.
175. R. Haverkamp, "God is at Work in Belgium," 3.

the elders at Wallenstein Bible Chapel. Haverkamp says that he and his wife were very burdened about going, but still were praying about assurance from God that they really should go. The family Bible reading in Hebrews 11, the accident on the way to talk with the elders, and the unanimous agreement and support of the elders finally constituted the end of the period of waiting and assurance of their specific prayer to God for His leading. All their ministry experience, and even the vision that Haverkamp had many years earlier, was not enough. They waited for a specific assurance of their call as an answer to prayer, even in the face of criticism by friends at their slowness to act, and in spite of their own burden for the planting of churches in Europe. Additionally, the Haverkamps refused to consider going to Europe unless all of the elders were in agreement.

The willingness of the Gellings to wait for answers to specific prayer requests had much to do with the removal of the practical obstacles to their move and the final night of prayer when Gelling received his answer from Mark 1. The sale of the milk transport business removed only part of the practical obstacles; someone was needed to take care of the chicken farm as well. The specific answer was provided quite pointedly as Mrs. Gelling's sister and her husband were not even converted when the Gellings began to pray about moving to Belgium. Their offer to run the farm for the specific purpose of the Gellings moving to Belgium answered the Gellings' prayer request for the Lord to take care of the farm if they were to go.

TWO CRUCIAL SHAPERS OF THE ECV: CONVERSION AND BACKGROUND

While every group has its founders, successful or long-lasting groups have those who effectively build upon what the founders have done, whether these later shapers are recognized or not. In the case of the ECV, workers came to be associated with this collection of newly planted Brethren assemblies, people whose fervor in many cases matched that of the founders, but whose ministry emphases and gifts were notably different. While the founders were committed evangelists primarily, the people who would build upon their foundation were gifted administrators, Bible teachers, and counselors. This is not to say that the founders did not exercise gifts in these areas, nor that those that followed them were not evangelists. This is to note the distinction in primary gifting and goals between the founders and the shapers of the ECV. Both the founders and those who followed understood and noted these differences.

Workers and Works of the Evangelische Christengemeenten Vlaanderen

This distinction in gifting and goals was perhaps one of the primary reasons why the ECV did not turn out as was expected by the founders. Certainly this distinction was at least a major contributing factor to the stop in explosive growth seen within the first decade or so by the founders of the ECV as increasing attention was given to the maintenance and strengthening of the work that had been founded. While the founders of the ECV were people who had come from outside Flanders, the shapers of the movement included people from Flanders, Canada, the United States, and the United Kingdom. The greatest number of these shapers would be Flemish as would be the most significant figure with respect to the change from a collection of like-minded local churches into a formally recognized, partially government-funded, organized denomination.

The material in this section and the final section of this chapter is not an exhaustive examination of all the background, activities, and gifts of the workers who would contribute to shaping the ECV into what it would become, but rather a selective history associated with those people who served as recognized workers with the ECV, either as missionaries or national workers.[176] Before considering the formation of each of the assemblies that became the ECV, two men will be introduced who each had a very important role in the shaping of the character of the ECV. The other workers are introduced in the final part of this section and will be considered as the planting and growth of each assembly is narrated.

Guido De Kegel, 1984–Present

The most significant person in the ECV outside of the Canadian missionaries was Guido De Kegel. He was responsible more than any one individual for the change of the ECV from an informal movement to a structured, governmentally recognized denominational organization. Whenever organizational changes, governmental recognition, or formal ties with other Christian organizations were encountered throughout the history of the ECV, the name of De Kegel was prominent. So how did this man come to be a part of ECV, and how did he grow to have such a pivotal role?

Guido De Kegel was born on 23 September 1948 into a nominal Roman Catholic family in the province of Oost-Vlaanderen. He was one of seven children. His father bought and sold cattle, and his mother ran a café. While they went to mass every week, the values of the church were not a part of everyday life. His childhood education was at Catholic boarding

---

176. A complete list of the recognized workers of the ECV and their dates of service is attached as Appendix 2.

schools, the first in Mater (a little village near Oudenaarde) and the second in Kortrijk. His unpleasant religious experiences at these very strict institutions left him hostile to the Catholic Church as well as to "anything to do with religion."[177] De Kegel said,

> In former days I had only one attitude toward belief, namely, deep contempt. In fact, the fables from the Bible, the religious goings on in the churches, the miserable wretches who looked to faith to solve their problems and who had a need for discipline—all this could cause only one reaction: a smile of pity and an internal feeling of aversion.[178]

De Kegel was a very good student, and his dream was to go to university to study Greek and Latin so that he could become a teacher. This dream would not be fulfilled, however, since he needed to help support the family after his parents divorced.[179] Upon completing school at age eighteen, De Kegel began work in an expedition and shipping company, a company for which he would work until he became a worker with the ECV at age thirty-six, seven years after he underwent evangelical conversion. During the beginning of this time at the company and before he was converted, he met his then sixteen-year old future wife, Marianne Steyaer. Born in Gent on 26 April 1950, Marianne spent most of her childhood in Zomergem.[180] Unlike De Kegel, Marianne was from a devout Catholic family. This family devotion was evidenced by activities such as her mother's pilgrimage to Lourdes.[181] De Kegel met Marianne via a teen newspaper, and his first real date with her was to meet her at a movie theater in Zomergem, a thirty-five kilometer bike ride from where he lived. De Kegel married Marianne three years later on 4 January 1969.[182]

Eventually, De Kegel's mother-in-law met Haverkamp and underwent evangelical conversion. As a result, she kept asking De Kegel if Haverkamp could come and visit him and her daughter. Finally, De Kegel relented, and during that first visit from Haverkamp on a Wednesday evening in April 1977, both Guido and Marianne underwent evangelical conversion. The De Kegels continued with the weekly Bible studies and attended a *Vrije Evangelische Gemeenten* (VEG) church in Gent, the *Evangelische Gemeente De*

177. Guido and Marianne De Kegel, interview, 12 August 2007.

178. R. Haverkamp, ed., *Nieuw: Vijftien Vlamingen vertellen hoe Jezus hun leven veranderde*, 21.

179. Schelstraete, "Handelingen (14)," 2.

180. De Kegel, email, 30 January 2008.

181. De Kegel, interview, 12 August 2007.

182. Schelstraete, "Handelingen (14)," 2.

Burg, since no other evangelical church was located nearby.[183] They continued until Haverkamp began celebrating the Lord's Supper in his home in Lovendegem on Sunday mornings. Once these Sunday gatherings began, the group immediately began looking for a place to meet as Haverkamp's home was not an ideal place for all the various meetings of the assembly on Sunday morning. This home meeting became the ECV church in Eeklo after three to six months as this was where a proper facility was secured.

After being very active with the ECV, De Kegel became a worker full time with them 1 January 1984.[184] His resignation as an expediter shocked his immediate boss, and initially the boss refused to forward the letter of resignation since Guido's work was behind the great success of the branch in Gent where he worked.[185] Once he began to minister full time, De Kegel wondered about whether he should become a classroom teacher. Part of his decision to seek a position at the BIB in Heverlee was influenced by reading the famous words of Donald Grey Barnhouse, "If I only had three years remaining to serve the Lord, I would spend two of them in study and preparation." Irrespective of his goal, De Kegel did not become a fulltime professor at the BIB.[186] Others noted that God did not need another professor. What was needed was a systematic manager to help the work begun by Haverkamp move beyond the pioneering stage.[187] So, from this time forward, De Kegel's ideas and goals would have a great influence on the organization and direction of the churches founded by Haverkamp and Gelling as well as being instrumental in the actual formation of the ECV. Additionally, De Kegel would be recognized almost universally as the best Bible teacher in the ECV, whether one asked members of the local church or those among the leadership of the ECV.

Peter Gifford, 1984–Present

Peter Gifford also came to Belgium from Canada. Along with Gelling, Haverkamp, and De Kegel, he is one of the most significant figures in the history of the ECV. Gifford grew up in Vancouver, BC, as the third of nine

---

183. This church is located on Burgerstraat 13, 9000 Gent, and was part of a church planted in the mid-1920s by the BEZ. Cf. Samuel Liberek, *Belgische Vereniging Van Vrij Evangelische Gemeenten*, 9. Cf. "Alg. Overzight," 1; this is a report which lists church planting by the BEZ since 1919 and was printed from a file named "Post Gemlyst 2."

184. "Gods strijders in de Vlaamse christengemeenten!", 2.

185. Schelstraete, "Handelingen (14)," 3.

186. De Kegel did, however, serve on the board of BIB in later years.

187. Ibid.

children.[188] His parents, Donald and Joan, underwent evangelical conversion when Gifford was about three years old.[189] He was converted at the age of seven during a series of "Daily Vacation Bible School" meetings held at the local Brethren assembly where the family was active. Gifford says that his life "bore little fruit" until the age of twenty-one during his third year of studies at the University of British Columbia when, "through the support of some caring friends, I was back on the path I started out on when I was seven."[190] Though Gifford had intended to use his Bachelor of Science degree in cellular biology as a basis of a career in medicine, his reorientation during his third year of university caused him to change his goals. Because his parents' marriage of twenty-six years ended in his last year of university, Gifford worked and stayed around home after completing his degree. During this time, he came into contact with an evangelistic organization related to the Brethren called Literature Crusades, and he "thought God was leading me to go overseas."[191]

Gifford's first exposure to Belgium came in a somewhat circuitous manner as a result of his relationship with the woman who would later become his wife, Joanna Groen. Unlike Gelling and Haverkamp, Gifford was not born in the Netherlands. Like the other two Canadian missionaries, however, Gifford had ties to the Netherlands as Groen's parents emigrated from the Netherlands to Montréal, Canada, just before she was born. This family connection later would be crucial since Joanna's ability to claim her Dutch citizenship kept the Giffords in Belgium at a time when the government was forcing others to leave.[192]

Joanna Groen grew up in a "large, loving Christian family" and attended the First Reformed Christian Church in Montréal for the first eighteen years of her life.[193] After high school, she went on to earn a diploma in

188. Ibid.
189. P. Gifford, interview, 25 August 2003.
190. P. and J. Gifford, "Personal Testimonies of Peter and Joanna Gifford."
191. P. Gifford, interview, 25 August 2003. Literature Crusades subsequently was known as International Teams and became an interdenominational, evangelical organization.
192. J. Gifford, telephone conversation with author, 08 February 2008. To gain a sense of the Byzantine regulations for citizenship in the Netherlands during the time the Giffords have been in Europe, one need only note that two of the Gifford children have Dutch citizenship, two have Belgian due to the inability to have Dutch citizenship, and Groen's brother was denied Dutch citizenship based on his particular year of birth as opposed to family standing or place of residence. Additionally, Dutch immigration laws changed very frequently, thus making living in the Netherlands uncertain and unstable for those without either a Dutch citizenship or, later, citizenship from an EU country.
193. P. and J. Gifford, "Personal Testimonies of Peter and Joanna Gifford."

medical sciences.[194] A time came, however, when she remembered being challenged about her relationship to God.

> The turning point of my life came in 1978. I had a good job, a nice apartment and good friends, things seemed to be going well for me, but I had given God second place. Circumstances had to change, and they did, to show me that the fulfilled Christian life is one totally yielded to God.[195]

At this point, Joanna set her sights on Holland, and she joined Literature Crusades as a member of a team headed there. Gifford met Joanna during the training time which began in 1978 prior to their departure for the Netherlands. They came to the Netherlands in May 1979 with Literature Crusades as part of a two year commitment to service outside of Canada. They were members of a seven-person team of young people from the USA and Canada who served with Literature Crusades in Eindhoven.[196] Their task was to help a small church, primarily with evangelism.[197]

Within a few months of arrival, the couple realized that their relationship was more than merely teammates or friends. Given their conviction that this was not a good thing in such a close knit team, Groen took the opportunity to go and work for Haverkamp as a secretary and Sunday School teacher in Belgium beginning in January 1980. Gifford would make frequent trips to visit Joanna during the remaining eighteen months of their commitment to Literature Crusades. These visits and Groen's work brought them into contact with the ECV. Gifford says, "This exposure through short-term missions left us with a real burden and desire to return to Belgium one day."[198] This also brought them into contact with one of the ECV missionaries who provided them with premarital counseling. Their very positive premarital counseling experience with Hal Threadcraft would become one of the motivators behind their firm commitment to a premarital counseling ministry when they returned to Flanders years later.[199]

After returning to Canada in May 1981, Gifford married Joanna on 20 June 1981.[200] For the next four years, they attended Westminster Gospel Chapel in Burnaby, BC, a suburb of Vancouver. During this time, Gifford

---

194. Schelstraete, "Handelingen (16)," 3.
195. P. and J. Gifford, "Personal Testimonies of Peter and Joanna Gifford."
196. P. Gifford, interview, 25 August 2003.
197. "Op de koffie . . . interview Pete en Joanna," 1–2.
198. P. and J. Gifford, "Personal Testimonies of Peter and Joanna Gifford."
199. More complete information on Threadcraft is found below.
200. P. Gifford, interview, 25 August 2003.

worked in a construction and lighting store, and he and his wife were both active at the assembly and ministered in areas such as youth work and camp work. They also came to understand that "the Lord was leading them" to return to the Netherlands as team leaders with Literature Crusades. Hence, the Giffords' letter of commendation reads,

> In preparation for this [return] Peter assumed additional training in the form of an "internship" working along with our full time staff worker and the elders. We believe this has been a profitable and valuable year adding much in the practical field of exposure to the operation and care of the local church gathering . . . We further commend them as the Lord directs after the team term is completed for it is their exercise to seek the Lord's leading in evangelical work in Europe.[201]

While they were commended initially to the Lord's care for His work in the Netherlands as team leaders for International Teams (IT), as Literature Crusades by then was called, the Dutch government refused to issue visas. This could have been a severe obstacle had not the makeup of their team changed as they waited and trained to go to the Netherlands. Their initial team would not have worked well in Flanders due to the lack of Dutch-language facility among the team members other than the Giffords; but this problem was not faced in the Netherlands given that English was spoken commonly. In fact, Haverkamp advised against coming with the initial team to Flanders due to this language deficit. While the Giffords waited, however, the team came to be comprised of the Giffords along with two young women, Marian Voskamp and Carmen Crana.[202] Both of the young women readily could learn the version of Dutch spoken in Flanders given the one's knowledge of her native Netherlands Dutch and the other of her native South African Afrikaans.[203] So in 1985, the Giffords arrived in Flanders with their team and became part of the work of the ECV.[204] While structurally the Giffords were part of an IT ministry team, they came as missionaries listed with MSC and never were part of the financial structure

---

201. Elders of Westminster Gospel Chapel, "Letter of Commendation." Until its last issue in June 1996, *Letters of Interest* was the North American magazine of the Open Brethren. *Letters of Interest* was formerly called "Letters of Interest from the Home Field," and was an apt description of its primary mission begun in July 1934. Thus, when someone left the "home field" for foreign service, *Interest* (as it eventually came to be known) would publish notice of the new worker's commendation. For the importance of the role of *Interest* to the Brethren in North America, cf. Baylis, *My People*, 247ff.

202. R. and M. Haverkamp, letter to supporters, Spring 1986.

203. J. Gifford, telephone conversation, 08 February 2008.

204. "Gods strijders in de Vlaamse christengemeenten!," 2.

Workers and Works of the Evangelische Christengemeenten Vlaanderen

of IT.[205] The Giffords came as part of the IT structure first because they liked the idea of a team, and second because they wanted to encourage others to become missionaries. Gifford said, "I was stuck by [contemporary Christian musician and evangelist] Keith Green's statement, 'You should be called to stay home.' That influenced our thinking. We saw the need. How can you stay home? It was unfathomable to me."[206]

PLANTING OF THE ECV

So what did the work of the founders and shapers of the ECV accomplish? How did these men come to found and build up a denomination which eventually had thirty-one churches? The first five churches planted by the founders of the ECV were the result of evangelistic home Bible studies. Each of these five studies was considered to be a local church at its first Sunday celebration of the Lord's Supper. The remaining ECV churches in Flanders mostly were the result of hive-offs from the original five churches planted by the founders of the ECV, meaning that people from one of the established churches left with the purpose of planting another assembly in another location.[207] The people who left departed with the full support of those who remained at their original assembly.

Exceptions to this pattern were the churches which existed for some time among the Belgian soldiers in Germany. Prior to their posting to Germany, these soldiers had known of the ECV assemblies. Another exception was one assembly which was planted as the result of a worker who underwent church discipline. During the time of his discipline, he planted a church in the Netherlands. Finally, the long-established Open Brethren assembly in Tienen also joined with the ECV.[208]

So how did the work of the ECV begin, and how did it progress?[209] Below is a roughly chronological record of the planting of the ECV assemblies as well as a short history of workers who shaped these local churches. The

205. J. Gifford, telephone conversation, 08 February 2008.

206. P. Gifford, interview, 25 August 2003.

207. R. Haverkamp, "Wie der Herr Jesus Christus Gemeinden baut," session 2.

208. Interestingly, Haverkamp noted that of the five long-established Open Brethren assemblies extant when he arrived in 1971, this one in Tienen joined the ECV, two closed, and the other two chose to have no contact with the ECV. Cf. R. Haverkamp, "Belgium—the Land," 349.

209. For simplicity, the churches and the work will be referenced as the ECV, even though this did not become the name of these assemblies until selected in a meeting on 25 November 1995. The assemblies officially incorporated as a *v.z.w.* on 11 March 1996 using the name ECV. Cf. chapter 4.

assemblies also are grouped according to the province in which they were planted, and the workers are listed with the assembly of their primary work with the ECV.[210]

Beginnings in Antwerpen: Berchem, Beveren, Beerse

The first two Canadian missionaries listed with MSC arrived in Flanders at the beginning of the 1970s. The Shindelkas arrived in Flanders from Canada in August 1971, and the Haverkamps moved from the Netherlands in December 1971 to Edegem, a suburb of Antwerpen. When specifically asked, one of the elders from Haverkamp's commending assembly noted that Richard moved to Belgium without needing the expressed permission or advice and consent of the elders. "We had commended him as a gospel preacher to the Dutch people, and he just moved from there to Belgium. We felt he was doing the Lord's work, and whether he stayed in Holland or moved to Belgium didn't concern us much."[211] Haverkamp's unwavering support from the elders of his commending assembly was proven to be well placed.

Initial contacts were gained through door-to-door evangelistic efforts, help from Operation Mobilization (OM) workers, and other ways. These contacts, however, were not made easily as people thought that Haverkamp and Shindelka might be Jehovah's Witnesses or from one of the known Flemish Protestant churches. Given the overwhelmingly Roman Catholic culture of Flanders, each option would have been viewed with equal wariness and suspicion. Additionally, the message and information that the missionaries related was completely unknown to most of the listeners, even once the missionaries were able to get a hearing. Haverkamp recalled,

> What shocked us most was the complete lack of understanding. People had never seen a Bible; when asked why Jesus died, most knew no answer or had a very strange answer . . . We were discouraged and wondered if we had done right to come here. Nevertheless, we were one hundred percent convinced that the Lord had brought us here with the purpose to build His Church.[212]

---

210. Cf. Appendix 3 for a chart showing the organic relationship of all the assemblies of the ECV, and Appendix 4 for a map locating all of these assemblies.

211. J. and M. Martin, interview, 01 September 2006.

212. R. Haverkamp, written response to questions from Koen Schelstraete, 09 September 1999.

Workers and Works of the Evangelische Christengemeenten Vlaanderen

Slowly the contacts came. As distinct from the usual large crowds Haverkamp had in Canada, a few here and there met to listen to him and Shindelka. These contacts eventually gathered in the Haverkamp home in Edegem for a study of the Bible, and a number were converted. As a result of these evangelistic Bible studies held in the Haverkamps' home, the first of the ECV churches began on 2 April 1972, less than four months after the move to Belgium. The Haverkamps wrote,

> We continue to thank the Lord for our co-workers, the Shindelkas. Together with them and two other young families we were able to start our own Sunday morning meetings, breaking of bread and Sunday school, on the second of April. The day before we had the joy of baptizing the first three converts. For the present, the meetings are held in our home. Since then at least five more have been saved and we soon hope to have another baptism. We are getting more and more contacts and are discovering that many are fed up with religion. Some have turned away, others are searching.[213]

As this assembly outgrew the Haverkamps' house, the meeting was moved to a storefront in the nearby town of Berchem in March 1973.[214] Haverkamp would note the interesting name of this location: *Uitbreidingstraat*, meaning extension or spreading street.[215] By the fall of 1975, the Haverkamps would report "about 100 believers" involved with this new church.[216] By 1977, this assembly had five recognized elders as well.[217] Eventually, Berchem would see a new assembly hive off and start in Beveren in 1981. Help was given from the ECV missionaries, and evangelistic outreaches going door-to-door were held. Nevertheless, this was a difficult area in which an evangelical church could grow as it had been heavily canvassed by the Jehovah's Witnesses.[218] This assembly in Beveren never grew very much, and it closed at the end of January 1998 though they continued to have an ECV Bible study in their town.[219]

At around the same time as the establishment of the first assembly of the ECV in 1972, Haverkamp and Shindelka began to distance themselves

---

213. R. and M. Haverkamp, newsletter to supporters, May 1972.
214. R. and M. Haverkamp, newsletter to supporters, Fall 1975.
215. R. Haverkamp, interview, 06 September 2000.
216. R. and M. Haverkamp, newsletter to supporters, Fall 1975.
217. R. and M. Haverkamp, newsletter to supporters, Winter 1977.
218. "Deur aan deur in Beveren en Berchem," 5.
219. "Verslag Nationale Vergadering," 22 November 1997.

from the long-established Open Brethren assembly in their area. This distancing took place over a six-month period. Haverkamp said,

> When we arrived here in Belgium, we discovered that there were about five "Open" assemblies, but in reality they were more like the closed ones we knew about in Canada . . . At that time we used the book of Hal Lindsay, *The Late Great Planet Earth* quite a bit. Many became interested in the Word through this book. One of these Brethren said that they could not use it as it was not written by a Brethren writer.[220]

Further, young men who had recently been converted were not allowed to celebrate the Lord's Supper because they had long hair.[221] Hence, Haverkamp rightly estimated that he indeed held closer to the beliefs of the early Brethren than those who strongly identified themselves as such in Belgium.[222] Haverkamp would agree with one of the original founders of the Brethren, who said, "the Church of God was one and that all that believed were members of that one body."[223] As another characterized the early Brethren, "The apostolic norm supplied the only true model for ecclesiastical life . . . [and this] was manifest in a desire to obey the instructions of the New Testament."[224] Accordingly, secondary or tertiary issues such as one's appearance or the pedigree of the books used for evangelism and teaching were not germane in Haverkamp's and Shindelka's thinking as they sought to follow the teachings of the New Testament as they understood them.

The second assembly was an outgrowth of an evangelistic Bible study that began in April 1973 in Beerse, a town located about thirty-five kilometers east of Antwerpen.[225] Contacts for this Bible study were given to Haverkamp and Shindelka by OM.[226] It met as a local church for the first time in August 1974 in the living room of the Haverkamps' home.[227] This location at Molenbergstraat 15 was formerly a windmill.[228] Prior to this first meeting, the Haverkamps had moved into the mill in July 1974 and had spent a great deal of effort making it suitable both for living and as a place

---

220. R. Haverkamp, email, 30 April 2008.

221. R. Haverkamp, interview, 25 April 2003.

222. R. Haverkamp, email, 30 April 2008.

223. Cronin, "Note regarding the remembrances of J. G. Bellet on the Early Years of the Brethren."

224. Callahan, *Primitivist Piety*, 153.

225. R. and M. Haverkamp, newsletter to supporters, Winter 1977.

226. R. Haverkamp, "God is at Work in Belgium," 3.

227. H. Gelling, interview, 25 April 2003.

228. R. and M. Haverkamp, newsletter to supporters, Fall 1975.

for meeting. After moving in, the Haverkamps realized that the mill had many leaks, and they wondered if they had made a good choice. According to Richard Haverkamp, his assurance came from a Bible verse which came to mind: Micah 2:12. The last part of that verse says, "the place will throng with people." Thus assured, the Haverkamps went about remodeling the facility, with helpers from Antwerpen and the Netherlands.[229] The Haverkamps lived in the house part of the facility, and the assembly met in the round part. When Haverkamp moved from the mill to Koersel in December 1974, he left the assembly in the care of his best friend from Canada, Martin Luesink. Luesink and Haverkamp had been friends from before both were converted; both went to the same Bible college after conversion, and both ended up in Flanders. Luesink worked with the ECV as an MSC-listed missionary from 1974 until 1977 when he and his family returned to Canada.[230]

The mill was used as a place of gathering until late in 1985 when an old warehouse was purchased and remodeled at Rijkevorselsebaan 42. While this never became a very large assembly, Beerse was the scene of many baptisms; hundreds were baptized over the years from Antwerpen, Beerse, Limburg, Eeklo, Gent, and even as far away as West Flanders.[231] Further, the believers in Beerse trusted the Lord for further growth even in the face of difficult times. Echoing the theme continually put forward by Haverkamp, Beerse would report in 1984 about the first ten years,

> The young assembly experienced rather difficult times, especially because of the lack of leadership. The Lord has said, however, "I will build my Church, and the gates of hell shall not overcome it." The Lord has been faithful and has built His Church in Beerse which has grown from approximately 10 adults in 1977 to 39 adults and 26 children now . . . And the Lord continues to build, even today.[232]

Beerse would not recognize elders until nearly thirty years after it began. Until then, they had a leadership team of men known as *verantwoordelijken* (responsible ones).[233] Finally on 19 January 2003, the assembly in Beerse

229. R. Haverkamp, interview, 06 September 2000.

230. H. Gelling, telephone interview, 02 December 2008. Cf. "Day 8," in *Missionary Prayer Handbook* (1975). For one year after his return to Canada, Luesink ran Gelling's chicken farm.

231. R. and M. Haverkamp, "The Haverkamp News," letter to supporters, Spring 1986.

232. "Daarbij die molen," 3.

233. H. Gelling, interview, 03 April 2003. Because of the awkwardness of translating this term, *verantwoordelijken* will be used throughout when leadership was recognized who acted much like *oudsten* [elders], but for various reasons were not yet formally

recognized two elders and two deacons.[234] One of the workers who would help with this assembly was Henry Heikoop.

Henry Heikoop, 1997–2000

Another Canadian couple, Henry and Cobe Heikoop, came and helped at Beerse, arriving on 1 May 1997 with nine of their twelve children. Henry and Cobe both were born in the Netherlands and immigrated to Canada when they were about five years old.[235] The Heikoops assisted for just over three years before returning to Canada in September 2000.[236] They were self-supporting missionaries sustained by an agriculture-related business in Canada, and thus they were not listed with any of the Brethren missions service agencies. They returned to Canada due to the needs of some of their older children who had not accompanied them to Belgium.[237]

Opportunities in Limburg, Belgium, and the Netherlands: Peer, Koersel, Overpelt, Heerlen, Tessenderlo, Ham, Leopoldsburg

While in Beerse, Haverkamp became aware of contacts to the east in the province of Limburg, relatives of a young man who came to the Beerse studies. As a result of following up on these contacts, two more evangelistic Bible studies had started in the villages of Peer and Koersel by the spring of 1974. These contacts would form the basis of Bible studies which would become separate churches in Peer and Koersel. Interestingly, among the first converts in Peer was a young woman who had been studying to become a nun.[238]

By the time the Gellings arrived in Flanders in June 1975, Peer had two evangelistic Bible studies, as well as plans for a third there and for a fourth one in a village nearby.[239] The study in the Gellings' new home in Peer would meet as an assembly for the first time on 26 September 1975.[240] The study from which the assembly in Peer started was among the ones be-

---

recognized as *oudsten*.
    234. H. and B. Gelling, letter to MSC, December 2002.
    235. De Kegel, "Nieuwe werkers uit Canada," 5.
    236. R. Haverkamp, "Heikoops," email, 06 January 2009.
    237. K. and E. Schelstraete, interview, 03 September 2007.
    238. H. Gelling, "23rd Belgium," email to MSC, 14 March 2004.
    239. R. and M. Haverkamp, newsletter to supporters, Winter 1977.
    240. H. Gelling, personal diary: green colored with color-code list on front, last pages.

Workers and Works of the Evangelische Christengemeenten Vlaanderen

gun by Haverkamp in 1974. In 1976, additional home Bible studies began in Overpelt for the people there as well as studies in Neerpelt and Hamont.[241] By the end of 1980, the resultant converts from these three towns no longer came to Peer to celebrate the Lord's Supper, but formed their own assembly. A year later, Martin Symons came to Hamont as a fulltime worker with the ECV. This assembly ultimately was located in Overpelt in 1986 when a suitable facility was acquired.[242]

Martin Symons, 1981–1983; 1990–Present

Symons was born in 1949 and grew up in a very devout Roman Catholic family whose father worked in the coal mines. The family attended mass every week, prayed before meals, had a crucifix in every bedroom, and even went twice a year on a religious pilgrimage.[243] Because of his father's busy schedule, Symons was raised primarily by his mother. Between her and his three sisters, his was a woman's world as he grew up. Still, he later considered this a good experience as he would raise five girls himself when he married.[244] In his early twenties, he worked as an electronics technician, and met and married his wife, Lydia Leurs, in 1972. His commitment to the Roman Catholic faith was challenged by a fellow trainee causing him to look at many options, including the Jehovah's Witnesses.[245] Coming in contact with Haverkamp in the early 1970s, the Symonses both were converted at the end of 1973.[246] By 1974, the couple were baptized, and they eventually became part of the assembly in Peer. They actively were involved with this assembly in areas such as Bible studies, youth work, and evangelization as well as Lydia's involvement with women's ministries. Additionally, they began a drug rehabilitation program along with another couple. This would be the groundwork for a ministry later to be entitled, Bethesda.[247]

Symons worked for a number of years in a meteorological office. His schedule was such that he could spend many hours in personal Bible study as long as he made his meteorological observations. During these years, his studies included works such as the Scofield Correspondence Course, *The Late Great Planet Earth*, books by Watchmen Nee, and books by Brethren

241. Gielen, "Overpelt, Hamont, Hamont-Overpelt?" 7.
242. Gielen, "10 Jaar Overpelt Geteld," 4.
243. Schelstraete, "Handelingen (10)," 3.
244. "Op de koffie bij . . . Martin en Lydia Symonds [sic]," September 2003, 3.
245. Schelstraete, "Handelingen (10)," 3.
246. "Op de koffie bij . . . Martin en Lydia," March 2001, 1.
247. Schelstraete, "Handelingen (10)," 3.

writers C. H. Mackintosh as well as the early works of Willem Ouweneel. Haverkamp asked Symons to become a full-time worker with the ECV in 1979, but it was not until 1981 that he would make this move.[248]

Symons' addition to the ECV was quite important as he was the first full-time Flemish worker. While he had the advantage of being a native Fleming, many of his friends and family thought he was a bit crazy or at least "flighty" [*jassendraaier*] to change both his religious beliefs and his work. He went from a stable job to one at which he only would receive his income as gifts, just like the Canadian missionaries.[249] This move was especially difficult for his father, who had worked hard to help him get a good job, and who now thought that his son had "thrown it all away." Symons' father considered this a "slap in the face."[250] Symons' financial arrangement could be particularly challenging, especially in the beginning. Symons recalled,

> We had moments when we thought I must return to work because we could not go on. Then at just the right time came a gift, and as a result we could go a bit further. How God did this, I do not know, but He never was late in providing.[251]

Eventually, Symons developed more and more into a pastoral worker, as distinct from one whose work was evangelization for the purpose of church planting, such as he was in the early years. He observed that this came about quite naturally given his empathetic nature, and many people were drawn to this type of needed ministry. Over time, this counseling ministry was used to benefit not just the people in his local assembly, but believers from other ECV churches, people from churches outside the ECV, and friends of friends who had heard about the work he did.[252] His main type of counseling involved marriage counseling as well as helping people deal with issues from their past. Additionally, he regularly worked with people whose lives he thought were influenced by the occult. Though he would serve as the head of the committee of the ECV workers, he observed that his gifts were not those of an administrator, and that he would have gladly passed these responsibilities to others more gifted in that area.[253]

---

248. Gielen and Symons, interview, 14 August 2007.

249. "Op de koffie bij . . . Martin en Lydia," March 2001, 2.

250. Schelstraete, "Handelingen (10)," 3.

251. "Op de koffie bij . . . Martin en Lydia," 2. For more information on how a commended worker is supported in the Brethren, cf. A. C. W., *Thanks for the Interest: A letter to a concerned saint about the support of commended workers.*

252. "Op de koffie bij . . . Martin en Lydia," March 2001, 2.

253. Ibid., 3.

Workers and Works of the Evangelische Christengemeenten Vlaanderen

Symons' ministry and the work in Overpelt-Hamont was shaken in 1983 as part of a year in which one observer said, "Satan shook our unity."[254] Symons was counseling a woman who he said was being "troubled by demons," and part of that counseling process was to have her come live in his home. The leadership from Peer, den Boer, and eventually the other workers in the ECV let Symons know that they disagreed with his methods. Further, some feared that the woman was having an unhealthy influence on his work as she began to make personal prophecies concerning various believers who came to Symons' house to visit her. Symons disagreed with the leaders and continued to try to help this woman. After repeated warnings and pleas to change, Symons was placed under church discipline, and he was removed as a worker with the ECV in 1983 as a consequence.[255] His counseling methods were not the issue; it was his refusal to obey the elders from his assembly and the other workers. Gelling noted that this discipline was a difficult thing, and not all in the assembly agreed with the action against Symons. The decision to place Symons under church discipline caused the work in Overpelt to split. A number of Symons' friends departed with him when he was put under discipline since he chose not to stay. During his seven years away from the ECV, Symons attended the Open Brethren assembly in Eindhoven, the Netherlands.[256]

The events surrounding Symons discipline and departure were traumatic for the ECV as well as the local assemblies with which he was involved, yet two beneficial events came about as a result. First, another assembly was planted and became associated with the ECV in Heerlen, a city in the southernmost part of the Netherlands, the province of Limburg near the German border. While Symons was no longer a worker with the ECV, he continued to be active in Christian ministry. Thus, much of the time he would have put into the work of the ECV he invested with these other people. He soon

---

254. Gielen, "Overpelt, Hamont, Hamont-Overpelt?," 7.

255. Church discipline was levied on people who continued in "open, unrepentant sin." Once under discipline, that person was no longer "in fellowship," meaning that he could neither partake of or participate in the celebration of the Lord's Supper, nor serve in any of the ministries of the assembly. Such discipline was for the purpose of repentance by the one disciplined so that complete restoration to fellowship could be achieved. At least all of the ECV assemblies would have supported a determination of church discipline and perhaps other evangelical churches as well.

256. Gielen and Symons, interview, 14 August 2007. Eindhoven would be in one of the unaffiliated of the Dutch Open Brethren assemblies. Cf. Plomp, "Re: Geschiedenis van de vergadering en Eindhoven," email, 10 July 2008. For a good overview of the history of the Open Brethren in the Netherlands and their various groups, cf. Hofman, "Open broeders in Nederland: Een onderzoek naar de geschiedenis en identiteit van open vergaderingen van gelovigen," 15–33.

discovered that if he became an Amway salesman, he could hold Bible studies with the Amway people. One Amway salesman in particular, Frank van den Brink, was instrumental in bringing family and friends to the Bible study that Symons held in Hamont. Very quickly, ten people were coming from Heerlen and the nearby city of Sittard for this Bible study. More people came over time, as the believers in Heerlen were anxious to share the gospel with their family and friends. After a while, Symons drove to two Bible studies—one in each city—rather than have all these people drive to him. As a result, a new assembly was planted in Heerlen in 1985. Their place of meeting was at the *Camignon*, Odiliastraat 1 in Heerlen.[257] This assembly would be listed among the ECV assemblies in the second half of 1991, but their official membership in the ECV would not come until a formal application was submitted and then a letter of acceptance was sent from the ECV in late 1997.[258] Eventually, this group would grow to about thirty adults with two elders leading the assembly.[259]

The second result of Symons undergoing church discipline was his complete restoration. After talking with Henk Prins, a Dutch commended worker from the assembly in Eindhoven, Symons realized the error of his actions when he refused to obey the elders and others.[260] Symons repented and was fully restored to fellowship with the ECV, resuming a very effective ministry as a full-time worker for the ECV. After meeting with the leadership of the ECV, another meeting was held with the people from the Hamont-Overpelt assembly in early 1986 at which Symons answered questions from those gathered. After hearing Symons, this assembly agreed to his restoration. As soon as the assembly in Peer also agreed, Symons was back in fellowship with the ECV.[261] Concerning this later meeting in Peer on 6 February 1986, Gelling wrote,

> [The Symons] openly admitted they were wrong. It was a great evening, there are details that have to be worked out yet but it is wonderful to have them back in fellowship . . . As I wrote a young couple from the U.S., praying about coming here:

---

257. "Nieuwe christengemeentes," 6.

258. "Nationale Commissie Agenda," 15 December 1997, point 3. This letter of acceptance was slated to be written by Rosario Anastasi since he was the *voorsitter*.

259. Gielen and Symons, interview, 14 August 2007.

260. Ibid.

261. H. Gelling, "Verantw. Verg. Hamont Overpelt Gebouw," personal diary: green notebook entitled "Overpelt." (The notes from this meeting are between entries dated 4 February and 4 April 1986.)

Workers and Works of the Evangelische Christengemeenten Vlaanderen

> "Belgium is a meat grinder for Christian workers. But God is able to keep us!"²⁶²

From that time forward, Symons enjoyed the full fellowship of the ECV churches. In May 1990, a letter went out from the ECV workers announcing that Symons could be asked once again for times of ministry in their churches. In part this letter read,

> We are glad and grateful that we can tell you that [the ECV workers and Symons] will together put their shoulders to the work that we believe the Lord has entrusted to us. This decision has come in consultation with the *verantwoordelijken* of the assembly in Peer from which Martin was initially commended.²⁶³

Looking back at these events years later, Gelling reflected that the friends going with Symons probably caused the discipline to go on for a lengthy period as it took longer for Symons to repent and return. Gelling also noted that while he and den Boer were certain that the steps they took were proper at the time, Gelling later wondered if perhaps Symons was treated too severely. Happily, not only did Symons return to continue as a vital part of the work of the ECV, but almost all his friends returned as well and continued in fellowship.²⁶⁴ Nonetheless, Symons' return to full-time service was one of the several grievances that caused den Boer to leave the ECV in later years.²⁶⁵

Despite these challenges, Overpelt grew over the years, and Gelling reflected on this growth nearly twenty years later when he wrote MSC:

> We had a lovely afternoon gospel rally in Overpelt. The weather was great and lots of people came. When you think back in 1995 there were only a handful of believers. The Lord has done great things. One of the groups who sang started in our basement many years ago. One man came to me and told me his brother had gotten saved by listening to tapes from our START studies coming home from his girlfriend at night so he would not fall asleep.²⁶⁶

Notably, this "gospel rally" was held on 15 August, a major date on the Roman Catholic calendar in celebration of "the Assumption of Mary." This scheduling of evangelistic outreaches on prominent Roman Catholic

262. H. and B. Gelling, letter to supporters, February 1987.
263. Workers of the ECV, letter to all in the ECV, May 1990.
264. H. Gelling, interview, 15 August 2007.
265. Vleugels, interview, 14 August 2007.
266. H. and B. Gelling, "44th," email to MSC, 15 August 2004. The START studies noted here are the same as the *Startstudies* mentioned in the remainder of the book. *Startstudies* are what the home evangelistic Bible studies eventually were called.

holidays was to be a practice of the ECV, much as it had been by the early Brethren in their efforts in Flanders in the previous century.[267]

The assembly in Peer continued to grow to the point where it divided into three assemblies: one in Peer, one in Meeuwen, and one in Wijchmaal. Thus, the first time that new assemblies met in Meeuwen and Wijchmaal to celebrate the Lord's Supper was 16 September 1984. The announcement of this divide in the newsletter for the ECV noted, "one pear divided by three does not equal pear sauce, but something far better!" It also challenged Houthalen and Berchem to follow suit.[268] Meeuwen met in Wijshagen at the *Gemeenschaphuis*, the Wijchmaal people continued to meet in Peer at the home of Ludo Cuypers at Achterstraat 108, and the Peer assembly also met in Peer at Burkel 28.[269]

Wijchmaal began with twenty-nine adults and twenty-one children. Initially, the assembly was led by three *verantwoordelijken*, but on 22 October 1989 two men were recognized as its first elders. A third elder would not be recognized until later. In 2001, a *verantwoordelijk* was added to the leadership team alongside the elders.[270] Meeuwen also saw good growth after hiving-off from Peer, and it doubled in size within the first three years of its existence.[271] Not until 24 November 2002, however, did Meeuwen finally recognize its first elders. At that time, two men were recognized at a service which also saw twenty new believers baptized.[272]

Peer continued to grow, and it recognized its first elders on 1 October 1991. Gelling wrote to MSC,

> Last Sunday we had the privilege of recognizing four brothers as elders in Peer. It was a happy time for the assembly. In 1975 the assembly in Peer started in our home while we were living in Peer. Since then the assembly grew . . . Yet for all kinds of reasons there weren't elders recognized until now. Sometimes it takes longer than we would like but we are happy this has happened now.[273]

The assembly in Koersel began through the efforts of Haverkamp and Gelling. Haverkamp had moved to Koersel on 1 January 1975 from Beerse. When the Haverkamps moved from Beerse, they placed the care

267. Cf. chapter 2.
268. "1 Peer gedeeld door 3= . . . ," 3.
269. "Nuttige inlichtingen," 7.
270. Dreese, response to written questions by Koen Schelstraete, 2002.
271. "Nieuws uit . . . Meeuwen," 7. Cf. H. Gelling, letter to MSC, Spring 1990.
272. H. Gelling, "Quarterly Report," email to MSC, 08 May 2003.
273. H. and B. Gelling, letter to MSC, 08 October 1991.

Workers and Works of the Evangelische Christengemeenten Vlaanderen

of the assembly in Beerse in the hands of the Luesinks, and they also had the Luesinks move into their old location in Beerse.[274] The Luesinks would stay and help for two years until the end of May 1977 before returning to Canada.[275] From January 1981, men began meeting who had leadership responsibilities.[276] The first four elders were recognized in January 1982.[277]

Haverkamp's move to Koersel would come about in rather different circumstances than one might expect as part of the work of the usual Brethren missionary. While driving his Volkswagen bus back and forth one night from Beerse to a Bible study in Limburg, Haverkamp related, "From the back of the bus came a voice—at least as far as I remember, maybe it was all in my mind—saying, 'You have to move.' Of course the bus was empty."[278] Returning home after the study that evening, Haverkamp found out that his wife had had the same impression that day. Still, Haverkamp says that he refused to look for housing as he drove back and forth between Beerse and Limburg. "Lord if this is from You, You'll have to find us a place."[279] Soon thereafter, someone from the study in Koersel came to Haverkamp with a quite suitable location, a big house with a sewing factory behind it which could be used as a place for meeting after some renovation. The facility was located at Posthoornstraat 48. Haverkamp and Gelling went to Antwerpen to rent the buildings from the owner, a prostitute. During the negotiations, the prostitute's male companion wryly noted, "This is really something. From a whorehouse to a church."[280] Haverkamp later moved from Koersel, and the place where he had lived became a house for the Gellings on 23 December 1976.[281] The Gellings moved to Koersel from Peer.[282] The assembly eventually moved to their permanent location at Linkestraat 89 in January 1983.[283]

The assembly in Koersel met to celebrate the Lord's Supper for the first time on 16 January 1977 in the Gellings' living room.[284] Gelling spoke on

274. R. Haverkamp, "God is at Work in Belgium," 3
275. R. Haverkamp, letter to supporters, May-June 1977.
276. "Christengemeente Koersel 15 Jaar," 3.
277. R. and M. Haverkamp, letter to supporters, February 1982.
278. R. Haverkamp, interview, 30 April 2003.
279. Ibid.
280. Ibid.
281. "In Koersel ann de toog," 2.
282. H. and B. Gelling, letter to MSC, Fall 1977.
283. "Christengemeente Koersel 15 Jaar," 3.
284. Ibid. Cf. H. Gelling, letter to supporters, Fall 1977. Gelling's personal diary: orange-brown spiral notebook labeled "Limburg-gemeente," on a page entitled "Koersel Broeder Vergadering, 9 December 1976," records a decision for the first Sunday of

"the Promise of Jesus Christ" from Mark 13:21ff after the Lord's Supper.[285] The assembly grew steadily, and in May 1979 the people from Houthalen hived-off to start their own assembly. An evangelistic Bible study begun in Houthalen in April 1977 also played a part in the establishment of this assembly. This study had quite a variety of peoples and nationalities. Gelling wrote in a letter dated Fall 1977,

> A real mixture of nationalities attend, the couple where the study is, he is a Greek who only reads Greek but speaks Flemish. Another man is Spanish who only reads Spanish but speaks Flemish. Last night another couple came, she is also Spanish. A Polish man came for a while but he is having problems at the moment.[286]

The assembly in Koersel continued to grow as the result of conversions which were the result of personal evangelism as well as regular evangelistic campaigns.[287] The first set of elders were recognized there in January 1982.[288]

People coming from Lommel hived-off from Koersel to begin an assembly in January 1979.[289] The first meeting to identify *verantwoordelijken* took place on 26 September 1982, and the last of these meetings was 27 September 1986.[290] Lommel would not become a very large assembly. It had only ten to twelve adults meeting for the Lord's Supper and no Sunday school by late 1987. Gelling noted in meetings notes for the *verantwoordelijken* in Overpelt that Lommel was in essence an "arm" of Overpelt. Twice a month, the believers would come to Lommel from Overpelt to celebrate the Lord's Supper and hold a Sunday school.[291]

In 1979, an evangelistic youth outreach from Koersel resulted in contacts being made with a family in Ham. Den Boer visited this family, and an evangelistic Bible study was formed. As was often the case in the early years

---

1977 as the time when the assembly in Koersel first would meet. No reason is given for the delay of two weeks.

285. H. Gelling, personal diary: mottled blue notebook labeled "Koersel," page dated 17 January 1977.

286. H. Gelling, letter to supporters, Fall 1977. The international flavor of this assembly continues at the time of this writing, as almost half of the assembly was either of direct Italian descent or immigrants from Italy, and one of the elders was from this group. Cf. H. Gelling, telephone conversation, 26 June 2009.

287. De Kegel, "In Koersel ann de toog."

288. R. Haverkamp, letter to supporters, February 1982.

289. R. and M. Haverkamp, letter to supporters, March 1979.

290. H. Gelling, "Gemeente vergadering, 27 September 1986," in a personal diary: purple Clairefontaine notebook labeled, "→Jan 86→ Lommel."

291. H. Gelling, "Verantwoordelijken vergadering, 3 December 1987," in personal diary: green denim-clored notebook labeled "Overpelt."

of the ECV, many were converted, and these new converts invited others to the Bible study. Around the same time, door-to-door evangelistic visits commenced in Tessenderlo. These visits saw a number converted, and others in Tessenderlo were converted through contact with newly converted friends and family. Initially, converts in both villages gathered in Koersel on Sunday mornings to celebrate the Lord's Supper. Very soon, however, the believers in both Ham and Tessenderlo decided to meet as a separate assembly from Koersel due to the growth in numbers. In 1980, the assembly began in Tessenderlo by meeting in the home of one of the new believers. When the assembly grew too large, they moved to a storefront, and then to a community center.

Meanwhile, contacts were made in the village of Leopoldsburg via an outreach of the BEZ using the ships "Ark" and "Ebeneezer." As with Ham, the names of these contacts were passed along to den Boer; he was instrumental in their conversion. Leopoldsburg was considered an especially good location for the wide spread of the gospel as an army garrison was quartered in the town. This also provided the challenge of explaining the evangelical faith to people from a variety of backgrounds and regions from throughout all of Belgium, both the Flemish and the Wallonian.[292] These new believers in Leopoldsburg met with the believers from Tessenderlo and Ham in Tessenderlo on Sunday mornings to celebrate the Lord's Supper. Later in 1980, however, the believers from Ham hived-off to start their own assembly under the leadership of some of the first converts. Leopoldsburg would hive-off from Tessenderlo in 1982. The challenge of finding and keeping a place to meet in Leopoldsburg was reflected by the frequent change of meeting locations. The Leopoldsburg assembly moved from a house to a restaurant owned by one of the believers, to a party hall, to an empty house—all within a few years. Various difficulties arose in later years such that a decision was made to combine the struggling assembly in Leopoldsburg with Ham in 1997.[293] Officially, this happened on 1 January 1997.[294]

While den Boer was very active in the work at Tessenderlo, he also took time to help a small church which was half-Flemish, half-Dutch, and located in Baarel-Nassau/Hertog.[295] Tessenderlo would continue to grow and stabilize, but not until January 1993 did Tessenderlo finally recognize elders. While most assemblies had only elders as part of the recognized

---

292. "Hoe het begon in Leopoldsburg," 7.

293. J. and M. den Boer, written interview with Koen Schelstraete, 14 August 2001. Cf. "Wijziginen," 7.

294. "Verslag Nationale Commissie," 21 April 1997, Punt 11: Fusie Ham-Leopoldsburg.

295. den Boer, "All-, Old-, en Full-timers," 7.

leadership, this assembly recognized three elders and three deacons on the same day.[296] One of the workers associated with Tessenderlo over the years was Eric Schraepen.

Erik Schraepen, 1992–2007

One of the people who would be affected by both the ministries of the BEZ ships in Leopoldsburg and the work of den Boer was Erik Schraepen, a man from Zolder.[297] A team from the ships came to his future mother-in-law's home and invited the Oeyen family to an evangelistic outreach on one of the ships. The family refused, but agreed to have den Boer come by for a visit. Den Boer came by a week later to talk with Schraepen's fiancée's parents, and his fiancée listened as she waited to go out with Schraepen. No decisions were made that evening, but den Boer was welcomed into the Schraepen home after he and Martine were married on 1 July 1982. Martine was converted soon thereafter, but Schraepen was not ready. He soundly rejected any talk concerning the evangelical gospel or attempts by his wife to get him to listen to its message. He did, however, read the Bible that she placed in the bathroom in hopes that he would read it. Looking back at that time, he said,

> I read things I could not believe; men nine hundred years old, etc. I became very upset, very angry. I told Martine, "you call this man. I will talk with him." He gave answers to those questions in a sense, that if I was honest with myself I had to say, "Maybe it went like that." That made me even more curious. Suddenly, it dawned on me that this was the truth.[298]

After a few more weeks of thinking and struggling, Schraepen, too, was converted. He was baptized in October of that same year. All this happened at a time that den Boer was just starting to plant the assembly in Leopoldsburg, and so the Schraepens were members of that church from the very beginning, 1982–1986. They also became part of another of the assemblies that den Boer planted about fifteen kilometers away in Tessenderlo, 1986–1992.

Schraepen would grow in the faith through being challenged by den Boer to practice good "Christian habits," habits such as daily Bible reading and prayer. Schraepen very soon was accompanying den Boer as he conducted door-to-door evangelistic efforts, and he also accompanied den Boer

---

296. H. Gelling, letter to MSC, January 1993.
297. "Op de koffie," December 1999, 2.
298. Schraepen, interview, 27 June 2007.

to his preaching appointments and other studies whenever he had the time. Initially, Schraepen worked as a coal miner who prepared the equipment for the other miners to take with them underground, but very soon he started working as a salesman of confectionaries.

From just after their conversion, the Schraepens felt that they had been called as missionaries to India. Mrs. Schraepen remembered seeing the need of the children in India when she was a child and telling her mother that one day she would go to help the children there. Schraepen remembered how, after they were married, Mrs. Schraepen continually bought books about India.[299] Accordingly, the Schraepens went to India in 1992 as some of the very first evangelical missionaries out of Flanders. Before going, Schraepen served as part of the leadership team of the assembly in Tessenderlo, having learned much through one-on-one training with den Boer and by accompanying him to various ministry events. Nevertheless, the leadership of the ECV, including den Boer, initially were opposed to Schraepen going out as a missionary. Den Boer thought that he was too new a believer, and he also thought that he would not have enough supervision once he was in India.[300] The other ECV leaders were uncomfortable with the sending agency, Youth with a Mission (YWAM), given its Pentecostal nature. To help break the impasse, a number of the full-time ECV workers suggested that the people in the church in Tessenderlo give their opinion. Den Boer expected that few would support the Schraepens' goal. To den Boer's surprise, however, all supported the Schraepens in their desire to go to India. One well-placed source who attended that meeting noted that den Boer summarized that evening by saying, "This is the worst meeting ever."[301] As the one who had worked closely with Schraepen, and given den Boer's principled commitment to make sure that a worker works under supervision whether in the local church or in another land when sent out, the ultimate decision to let the Schraepens go to India was very troubling to den Boer and a further part of den Boer's reasoning to leave the ECV in 1996.[302]

After a fruitful number of years in India as a church-planter, Haverkamp asked Schraepen to return to Belgium in 1997 as the ECV needed workers. Schraepen eventually agreed in 1999, as his twin girls were now of an age that they needed to be back in the Flemish educational system.[303] On 1 September 1999, Schraepen became a full-time worker with the ECV. His

299. "Op de koffie," December 1999, 1.
300. Vleugels, 14 August 2007.
301. Anonymous, interview by author.
302. Vleugels, interview, 14 August 2007.
303. "Op de koffie," December 1999, 3.

contract was for a minimum salary according to government standards plus whatever gifts he might receive. While his contract described his work as that of an evangelist, Schraepen was very active leading Bible studies for believers and preaching on Sunday mornings as well. Other ministry that both he and his wife conducted involved youth work, and they especially led this age group in creative evangelization projects, using such methods as drama, dance, and singing groups.[304] Schraepen worked primarily with the assembly in Tessenderlo from 1999 until 2004, and then at Koersel from 2004–2007. Schraepen would leave the ECV in 2007 for a number of reasons, including what he felt were limits on his ministry. In particular, Schraepen had a group of twenty-five English-speaking people in Antwerpen ready to start a church, but the ECV asked him to stop with this and concentrate on the Dutch-speakers.[305]

Before and while all this was happening with the Schraepens and den Boer, the work of planting churches continued in Limburg. The Gelling family moved to Houthalen in July 1979 and lived there for only eighteen months, though later they would return and stay.[306] The choice to move to Houthalen the first time was a difficult one for the Gellings as they had to choose between moving to Houthalen and helping the new assembly there, or moving to Geel and helping a Bible study in that town become a new assembly. The Bible study in Geel had begun as the result of a contact through the sister of one of the hosts of the Bible study in Lommel. It met for the first time on 1 September 1977 in the Riviera, a dance hall.[307] This woman and her husband, as well as the top waiter at the Riviera, became believers, so they held the Bible study on Thursday evenings in their place of business.[308] When asked, Gelling wrote,

> Why did it never become an assembly? In [1979] we had to make a choice as to where we would move, either Geel or Houthalen where we also had a Bible study. It became Houthalen. I still had a study in Geel but did not have the time to visit there as much . . . It is a shame there was no one to follow up on these contacts.[309]

Ultimately, the move to Houthalen rather than Geel meant that the assembly in Houthalen grew well, and the people from the Bible study in Geel

304. "Op de koffie," September 2002, 2.
305. Schraepen, interview, 27 June 2007.
306. H. Gelling, letter to MSC, April 1989.
307. H. and B. Gelling, letter to supporters, Fall 1977.
308. H. Gelling, interview, 01 May 2003.
309. H. Gelling, email, 26 May 2008.

slowly drifted away, though a few ended up at the assembly in Tessenderlo. Interestingly, later efforts by Adri and Petra van de Berk of the BEZ over a five-year period did not see one person converted in Geel. Additionally, a couple from the US planted a Pentecostal church early in the twenty-first century, but returned to the US after a few years, discouraged with the situation in Geel. Nonetheless, Gelling noted that a man from Geel who was almost 80 years old underwent evangelical conversion during the years of the ECV Bible study. When he died, "probably 300 heard the gospel" at his funeral. "What did they do with it? The Lord knows!" Still, Gelling believed that "we will meet some of them in heaven."[310]

After moving to Zutendaal in 1980, the Gellings lived at Boogstraat 24. In 1980, Gelling wrote, "The reason we came to Zutendaal is because the assembly in Houthalen can get along without us being there. Here in this area there are 15 saved and they have a real desire to also start with the Lord's table."[311] Later that year, the assembly in Lanaken (Zutendaal) began to celebrate the Lord's Supper as they met in the Gelling home. By 1981, Gelling would report about this assembly, "at the moment about twenty adults are born again." Further, he noted active evangelistic efforts in Lanaken, such as an evangelistic film at which 100 were unconverted out of 175 who attended.[312]

The Gellings later returned to Houthalen and bought a dance hall in 1985. Reporting on this new location, Haverkamp quipped in a letter to supporters, "Imagine, even dancing halls can get converted in Belgium!"[313] The downstairs was used for the assembly, and the Gellings lived above it.[314] While the assembly began to meet in this building on 5 May, the Gellings did not move back to Houthalen until July. This new facility was much appreciated as the assembly of ninety adults had been meeting in an area of less than forty-seven square meters. The new facility had nearly 186 square meters for the meeting, an additional 186 square meters for the Sunday School rooms, and then two additional floors of living quarters for the Gellings.[315] By the time the assembly recognized four men as its first elders in December 1991, the assembly had grown to almost one hundred adults "in fellowship" and around seventy children. Gelling had worked

---

310. Ibid.
311. H. Gelling, letter to MSC, 12 September 1980.
312. H. Gelling, letter to supporters, Fall 1981.
313. R. Haverkamp, letter to supporters, Spring 1986.
314. R. and M. Haverkamp, "The Haverkamp News," letter to supporters, Spring 1986.
315. H. and B. Gelling, letter to MSC, May 1985.

with these four men for ten years before they were recognized by the assembly.[316] The Gellings sold the building to the assembly in the spring of 2008 with the intention of moving to smaller quarters as soon as suitable housing could be found.[317]

Julie Gelling, 1997–2009

By the end of the 1990s, another worker came out of Limburg to serve the ECV, Julie Gelling, the daughter of Henk and Beryl Gelling. Born in Clinton, ON, Canada, on 8 October 1969, Julie grew up in an obviously committed evangelical Christian household. Such was the atmosphere that she could not recall a specific date of her conversion as she never really questioned it. She noted that believing in God, Christ, etc., were facts that she learned along with her ABCs. "Because I was brought up in a Christian home and saw what it meant to be a Christian, depending on Christ, and God's providence, it all became very real to me."[318] By age 13, she was a Sunday School teacher at the ECV assembly where her family were members. During the 1989–1990 school year, she attended the US Brethren Bible school, Emmaus Bible College in Dubuque, IA.[319] Like many children raised in committed Christian homes outside their parents' home country, she said, "I wanted to see if my faith was my faith or my parents' faith . . . and I wanted to see if I wanted to stay in Belgium or if I felt drawn to the North American way of life."[320] She also used this time to take courses in Christian camping.

Returning to Belgium, Julie completed a nine-month secretarial course in Hasselt, Limburg, and subsequently continued to live with her parents.[321] She also continued her active involvement with the work of the ECV as a volunteer, primarily as a worker at the youth camps as well as in the local church doing ministry with the children and youth. In 1996, Julie and Rosario Anastasi became part of the *Evangelisch Jeugdverbond* (EJV), an organization which worked with youth throughout Flanders.[322] The ECV

---

316. H. and B. Gelling, letter to MSC, December 1991.

317. H. Gelling, telephone conversation, 22 April 2008.

318. J. Gelling, interview, 12 August 2007.

319. Though now a fully recognized four-year undergraduate institution accredited by the US governmental educational authorities, Emmaus only offered a one-year Bible certificate and a three-year study in Bible, and was not accredited when Julie attended. For more information, cf. http://www.emmaus.edu/.

320. J. Gelling, interview, 12 August 2007.

321. Ibid.

322. Cf. http://www.ejv.be/ for more information. For more information about Anastasi, cf. this chapter, "Rosario Anastasi."

Workers and Works of the Evangelische Christengemeenten Vlaanderen

was invited to become part of this organization because of a change in rules by the Belgian government for this type of organization.[323] The ECV was asked to become a part of this organization along with the VEG, BEZ, and others. Subsequent to these organizations having representatives on the oversight of the EJV, the EJV became an organization recognized by the Flemish government.

Around this same time, Julie began to work full time with the ECV. She was hired as a half-time worker in June 1997. She was recognized for her tireless activity in a variety of areas within the ECV, including administration, publicity, and the planning and execution of a variety of ECV social gatherings. She noted that her unmarried status made it possible for her to commit more energy to the work of the ECV than some could. Her gifts in organization and administration, as well as a creative flair, made her contribution important to the overall work of the ECV.[324]

Oost-Vlaanderen and West-Vlaanderen: Eeklo, Gentbrugge, Ieper, Wevelgem, Roeselare

The assembly in Eeklo began as the result of an evangelistic Bible study which met first on 7 January 1977 in the Haverkamp home at Kort Eindeken 73 in Lovendegem.[325] In a short time, thirty people came to study and most were converted. A new assembly began to meet on 9 October 1977 in the Haverkamp home as a result. By the fall, sixty to seventy adults, youth, and children regularly attended the assembly.[326] This group soon moved to a more permanent location, a storefront on Collegestraat 21 in Eeklo.[327] This move came in June 1978.[328] In the summer of 1988, the assembly in Eeklo would buy a large building in which to meet.[329] This became their permanent location at Molenstraat 53.[330]

In the summer of 1978, the assembly in Gentbrugge began as a hive-off from the Eeklo assembly. In just one year, the Eeklo assembly had grown

323. J. Gelling, interview, 12 August 2007.

324. "Op de koffie bij . . . Julie Gelling," 2.

325. "Christengemeente Eeklo bestaat 25 jaar!," 5. This is the same assembly mentioned earlier associated with the section on De Kegel above.

326. R. Haverkamp, letter to supporters, September-October 1977.

327. "Eeklo 7 Jaar Gemeenteleven," 2.

328. "Christengemeente Eeklo bestaat 25 jaar!," 5.

329. R. Haverkamp, letter to MSC, 4 August 1988. Cf. R. and M. Haverkamp, letter to supporters, December 1988.

330. "Christengemeente Eeklo bestaat 25 jaar!," 5.

to the point that around twenty-five adults were able to leave and form this new assembly.[331] This group of believers from the Eeklo assembly began with a Bible study and celebration of the Lord's Supper, and the Threadcrafts helped with this work.[332] Quite a number of the early converts were people whose common background was being from a close-knit group of "bikers," a somewhat rough group of motorcycle riders.[333] Initially, Bible studies were held in the apartment of Jean-Pierre and Carrie Borgonjon, and the celebration of the Lord's Supper was held at the apartment of Fabri and Ann Ferri. Especially helpful in the growth of the children's Sunday school was the work of Marina Haverkamp and Joanna Groen (later to be the wife of Peter Gifford). Not until 1981 would the assembly find a more permanent place to meet. They remodeled a facility on Gontrodestraat 72, and this would be their place of meeting for many years to come.[334] In 1985, the Giffords returned to help out at Gentbrugge along with Marian Voskamp and Carmen Crana as part of a team from International Teams. While Voskamp had to return to Canada due to health problems, Crana finished out her two year commitment, and the Giffords stayed on as long-term ECV workers.[335] Gifford worked at Gentbrugge in the areas of evangelistic Bible studies, discipleship, camp work for youth, and counseling. He also assisted later when he could at Mariakerke and Beveren.[336]

The first *Startstudies* in southwest Flanders were instrumental in helping to plant several assemblies, studies which began in 1979 in Moorsele.[337] The reason these studies began is that Haverkamp went to visit the pen pal of a doctor's wife from Oost-Vlaanderen, and a Bible study was established in that home. This first study grew so fast that another had to be started.[338] By 1981, assemblies were planted in Ieper, Wevelgem, and Roeselare. Various locations of the Ieper assembly over the years included a house in Izegem and later a school in Wevelgem. After about four years, the meeting place in Ieper was too small, so a new assembly was planted in Wervik as a hive-off in 1987.[339] Thus, the twenty-fourth ECV church was started in Wervik on

331. "Eeklo 7 Jaar Gemeenteleven," 2.

332. R. Haverkamp, "God is at Work in Belgium," 3. Cf. this chapter, section below, "Hal Threadcraft."

333. P. and J. Gifford, interview, 20 August 2008.

334. "Gent, van huisgemeente tot . . . ," 2.

335. R. Haverkamp, "God is at Work in Belgium," 3.

336. P. Gifford and J. Gifford, "All-, Old-, en Full-timers," 4.

337. A. Biesbrouck, "Een eigen gebouw voor Ieper," 3. For an extended explanation about the *Startstudies*, cf. chapter 4.

338. R. Haverkamp, "God is at Work in Belgium," 3.

339. A. Biesbrouck, "Een eigen gebouw voor Ieper," 3.

Workers and Works of the Evangelische Christengemeenten Vlaanderen

3 May 1987, a town on the border of France. Thirty-five adults and their children began meeting as a separate church in on this date.[340] By 1988 two elders were recognized, Robert Blondeel and Antoon Biesbrouck.[341]

Eventually, the assembly built its own facility and begin using it on 5 April 1992. This assembly struggled in later years. Gelling reported, "People kept leaving because of extreme charismatic influences and the resulting division, so sad!"[342] This assembly closed in November 2004 when it had to sell its building because too few remained to pay the costs. Initially after the sale, the believers gathered in a home, but their few numbers and advanced age made continuing not a realistic option. At the time of the sale of the meeting place in Wervik, Haverkamp wrote, "*Please pray. In some places we are making headway, in others we are losing ground, which really hurts.*"[343] In contrast, Ieper continued to grow; a new building was found in 1992, their first meeting being 5 April.[344] This building later was expanded in 1997.[345]

The assembly in Roeselare initially met together with the assembly at Moorsele, then meeting in Wevelgem. Within a year, some of the people from Wevelgem hived off and moved to begin a new assembly in Moorsele due to the rapid growth. The assembly in Roeselare also would begin as a hive-off from the assembly in Wevelgem in 1981.[346] By spring 1982, Roeselare had thirty-five adults plus children.[347] On 9 April 1984, the first elders' meeting was held.[348]

Eric Rutten, 1991–1997

One of the men who would help with the work as a full-time Christian worker in West-Vlaanderen was Eric Rutten. Rutten was born in Eksel, Limburg, and was converted in 1975 through a *Startstudies* held in the Symons' home in Limburg. Though only sixteen at the time, Rutten was already living a troubled life. His contact with the claims of Jesus Christ at these studies convinced him of his need for conversion. Lut Helsen, the

340. R. and M. Haverkamp, letter to supporters, Fall 1987.
341. Blondeel, "artikel niewsbrief [sic] Ieper," email, 12 October 2002.
342. H. and B. Gelling, "Belgium—A Mission Field!," 3–5.
343. R. and M. Haverkamp, letter to supporters, March 2004.
344. A. Biesbrouck, "Een eigen gebouw voor Ieper," 4.
345. H. Biesbrouck, "En Ieper bouwde voort," 10.
346. Schelstraete, "Handelingen (6)," 3.
347. R. and M. Haverkamp, letter to supporters, Spring 1982.
348. "Gemeentekaantje in Roeselare," 2.

woman who was to be his wife, also was converted through these same Bible studies. As this study grew to be the assembly in Peer, these young converts went to the youth group and eventually became its leaders. Also during this time, Rutten earned his undergraduate degree at BIB while Lut studied psychiatric nursing. During his studies at BIB, Rutten met den Boer. Rutten would be responsible for introducing den Boer to the ECV. After completing his studies, Rutten served as a chaplain in the Belgian armed forces at the post in Leopoldsburg. Meanwhile, Lut studied at the Capenwray Bible School in the UK, and then she completed studies at BIB.[349]

In 1982, the Ruttens were married. He worked as a teacher of Protestant religion in West-Vlaanderen half time and provided pastoral care for the assemblies in Ieper, Roeselare, and Moorsele. At Haverkamp's urging, Rutten became a full-time worker for the ECV in 1991. While primarily providing pastoral care, Rutten also helped with the founding of the assemblies in Wervik and Kuurne.[350] During his time in the ECV, the ECV made major changes from an "organism to an organization." These structural changes were not welcome by Rutten, and so he left the ECV in 1997.[351]

Back to Antwerpen: Boom

The assembly in Boom began due to the work of a man from the *Evangelische Gemeente* in Hemisem, a Dutchman named Rinus Pieper from the VEG, and Theo Le Jeune, an elder from the assembly in Berchem. The initial contacts were gained in 1980 through a series of outreach efforts in conjunction with OM, primarily a door-to-door evangelistic campaign. As with many other ECV churches, this work began as home Bible study. On 25 September 1980, the first three people came to this study. It was held in Reet, a small village a few kilometers northwest of Boom.[352] Pieper primarily helped as an evangelist and Le Jeune as an administrator. On 12 November 1981, the assembly met for the first time of public worship.[353] The location was Pieper's home.[354] In April 1981, the assembly relocated to the *Christelijk Centrum* at Advokaatstraat 2 in Boom. The first six people were baptized on 23 May 1982.[355] Soon thereafter, they had to choose to become affiliated

349. Schelstraete, "Handelingen (17)," 3.
350. Ibid.
351. K. and E. Schelstraete, interview, 03 September 2007.
352. Le Jeune, "Boom," 6. Cf. "Feestzaal wordt Christengemeente," 1.
353. "Feestzaal wordt Christengemeente," 1.
354. Schelstraete, "Handelingen (16)," 2.
355. Le June, "Boom," 6.

with either the VEG or the ECV, and they chose the latter. In 1986, Pieper returned to his home country and continued an active ministry as an evangelist.[356] On 1 August 1987, Le Jeune accepted his pension from work and committed himself full-time to the work at the assembly in Boom, though he officially never became an ECV worker.[357] He also was instrumental in the organizational changes that later came to the ECV.[358]

Again in Oost-Vlaanderen: Maldegem

The assembly in Maldegem grew very slowly in the first years. Just a handful of believers could be found in Maldegem after ten years of work. Initially, these new believers would have a Bible study in one of their homes, and then attend Sunday services elsewhere. The new believers went to the BEZ church in Gentbrugge until the assembly started in Haverkamp's house in Lovendegem. From a Bible study of some forty interested people, only ten were converted. In 1980–81, however, a sudden change came about; in a very short time, over thirty people were converted. By this time, the believers from Maldegem gathered with the assembly at Eeklo on Sundays to celebrate the Lord's Supper. The meeting place in Eeklo, however, was too small.[359] As a result, the believers from Maldegem began meeting as a separate assembly in March 1982, hiving off of the assembly in Eeklo. This was the fourteenth church planted in a ten-year period. The Threadcrafts from the USA went with this new group to help with its establishment.[360] They also helped with a Bible study planted in Oudenaarde.[361] Though only in Maldegem for a relatively short period of time, the Threadcrafts' help was important in the early years of the Maldegem assembly. Over the years, the assembly in Maldegem met in a house, a chiropractor's office, and in an apartment. In their sixteenth year, the assembly finally were able to build a facility at Karrewegel 47 in Maldegem.[362]

Hal Threadcraft, 1979–1983

Hal Threadcraft was raised in Birmingham, AL, USA. He was converted during his studies at the University of Alabama, where he earned a Bachelor's degree in Civil Engineering. In contrast, his future wife, Marion, was

---

356. Schelstraete, "Handelingen (16)," 2.
357. "Stap voor stap verder in Vlaanderen," 5.
358. These changes and his role will be covered in more detail in chapter 4.
359. "Maldegem, twee jaar op eigen benen," 5.
360. R. Haverkamp, letter to supporters, February 1982.
361. R. Haverkamp, letter to supporters, April 1983.
362. "Karrewegel 47," 7.

converted at about five years old. In fact, his future wife was the catalyst for his conversion. Though Threadcraft believed in God, he "could not accept the Bible as being anything more than a book written by men because it contained so many blatant and obvious errors." Marion challenged him to study and see if these errors really existed, and several months into his reading while in the seventh chapter of Romans, Threadcraft was converted.[363] When he finished this first degree, he and his wife moved to Dallas, TX, USA, where Threadcraft earned his ThM at Dallas Theological Seminary.

During his studies at Dallas Theological Seminary, the Threadcrafts "became aware of the vast spiritual vacuum" in other parts of the world. He recalled that once they became aware of the need, the only question was whether they were to go personally or "intercede for others that were already there."[364] He said,

> To determine God's will in a matter, we did then what we continue to do today when faced with a question. The first thing is to go to God's Word. Many times the answer will be clearly [revealed] by a certain verse or passage . . . We learned from the Bible what we were supposed to do, but nowhere did He say where He wanted us to do it.[365]

The Threadcrafts bought a map of the world and began to pray over it, and Threadcraft contacted a number of missionaries. One of those contacted was a man from "a Bible school in Belgium," Theo Kunst, the man who later would head the *Evangelische Alliantie Vlaanderen* as well as *Evangelische Theologische Faculteit* (ETF). Kunst also was a graduate of Dallas Theological Seminary. As a result of this contact, Threadcraft went over to the Netherlands and Belgium to see more, and one of the families with whom he stayed was the Haverkamps. After that trip, he continued to correspond with Haverkamp, and made a decision to go to Belgium. On 4 December 1979, the Threadcrafts arrived in Belgium.

The time in Belgium was difficult for Threadcraft as his gifts were more that of a first-rate teacher and counselor than as a church planter. Additionally, the cultural adjustment was a great challenge.[366] Nonetheless, Threadcraft did teach courses in homiletics, pedagogy, and New Testament Greek at ETF. "It was a wonderful experience and the graduates of that [first] class have gone on to minister in Belgium, Holland, and into Africa."[367]

363. "May we introduce . . . Hal and Marion Threadcraft," 24.
364. Ibid.
365. Ibid.
366. H. Gelling, interview, 01 May 2003.
367. Threadcraft, "Re: ECV in Belgium," email, 02 September 2008.

Workers and Works of the Evangelische Christengemeenten Vlaanderen

Though in Belgium for only four years, Threadcraft gave a course of premarital counseling which was instrumental in the life of Peter Gifford and Joanna Groen as they contemplated marriage.[368] While the Threadcrafts did not stay long term, Threadcraft became convinced during this time period of the Lord's leading to improve on His gifts to him by pursuing doctoral studies as a counselor. Accordingly, the Threadcrafts returned to North America in 1983, initially to Edmonton, AB, Canada, where Threadcraft served as a resident worker at a Brethren assembly.[369] Among his activities was a series of Bible studies at the nearby university.[370] He and his family later moved to the US where Threadcraft eventually earned his PhD in Marriage and Family at the University of Alabama.[371]

Flemish Assemblies in Germany: Soest, Brakel, Arolsen

Though Flanders was the primary place of ministry for the founders of the ECV, three churches also were planted in Germany as a result of Belgian military men being stationed there. About six months after his conversion in 1981 at the assembly in Eeklo, Dominique Vandelannoote was stationed in Soest, Germany, a location about fifty kilometers east of Dortmund.[372] Once there, Vandelannoote began to challenge his fellow soldiers with the claims of the evangelical gospel, and people responded. The first Bible study was held, and just two gathered to learn more about the message of the evangelical gospel. More and more came to the studies over time. Around the same time, people began to gather to study the Bible in Arolsen due to the efforts of Johan Allaert.[373] Eventually, Vandelannoote, Allaert, and Hugo de Bock prayed about starting a new assembly.[374] By the end of 1982, the assembly was established. In a very short time, assemblies were planted not only in Soest, but also in Brakel and Arolsen—places about one hundred kilometers from Soest. Vandelannoote was the contact point in Soest, de Bock in Brakel, and Allaert in Arolsen.[375] Initially, a Thursday meeting was held

---

368. J. Gifford, interview, 08 February 2008.

369. "Deletions," 24.

370. "Groeten uit Canada," 1.

371. Schelstraete, "Handelingen (18)," 3; Threadcraft, email, 11 January 2009.

372. Haverkamp, "God is at Work in Belgium," 5.

373. Vandelannoote, email, 18 August 2008. In turn, Haverkamp forwarded this email to author, 18 August 2008.

374. Vandelannoote and Allaert were lieutenants, and de Bock was a 1st Sergent Major. Cf. "Legerdienst," 4.

375. Vandelannoote, "Bei uns in Deutschland," 3.

to celebrate the Lord's Supper, and this celebration rotated among the three garrison locations.[376] However, believers gathered in various homes in these three locales to study the Bible and pray each week as well.[377] The assemblies also scheduled evangelistic campaigns, Bible study weekends in Soest and Brakel, film nights, and other events to help the assemblies grow. They even had professors from a German Bible school come and teach the new believers, and they had preachers come from Flanders for Bible conferences. They were not just interested in the areas near these Belgian assemblies in Germany, however. They also were interested in Christian work in other lands. Arolsen, for example, in 1984 "financially adopted" Rosimeide, a nineteen month old girl living in Brazil, as a part of the work of *Evangelische Zending Brazilië*.[378] Over time, the number of believers in Soest grew to the point that Sunday morning meetings were scheduled for the Lord's Supper as well as a Sunday school for the children.[379] These assemblies closed after 1 July 1991 due to a reorganization of the Belgian military which included a withdrawal of forces from most places outside of Belgium.[380] At this time, the military members and their families returned to Belgium.[381]

More Work in Limburg: Zwartberg

The Zwartberg assembly began as a hive-off from the one in Houthalen. Approximately twenty adults from Winterslag and Houthalen-East combined with another eight from Waterschei for a Bible study and time of prayer. At a meeting on 6 March 1982, a decision was made to rent an old school building on Heizeisstraat in Waterschei as a place to house the new assembly. This facility had but four rooms for use. On 25 April 1982, the assembly met to celebrate the Lord's Supper for the first time. When this first facility was outgrown, another school building was found in Zwartberg at Arbeidstraat 56. This one was purchased by the assembly, remodeled, and used as a place for the assembly activities beginning in the fall of 1984. This was a much larger facility and comfortably could house up to one hundred and fifty people in the

---

376. Because the Lord's Supper was held at all three locations, "three assemblies" are counted. Nonetheless, in many ways these three locations acted in closer concert with one another than was the norm for other ECV assemblies. Because of this close association, others count these three as one. Cf. H. Gelling, "RE: Wellen assembly," email, 05 September 2008.

377. "Hallo, wie geht es ihnen," 2.

378. "Nieuws van het oostelijk front," 5.

379. "Hallo, wie geht es ihnen," 2.

380. "Adreswijzigingen," 6.

381. Vandelannoote, "Bei uns in Deutschland," 3.

Workers and Works of the Evangelische Christengemeenten Vlaanderen

main meeting room as well as provide a place for classrooms, a kitchen, and a nursery. Given the needs of the surrounding community, Zwartberg eventually had ministries for youth with drug and alcohol problems.[382] Elders were recognized in Zwartberg after a day of prayer and fasting in early 1988. One of the elders was Flemish and the other was Italian, a reflection of the half Flemish and half Italian composition of this assembly.[383] Gelling wrote to MSC,

> Both men are young but are shepherding the flock . . . I will be working with them for a period of time yet as we feel we have arrived at the I Tim. 3:10 stage. This is our whole purpose—to plant assemblies that will become autonomous. Much wisdom and patience is needed. We are going step by step ourselves as to how to train these men.[384]

The Italian elder, Rosario Anastasi, later became a full-time worker for the ECV in 1990.

As the assembly in Zwartberg grew, finding and keeping leadership became a challenge. Anastasi even had to serve as a lone elder of the Zwartberg assembly for a two-year period since the men of Limburg did not readily seek or exercise leadership. His time as a coal miner and his heritage as a first generation Italian born in Belgium made him more inclined toward leadership than the average man in Limburg.[385]

Rosario Anastasi, 1990–Present

Anastasi was converted from a nominal Roman Catholic background. He grew up as one of seven children, the child of Italian immigrants.[386] He was converted at age twenty-two through the ministry of Gelling in 1982. His sister had set up a meeting in the home "without [his] permission."[387] The

---

382. "Gods wondere wegen van Houthalen over Waterschei naar Zwartberg," 2.

383. In the 1970s, 35.8 percent of the foreign population of Belgium was Italian. By 1990, this had decreased to 27.3 percent, though their overall numbers had increased moderately. Nevertheless, Italian immigrants remained the largest group of foreigners in Belgium. Cf. Thränhardt, ed., *Europe—A New Immigration Continent,* 251. For an analysis of the socioeconomic conditions and attainment of the Italian immigrants and the direct Italian descendents in Flanders, cf. Phalet and Swyngedouw, "Measuring immigrant integration: the case of Belgium," 781ff.

384. H. and B. Gelling, letter to MSC and supporters, February 1988.

385. Anastasi, interview, 01 July 2005.

386. Although he was born in Belgium, Anastasi would be born as and remain an Italian citizen.

387. Anastasi, interview, 30 June 2005.

timing was auspicious since Anastasi was dealing with the aftermath of a serious accident in the coal mines which had left him handicapped in his right arm and hand. As Anastasi said,

> I was touched by the person of Jesus and His saving work, but I did not want to admit it as I was firstly a proud Italian! However, the more I saw, the more my opposition disappeared. Finally I gave my life to the Lord. I sometimes feel a little bit like Paul whom the Lord had to call in a dramatic way.[388]

Association with the ECV brought more than just conversion to Anastasi, however, as he met his wife, Anita Milazzo, at the assembly in Zwartberg. She was born in Sicily and had grown up in a household of believers. She herself had been converted at age fourteen.

After they were married, the Anastasies became very active in the assembly in Zwartberg. They helped with the youth and started a ministry for young adults. Summers were spent helping out at the youth camp in Gierle, he as one of the youth leaders and she in the kitchen. Gelling initially asked Anastasi to teach a Bible study in Zwartberg, but soon he invited him to teach at the other assemblies in nearby towns as well. Both of the Anastasis enjoyed their increasing involvement with the ECV. Then, because of a 1989 court ruling by the labor court in the aftermath of his 2 March 1982 accident in the mines, Anastasi received a monthly disability compensation. This compensation made it financially possible for him to become a full-time worker with the ECV in 1990.[389]

After becoming a full-timer, Anastasi's main ministries were at the local church in Zwartberg and with youth work locally. Additionally, he worked with the Flemish youth organization *Evangelisch Jeugdverbond Vlaanderen* (EJV) in addition to other cooperative efforts with various evangelical organizations and outreaches in Limburg and Flanders.[390] He also completed a bachelor's degree in Bible over six years at the BIB Saturday school.[391] Ultimately, Anastasi's service with the ECV was primarily according to his gifts of teaching and administration since he did not see himself having the gifts of a pastoral worker.

---

388. "Op de koffie met . . . Rosario en Anita," 2.
389. Schelstraete, "Handelingen (22)," 3.
390. "Op de koffie met . . . Rosario en Anita," 2.
391. K. and E. Schelstraete, interview, 03 September 2007.

Workers and Works of the Evangelische Christengemeenten Vlaanderen

David Dunlap, 1983–1989

Another Brethren missionary from the US was involved with the assembly in Zwartberg almost from the beginning as well as helping out with the work of the ECV throughout Limburg. David Dunlap was born 24 August 1956. He grew up in a Brethren family because his father had met and associated himself with assembly people during his years in Columbia, SC, US, as he attended seminary at Columbia Bible College. While growing up in New Jersey, Dunlap attended a Tunbridge Wells assembly, and had no knowledge of the Open Brethren.[392] Although he made several "professions of faith" at Christian summer camps run by Word of Life at Schroon Lake, New York, Dunlap said that he truly was not converted until the age of twenty-three while he was in university.[393]

Of his years before university, Dunlap notes, "Sport became my passion and consumed most of my time and energy. My desire for Christ was replaced by alcohol and friends. But the further I went from the Lord, the more pointless my life became."[394] Eventually, the truth claims of the world's great religions drove Dunlap into deeper study of the Bible. Also during this time, Dunlap was involved with university Bible studies run by InterVarsity Christian Fellowship (IVCF).[395] Through these influences, Dunlap was converted in 1979.

Dunlap said that he immediately was filled with the desire to serve God. He attended Bible studies, told others about his evangelical faith, and worked at a Christian book table in the student center.[396] Off campus, he accompanied an older Christian to an inner city mission to see if this would be a place for him to minister. While there, the leader of the mission said, "Whatever you do decide to do make sure God gets all the glory." Dunlap said that from then on, he tried to make those words the goal of his life.[397] In a short period of time, Dunlap was involved as a leader with the local branch of IVCF as he completed his Bachelor of Science degree in Business Administration and Psychology. During university, Dunlap also attended Grace and Truth Chapel in Mahwah, NJ, an assembly that was part of the

---

392. Tunbridge Wells was a division of the Exclusive Brethren, so named because of the geographical location in England associated with the beginnings of this branch. Cf. Noel, *The History of the Brethren*, 2:633–64; Dronsfield, *The "Brethren" Since 1870*.
393. Dunlap, interview, 19 September 2006.
394. "David: een hart voor België," 6.
395. IVCF is known as InterVarsity Fellowship (IVF) in the United Kingdom.
396. "David: een hart voor België," 6.
397. "May we introduce . . . David Dunlap," 4–5.

Kelly Continental Brethren's worldwide network.[398] While not as strict as the Tunbridge Wells assembly in which he grew up, this still would have been an Exclusive assembly.

Right after graduation, he became a paid, half-time worker with IVCF, though he noted that he really worked for IVCF full time from 1979–1982. He also took some courses at Alliance Theological Seminary in Nyack, NY, during the same period. Concurrently, he worked in New York City for Merrill Lynch.

While Haverkamp was visiting at CMML headquarters in Wall, NJ, during furlough in 1982, Dunlap became reacquainted with him from an earlier summer time with OM in Belgium, and Haverkamp asked Dunlap to come to Belgium long term. A few years earlier, Dunlap had become a member of his first Open Brethren assembly, Bethel Bible Chapel in Middletown, NJ, where his uncle, Gerald Dalamore, was a resident worker.[399] This chapel had hived-off from a long standing, Italian language assembly, Long Branch Gospel Hall, many years earlier.[400] Over an eighteen month period which included discussions with the elders of Bethel, men's meetings at Bethel, and finally an assembly-wide meeting, Dunlap was commended to the Lord's care for His work in Belgium. In their letter of commendation, the elders said in part,

> Christians at Bethel Bible Chapel, have commended Mr. David Dunlap to full-time Christian service in Belgium and to work among the assemblies who are seeking to carry on New Testament church principles. We are aware that it is only the holy Spirit of God that calls out and separates unto Himself, those for His service (Acts 13:2–4) . . . [David's] gift of teaching and ministry became evident in the local assembly and has gained the confidence of the elders and of the Christians at Bethel Bible

---

398. Dunlap, interview, 19 September 2006.

399. A resident worker among the Brethren is a commended worker who commits the bulk of his time to ministry in one local assembly. In contrast, a commended worker who works outside his home country is a missionary, such as were the founders of the ECV.

400. Long Branch Gospel Hall began through the personal work of Nunzio Pizzulli and an extended evangelistic outreach by Louis Rosania. The first Lord's Supper was held in Pizzulli's home in 1925 after a baptismal service. Because of growth through new converts, this assembly rented an upper room on Branchport Avenue, and then on 7 August 1932 moved into their own building at 635 Art Street. For this and more information, cf. "Historical Sketch of a Movement of the Spirit which resulted in the Establishment of Italian Assemblies in the U.S.A. and Canada," in *La Voce Nel Deserto*, 22–23. Cf. Diorio and De Carlo, *La Storia Delle Assemblee Italiane In America*. Cf. "United States—New Jersey: Long Branch," in *2006 Address Book of Some Assemblies of Christians in the United States, Canada, and other countries*, 101.

Chapel. David utilized his teaching gift and then was exercised about more participation in God's service. He has demonstrated good Christian character, maturity and sincerity of purpose since working with us.[401]

During the time before his commendation, Dunlap also corresponded with ECV missionaries Haverkamp, Gelling, and Threadcraft.[402] Threadcraft had some particularly pertinent comments as he wrote in response to Dunlap's inquiry,

> There is but one reason one may have in coming and only one which will keep one after coming and that is knowing that he is in the will of God. To come does not commit you for life but it will keep you while the going gets tough—and it will be tough.[403]

Dunlap moved to Belgium on 12 October 1983 and began a time of language learning, as well as a time of being mentored by Gelling. His hard work was rewarded as he would preach his first sermon in Dutch on Sunday, 11 March 1984.[404] He said that Gelling was like a spiritual father to him. Gelling taught him ways to evangelize to include one-on-one witnessing, how to organize and lead evangelistic Bible studies, how to work with people, and how to nurture an assembly once it was begun. As a part of his work, Dunlap also helped to mentor Anastasi. Reflecting on his years in Flanders, and especially during his time in Limburg learning from Gelling, Dunlap later would say that he learned a valuable principle which helped him as a commended worker when he returned to the US. He learned that

> when you have a thriving assembly work, it's contagious. People come and look and say, "This can be actually done." I got the impression that when an assembly movement is struggling and says, "This is what the Bible teaches," it is much harder to convince others. But when it's thriving and it's dynamic, and people are being saved, and appears like it is meeting like the New Testament, others say, "Well maybe we can do this, too."[405]

Dunlap returned to the US in November 1989 on what was supposed to be a furlough. During this visit, he met his future wife. After prayerful consideration, and given the opportunities to minister among the

---

401. Bethel Bible Chapel, letter of commendation for David Dunlap, 27 June 1983, as signed by John H. Pinkham, Reuben Tirado, Pat Truglia, and Edward Risden.
402. Dunlap, interview, 19 September 2006.
403. Threadcraft, letter to David Dunlap, 14 April 1982.
404. "Arbeiders," 6.
405. Dunlap, interview, 19 September 2006.

assemblies in New Jersey and Pennsylvania, Dunlap decided to remain in the US.[406] Though he did not remain in Belgium past 1989, Dunlap maintained contact with the work there and especially with the Gelling family. He eventually moved to Land O' Lakes, FL, both to plant an assembly and to have a base from which he conducted an active Bible conference ministry as a full-time worker among the Open Brethren.

New Assembly in West-Vlaanderen: Kortrijk

Kortrijk, the twenty-second assembly in Flanders, came as a hive-off from Wevelgem and Roeselare.[407] They met for the first time on 19 January 1986 in the *Stedelijke Tuinbouwschool* in Kortrijk, beginning with approximately thirty adults and twenty-five children.[408] As with many of the assemblies, they used *Startstudies* as a way to increase their numbers through evangelical conversions. *Startstudies* were held both in Kortrijk as well as the nearby village of Avelgem. Within eighteen months, the assembly grew to sixty adults and fifty children.[409] When this gathering grew to about one hundred adults and eighty-five children, they built a new place to meet in Kuurne. Over time, this assembly would recognize elders, deacons, and even send out Noel and Manja Soetaert as missionaries to Burkina Faso.[410] Still, this assembly was not without times of difficulty. They went through a period of great unrest due to some of the members actively propagating charismatic beliefs and practices among the rest of the assembly. Reporting this in the ECV newsletter, the assembly leaders wrote,

> For three years we went through a painful and difficult period . . . We were unprepared and taken by surprise; the tension, conflicts and eventual separation caused by this burden has left behind scars. Still, God had taught us much. He has made us to know our frailty and sinfulness. He has shown us as assembly leaders that we must keep in continual touch with those in the assembly.[411]

---

406. Dunlap, "Re: Pictures arrived," email, 17 July 2008.

407. "Kortrijk: 'We zijn benieuwd,'" 6. While R. and M. Haverkamp, letter to supporters, Spring 1986, lists 05 January 1986 as the date of the first Lord's Supper in Kortrijk, contemporaneous reports and this historical essay list 19 January 1986 as the first week.

408. "Weeral een nieuwe gemeente? Ja, te Kortrijk," 8.

409. "Gemeentenieuws," 4.

410. Schelstraete, "Handelingen (21)," 3.

411. "Kortrijk: 'We zijn benieuwd,'" 7.

Workers and Works of the Evangelische Christengemeenten Vlaanderen

Though some left, the assembly continued well such that, in early 1995 they reported sixty-eight adults and seventy-five children at the assembly.[412]

Once More in Limburg: Wellen

After a pause of nearly eight years, the ECV planted two assemblies in 1990 and 1991. The first of these was started in Limburg by Luc Vandevorst and Gelling. Vandevorst had become a full-time worker with the ECV on 1 September 1984.[413] The work in Wellen began as an evangelistic outreach and a series of *Startstudies*. The first meeting was held on a Sunday afternoon in the village of Riksingen. Soon, another study was begun in Vliermaal. Other outreaches were held in Blizen and in Guigoven. While the Lord's Supper was celebrated twice a month in Riksengen before the official beginning of the assembly, ultimately, the first official meeting was held on 4 November 1990 in Guigoven.[414] They had twenty-five adults and forty children.[415] Vandevorst was the main ECV worker to help out with this assembly once it became an established church, though Gelling also helped out.[416]

Vandevorst eventually had to leave full-time Christian work due to health problems for both him and his wife. He served at the assembly until his return to secular work in 1992, a period of seven and a half years.[417] In 1995, this assembly moved to Wellen.[418] For Sunday meetings and Bible studies, the assembly met in a "town hall type of building," and prayer meetings were held in the homes of various believers.[419]

Final New Assembly, Oost-Vlaanderen: Mariakerke

A year later at the other end of Flanders, the assembly at Mariakerke met for the first time on 13 October 1991.[420] Initially, about ninety were

---

412. Ibid.
413. "Luc en Nicole 'fulltime,'" 3.
414. H. and B. Gelling, letter to MSC, Fall 1990.
415. "Nieuwe gemeente in Guigoven," 1.
416. H. and B. Gelling, letter to MSC, 31 January 1991.
417. H. and B. Gelling, letter to supporters, Spring 1992. In a telephone interview of 08 December 2008, H. Gelling noted that Vandevoorst remained active in the work of the ECV to the time of this writing, including leading *Startstudies* even after ceasing to be a fulltimer.
418. H. and B. Gelling, letter to MSC, 25 September 1995.
419. H. and B. Gelling, letter to MSC, 25 January 1996.
420. R. and M. Haverkamp, letter to supporters, January 1992.

in attendance.⁴²¹ This assembly began as a result of a hive-off from the assembly in Gentbrugge as well as through evangelistic outreach.⁴²² The meeting place in Gentbrugge had become too crowded, and this created a difficult challenge for children's work on Sunday mornings. *Startstudies* led by Haverkamp and other evangelistic outreaches involving believers from a number of nearby ECV churches helped to increase the numbers. While the primary assembly from which most came was in Gentbrugge, believers also came from Eeklo.⁴²³

Because of the high costs of renting a suitable location or buying a new building, Mariakerke and Gentbrugge eventually would reunite. This worked well, however, as one of the nights of opening weekend of the new facility was attended by the mayor of Gent. Thus, on 5 May 2000 the mayor came to the assembly building at Gent.⁴²⁴ The assembly had expected some low-level functionary, but the mayor and his wife came, and the mayor publicly was presented with a Bible by Paul Eeraerts, one of the leaders.⁴²⁵ Writing on this two days of "opening festivities," Gifford reported, "The mayor of Ghent did indeed attend . . . We had several local newspapers report the event and we are hoping that this helps dispel the rumors of us being a sect."⁴²⁶ This type of official acknowledgment and welcome never would have been imagined when the ECV began meeting in Gentbrugge twenty-two years earlier.

Anne Dryburgh, 1999–Present

One of the later Brethren missionaries helping out at the assemblies in Gentbrugge and Maldegem was Anne Dryburgh. Dryburgh was raised in a theologically liberal Christian home as part of the Church of Scotland. While religious practices were observed, such as weekly Sunday services, and though her grandfather was a Church of Scotland minister, she did not hear the evangelical gospel until her teen years.⁴²⁷ She was converted at age seventeen on 1 December 1989 through the influence of Christian

---

421. Derweduwen, "Gentbrugge en Mariakerke: de fusie," 7.

422. R. and M. Haverkamp, letter to MSC, 20 March 1991. Cf. Haverkamp, letter to supporters, January 1992.

423. De Kegel, letter to the National Vergadering van christengemeenten, 05 October 1992.

424. R. Haverkamp, email to supporters, 22 April 2000.

425. Derweduwen, "Officiële Opening Gemeente Gent," 1.

426. P. Gifford, "prayer letter," email to MSC, 06 September 2006.

427. Dryburgh, interview, 25 August 2003.

Workers and Works of the Evangelische Christengemeenten Vlaanderen

friends from the assemblies, and from that time on she wanted to tell everyone about her evangelical faith. She knew these friends through the local chapter of the Scripture Union Scotland.[428] After her conversion, Dryburgh helped lead a coffee bar outreach as well as street work, both aimed at evangelizing youth. Dryburgh's interest in mission work came about from the general mission focus which was present at her local assembly.[429] In addition, a representative from BEZ came to her local assembly and challenged her with the needs in Belgium. Her background in an area of Scotland whose inhabitants were seventy percent Roman Catholic also was a good fit for the work in Belgium.[430]

After leaving school and three years of working as a Grade 2 Bank officer for the Royal Bank of Scotland, Dryburgh began full-time service with Operation Mobilization in 1991.[431] OM assigned her to Zelzate, Belgium, on the border with the Netherlands. She associated herself with the VEG church on the outskirts of Gentbrugge for her first two years, and then spent the next five years at the VEG church in the center of Gentbrugge.[432] During her time with OM, Dryburgh helped with the daily bookkeeping tasks and was responsible for the financial details of the summer campaigns. These were in addition to her work in a variety of evangelism schemes. In the local church, she was involved in personal work with a number of the women of the church, youth work, and as a co-leader of a cell group with responsibilities for working with the women in that cell.[433] Dryburgh left OM in 1998 and spent the next six months with the Brethren evangelistic agency, Global Literature Outreach (GLO) in Motherwell, Scotland.[434] She would return to Gentbrugge on 16 March 1999 as a commended missionary listed with Interlink.[435]

---

428. "Our History," http://www.suscotland.org.uk/about_us/about_us.html. Scripture Union (SU) was founded in 1868 in Wales with the primary focus of reaching children and young people. SU Scotland was formed in 1902 and became an autonomous movement in 1972. SU is found presently in 130 countries.

429. Dryburgh, "RE: Letter of Commendation??," email, 24 June 2008.

430. "Op de koffie," 1–2.

431. Dryburgh, letter to Richard Haverkamp, 13 January 1998.

432. Dryburgh, interview, 25 August 2003.

433. Dryburgh, letter to Richard Haverkamp, 13 January 1998.

434. "History of Global Literature Outreach." GLO was established first in Australia in 1965, and the GLO Europe headquarters was established in 1974 in Motherwell. GLO describes themselves by saying, "Through partnership in mission, our purpose is to engage in evangelism and the establishing of local churches."

435. Dryburgh, interview, 25 August 2003.

Dryburgh was commended from the Dumbarton assembly in Scotland in 1999.[436] Upon her commendation, Dryburgh was listed with the Scottish Brethren service agency, Interlink, as well as the overall Open Brethren service agency in the UK, Echoes of Service (EOS). While maintaining very close relations with EOS, Interlink had an almost equally long history of service to Brethren missionaries as it was started about ten years later than EOS in the late nineteenth century. One well-placed observer noted that Interlink is perhaps just a bit more conservative than EOS as is in keeping with the slightly more conservative nature of most of the Scottish assemblies versus those of England and Wales. Scottish missionaries such as Dryburgh would have been listed in the *Echoes of Service Daily Prayer Guide* as well as had their reports published in the *Echoes Missionary Magazine*, but designated financial gifts would come primarily through the Interlink office in Glasgow.[437]

Her work was related to discipleship and evangelism, tasks consistent with the work of the ECV. Dryburgh said that her work was to build up the believers, "taking them from the past and helping them to build their life on Scripture."[438] She especially was active among the women of the assembly through small group meetings and one-on-one sessions in both planned and less formal settings.[439] She viewed her situation as an unmarried woman especially helpful in being sensitive to the needs of other singles and those women married to unconverted men. She understood that these women needed "to not be emphasizing life's circumstances, but to emphasize Christ and His sufficiency."[440] Her vision for this type of ministry went beyond just Belgium, however, as she was active in an annual women's missions conference sponsored by the Scottish assemblies.[441]

Like all of the later full-timers, Dryburgh placed a high value on formal education commensurate with her work in the ECV. Accordingly, while she received some biblical and theological training while she was with OM, she later pursued a more formal course of studies via distance education through Trinity College of the Bible and Theological Seminary in Newburgh, IN, US.[442]

---

436. *Echoes Daily Prayer Guide 2008*, 48.

437. Burness, "Message from Dr J H Burness, Trustee, Echoes of Service," email, 01 August 2007.

438. Dryburgh, interview, 25 August 2003.

439. Dryburgh, letter to Echoes of Service, 31 December 2007, 127.

440. Dryburgh, interview, 25 August 2003.

441. "Op de koffie bij . . . Ann [sic]," 4.

442. Dryburgh, interview, 25 August 2003.

Brabant: Tienen, an Open Brethren Assembly Joins the ECV

The last assembly to become associated with the ECV was the result of ministry done by Ghislain Piérard just after the First World War, as noted earlier in this work.[443] Over the years, this assembly felt itself more and more linked to the Open Brethren in Wallonia, due to the background of Piérard with the *Assemblees de Freres*.[444] Because of positive contacts with the ECV assembly in Boom, however, Tienen made a formal application to become part of the ECV on 27 October 1991 through a letter written by its elders, Luc Maeyens and Pierre Denville. This created quite a discussion among the national leaders, as this type of situation had not presented itself previously for consideration. The first attempts at accession methodology were rejected as too cumbersome and lengthy, but the national leadership did finally agree on a more simplified process.[445] Freddy Mantels wrote to Tienen on behalf of the national leaders after a meeting in January 1992, and he and De Kegel visited with Tienen's elders on 25 February 1992. Mantels and De Kegel recommended that the national leaders accept Tienen into the ECV. In part, their positive recommendation read,

> From our conversation it was clear that their identity is the same as that of the *christengemeente*. Baptism, the Lord's Supper, the role of women, the recognition of elders, and the independence of the local church are completely in line with what is believed and practiced in the *christengemeente*.[446]

Nonetheless, Tienen did not become part of the ECV structure until 1993 after the next national leaders meeting.[447] Among those active in the Tienen assembly was Vandelannoote, one of the men who had helped to start the ECV work among the Belgian soldiers in Germany.[448] For a time, the assembly grew, and it grew to the point that its building was full on Sunday mornings. Nonetheless, the Tienen assembly closed in the summer of 2001

---

443. Cf. chapter 2, "Open Brethren in Flanders."

444. "Regarding: The Accession of the Assembly in Tienen."

445. "2. Accession methods for a new assembly."

446. "Regarding: The Accession of the Assembly in Tienen."

447. The first mention of Tienen on an address list of the ECV is found in the *Nieuwsbrief van de christengemeenten*, ed., Marc Van Den Bogaerde, November 1993, 10. Interestingly, this Tienen assembly is listed by one of the German Brethren groups in their 1998 handbook. None of the other ECV assemblies is in this book. Cf. "Belgien: Tienen," *Wegsweiser: Ausgabe Herbst 1998*, 90.

448. H. Gelling, interview, 01 September 2008. For more information about Vandelannoote, cf. above, this chapter, "Flemish Assemblies in Germany: Soest, Brakel, Arolsen."

due to its dwindling numbers, most likely the result of personality clashes and divergent views on the nature of Christ.[449]

Summary Statistics

By 1997, the ECV would note the lack of active growth in the past five years and that the newest assembly had been begun in 1991. The total number of people who were part of the ECV in 1997 were 1486 adults, 381 youth, and 825 children spread across twenty-six assemblies. The assemblies were found in the provinces of Flanders as follows: thirteen in Limburg, four in Antwerpen, four in East Flanders, and five in West Flanders. Five assemblies had less than 30 adults, eight between 30 and 50 adults, eight between 51 and 74 adults, two between 75 and 99 adults, and three between 100 and 125. Fourteen of the assemblies had recognized elders, three had only one recognized elder and one *verantwoordelijke*, seven assemblies had a team of *verantwoordelijken*, and two had no type of recognized leadership.[450] By 2006, the number of assemblies had fallen to twenty-two.[451]

During the years from the planting of the initial assembly in 1972 until the early twenty-first century, the ECV developed from a collection of like-minded local churches tied together by the ministry of the Canadian missionaries to a government-recognized denomination. By 2008, discussions were well underway to effect a union with the VEG churches, and a vote was scheduled in late 2008 by the elders of the ECV to decide if this was the future direction to take.[452] Eventually, a decision was taken not to merge with the VEG.

---

449. De Kegel, "RE: Waregem: Paul Huygens," email, 08 July 2008; H. Gelling, interview, 01 September 2008.

450. De Kegel, "Enkele gegevens over de Christengemeente," 3–4. Though listed in the address directory in this same issue of *Nieuwsbrief*, 7, the assembly in Heerlen was not included in these statistics, since it was not a Flemish church. Thus, the total number of ECV assemblies was twenty-seven in 1997. Cf. "Verslag Nationale Commissie," 21 April 1997, point 12; "Nationale Commissie Agenda," 15 December 1997, point 3.

451. "'Om U te dienen': Beleidsplan, 2008–2011," *Evangelische Christengemeenten Vlaanderen*, November 2007, 4. This total does include the assembly in Heerlen, Netherlands.

452. Dryburgh, "Re: Anne or Ann?," email, 24 June 2008.

4

Ecclesiology of the *Evangelische Christengemeenten Vlaanderen*

THE ECV HELD TO a mainstream ecclesiology within the Open Brethren. David J. MacLeod, Brethren theologian, author, and professor of systematic theology, presents a good summary of this Brethren ecclesiology:

> "Ecclesiology," says university of Basel professor, Karl Ludwig Schmidt, "is simply Christology." He argues that all sociological attempts to explain the church are futile because the church can only be explained by its link to the person and work of Christ (σῶμσ Χριστοῦ, *sōma Christou*) and Christ is the head (κεφαλή, *kephalē*) of the body (Eph. 5:23; Col. 1:18; cf. 1 Cor. 12:12–13, 27). These metaphors stress the unity of Christ and His people, and the term *head* specifically stresses that He is leader or ruler over the church. He exercises a position of power and authority over His people. The early church witnessed to the headship of Christ by recognizing no individual man as the head of the church. Leadership was always invested in a plurality of leaders (first apostles and soon elders). This was true of the universal church and the local church, which is a replica or a miniature of the universal church.[1]

In a footnote attached to this paragraph, MacLeod adds, "Significantly both the universal church (Eph. 1:23) and the local church (1 Cor. 12:27) are

---

1. MacLeod, "The Primacy of Scripture and the Church," 20.

described as the body of Christ."[2] MacLeod's observation contains important elements of the overall understanding of the Church as seen through the eyes of the Open Brethren. Key elements include the Christocentric nature of the Church in its definition, the Christocentric nature of the ultimate leadership structure, and the relationship of the universal Church with the local church. These emphases will be elaborated below.

In the same vein, the understanding of the universal Church within the ECV was simply that the Church is the body of people who have undergone evangelical conversion and have Christ as their Head. These people are called believers, and the common bond between them was the indwelling Holy Spirit. Very notably, Haverkamp seemingly would have blurred the distinction between the local church and the universal Church in his teaching. In fact, this was not a blurring but rather the outworking of belief as seen also in MacLeod's statement above. Other Brethren writers commonly held the same view as seen in a book that was widely disseminated among the Brethren: "Each local Assembly was a miniature of the whole Church. As the Church universal embraces every believer, so the local Assembly embraced all the saints living in any given locality."[3] This idea was not unique to the Brethren but in line with other free church thinking contemporary to the founding of the ECV assemblies. This thinking, for example, was found in the writings of Robert Saucy, seminary professor and minister of the North American Baptist General Conference:

> Predominantly, *ekklesia* applies to the local assembly of all those who profess faith and allegiance to Christ . . . *Ekklesia* also designates the universal church. In this usage the concept of a physical assembly gives way to the spiritual unity of all believers in Christ . . . The universal church was the universal fellowship of believers who met visibly in local assemblies.[4]

Haverkamp taught that when the tabernacle was built by Moses, the glory of the Lord came down and filled it; when the Solomonic temple was dedicated, the glory of the Lord came down to fill it; when Jesus was born in Bethlehem, the glory of the Lord came down in the form of man; at Pentecost in Acts 2, the glory of the Lord came down and filled "the New Testament temple, and now we individually and as the Church are the temple of God."[5] Believers since the descent of the Holy Spirit at Pentecost also have

---

2. Ibid., 20n39.
3. Hitchman, *Some Scriptural Principles of the Christian Assembly*, 28.
4. Saucy, *The Church in God's Program*, 16–17; Cf. Volf, *After Our Likeness*, 135ff.
5. R. Haverkamp, "Wie der Herr Jesus Christus Gemeinden baut," session 1.

been indwelt from the time of their evangelical conversion as supported by such texts as 1 Corinthians 12:12–13.[6] He goes on to say that God gave Moses the pattern for the tabernacle and David the pattern for the temple, and then observes, "I personally believe that God has given the Apostles the pattern for the New Testament Church. I believe that the closer we can stay to the Apostles and the Early Church, the safer we are."[7]

The gathering of believers in the local setting is called an assembly. This term among the Brethren for the local church is defined clearly in many places. For example, one of most widely known of Brethren writers, J. N. Darby, wrote in the opening paragraphs of an article about the body of Christ,

> The first general idea, that of which we are to speak, is the Church (*ekklesia*) . . . [The church] is applied, as all know, to buildings appropriated to ecclesiastical services. But the church is the house of God; and the building is treated as the house of God, though God has expressly declared that, under the Christian system, He will not dwell in temples made with hands; that where two or three are gathered together in His name—the true church so far, and so called in the passage—there Christ is in their midst. I shall speak therefore of the Assembly, the real meaning of the word.[8]

Former President of Emmaus Bible College William MacDonald wrote concerning the local church and the universal Church,

> In the New Testament, the word *church* is a translation of the Greek word *ekklesia*, which means "a called out company," "a gathering" or an "assembly." . . . The Church is a fellowship of all those who share the life of Christ and who are linked together in living union by the Holy Spirit.[9]

The Brethren believe that the one around whom the assembly gathers is "Christ alone." "The early disciples were held together, not by membership in an organization, but by devotion to a Person."[10] Accordingly, frequent reference is made in Brethren writing to Matthew 18:20 as the basic under-

---

6. MacDonald, *Christ Loved the Church*, 1/5.

7. R. Haverkamp, "Wie der Herr Jesus Christus Gemeinden baut," session 3.

8. Darby, "The House of God; The Body of Christ; and the Baptism of the Holy Ghost," 16.

9. MacDonald, *Christ Loved the Church*, 1/1–1/2. For a sampling of similar twentieth-century Brethren thinking on the local and universal church, cf. Davies, "The Church: Its Formation, Fellowship and Features," 15–25; Norbie, *New Testament Church Organization*, 22ff.

10. Norbie, *The Early Church: Rediscovering Truth for the Churches*, 8.

standing of the assembly.[11] This Christocentric understanding of the local church as it gathered was not unique to the Brethren, but in line with the thinking of others within the wider history of the free church movement. As Volf notes, "In fact, it was [Matthew 18:20] that shaped the entire free church tradition."[12] Volf also notes that this tradition can be traced back at least as far as the early second century to Ignatius of Antioch as well as to Tertullian.[13]

Haverkamp's concept of the local church, as expressed in lectures and in studies, echoed the teachings of Darby. While no direct link was found, the parallels were clear and thus demonstrated that Haverkamp held to Brethren thinking in this area. As Darby writes:

> According to Scripture the whole sum of the churches here on earth (or, rather the Christians of whom they consist) compose the church, at least the church on earth; and the church in any given place was no other than the regular association together of whatever formed part of the entire body of the church, that is to say, of *the complete body of Christ here on earth* . . . There was no idea of any such distinction between the little churches of God in any place, and the church as a whole.[14]

Yvan Thomas, an elder of an ECV assembly, wrote a two hundred page manual for the training of elders. As part of that manual, a definition of the Church was included. Thomas drew from numerous sources, including Open Brethren writer William J. McRae of North Park Community Chapel in Canada (as quoted by American free church pastor and author John MacArthur) and Alexander Hay's book which greatly influenced Haverkamp, laying out a clear definition of the Church in a pattern of "what the Church is" versus "what the Church is not." This back and forth definition demonstrated his belief that the Church is not an organization existing from programs and methods, not made of buildings and offices, not a hierarchical organization, and not an "other worldly institution" merely trying to solve social and personal ills. The Church is a living organism, "a body with personality that lives, breathes, feels and acts . . . people who together are living and loving, learning and working, leading and following to the glory of Christ."[15]

---

11. Cf. Ironside, *Expository Notes on the Gospel of Matthew*, 228f; Mackintosh, "The Assembly of God," 1–47; Naismith, "Christ the Centre," 13f; J. N. Voorhoeve, *Gelovigen vergaderd in de Naam van Jezus*, 3–4.

12. Volf, "Community Formation as an Image of the Triune God," 216.

13. Ibid.

14. Darby, "On the Formation of Churches," 143.

15. Thomas, "Cursus Oudstenbegeleiding," 60–61.

Ecclesiology of the Evangelische Christengemeenten Vlaanderen

This very Christocentric understanding, which influences the understanding of the universal Church and local church, was crucial to the ECV ecclesiology. A study of functional emphases as a result of this Christocentric understanding is in line with the manner in which Brethren commonly define themselves. Quite simply, Brethren assemblies often recognize or identify themselves, as well as other assemblies, by what they do as the local church gathers. For example, the understanding of Christ as the literal head of the Church and its local manifestations is such that an authoritative local pastor, a presbyterian form of church government, or an episcopal style of church government normally is rejected as unbiblical. Within the Exclusive Brethren, even the recognition of elders as seen in the New Testament is rejected because of Darby's view that the failure of the Church to follow the commands of Scripture in this dispensation has caused the Church to be "in ruins." Thus, as with every other dispensation, man cannot go back and undo the damage of this sin and recover God's pattern for Church government.[16]

This also meant that without any of the apostles, today's believers could not recognize elders.[17] In a discussion with some Exclusive Brethren, Haverkamp responded to this charge of the absence of the apostles by saying, "Did the apostles have helpers? Of course they did! We are just more of those helpers!"[18] While the ECV certainly would not have held to this extreme outworking of a dispensational viewpoint, they did teach from a dispensational viewpoint. Additionally, the ECV founders would have been opposed to a designated person as the single leader of any particular local church, at least initially. So, within this clearly Christocentric outlook, how did the ECV function? What was the functional ecclesiology of the assemblies which became known as the ECV?

---

16. Darby taught that the expanse of human history is divided into seven ages or dispensations as revealed in the Bible. "As a system dispensationalism was largely formulated by Darby, but . . . outlines of a dispensationalist approach to the Scriptures are found much earlier." Ryrie, *Dispensationalism*, 66. Darby often is called the father of dispensationalism or at least its systematizer. Dixon, "The Importance of J. N. Darby and the Brethren Movement in the History of Conservative Theology," 43–44. For a rehearsal of interpreting the Bible dispensationally, cf. Scofield, ed., *Scofield Reference Bible*, 10n1, and subsequent references; Chafer, "The Dispensations," 129–38.

17. Darby, "Scriptural Views Upon the Subject of Elders, in answer to a tract entitled 'Are Elders to be Established?'"; Darby, "Examination of a Few Passages of Scripture, the force of which has been questioned in the discussion on the New Churches; with remarks on Certain Principles Alleged in Support of their Establishment"; Darby, "What Has Been Acknowledged? or the State of the Controversy about Elders, followed by a Short Answer to an Article of Mons. de Gasparin"; and Darby, "An Appeal to the Conscience of those who take the Title of 'Elders of the Evangelical Church at Geneva'; and a Reply to one of them," 181–270, 286–338.

18. H. Gelling, interview, 11 September 2002.

When studying a late-twentieth century group such as the ECV which has no formal archives, no rigid form, and no written liturgy, the words and ensuing works of the people who founded and shaped the denomination provide the main clues as to the functional ecclesiology. Particularly helpful is to review the teachings of the principals, either through recorded and written lectures or by reviewing the notes of those present when the principals lectured. By looking at a sampling of public lectures and writings of the founders and shapers, the diaries of one of the founders, the notes of meetings, and the popular publications of the ECV, a picture is presented which is consistent with the information related in personal interview.

In addition, the relationship of the ECV with other Christian groups in Flanders during the time under investigation and the change in this relationship is important. An even more radical change of the functional ecclesiology was seen as the ECV changed, in their words, from "organism to organization." An examination of their four functional ecclesiological emphases, the relationship the ECV with other Christian groups in Flanders, and the change from organism to organization is followed by an appraisal based on the four traditional marks of the Church.

FOUR FUNCTIONAL ECCLESIOLOGICAL EMPHASES OF THE ECV

At least four emphases comprised the functional ecclesiology of the ECV. While these four emphases are consistent with what was taught and practiced in the ECV, they are not necessarily unique to the churches of the ECV as distinct from the evangelical churches in Flanders or indeed the body of Christ since its inception at Pentecost. The prominence given some of them, however, is what set the ECV apart from similar evangelical groups in Flanders. Even though organizational changes and methodological variances can be traced in these assemblies since their inception in 1972, the ECV continued to keep at least four emphases as primary in its thought and actions. These four emphases were the purposeful, unwavering commitment to the proclamation of the gospel for the purpose of Church planting; the centrality of the Lord's Supper consistent with Open Brethren thinking; the emphasis on pragmatic, sound teaching; and the types and selection of leadership.

Ecclesiology of the Evangelische Christengemeenten Vlaanderen

The Unwavering Commitment of the Proclamation of the Gospel for the Purpose of Church Planting

From the beginning of the Bible studies which would become the ECV, right through the formation and governmental recognition of the ECV and beyond, the proclamation of an evangelical gospel had a central role. The three components which comprised this commitment to a proclamation of the gospel with the purpose of planting churches revolved around the ones who told of their faith, the message that they preached, and the methods which they used to transmit their message.

Both as a passion and in giftedness, Haverkamp and Gelling were committed to evangelism—openly and unwaveringly.[19] One family member noted, "[Gelling] is an evangelist. That's what he lives for; he thrives on it. I am amazed that, any conversation he gets into, he can turn it to Christ."[20] He also involved his family in the work, as his daughter Julie, for example, remembered going door-to-door with him. She especially remembered his ability to tell a story and make an illustration, and she noted that this was very effective as he met people face-to-face on their doorstep.[21] Another family member said, "Henk is an evangelist. The more [unconverted people present], the more excited he gets."[22] Gelling himself confirmed these multiple observations when he wrote to MSC, "It is thrilling to be into evangelism again. As we see more gift develop in each assembly we can be busy in our main field of work. As I have been busy with many things through the years I am happiest in evangelism and working with new believers."[23] Yet, his passion was not merely for evangelism, but that the new converts could be gathered together to form new assemblies. "I long to start new assemblies, that is more my gift, but we need to see the existing ones come to maturity."[24]

Haverkamp was equally gifted and passionate about evangelism, especially for the purpose of planting churches. For example, some of Mrs. Haverkamp's earliest contact with Haverkamp was through his leading evangelistic outreaches in Canada.[25] One very experienced and respected church planter noted of Haverkamp and his work in Belgium, "I felt that there was nobody at that time that could preach the gospel as well as he

19. R. Haverkamp, interview, 25 April 2003.
20. J. Gelling, interview, 12 August 2007.
21. Ibid.
22. B. Gelling, interview, 15 August 2007.
23. H. Gelling, handwritten letter to MSC on the reverse of a letter to supporters, Spring 1990.
24. H. and B. Gelling, letter to supporters, January 1989.
25. M. Haverkamp, interview, 30 April 2003.

did."[26] Additionally, Haverkamp's wife was involved as much as she could be as an evangelist.[27] Her work was done primarily with the children.[28] In a particularly prescient writing entitled "The Missionary of the Seventies," veteran missionary and missiologist George W. Peters wrote of seven necessary characteristics for missionaries. Haverkamp modeled these seven characteristics though he had never read Peters' work. Particularly pertinent was Peters' observation that the missionaries of the seventies

> must be men of order, purpose, and dynamic function rather than of a fixed organization and program . . . We are living in a dynamic society that is moving at a rapid pace . . . Culture is in convulsion and society in explosion . . . Live imagination, original creativity, discerning adaptation, flexibility, and resourcefulness are demanded . . . Only dynamically functioning, well integrated, and purposeful men will be able to function effectively in an ordered manner in such a world and achieve worthy goals.[29]

Haverkamp recognized the dynamism of his era in Flanders, and he was creative and flexible in his methods by which the message of the evangelical gospel was presented.

Beyond these two primary figures, another of the founders, den Boer, also had a passion for evangelism. A man who said he was "led to Christ" through the work of den Boer noted that he liked people, was good at making contacts, and was an effective worker presenting the gospel one-on-one.[30] Another man who eventually became a worker with the ECV recorded that he learned his door-to-door evangelism from den Boer during his internship as part of his education at ETF.[31] How then did the ECV understand the goal of evangelism? What methods and emphases did they follow as they evangelized?

Initially, not much thought went into an overall strategy as what to do with the new converts.[32] The general goal was "to plant churches all over Belgium" in line with Haverkamp's call to Belgium. However, the work was

---

26. Anonymous, interview by author.

27. B. Gelling, interview, 15 August 2007.

28. Dryburgh; H., B., and J. Gelling; P. and J. Gifford; and D. and E. Tinder, Netherlands/Belgium roundtable discussion at the Brethren European Christian Workers Conference, 26 August 2002.

29. Peters, "The Missionary of the Seventies," 53–54.

30. Vleugels, interview, 14 August 2007.

31. K. and E. Schelstraete, interview, 03 September 2007.

32. B. Gelling, interview, 15 August 2007.

Ecclesiology of the Evangelische Christengemeenten Vlaanderen

so difficult at first that Haverkamp despaired of any results at all; then, when so many were converted, the founders were overwhelmed. Haverkamp said,

> When I came to Belgium in 1972, I had never built a church in my life. I'd never talked to a Catholic in my life. I had never done personal work in my life. I didn't know anything about church planting. I don't know why God called me to do that. I don't know why God called me to a Catholic country. But I took these words [Mt 16:18], and I got down on my knees, and I said, "Lord Jesus, I know why You brought me. You said You want to build Your Church here in Belgium, and You brought me here to use me in that. And so, very respectfully, let's go, Jesus." And a few years later I said, "Please slow down a little bit, Jesus, I can't keep up."[33]

Gelling, too, had his doubts initially, especially after he made a trip to Belgium in 1974 to determine if this was a place to where he wanted to move.[34] Once people began to get converted, however, he, too, was overwhelmed by what was happening. Gelling wrote, "I remember when we came here in 1975, that Richard and Marina [Haverkamp] complained of being overtired and I wondered how that could be. Well, we know all about it now."[35] In that same letter, Gelling relayed that he was involved in ten Bible studies a week as well as "the Lord's Table in Peer and Koersel every week."[36]

In the ensuing years, the ECV founders and shapers were involved in a variety of evangelistic outreaches. The various methods included (but were not limited to) door-to-door work, evangelistic outreaches using barges on the Flemish canals, evangelistic teams brought in for campaigns, tent evangelism, drama and music, open air campaigns, films such as *Jesus*, and all manner of literature, both in short tracts and longer booklets. Both this emphasis on evangelism and the various methods used were seen in every issue of the periodic newspaper which circulated among the churches of the ECV, from the inception of the newspaper in 1984 until 2000. Ready evidence also was found among the personal diaries of Gelling and the newsletters sent out by Haverkamp and Gelling to their supporters in Canada and the US. The letters to supporters from Gifford also recorded evangelistic efforts, though his references were not as frequent as those of Haverkamp and Gelling.

---

33. R. Haverkamp, "Wie der Herr Jesus Christus Gemeinden baut," session 7.

34. H. Gelling, interview, 25 April 2003. For a more complete description of this event, cf. chapter 3, "Gelling's Call to Belgium."

35. H. and B. Gelling, letter to supporters, Fall 1977.

36. Ibid.

New Brethren in Flanders

An evangelism committee was formed within every assembly planted by the founders of the ECV and the assemblies that hived-off in the ensuing years. Every ECV newsletter and every church meeting devoted a section to noting the plans and results of these efforts. The creativity and flexibility of the founders and the assemblies they planted was seen in a number of areas, but especially those efforts designed to find contacts. For example, when the assembly in Houthalen held a showing of the film *Jesus*, they followed this movie first with a talk in Italian and then one in Dutch because of the many Italian immigrants who came to the showing.[37] The assembly in Berchem held a series of evangelistic efforts aimed at both adults and children from Turkey and Morocco, noting that the message of the evangelical gospel was "a precious pearl" for all those in the neighborhood, not just the Flemish.[38] The Maldegem assembly held an evangelistic outreach during Pentecost weekend to include street drama, a book table, gospel music, and even a model of the Old Testament tabernacle to explain to interested passersby. Later that year, they planned another city center outreach which included a presentation of Flemish and Norse gospel music.[39] Those involved with evangelistic outreach included all ages as seen in the example during the last week of Easter vacation in 1996. During this six-day outreach, fifteen young people aged fifteen to twenty went door-to-door handing out Gospels of John and "small Easter gifts." One of the young people reported that her group "went out nine times . . . [and] spoke with 263 people of whom 67 asked us to come back for a return visit."[40]

Letters to supporters often noted that various of the assemblies had displays or outreaches on major Roman Catholic holidays, such as 15 August, the Feast of the Assumption of the Blessed Virgin Mary. The assembly in Gent, for example, would go each year to the Festival of Gent to serve breakfast to the less-than-sober revelers, even as they tried to make a contact or share the gospel.[41] This scheduling of evangelistic outreaches or the raising of awareness of the ECV churches at local festivals and Roman Catholic holidays characterized all of the ECV churches, and thus continued a pattern begun by the Brethren in Flanders in the nineteenth century.

While creativity and variety marked the evangelistic efforts of the ECV to make contacts, one of the primary evangelistic tools was the *Startstudies* in the first decades of the ECV once a contact was gained. This was a

37. "Met zijn allen naar de film," 3.
38. "De Parel," 5.
39. "Nieuwe aanpak voor Maldegem," 1.
40. Christel, "Evangelisatieweek Zwartberg," 10.
41. P. Gifford, email to MSC, 21 July 2002; S. Gifford, conversation, 26 August 2007.

Ecclesiology of the Evangelische Christengemeenten Vlaanderen

ten-lesson, evangelistic Bible study from the first three chapters of the Gospel of John held in the home of a contact. After finding a contact, the Bible study leader would tell the person hosting the study to invite family and friends. Haverkamp noted that he would make outrageous statements in order to draw an audience.[42] "One of the methods Richard used was to say, 'I am a guru.' And people were shocked, thinking, 'How can that be?' 'I come to you tonight explaining what that means,' and he did."[43] Once arriving, the Bible teacher would begin by giving everyone present a free copy of the Bible. The "Practical Tips" section of the *Startstudies* booklet particularly emphasized not charging for the Bible in order to prevent the new contacts from thinking that these Bible studies were some sort of scam to get money. Also, by having all use the exact same edition and text, listeners would not be embarrassed; the many Bible references in any night's study would be referenced not merely as chapter and verse but according to the page numbers.

The lessons were a methodical, biblical presentation of the claims of the evangelical faith. They were: 1) the existence of God and the veracity of the Bible; 2) the person of Christ; 3) the three kinds of life and death; 4) how to become a child of God; 5) sin; 6) the Lamb of God; 7) the Holy Spirit; 8) four testimonies confirming Jesus as the Christ; 9) the lessons of the wedding miracle at Cana and the cleansing of the temple; and 10) the new birth.[44] The tone of these studies had a definite apologetic edge to them, as did presentations which took the listener from one end of the Bible to the other. Haverkamp began his time in Belgium believing in the power of the Bible, and he said it only increased with time. Accordingly, the lessons went from text to text to text as the teacher was told to expect that the Holy Spirit would use the Bible in the lives of the listeners. "God's Word is a hammer, a fire, and a sword; learn to use it."[45] One careful observer said,

> The home Bible study was [Haverkamp's] strength . . . Once he has a little group in the home, he would explain the gospel to them in different ways, and challenge them to bring others along . . . And so in the home, challenging people, and just going

---

42. R. Haverkamp, "Wie der Herr Jesus Christus Gemeinden baut," session 6.

43. Nullens, interview, 10 September 2003. Cf. R. Haverkamp, "Wie der Herr Jesus Christus Gemeinden baut," session 6.

44. R. Haverkamp, "Startstudies." While Haverkamp was the sole author, this series of Bible studies later was published as the book, Thomas and R. Haverkamp, *10 startstudies, handleiding voor het doorgeven van geloofsprincipes.* Cf. R. Haverkamp, "RE: Startstudies," email, 31 July 2008.

45. R. Haverkamp, "*Startstudies*," 2.

back and forth through the Bible . . . he was like a locomotive going through.[46]

This same observer also noted about Haverkamp, "He is a Dutch Canadian. He comes to Flanders with his Dutch Canadian accent, and people would give money just to hear him talk! For a salesman or an evangelist, it gets an audience."[47] Still, Haverkamp's Dutch roots could have created an obstacle given the historical and cultural tensions between the Netherlands and Belgium. When he was challenged by a listener as to his Dutch roots, Haverkamp commonly would defuse the situation effectively with a response that elicited laughter from the listener by stating, "I was born there, but I had nothing to do with it!"[48]

Because of the apologetic tone of the studies, a careful progression was followed; the central tenets of Roman Catholicism were not challenged directly until the leader of the studies was sure his contacts were committed to coming and listening.[49] For example, challenges to the traditional Roman Catholic teachings on the role of Mary were not put forward until the ninth lesson.[50] This would have been after at least sixteen hours of teaching plus times of question and answer over the eight previous sessions. The ECV Bible teachers used this time to teach the tenets of evangelical belief as well as to develop a relationship with those who attended. Over time, these studies were led by the Brethren missionaries from North America as well as the Flemish and Dutch workers associated with the ECV.

The *Startstudies* instructions also emphasized that the condition of the worker who would lead the sessions was as important as the content of the study. Echoing what he said many times in public lectures concerning church planting, Haverkamp writes,

> Be sure that you are filled with the Holy Spirit when you give a study. Before leaving home, confess your sins, surrender yourselves completely to the Lord, and in faith accept the filling of the Holy Spirit. Study as though all depends on you; teach as though all depends on Him.[51]

---

46. Lukasse, interview, 05 December 2003.

47. Ibid. While Lukasse did not always agree completely with what was done by Haverkamp, Lukasse was a great admirer of the work that Haverkamp accomplished and considers Haverkamp a friend and coworker.

48. R. Haverkamp, interview, 25 April 2003.

49. R. Haverkamp, "Wie der Herr Jesus Christus Gemeinden baut," session 6.

50. R. Haverkamp, "*Startstudies*," lesson 09.

51. Ibid., 2.

Ecclesiology of the Evangelische Christengemeenten Vlaanderen

Other tips included being sure that the teacher was aiming for the "hearts" of the listeners and not merely their "heads." Gelling noted that in the late 1970s, the founders went from one *Startstudies* location to another as people were anxious to hear what the ECV was teaching.[52]

Why might have the Flemish listeners been so receptive to the *Startstudies*? One cannot consider the answer without attention to the effects of the Second Vatican Council. So far-reaching were the effects of the Second Vatican Council that one participant wrote

> It fell upon us like a thunderbolt, called by a charismatic Pope, John XXIII, in a moment of extraordinary insight. As the sessions unfolded from 1962–65, it gathered energy of its own . . . Vatican II left all concerned from Paul VI and the Fathers of the Council itself, down to the simplest practicing Catholic, somewhat breathless in its aftermath.[53]

A veteran BEZ missionary made four observations about the times in view of this, observations often repeated by others.[54] All of these were the result of the pronouncements of the Second Vatican Council or the popes associated with this council.[55] First, "[Protestant Christians] were no longer heretics anymore, but separated brethren."[56] This created an opening for evangelical Christians such as the ECV to meet with Roman Catholics. Second, Pope John XXIII, the convening pope, said that Catholics should read their Bibles.

> All Sacred Scripture ought to furnish spiritual nourishment for all the Catholics in the world. We welcome this opportunity to invite the faithful to answer the challenge and live up to the Roman Synod's directions to everyone to read the Sacred Book; for nowadays ignorance of it on the part of any Catholic with self-respect is truly unforgivable.[57]

Accordingly, Haverkamp and others would ask their listeners if they were good Catholics, and if so, why not do as the Pope asked? Haverkamp even kept handy a copy of Pope John XXIII's encouragement for Roman Catholics

---

52. H. Gelling, interview, 11 September 2002.

53. Moloney, "Vatican II: The Word in the Church Tradition." (NB: When first released, this article was entitled "Vatican II: The Word in the Catholic Tradition.")

54. Lukasse, interview, 05 December 2003.

55. Cf. Abbott, ed., *The Documents of Vatican II*.

56. Ibid., 33–34.

57. Pope John XXIII, "The Roman Synod And The Priest." Cf. Cronin, ed., *Encyclicals and Other Messages*, 112–28.

to read their Bibles, as reported in a Roman Catholic newspaper. Not only did the Roman Catholic Church encourage her followers to read the Bible, however, but one of the documents of the Second Vatican Council pointedly pushed for greater availability of the Bible "for all the Christian faithful."[58]

Third, the Mass was now read in the vernacular after centuries of teaching that it could be said only in Latin.[59] This removed some of the sense of mystery associated with the Mass.[60] Finally, Pope Paul VI, the pope at the end of the council, released his encyclical *Humanae Vitae*. This clearly stated the Roman Catholic Church's position with respect to human reproduction and life. The positions concerning contraception and abortion, for example, were directly opposed to the cultural climate in Belgium at the time of the arrival of the ECV founders. As a result, these four points created a climate where "everybody was confused" by the sudden change to centuries of teaching, and "everybody was disappointed" because the teachings on human life did not change.[61] Into this setting came the founders and shapers of the ECV who presented the evangelical gospel with a slightly apologetic edge, and the results were remarkable. Additionally, Haverkamp and the other ECV founders told people that they had not come to Belgium to start a new organization, but that they just wanted to return to the Bible.[62]

Gelling noted that the ECV people often used a form of "friendship evangelism" before any of them had ever heard the term.[63] In a personal example in Peer, Gelling slowly won the trust of his landlord and his wife over a period of time. His initial contact was to tell the landlord and his wife that he had been a chicken farmer, but now was "a fisher of men." While this made no sense to the listeners, the wife did remember the chicken farmer aspect, and as the Gellings moved into their rented home, the landlord and the neighbors were concerned that he might use the adjacent lot to create the "noise, mess, and smell of a chicken farm." At first, the landlord came

---

58. Abbott, ed., *The Documents of Vatican II*, 125; and see ibid., n50, on this same page and the following comment, "This is perhaps the most novel section of the Constitution. Not since the early centuries of the Church has an official document urged the availability of the scriptures for all."

59. Ibid., 159.

60. This author found this change to the vernacular a shattering experience for a number of Roman Catholics present in a religion class he taught in the US. The Catholics and former Catholics in the class reasoned that if such an important practice could be changed after so many centuries, what else could and would be changed?

61. Lukasse, interview, 05 December 2003.

62. R. Haverkamp, interview, 25 April 2003. This statement is ironic given the change in the character of the relationship between the ECV churches that the founders planted.

63. H. Gelling, interview, 11 September 2002.

Ecclesiology of the Evangelische Christengemeenten Vlaanderen

personally to collect the rent each month as he was uncertain of his foreign renters' intentions. Over time, Gelling witnessed to the wife and she became converted. The husband was unhappy with this as he was the head of the local committee which led the local *Carnivale* celebrations just before Lent. Gelling continued to win the trust of this man, and eventually, he, too, underwent evangelical conversion.[64]

After the founding of the first few assemblies, evangelistic efforts almost always were connected with and under the direction of one of the ECV assemblies. Accordingly, one American Brethren missionary and author referenced the work of the ECV as a prime example of those which "understood the biblical centrality of the local church in New Testament practice."[65] Some evangelical writers outside of the Brethren would have viewed the ECV assemblies as "gospel-centered," meaning that they were committed to a "word-centered" and "mission-centered" identity. "Within history, the church glorifies God by making him known to the world. Within history, mission must be central to every local church."[66] The commitment to mission indeed was central to the identity of the ECV assemblies. Similarly, one could characterize the nature of the assemblies planted by the founders as in line with the Apostle Paul's sense that his apostolic vocation as a church planter was not complete until the newly planted church was a center for evangelistic outreach in its own right.[67]

Commonly, the announcements of a coming evangelistic effort in the ECV newsletter encouraged the reader to pray about the effort as well as to become part of the outreach that the assembly was planning. The newsletter also reported the outcome of these efforts, normally the establishment of an evangelistic home Bible study which would be taught by one of the ECV workers. Noticeably absent from these reports was a head-count of how many people had been converted since mere conversion was not considered the goal. Especially before the planting and maturing of the first assemblies, Haverkamp and Shindelka followed leads which came from many quarters, usually a friend or family member of someone in one of the *Startstudies*. People inside and outside of the ECV called this a "strawberry plant" methodology.[68] The ECV founders followed whatever "runners" came out from a study or assembly to wherever this lead might take them.

64. H. Gelling, interview, 25 April 2003.
65. Fleming, *Essentials of Missionary Service*, 109.
66. Chester and Timmis, *Total Church*, 16, 86.
67. Ware, *The Mission of the Church*, 271. For a discussion pertinent to Ware's translation of Philippians 2:16, cf. Eadie, *Commentary on the Greek Text of the Epistle of Paul to the Philippians*, 142–44; Hawthorne, *Philippians*, 103.
68. Lukasse, interview, 05 December 2003.

This meant that especially Haverkamp crisscrossed Flanders as he drove from one study to the next each week. So full was this travel schedule that the elders from Haverkamp's commending assembly joked, "The impression was a man with a private jet. He was *very* mobile."[69] While Gelling's schedule was equally intense, his evangelistic Bible studies by design were limited primarily to Limburg after a few years even as Haverkamp continued to travel throughout Flanders.

ECV evangelistic efforts were not done in isolation from other evangelistic activities in Flanders, however. Over the years, the ECV churches cooperated with crusades by Billy Graham and Luis Palau as well as the work of OM, especially when OM sent teams of young people on barges throughout Flanders or conducted door-to-door evangelistic campaigns. These efforts most often were used to find contacts from which *Startstudies* or another type evangelistic home Bible study could be formed.

As early as 1973, Haverkamp had a tract printed which was a challenge to the reader from his own experience, a personal testimony of his evangelical conversion.[70] In 1980, the ECV produced a book of fifteen "personal testimonies" collected by Haverkamp. Stories were collected of Flemish Christians from all walks of life, ages, and educational backgrounds to tell "how Jesus changed their lives."[71] This idea of a *personal* testimony was central to all the evangelistic work done by Haverkamp, Gelling, and den Boer as well as the writing of Yvan Thomas. This personal testimony was to be presented in an enthusiastic manner. Accordingly, Haverkamp wrote in his practical tips section to workers who would lead *Startstudies*,

> Speak with enthusiasm! Do you believe what you are saying?!
> It is not always *what* you say that will persuade people (though this is important, too), but how you say it! Don't forget, we have the most beautiful and powerful message on earth."[72]

He also stated in one public lecture, as was typical, "Some people are born with more enthusiasm than others, but, come on, every Christian should be enthusiastic!! . . . How can you *not* be excited!!"[73]

The ECV evangelistic work, as mentioned above, had an apologetic edge to its presentation, especially until the end of the twentieth century. This apologetic edge was not limited to the *Startstudies*, however. For example, a

69. Former elders of Wallenstein Bible Chapel, interview, 1 September 2006.

70. R. Haverkamp, "Mijn weg naar de realiteit."

71. R. Haverkamp, ed., *Nieuw: Vijftien Vlamingen vertellen hoe Jezus hun leven veranderde.*

72. R. Haverkamp, "*Startstudies*," 1–2.

73. R. Haverkamp, "Wie der Herr Jesus Christus Gemeinden baut," session 9.

popular choice of literature for distribution by the ECV founders was *Meer dan een timmerman*, a translation of Josh McDowell's *More than a Carpenter*, "a hard-headed book for people who are skeptical about Jesus' deity, his resurrection and his claims on their lives."[74] The ECV also used *Geloven— Waarom eigenlijk?*, Haverkamp's translation of Paul Little's *Know Why You Believe*, published by the main Dutch Brethren publisher.[75] Thomas' first book was an apologetic work entitled *En jij gelooft dat?!!* [*And You Believe That?!!*] to help the person who was telling about his faith to answer "common arguments used to avoid the Gospel."[76] This book contained answers to a series of twenty questions defending the existence of God, the truth of Scripture, the deity of Christ, and challenging the Roman Catholic teaching on Mary, among other topics. Another mainstay of the ECV founders and their early Flemish converts as they challenged their Roman Catholic listeners was *De planeet die aarde heette*, a translation of Hal Lindsay's *Late Great Planet Earth*.[77] This dispensational, pretribulational look at the "end times" confronted the readers with the idea that the "end times" were really in the very near future. The readers would be asked by the ECV worker if they were ready for this time. While not an apologetic work for Christianity per se, this book was another apologetic for why the ECV Christians were so passionate about their goal of evangelism with the purpose of planting churches. If indeed the "end times" were close, then the Christians needed to be diligent in their witness, and the unbelievers needed to respond before it was too late. Nonetheless, the founders of the ECV did not speak in grand generalities or base their work merely on providing answers to a basket of commonly asked questions. Their motivation was personal and heartfelt.

Questions and challenges to raise the interest of the listener were not limited to books and pamphlets. Haverkamp personally would ask shocking questions to potential contacts, such as, "Do you know that Jesus had brothers and sisters?" and then show them from the Bible. He would follow this question with, "Did you know that your first pope, Peter, was married?" Haverkamp noted that "fifty percent of the time the reaction was, 'What else

74. "More than a Carpenter," Campus Crusade for Christ. One bookseller described this book by saying, "By addressing questions about scientific and historical evidence, the validity of the Bible, and proofs of the resurrection, McDowell helps the reader come to an informed and intelligent decision about whether Jesus was a liar, a lunatic, or the Lord." "More than a Carpenter," Amazon.com. McDowell, *Meer dan een timmerman*.

75. Little, *Geloven—Waarom eigenlijk?* This was translated from the 1968 2nd ed. English version.

76. Thomas, *En jij gelooft dat?!!* This work has gone through four editions, and the most current edition is from August 2007.

77. Lindsay, *De planeet die aarde heette*.

is in the Bible?'"[78] Gelling did similar questioning, though he liked to ask less shocking questions, going door-to-door as part of a "survey."[79]

Haverkamp clearly outlined what he believed was the message and method of the workers and their work whenever he spoke on the topic. Two thoughts were central with respect to those who would do the work, the ones who would witness. First, the most important part of church planting was the church planter himself. Second, relationship with God was the most important part of the church planter.[80] Haverkamp understood that the summary of the relationship of the church planter with God was found in the Westminster Shorter Catechism's purposes of "to glorify God, and to enjoy Him forever."[81] To glorify God, the church planter needed to praise God (Psalm 50:23), bear fruit (John 15:8), use his spiritual gifts (1 Peter 4:11), and fulfill the work God had given him (John 17:4). In explanation, Haverkamp noted that bearing fruit meant to exhibit the fruit of the Spirit in Galatians 5, "not bringing people to Christ as many evangelists believe."[82] This identification and use of spiritual gifts was a continual theme in the work of the ECV, a theme which went beyond even its importance to the church planter. Certainly as early as 1979, clear evidence was seen of this emphasis on identifying one's gifts in Haverkamp's teaching. He noted that when people asked him what God wanted them to do, he told them to find their spiritual gifts, and "then it is easy." Gifts were defined by Haverkamp as "a manifestation of the Holy Spirit that comes to live and work through us." He also differentiated spiritual gifts from natural talent, something which may seem to be the same. He taught that the exercise of a spiritual gift comes with power. "The spiritual gifts come with your second birth but it may take some time before you discover them. It depends partly on how much of a surrender there is in your life."[83]

Haverkamp saw these gifts in two categories as found in 1 Peter 4:11—namely, those acts for which one uses his mouth and those acts for which

78. R. Haverkamp, "Wie der Herr Jesus Christus Gemeinden baut," session 6.

79. E.g.: During January 1980, Gelling and his helpers used a survey entitled "Opinieonderzoek" to make contacts in and around the town of Lanaken. Completed copies of this survey are found in one of Gelling's personal notebooks with a series of black, white, red, and blue geometric angles on the cover. The first notebook entry is a lecture on "Church Planting" by Haverkamp, dated 20 August 1979.

80. H. Gelling notes of Haverkamp lecture, 20 August 1979.

81. "Westminster Shorter Catechism, AD 1647," answer to question 1. One of the many places at which Haverkamp taught this idea was the conference "Wie der Herr Jesus Christus Gemeinden baut," session 2.

82. R. Haverkamp, "Wie der Herr Jesus Christus Gemeinden baut," session 2.

83. Ibid., session 8, question and answer. "Second birth" is a common way to speak about evangelical conversion and should not be confused with theories of reincarnation.

Ecclesiology of the Evangelische Christengemeenten Vlaanderen

one used his hands. He went on, "As a whole, God wants us to function according to the gifts He has given us."[84] To use these gifts was to fulfill the work one is given by God. Of himself, Haverkamp passionately stated, "One of my gifts is evangelism. I have to be involved in that work. That is fulfilling the work He has given me."[85] Expanding on this idea, he then observed that the work given to the Church was found in Matthew 28:18–20, and that this work had never changed since its identification by the Lord. This commitment to evangelism was given as the outworking of the "Seven Great Words of Christ" in Matthew 16:18, what Haverkamp on many an occasions called his life's verse.[86] "I - will - build - my - Church- and the gates of hell - shall not overcome it." Looking at these seven sections, Haverkamp emphasized that 1) the worker evangelizes, but God does the building; 2) the work of building the universal Church was guaranteed, even if the local manifestations come and go; 3) the local church is God's, not the worker's; 4) the goal was planted churches, not merely built-up individuals through existing Bible studies; 5) the work of planting a local church will be completed, not merely begun; 6) the devil will oppose this work; and 7) the devil will fail to stop it.[87] In fact, Haverkamp couched church planting in terms of warfare, both in his lectures and his letters to supporters.[88] Nevertheless, this outlook was unshaken, grounded firmly in his understanding of Matthew 16:18. This outlook proved especially important during the first months the Haverkamps were in Flanders, given the nature of the work they attempted. "The work was difficult and seemed to be in vain. God encouraged Richard and Marina [Haverkamp] with the idea that He will build His Church."[89]

Haverkamp was not alone in his emphasis on the character and preparation of the worker who would do evangelism. In his 1993 book on evangelism, Yvan Thomas also emphasizes the importance of the worker's relationship with God. He lists five characteristics which a person must

84. Ibid., session 2.

85. Ibid. In fact, Haverkamp was so consumed with exercising this gift of evangelism that he preached the gospel at every opportunity. This includes events such as Brethren missionaries gathered at their celebration of the Lord's Supper as well as conferences of church planters.

86. Schelstraete, "Handelingen (1)," 4. Cf. R. Haverkamp, "Wie der Herr Jesus Christus Gemeinden baut," session 2. The designation of these words as only "seven" is Haverkamp's nomenclature.

87. R. Haverkamp, "Wie der Herr Jesus Christus Gemeinden baut," session 2. Listening to Haverkamp lecture on this topic of building the Church is to hear him shift seamlessly between the universal Church and local church at times, though later in the series he does clarify the difference.

88. Ibid., session 9.

89. Schelstraete, "Handelingen (1)," 4.

possess if he is to evangelize. 1) The messenger must be "born again." Thomas writes that a witness to a new life can come only from one who has this new life. 2) The messenger must have a good relationship with God. Thomas defines a good relationship as a "living relationship," as seen by a life characterized by prayer, Bible reading, and no unconfessed sin. 3) The messenger must be filled with the Holy Spirit. To be filled, the messenger must be "unconditionally surrendered" to God. 4) The messenger must have a practical knowledge of the Bible. He notes that theoretical knowledge is not enough. 5) The messenger must belong to a local church. This was consistent with the ECV's view of the importance of the Church as God's special creation. The local church was understood as a manifestation of that special, universal creation.[90]

While the importance of the messenger or worker made by Haverkamp and Thomas was not unique as such, the strength of the language and centrality of the character of the messenger were not common to many contemporaneous evangelistic seminars and books within the Brethren milieu. Within Open Brethren assemblies at the end of the twentieth century in North America, commonly found books on evangelism, as seen in lists of recommended books on evangelism at the local Brethren assembly, might include Brethren missionary Floyd Schneider's, *Evangelism for the Faint-hearted*, Jim Peterson's, *Evangelism as a Lifestyle*, Robert Coleman's, *The Master Plan of Evangelism*, Paul Little's, *How to Give Away your Faith*, and Lorne Sanny's, *The Art of Personal Witnessing*.[91] While all these sample books and others emphasize the proper content of the evangelical gospel and teach various techniques as how best to evangelize, only Sanny's 1957 work contains a heavy, central emphasis on the preparation of the evangelistic witness or worker himself in line with the same emphasis found in the ECV. More commonly, the personal life of the worker had become the domain of emphases on Christian living rather than the fundamental basis upon which the worker did his work.[92] That said, Hay's book, the one book

---

90. Thomas, *Evangelisatie? Wat doet u eraan?*, 21–23.

91. Schneider, *Evangelism for the Faint-hearted*; Peterson, *Evangelism as a Lifestyle*; Coleman, *The Master Plan of Evangelism*; Little, *How to Give Away your Faith*; Sanny, *The Art of Personal Witnessing*. For a more complete list in a Brethren context, cf. Knott, "Additional Reading on Evangelism," an insert attached to Sanny's work which was used as the basis of evangelistic training, Lubbock Bible Chapel, TX, January 1978.

92. Searches through the *Emmaus Journal* (the journal of Emmaus Bible College), as well as the most well-known North American English-language, non-charismatic evangelical journals (e.g., *Bibliotheca Sacra*, the *Journal of the Evangelical Theological Society*, *Trinity Journal*, and the *Master's Seminary Journal*) from the 1970s until the end of the century show no articles emphasizing the holiness of the Christian worker and its importance to evangelism. While many articles deal with evangelistic methods

Ecclesiology of the Evangelische Christengemeenten Vlaanderen

that Haverkamp noted he read before going to Belgium, did emphasize the condition of the worker in line with what Haverkamp taught.[93]

Unlike a number of evangelists, the founders of the ECV saw evangelism as the means to an end, not an end in itself. This was consistent with the views of some within the North American Open Brethren community such as Kenneth Fleming, veteran missionary and Professor of Missions at Emmaus Bible College. In an article entitled "Missionary Service in the Life of Paul," Fleming notes that the Apostle Paul's two general objectives were "the individual salvation of as many as possible," and "the establishment of churches (assemblies of converts)."[94] Whereas the founders of the ECV did their work in an era when the stadium evangelistic crusades for the purpose of "winning converts" were still very popular, as was the annual "week of revival" in many conservative North American churches, the goal of the ECV's founders was to create "a living, active, independent, multiplying [local] church" as the result of successful evangelism.[95] The ECV founders considered the work of the worker incomplete until this goal was attained. Further, Haverkamp anchored the founding of the Church in creation principles when he passionately emphasized

> Evangelicals may say Jesus came to die for our sins. They are right, but this is not the first reason. Jesus came to build His Church, and He went to the cross to die to make it possible. The first thing God built was a woman. The thing that Jesus came to build was a Bride for Himself.[96]

So, the obvious goal of a church planter was to start a local church, the localized gathering of what was part of the universal Church, but how was this accomplished? What were the methods of the church planter beyond merely evangelism?

Methodologically, Haverkamp laid out a three-point process bounded by when the worker "gets in" and "gets out" as an assembly was planted. First, the worker was to get the people saved. This was the process of evangelization. Second, the worker was to teach them. This was the process of edification. Finally, the worker was to get the people trained. This was the process of multiplication.[97] Theologically, Haverkamp understood that God

---

or the message that should be preached, none deal specifically and pointedly with the worker who carries the message.

93. Hay, *The New Testament Order for Church and Missionary*, 401ff.
94. Fleming, "Missionary Service in the Life of Paul—Part 1," 109.
95. R. Haverkamp, "Wie der Herr Jesus Christus Gemeinden baut," session 3.
96. Ibid., session 1.
97. R. Haverkamp, "Church Planting," lecture, 21 August 1979. (NB: All the notes

has given His Word, and then the Holy Spirit uses God's Word through the instrumentality of the workers as they take the message of the Gospel to the unconverted.

During the process of evangelism, the worker must make the listener "mad, sad, or glad."[98] Haverkamp's expected threefold response can be heard from the lips of those inside and outside the ECV as they talk about its process of evangelization over the years. Haverkamp, Gelling, Shindelka, and den Boer all confronted their listeners with a clear choice when sharing the gospel with them. As is consistent with the personalities, however, Gelling and den Boer were more relational while Haverkamp and Shindelka were more confrontational. Nonetheless, all four presented the message in what most saw as a winsome way since people could sense the genuine nature of their belief. In one of the more memorable confrontations, Haverkamp asked a very devout Roman Catholic man what he thought after this man had attended his first night of an evangelistic Bible study. This man came from a family of many priests and nuns among his parents' and his own generation. This "quiet Belgian" responded that he believed in "our dear Lady." Haverkamp responded, "That is an abomination," opened his Bible to Deuteronomy 18 and said, "Here, you pray to the dead. That is an abomination to God!"[99] This man was taken aback, but he considered what Haverkamp and Gelling presented in subsequent studies and in one-on-one times of question and answer; he noted that the answers always were based on, "the Bible says." The local priest would respond to the same questions with "the [Roman Catholic] Church says." After a few months, this man underwent evangelical conversion and later would serve as an elder in one of the ECV assemblies near his home.[100]

So why might even strong confrontations have been countenanced by the listeners in Flanders? In an earlier chapter, the uncertain, changing times were noted as an important cultural reason for the openness to the message of the founders of the ECV. Added to this was the uncertain, changing attitudes toward the Roman Catholic Church among her adherents in Flanders. Nonetheless, more than just the uncertain, changing times seemed to be the reason for the willingness to listen of the unconverted Flemish. The underlying attitude of the ECV missionaries had much to do

---

from this conference come from a personal notebook/journal written by H. Gelling.)

98. R. Haverkamp lecture, 20 August 1979. Cf. Lukasse, interview, 05 December 2003. While Haverkamp credits this threefold response to Charles Spurgeon in a 2002 lecture, only a quotation by Vance Havner seems to match this "mad, glad, sad" response.

99. H. Gelling, interview, 11 September 2002.

100. Gielen and Symons, interview, 14 August 2007. The story above refers to Gielen.

Ecclesiology of the Evangelische Christengemeenten Vlaanderen

with their success with their unconverted "contacts." In fact, Haverkamp said that he disliked the coldness of the term "contacts," noting that it was a salesman's term—a salesman who was looking for financial gain. Haverkamp strongly emphasized the need for the church planter to love those to whom the gospel was presented. "We see people as God's creatures for whom Christ died . . . When you love them and have prayed for them, it is much easier to win them. Love is a weapon, and love can break down the most hardened hearts."[101] In practice, this ability to confront in a strong but loving way was noted repeatedly by those who were confronted as well as those who witnessed various evangelistic confrontations. Anastasi observed that the assemblies in Flanders grew because of the charismatic personality of Haverkamp in a friendship-evangelism setting.[102] As mentioned earlier, Shindelka was one who took twenty minutes to enter a room because he went around greeting everyone, and during those greetings that person had his undivided attention, not the feeling that he was going through the motions before going on to the next person.[103]

Gelling remembered that the people were very touched by the nature of the extemporaneous prayers of the ECV missionaries since these Roman Catholics only had seen priests use scripted prayers. These Roman Catholics said, "Something is going on here. They are in contact with God."[104] Gelling related the story of an old man, the grandfather of Eric Rutten. (Rutten later became an ECV worker.) "[The grandfather] was a tough guy. He threw the nuns out . . . We had a Bible study in the home, and he spent the evening just glaring at me from his chair. After a number of times of coming, he suddenly said, 'I want to be baptized.'"[105] Gelling's subsequent visit with him confirmed that this "tough guy" indeed had been converted and that he knew his Roman Catholic baptism was of no consequence for a convert to the evangelical faith. Shortly thereafter, this man in his seventies was publicly baptized.

Closely related to this love of people was the desire that the founders not be idolized or held up in what they viewed as some unbiblical manner. While the founders certainly were the human cause of the making of the ECV, and some observers referred to the churches as "the Haverkamp churches" or "the Haverkamp/Gelling churches," these men actively took steps to see that the churches were not seen as their churches, but rather

---

101. R. Haverkamp, "Wie der Herr Jesus Christus Gemeinden baut," session 4.
102. Anastasi, interview, 30 June 2005.
103. H. Gelling, interview, 25 April 2003; cf. chapter 3, "Herb Shindelka, 1971–1976."
104. H. Gelling, interview, 12 August 2007.
105. H. Gelling, interview, 12 August 2007.

God's churches.[106] At the beginning of church planting in the early 1970s during a baptismal service, Haverkamp would preach and Shindelka would baptize. Once Shindelka left, however, the founders seldom if ever baptized any of the converts. Haverkamp and Gelling baptized few if any of the converts to prevent what they would have viewed as an unhealthy dependence upon certain persons for public ordinances as well as a potential for an unhealthy lifting up of the missionaries. Haverkamp would emphasize his practice of not baptizing the converts himself as he taught about church planting.[107] Both Haverkamp and Gelling wanted to avoid pride on the part of some who would place themselves above others if they had been baptized by either of them.[108] Also, while a number of evangelical church groupings in Flanders allowed the new converts to request that certain people baptize them, one of the men of the local ECV assembly baptized all who were scheduled to be baptized at a given service once the first churches were formed and after the departure of Shindelka.[109]

The speed with which the ECV grew was readily apparent, not just through the establishment of new churches, but through the many new converts baptized each month. In early spring 1981, for example, Haverkamp wrote, "God is blessing the work, it's hard to keep up. In January we baptized 26 and on the 8th of March 31 new believers."[110] Nevertheless, the work did not proceed without opposition and at times at a cost to the new converts. In a letter of 1987, Haverkamp wrote thanking the Lord that "quite the number of new believers have been saved the last couple of months," but then went on to say, "Some experience real opposition, from their relatives or at work. Some have even lost their job because of their 'new faith.'"[111]

Haverkamp's desire for the building of the Church was not limited to evangelization alone nor to Belgium alone. Given his conviction that the Church of Jesus Christ is a worldwide entity, he happily worked hard in whatever place opportunity was provided, either to evangelize or to recruit new workers for the purpose of planting churches. Over the decades, Haverkamp traveled to a minimum of thirteen countries on three continents to speak at some forty conferences.[112] Both Haverkamp's gifts and

---

106. C.f. Heyman, "Verslag van de vergadering."

107. R. Haverkamp, "Wie der Herr Jesus Christus Gemeinden baut," session 4.

108. R. Haverkamp, "Re: Question on the Brethren," email, 30 April 2008. Cf. H. Gelling, telephone conversation, 22 April 2008.

109. H. Gelling, telephone conversation, 22 April 2008.

110. R. Haverkamp, letter to MSC, March 1981.

111. R. Haverkamp, letter to MSC, 12 July 1987.

112. R. Haverkamp, "Haverkamp History," 2.

Ecclesiology of the Evangelische Christengemeenten Vlaanderen

vision were put to use by MSC when it asked him and his wife to represent MSC at a missions conference at Ontario Bible College. In an early 1990 letter thanking MSC for a gift and for the opportunity to represent MSC at the conference, Haverkamp writes,

> I believe our being there was worthwhile. Our purpose for being there was: to meet the students and create an interest in missions, to influence them to live their lives for Christ and also to make M.S.C. known . . . We had expected to see more assembly young people . . . Most of these young people come from churches where they have their own missions conferences and meet their own missionaries. Again, I believe our being there was worthwhile, ministering to the wider body of Christ and only eternity will reveal how much was accomplished.[113]

Even while on a furlough in Canada for rethinking the ability to return to Belgium, Haverkamp practiced his commitment to evangelism for the purpose of planting churches. In the fall of 1988, he preached a six-week series of meetings at the request of his commending assembly, Wallenstein Bible Chapel, to help plant a church. These meetings were in part responsible for the formation of Alma Bible Church, ON, an assembly which met for the first time on 26 March 1989.[114] By the time he and his wife departed again for Belgium, this assembly had 120 adults and children as well as three elders.[115]

Evangelism was not limited to native Belgians as efforts were made to reach out to immigrant communities. Specifically, efforts were made to evangelize Muslims and English-speakers. The Haverkamps asked for special prayer for "the thousands of Muslims in Ghent, mainly from Turkey and Morocco."[116] Mrs. Haverkamp and others specifically had Bible classes for Muslim children in Gent. Other evangelistic outreach efforts were held among Muslim children in Berchem. The assembly bought the house next to the place where they met on Sundays, and between sixty to seventy children came each week during this long-term effort. Gelling's comments supported this forward thinking strategy when he reported, "It is a great opportunity to reach out to the next generation growing up in Belgium."[117] Additionally, BEZ courses on how to reach Muslims were made known in the main ECV

---

113. R. and M. Haverkamp, letter to MSC, 13 February 1990.
114. "Wallenstein Bible Chapel: The first thirty years, 1968–1998," 13.
115. R. and M. Haverkamp, letter to supporters, June 1990.
116. R. Haverkamp, New Year's letter to supporters, [21] January 1992.
117. H. Gelling, letter to supporters, November 1987.

publication, *Nieuwsbrief*.[118] Nonetheless, the reach of the ECV was limited by design to Dutch speakers or those who potentially would integrate into Flemish society. Hence, Schraepen was asked by the leadership structure of the ECV to cease his work with a church plant which targeted English-speaking expatriates in the area of Antwerpen.[119]

The ECV missionaries were not satisfied merely with professions of faith as they reported numbers of believers. Wisely, they frequently mentioned numbers baptized as they counted converts, since "it is quite a step for a Roman Catholic Belgian to get baptized in front of a group of people."[120]

The Centrality of the Lord's Supper Consistent with Open Brethren Thinking in the Assemblies of the ECV

As with any local church associated within the mainstream of the Brethren, the ECV emphasized the importance and indeed the centrality of the Lord's Supper in the meetings of the assembly. The three parts which comprised the understanding of the Lord's Supper in the ECV related to those who were allowed to participate, how they participated, and the theological underpinning of this New Testament practice.

In keeping with the outlook of the Open Brethren, the ECV founders and shapers held to a nonsacerdotal, nonsacramental, memorial view of the Lord's Supper, which served as a mark of both identity and unity within the body of Christ. So central to their identity was this "breaking of bread" meeting that the founders of the ECV and the assemblies they planted used the first Sunday celebration of the Lord's Supper as the date on which each of their home Bible studies was considered as a local church. This was clearly evident in the personal correspondence and diaries of the ECV workers as well as the newsletter published by the ECV. For example, concerning the thirtieth anniversary of the assembly at Koersel, Gelling wrote, "In the Koersel notebook . . . I have what brothers read at the Lord's table. I need information from the first Sunday we came together. It will say a name and then what the brother read."[121] The request came as Gelling prepared to preach at the thirtieth anniversary Sunday, and thus shows both the importance of the event as well as his general practice of keeping a record of what was said by whom when the believers gathered at the Lord's Supper. Haverkamp also clearly marked the beginning of an assembly by the first Sunday celebration

---

118. "Waar naar toe?," 2.
119. Schraepen, interview, 27 June 2007.
120. R. and M. Haverkamp, letter to supporters, February 1982.
121. H. Gelling, email, 11 December 2007.

Ecclesiology of the Evangelische Christengemeenten Vlaanderen

of the Lord's Supper as the time when a Bible study became a local church. In response to a public question at a church planting conference at which he was teaching, Haverkamp said,

> When we started in our pioneer phase—and we began with all new converts—we had two missionary couples, and we had about ten converts, and we had met with them for a while for Bible study, then we had a baptism on the first of April. On April second, we started meeting in our home on Sunday morning with the Breaking of Bread. For us that was the beginning of the church.[122]

The ECV also held that all believers were welcome at the Lord's Supper. As Haverkamp said, "We did not receive people into fellowship, because the moment a person was converted, he was baptized. He was part of the universal Church, and he also was *automatically* part of the *local* church."[123] For example, in an all-church meeting in Lommel in 1986, the believers had a public discussion as to who would be allowed to participate in the Lord's Supper. The only requirements were that the person be "born again" and be "in fellowship" with God. Thus, evangelical conversion and a life free of known, unrepentant sin were the only hurdles to participation.[124] That said, the discussion in Lommel assumed that the believer was baptized as this was done commonly with all the new believers shortly after they were converted. Going further, Haverkamp taught that three conditions must be met to participate in the Lord's Supper, and he based his understanding on Matthew 28:19 and Acts 2:41–47, both of which he saw as teaching the same three requirements. First, the person must be born again, "otherwise he has nothing to remember." Second, the person must be baptized, as this was the first step of obedience. This was not an obstacle for the new believers in the pioneer phase of the ECV, but as the ECV matured, they faced some practical limitations with respect to baptism. Accordingly, Haverkamp taught that, to participate in the Lord's Supper, a visitor need not be baptized, as well as a new believer who had not had a chance to be baptized, nor a wife who had been forbidden by her husband to be baptized, nor a child whose parents have not yet allowed it to be baptized. Since baptism was a definite mark of departure from the Roman Catholic Church, these prohibitions by family members were quite real. Third, the person must have a good relationship with God and with other Christians. Unconfessed sin or unre-

---

122. R. Haverkamp, "Wie der Herr Jesus Christus Gemeinden baut," session 8.

123. Ibid., session 2.

124. H. Gelling, personal diary, "→Jan 86→ Lommel," notes from church meeting of 14 June 1986.

solved strife with another Christian prevented a person from being allowed to partake of the Lord's Supper. They could come to the meeting, but they had to observe only.[125]

As the assemblies that were planted formally became the ECV, statements of theological belief were constructed. In a section entitled "The Identity of the *Evangelische Christengemeenten*," subsection 1.2 entitled "Theological Emphasis," the ECV clearly laid out their beliefs concerning the Lord's Supper in a few simple sentences.

> The Lord's Supper must take place regularly(a). The purpose of the Lord's Supper is to remember Christ. The bread and cup are symbols of His body and blood(b). When we partake of the bread and cup, we confess that we share in the sacrifice of Jesus Christ(c), a privilege only for those who are born again believers. It is expected that they are in good fellowship with God and with their brothers and sisters(d) so that they can partake in a worthy manner(e).
>
> (a) Acts 2:42; 2:46; 20:7 (b) Lk. 22:14–20 (c) 1 Cor. 10:16; 11:26
> (d) Mt. 5:23–24; 1 Cor. 5:7–8; 10:21 (e) 1 Cor. 1:27[126]

The format of the ECV Lord's Supper was an open meeting during which any believer could ask for a song to be sung, give a prayer, or read a passage from Scripture, with or without commentary, in line with the traditional Brethren customs for conduct during a Lord's Supper service.[127] The meeting would not be led by a clergyman, an elder, or one of the ECV workers because of the commitment in the Brethren to the priesthood of all believers, especially as practiced with a historical aversion to any sort of clergy-laity division in practice or even through recognition of such a division.[128] Additionally, the tradition among the Brethren normally was to have no sort of preplanned course of the service other than a set start time and a general ending time. These "remembrance meetings" culminated with the passing of the bread and cup. Haverkamp emphasized the simplicity of the celebration of the Lord's Supper as commonly practiced among the Brethren by outlining the meeting itself in four points: 1) "There is to be no *human* leader;" 2) there is to be no preset order, but the meeting is to be

---

125. R. Haverkamp, "Het avondmaal—de samenkomst van de gemeente," lecture.

126. Evangelische Christengemeenten Vlaanderen, "geloofsbelijdenis. "

127. "Samenkomst van de gemeente." In contradistinction with the common practice at the assemblies from which the founders came, women believers also were allowed to participate in much the same manner as the men. For a more complete explanation, cf. chapter 4, "The Centrality of the Lord's Supper."

128. Fraser, *The Lord's Supper*, 5/2–5/3.

Ecclesiology of the Evangelische Christengemeenten Vlaanderen

conducted with "complete freedom" because the Holy Spirit is the leader; 3) because of the priesthood of all believers, all come as priests with something, "not with empty hands;" 4) all should come as a priest would with a spiritual sacrifice (1 Pt. 2:5).[129] Reviewing the early Lord's Supper meetings in the ECV assemblies, Haverkamp remarked,

> We had fifteen or eighteen believers in our living room, or sometimes in another area just ten. We put a table in the middle of the room. We put a piece of bread and a glass of wine there. We took out Bibles and someone would read something, someone would pray, we would sing, and we would break bread and pass it around . . . I sort of feel that's New Testament Christianity.[130]

Another Brethren writer noted much the same when he wrote, "As originally instituted and observed, the ordinance was simplicity itself. Totally absent were rites, vestments and priestly assumption, deemed sacred and essential by so many churches today."[131]

Reading through handwritten notebooks of the ECV workers provides a clear insight as to the number of participants as well as the nature of how they participated. A congregational meeting in Lommel, for example, emphasized once again the need for the Lord's Supper to be a time of worship, not a time to present a Bible study.[132] At the same meeting, a caution was mentioned as one of the men was praying very long prayers.[133] A common challenge was the need for well prepared, longer preaching after the end of the Lord's Supper. Dunlap's diary expressed this as a goal, and others noted that the teaching could be very shallow when the ECV workers were not present.

How would this type of meeting be explained to newcomers and those who attended the Lord's Supper? Visitors who came to the Lord's Supper celebration at one ECV assembly were told, "You will see several people read something from the Bible and give a short thought, ask for a song to be sung, or to pray. All of these will be to praise and worship the Lord Jesus Christ."[134] De Kegel also taught,

---

129. R. Haverkamp, "Het avondmaal—de samenkomst van de gemeente," lecture.
130. R. Haverkamp, "Wie der Herr Jesus Christus Gemeinden baut," session 8.
131. Fraser, *The Lord's Supper*, 2/5.
132. H. Gelling, notes from church meeting of 14 June 1986.
133. Dunlap, personal diary, notes from church meeting of 14 June 1986.
134. "Evangelische Christengemeente Houthalen," a pamphlet given to visitors to this Limburg assembly.

> What specifically can we think about during the celebration of the Lord's Supper? In fact, we can think about everything that has to do with the Lord, but specifically — His humiliation and His suffering — His death and His sacrifice — His resurrection — His forgiveness for our sin — His covenant, sealed with His blood — and above all His love.[135]

These themes were seen readily in Gelling's diary on the pages on which he recorded the believers who participated and what passages they read from the Bible. In the first two months of Koersel's Lord's Supper, for example, men read a number of Psalms referring to God's redemption of and care for His people, the role of Christ as high priest in Hebrews, and passages referencing the sufferings of Christ from the Gospels.[136] Haverkamp also taught that five ways existed by which thoughts could be shared on the person and work of Christ in such a manner as to glorify God. One of those gathered could ask for a Psalm, either as a song or reading from Scripture; one could share a short teaching; one could offer an insight new to themselves that "glorifies Him and builds up the others present;" one could give a message miraculously in another language; and one could translate the other's miraculous gift of speaking in a previously unlearned, known language. However, Haverkamp was careful to note,

> The last two very seldom happen today because we have something that they did not have, namely, the complete Word of God. Generally, God speaks to us now through his Word, whereas then He talked directly to His Church through the Apostles and prophets, the foundation of the Church.[137]

For some, this commitment to the centrality of the person and work of the Lord Jesus at the celebration of the Lord's Supper was important enough for public rebuke if this pattern was not observed. Den Boer issued such a public rebuke at one of the assemblies at the end of the celebration and consequently caused quite a commotion. In the ensuing ECV workers' meeting, the other workers asked den Boer to issue a public apology.[138] While the other ECV workers agreed with the centrality of the person and work of the Lord Jesus at the celebration of the Lord's Supper, they had not agreed with the manner in which den Boer had handled the situation. While a public

---

135. De Kegel, "Het doorgeven van een avondmaalsgedachte." R. Haverkamp had the exact same items in his teaching notes on the Lord's Supper.
136. H. Gelling, "Koersel avondmaal," personal diary.
137. R. Haverkamp, "Het Avondmaal—De samenkomst van de gemeente."
138. H. Gelling, interview, 15 August 2007.

Ecclesiology of the Evangelische Christengemeenten Vlaanderen

rebuke such as den Boer issued was not an unknown practice among the Brethren, and especially among the Exclusive Brethren, the more normal course of events among the Open Brethren and indeed the ECV would have been for one of the leaders gently and privately to correct those who had used the Lord's Supper as a time for sharing personal experiences or to pray for specific needs of which they were aware rather than to center on the person and work of Christ. This need to focus on the person and work of Christ was a common topic of discussion in almost all church meetings as well as meetings of the ECV workers. Additionally, the ECV newsletter and teachings on the Lord's Supper by Haverkamp and De Kegel emphasized the remembrance nature of the Lord's Supper as opposed to letting it become a general meeting for prayer and a time of preaching.

Anastasi noted that the former Roman Catholics really liked the participatory nature of the ECV and particularly its manner of celebrating the Lord's Supper. This was in sharp contrast with the services at the Roman Catholic churches during which the parishioners mostly were spectators. Still he also observed that his own children, as well as many of the children of the original members of the ECV, did not continue with this same appreciation since they grew up in the ECV assemblies.[139] Nevertheless, one of these children of those who were converted as adults, because of the work of Haverkamp and Symons, remembered that he was encouraged at a young age to take part in the public expressions of worship associated with the Lord's Supper. As young as sixteen, he remembered participating. He did so due to the "openness for the young people [to participate].[140]

Although this type of open meeting was common in both the Exclusive and Open Brethren, the more usual practice was to allow only the men to lead the meeting by asking for a song to be sung, praying, or reading a passage from Scripture. In the case of the ECV from the earliest years, however, the women also were allowed to participate in this manner. Gelling noted that in Belgium among the ECV, the role of women at the Lord's Supper was not an issue. In practice, the women's participation was both in balance and in contrast with what he had seen in Pentecostal churches where the women often dominated the gatherings.[141] Since neither of the Canadian commending assemblies associated with Haverkamp and Gelling allowed women to participate in this manner or to pray in a mixed-gender group during the midweek prayer meeting, a bit of anxiety was present when the first of the elders from Haverkamp's commending

---

139. Anastasi, interview, 30 June 2005.
140. Creemers, interview, 06 September 2007.
141. H. Gelling, interview, 11 September 2002.

assembly came for a visit. In fact, the Canadian assemblies which did allow women to participate in this manner probably would have been frowned upon by most other Canadian assemblies, especially in the first decades of the ECV.[142] Nonetheless, the visit by the Canadian elders, Ezra Frey and John Martin, went well. During this visit, Haverkamp took these men to an assembly prayer meeting where women had not yet publicly prayed, but that very week was the first time they would have been permitted. Half of those who prayed that evening were women. Nonetheless, the elders reportedly were thrilled by what they saw overall because of the planting of all the churches as a result of all the converts.[143] As Gelling said, "The commending assemblies in North America know or accept that, on the field, there's some things happen that really wouldn't go over in the commending assembly."[144] Haverkamp also noted that these elders more readily could accept this outworking of the cultural differences between Canada and Belgium since both of these men "either had been on the mission field themselves or had children on the mission field."[145]

The ECV's prohibitions as they understood the Bible for the women's role were only that she could not teach a mixed-gender group and she could not be in a position of authority, either as an elder or as a *verantwoordelijke*.[146] Most of the ECV assemblies also encouraged the women to have their heads covered as they participated in the Lord's Supper. The concept of the women covering their heads had been a historical belief of the Brethren going back to the nineteenth century. This was based on a literal understanding of the instructions of 1 Corinthians 11 as bound neither by culture nor era.[147] Initially, this practice of the woman's head covering was taught very strongly, but over time the emphasis decreased.

The Emphasis on Pragmatic, Sound Teaching throughout the ECV

Since nearly all of those who would associate themselves with the churches planted by Haverkamp and Gelling were new believers, the ECV assemblies had a significant need for Bible teaching in order that these new believers

---

142. For the prevailing view on the role of women speaking in the assembly, cf. Fish, "Women Speaking in the Church," 214–51.

143. R. Haverkamp, interview, 25 April 2003.

144. H. Gelling, interview, 15 August 2007.

145. R. Haverkamp, interview, 25 April 2003.

146. H. Gelling, interview, 11 September 2003.

147. For example, cf. Cataford, *"Because of the Angels" A Biblical look at the Women's Headcovering*; Linsted, *The Women's Head Covering: Fact or Fallacy*.

Ecclesiology of the Evangelische Christengemeenten Vlaanderen

could learn more about the faith to which they had converted. While the new converts had some familiarity with Christian ideas, the knowledge they had primarily was that which might have been learned when catechized as members of the Roman Catholic Church. Accordingly, a fundamental knowledge of the content of the Bible and most of the tenets of an evangelical faith were absent from the minds of the new believers. In the ensuing years, the founders and shapers of the ECV taught the new converts the fundamentals of evangelical Christianity as well as the basic content of Scripture. In addition to basic biblical knowledge, a continual emphasis on putting this knowledge to use in practical ways was seen, such as working with drug addicted youth, dealing with the occult, and counseling. While this emphasis on providing biblical knowledge and teaching its practical outworking which addressed the perceived needs of those within the ECV was not a unique approach for a conservative, evangelical group such as the ECV, this emphasis continued well past the early years and up through the date of this writing many decades after the founding.

The manner was a bit surprising in which this two-fold emphasis on knowledge and application often was delivered, given the lack of formal theological education for Gelling and the friendly teasing that Haverkamp consistently delivered to those with formal theological education beyond his own four years of Bible college.[148] Nevertheless, many of those who would be converted through the work of Haverkamp and Gelling, and especially those who became full-time workers for the ECV, sought and received at least a bachelor's degree in Bible and theology. Further, the children of these workers and those who became ECV workers from families whose parents were converted through the work of Haverkamp and Gelling even sought a master's degree or higher. As the years passed, a significant emphasis also was added on biblical truth related to marriage and family. How did the founders and shapers of the ECV meet this challenge? What did they do to help these new believers learn about their new faith?

Early on in the work, the missionaries began a time of organized Bible teaching and study for all the new believers associated with the ECV throughout Flanders. In a letter of November 1977, Haverkamp reported,

> The "one day a month" Bible school has been going for two months now. About 100 are taking part, 85 are following the classes, while another 15 are following the lessons at home,

---

148. A good example of this teasing was evident in several of Haverkamp's lectures, "Wie der Herr Jesus Christus Gemeinden baut," during which he mentioned his lack of education versus those with doctorates or those who held teaching positions on theological faculties.

using the stencils. It means an awful lot of extra work for us, but we believe it is worth it. Already it is bearing fruit.[149]

In addition to these large gatherings, the newsletters of the ECV in the early 1980s listed a plethora of Bible studies based in an assembly or perhaps among two or three assemblies which were located within a few kilometers of each other. Most often these studies worked through a New Testament book or another section of scripture, such as the parts of Genesis which contain the life of Joseph. Commonly, these studies were taught by the founders of the ECV or some of the shapers who became full-time workers with the ECV. That said, teachers from the Dutch assemblies as well as other evangelical groups from Flanders taught these studies. These Bible studies were in addition to *Startstudies* that the founders of the ECV continually sought to have.

Methodologically, the ECV saw the importance of putting to work the ideas of 2 Timothy 2:2 as a way of multiplying teaching and teachers. Haverkamp pointedly asked for prayer for "the *training* of men for *teaching*." He then went on to write,

> We have had Dr. Gooding from Belfast with us twice now, one week last year when he took us through the Gospel of Luke and one week this year going through Acts and Romans. Our Belgian co-worker, Guido De Kegel is using this material to teach it to a number of men in different churches, who in turn teach it to their own church. This system works real good and we are seeing the development of some teachers.[150]

A regular time of teaching was not the only method used to teach about the faith. In the spring of 1979, the assemblies planted by the Canadian founders gathered for a men's Bible conference. As Gelling reported,

> About ninety brothers came from the nine assemblies. It was great to be together and Ps 133 really fitted the occasion. The Flemish brethren ministered plus Richard and I. The theme was God's purpose with the church and its members."[151]

This men's conference would become an annual event; speakers were invited from a variety of Brethren sources initially, and then more widely by the mid-1980s. During the early 1980s, speakers often were those from within the ECV, such as De Kegel, Haverkamp, Gelling, and Symons. Within a few years, national women's conferences were added as well.

---

149. R. and M. Haverkamp, letter to supporters, November 1977.
150. R. and M. Haverkamp, "The Haverkamp News," letter to supporters, Spring 1986.
151. H. Gelling, letter to MSC, 11 June 1979.

Ecclesiology of the Evangelische Christengemeenten Vlaanderen

An examination of the teaching topics of one of the main teachers within the ECV gives insight as to the balance between basic biblical knowledge and practical topics which applied this knowledge. The main thrust of the teaching provided by De Kegel was that of basic Bible knowledge. Of the more than 230 times De Kegel preached as part of a series, only around thirty were not what could be called basic Bible knowledge. The list of basic Bible knowledge included studies through the Psalms, Daniel, Ephesians, Romans, and Revelation as well as the life of Abraham, kings of the Old Testament, and the parables. Among the series geared to a more practical application of biblical knowledge were those on the gifts of the Holy Spirit, discipleship, "the basis of our faith," and lessons on the Church. In addition to these series, De Kegel also preached around thirty thematic messages specifically geared to the perceived needs of the assemblies to which they were delivered. These messages included, but were not limited to, teaching on the Lord's Supper, baptism, the doctrine of election, God's purpose in suffering, prayer, anointing the sick, and reincarnation.[152] These messages were in addition to any teaching done at men's conferences or other days of Bible training.

The more formal days for Bible study began with a plan for Saturday classes in Limburg known as the *Limburgse Studiedag Toerusting* (LST).[153] While this provided a practical solution to the need for a more in-depth understanding of the Bible, the reach was limited geographically. A national program eventually was proposed by Patrick Nullens, and he and De Kegel and den Boer brought this proposal to fruition as the *Toerustingscentrum Christengemeenten Vlaanderen* (TCV).[154] As Patrick Nullens, one of the main proponents, wrote in 1990

> In Flanders in the past years, we have experienced a spectacular growth of the *christengemeentes*. This is a wonderful example of how the Holy Spirit has worked. At the same time, we are aware of our great responsibility. Now we must take what has grown and strengthen it. We must equip the young assemblies for further growth and development. Here lies the reasons for and the task of the TCV. It is, therefore, a form of stewardship. We are burdened for the future of the *christengemeentes*. Presently in the *christengemeentes*, there are generally no Pastors. This makes

---

152. De Kegel, list of sermon topics, August 2007.

153. H. Gelling, telephone interview, 08 December 2008. Interestingly, the initial name of this program was to be *Limburgse Studie Dag*, but the resultant initials, "LSD," were deemed inappropriate.

154. "Eindelijk wat ik zocht!," 7.

the *verantwoordelijken* or elders very busy. This means they have almost no time left over for training. We want to fill that gap.[155]

The studies were advertised as practical and the course schedule as flexible.[156] For example, courses on Church history might examine the working of the Roman Catholic Church in the Middles Ages, but the lessons would be applied to help the listeners better understand the contemporary Roman Catholic Church.

Nullens further noted that the TCV was a structured curriculum which would take two years to complete, though students could pick and choose courses rather than come for the whole program. He also specifically emphasized that the courses were not only for elders or those thinking about formal theological studies or becoming an elder. Nevertheless, the TCV was formed in the hope that those who came would grow in knowledge, and then put this knowledge to use in the local assembly from which they came.[157] During the four or five years of the TCV's existence, it helped accomplish those goals, though the TCV ended eventually due to lack of enough students to continue.[158]

Preaching and courses taught throughout the ECV were not, however, the only means of pragmatic, sound teaching. In 1994 and 1995, De Kegel would have his only two books published. In contrast to his normal preaching, both books contained teaching of a pastoral, practical nature.[159] *Zalf voor je ziel* [*Salve for Your Soul*] contains pastoral principles taken from the Psalms and then observed in the life of David in 1 and 2 Samuel. De Kegel's direction is made evident in the acknowledgements in the front of the book, where he thanks Brethren author and Septuagint scholar David Gooding for the insights into the life of David and Saul in the books of Samuel, and by acknowledgment of insights from psychologists Larry Crabb and Jef De Vries. He especially notes that Crabb's work "opened my eyes to the hidden parts and craftiness of men's heart."[160] The book's twenty-eight chapters combine biblical teaching with psychology from a Christian perspective. This very practical approach is reinforced by questions for the reader at the

---

155. "Nieuw initiatief voor de christengemeentes," 6.

156. "Eindelijk wat ik zocht!," 7.

157. "Nieuw initiatief voor de christengemeentes," 7.

158. De Kegel, email, 30 June 2009.

159. The pastorally themed books were the only ones authored by De Kegel. The more complete record of his characteristic teaching emphasis is garnered by perusing the list of his preaching/teaching topics as well as his personal notes which were made for these lectures.

160. De Kegel, *Zalf voor je ziel*, 4.

Ecclesiology of the Evangelische Christengemeenten Vlaanderen

end of each chapter, questions designed to make the reader examine who he is and how he is living.

De Kegel's second book, *Splinters in je hart* [*Splinters in Your Heart*], is a twelve chapter presentation dealing with failures and problems as seen in the lives of various biblical characters, such as Abraham, Moses, Joshua, Elijah, Peter, and others.[161] De Kegel notes the hesitation of many believers to admit failure and the resultant struggles with discouragement. These books certainly were in line with the changes evident within the ECV assemblies, as they altered in membership from primarily new coverts to those who had been believers for a decade or more. This pastoral emphasis also coincided with the focus on marriage and family teaching brought to the fore with the arrival of the Giffords. This emphasis was as a result of the Giffords' good experience with their premarital counseling from Threadcraft as well as their observation of the marriage and family needs of the new converts.

The Giffords also saw a great need for solid teaching aimed at the youth. Accordingly, Gifford designed material specifically aimed at training young men and women who led camps that he oversaw. Foundational to that teaching was the need to help the campers become believers and to mature in the faith (Colossians 1:28–29), as well as an emphasis on teamwork predicated upon the individual gifting provided each believer by the Holy Spirit (1 Corinthians 12:4-6; Ephesians 4:11-16). Building on this foundation, Gifford then provided practical and sociological insights into the age group with which these young leaders would be working.[162] The youth camps which the Giffords led, and especially the lessons that Gifford taught at these camps, were well received, to the point that extra camp weeks needed to be scheduled. The mere transmission of biblical information was not the final goal, however, as the reason for the additional camp weeks was so that the number of campers per camp could be limited. Gifford wanted to be sure that a "personal touch" was part of the teaching effort—namely, the contact he would have outside the lectures he delivered.[163] He said,

> I really believe that if you can encourage young people at a young age to make choices for Christ, and make wise choices as they get older, you are going to avoid a lot of the problems we end up dealing with in families and marriages and relationships.[164]

---

161. De Kegel, *Splinters in je hart*, 5–6.
162. P. Gifford, "Tienerkampen."
163. P. and J. Gifford, letter to MSC, December 1996.
164. P. Gifford, interview, 25 August 2003.

Teaching times for the new churches were not all that would be a part of the teaching work of the missionaries of the ECV. As a result of the rapid planting and growth of the Flemish assemblies, Haverkamp was in high demand as a conference speaker, especially conferences dealing with church planting. This happened from the earliest times of the efforts in Flanders. For example, Haverkamp wrote to his supporters that he had been to France seven times in a fifteen-month period, stretching from late 1978 until early 1980 for conferences which lasted from one to five days.[165] Especially noteworthy was the consistent message preached by Haverkamp when the topic was evangelism, with a goal toward planting a local church, as well as the nature of the local church that was planted. Haverkamp himself confirmed this when he said to an audience, "If you have heard me speak before or you've listened to my tapes, you will not hear much different."[166]

At the end of the 1990s, the *Nieuwsbrief* also began to take on a role as an instrument through which teaching was delivered. Prior to this time, this publication primarily was for information of interest for the believers of the ECV. This information might have included personal testimonies of conversion, requests for prayer, announcements of new *Startstudies*, announcements of the beginning of a new assembly or the anniversary of one already in existence, notices of upcoming conferences, or the appointment of a new full-time Flemish worker or a foreign missionary to work with the ECV. The *Nieuwsbrief* eventually added sections on marriage and family teaching. In the early parts of the twenty-first century, an extended series was given in the *Nieuwsbrief* which covered the tenets of the Roman Catholic faith; these were compared and contrasted these teachings with evangelical Christianity. The topics covered included infant baptism, burial of a loved one, the eucharist, images, and two on Mary the mother of Jesus.[167]

The emphasis on sound, practical teaching within the ECV led to their cooperation with the BEZ and the VEG to form the *Evangelische Toerustingschool Vlaanderen* (ETV) in 2005. The ETV was an outgrowth of the *Evangelische Bijbel Scholen*, a practical Bible training effort in the Netherlands which began in 1972.[168] This four-year course of studies would take the student through the entire Bible "to increase the knowledge and experience of the Christian faith." The collaborative nature of the ETV meant that it had a wider aim than just those associated with the ECV. Nonetheless, three of the

---

165. R. and M. Haverkamp, letter to supporters, Spring 1980.
166. R. Haverkamp, "Wie der Herr Jesus Christus Gemeinden baut," session 1.
167. Van Wijngaarden, "Rooms Katholieke Gebruiken Onze Houding?," 2, 3.
168. "Welkom," Evangelische Toerustingschool Vlaanderen.

Ecclesiology of the Evangelische Christengemeenten Vlaanderen

five teachers were full-timers from the ECV.[169] Courses emphasized biblical studies, systematic theology, and practical theology.

While other groups within Flanders also noted the importance of sound teaching, perhaps a summary of the strong emphasis on pragmatic, sound teaching as a fundamental part of the identity of the ECV was found most clearly in the observation of one of its workers. He noted that, while many solid, evangelical works had come to his part of Flanders, the ECV remained the only group which continued to hold and promote a corporate, weekly Bible study such as was held in his assembly.[170] Indeed, this aspect of the ECV was not a passing fad or a church planting technique, but was part of its "DNA" from its founding.

The Types and Selection of Leadership Within Individual Assemblies and Throughout the ECV

One of the earliest challenges in the planting of assemblies by the founders of the ECV was to provide leadership for the local churches after they had been planted. As could have been expected, the leaders of the evangelistic Bible studies were the initial leaders of any subsequent churches. Thus, the founders were the initial leaders of the individual churches, and the ones who came and shaped the movement or became full-timers from among the Flemish later became leaders also. Clearly the ECV held that good, biblical leadership was essential for each assembly, and that the proper leadership structure was described in the New Testament in 1 Timothy 3 and Acts 20 among other places.[171] As Hay wrote, "The fact is that the Apostles, fulfilling the ministry which God gave them, laid a complete and perfect foundation for the Church, both as regards structure and doctrine."[172] Accordingly, the founders and shapers of the ECV were committed to the recognition of elders in each local church. Ideally, elders and deacons both would be recognized. Further, the requirements for those who held the position of elder were understood to be located in 1 Timothy 3 and Titus 1. "The qualities of leaders are not so much what they can do, but who they are. It is a matter of character."[173]

As noted earlier, an evangelistic Bible study was considered a local church once the celebration of the Lord's Supper on Sunday had commenced

---

169. "Programma," Evangelische Toerustingschool Vlaanderen.
170. P. Gifford, interview, 19 August 2008.
171. De Kegel, "Leiding in de gemeente," 5–6.
172. Hay, *The New Testament Order for Church and Missionary*, 133.
173. De Kegel, interview, 13 August 2007.

as a regular meeting of the believers in an area. While some of the studies had met on Thursday for a celebration of the Lord's Supper, the first Sunday celebration marked an assembly's birth. The challenge for the founders then was to provide adequate leadership for each local church. While the vision of the founders was to plant churches widely and continually, not much thought had gone into the planning for leadership once the assemblies formed. The founders had assumed that leaders would be recognized in a quite natural process as the Holy Spirit made known which men should lead. As Hay wrote concerning the appointment of elders,

> Since each one is put in his place by God, the only thing the church can do in the matter is to find out what God's choice is and acknowledge it. This is what happened at Antioch . . . The action was taken by the Holy Spirit. The church obeyed His guidance."[174]

Similarly, the ECV's Yvan Thomas wrote, "There is no argument that God is the One who calls elders, and the Holy Spirit appoints them as is seen in Acts 20:28."[175] Thus, the assembly merely had to recognize those whom the Holy Spirit had appointed. How was this recognition to be accomplished, however?

While the ECV's beliefs were those which had long been taught by the Open Brethren, not much was available in Brethren thinking as to how the actual process of recognizing elders would be accomplished, especially in new assemblies. Additionally, what teaching and models were available were not unanimous in outlook. Historically, the Brethren had leadership models from their earliest days which ranged from a local worker whose primary ministry was one assembly, all the way to an unstructured meeting of the men who were "in fellowship" deciding the affairs of the local church.[176] Among the Open Brethren, governance beyond the local church was not practiced in view of the wholehearted commitment to the autonomy of each local church. Over time among the Exclusive Brethren, however, a system developed whereby "leading brothers" had a great influence over local churches. Usually, these "leading brothers" had ministries in the areas of writing and itinerant preaching. This meant their influence was multiplied the more they wrote or traveled, provided that their teaching was accepted. Darby, for example, produced a prodigious body of literature, including

---

174. Hay, *The New Testament Order for Church and Missionary*, 306.

175. Thomas, "Cursus Oudstenbegeleiding," 18.

176. For a good survey of the various practices, cf. Fleming, "Leadership in the Open Brethren Assemblies of North America," 57–66.

Ecclesiology of the Evangelische Christengemeenten Vlaanderen

books, pamphlets, tracts, and personal correspondence; all this was in addition to a well-traveled preaching and teaching ministry.[177]

Initially, an ECV worker or workers would act as the pastoral leaders and primary teachers of the new assembly. Over time, an assembly would recognize church leadership of some sort, usually *verantwoordelijken* or elders. The ultimate leadership goal was the recognition of elders, though even after ten or more years some of the churches did not have recognized elders. By 1982, the pressing need for godly, recognized elders certainly was in the forefront of the mind of the founders as they and other full-time workers ministered among the churches of the ECV. Haverkamp even labeled this as "the greatest need" in correspondence with supporters as he asked for prayer.[178]

According to Haverkamp, this process of selecting elders involved four parties: the Holy Spirit (Acts 20:28); the man himself (1 Timothy 3:1); the founding missionaries or their delegates (Acts 14:23; Titus 1:5); and the local assembly (1 Thessalonians 5:12; Hebrews 13:7, 17).[179] "We believe that the Holy Spirit appoints the elders . . . How do we know who the Holy Spirit has appointed? By the other three parties!"[180] While the ECV acknowledged that the Bible did not give clear instructions as to the exact process whereby elders were recognized, it looked to the New Testament for principles whereby a process could be designed and followed. Over time, the elders replaced the founding missionaries or their delegates as one of the four parties involved in selecting elders, as listed above. Haverkamp was careful to note, "If one of the parties does not agree, you must wait."[181]

In addition to the four parties, the wife of a prospective elder was part of the process of selection. In fact, both Haverkamp and Gelling emphasized the need for elders to be married men as they believed that "the home life is the 'training' ground for work in the assembly."[182] One of the ECV missionaries would meet with a team of couples as they explored potential elders of any local church. For very practical reasons, the wholehearted support of the

---

177. A sample of Darby's writing on a variety of topics commonly is found in a thirty-four volume set. An additional three-volume set of letters also is commonly found. This is but a sampling and does not exhaust or include all his writings written in a number of languages as he traveled throughout the world. For a discussion of Darby's impressive output, cf. Weremchuk, "Ministry: Written and Oral," in *John Nelson Darby*, 163–92.

178. R. Haverkamp, letter to supporters, February 1982.

179. R. Haverkamp, "Wie der Herr Jesus Christus Gemeinden baut," session 9.

180. Ibid.

181. Ibid.

182. H. Gelling, email, 30 June 2009.

wife of the prospective leader was deemed necessary. Unnecessary marital tension, in addition to what was already a difficult job, was not viewed as a good dynamic for the leadership team or the local church. Further, this type of tension would harm the marriage of the potential leader. As Gelling pointedly observed,

> In the beginning, we only worked with the men, and that was a mistake; it was stupid. There are some charismatic/Pentecostal groups that have elder couples. We do not believe that the wife is an elder. We do believe that the wife is one flesh with the husband. If the wife is not behind it, if the wife is not in on it, if she doesn't know what is going on, if she isn't prepared for it, then you might as well forget it. You are only doing half a job.[183]

Accordingly, the ECV missionary would gather with this team of potential elders to pray and consider whether or not the Lord had "raised up" these men. Once the ECV missionary and the man both were convinced that the Holy Spirit had indeed raised a man to be a leader, this conviction was tested further by getting input from those in fellowship at the local church. Once all four groups listed above agreed, then the man was recognized as an elder. The full fourfold process was not followed to completion when leaders other than elders were understood to be the leaders of the local church. In this case, the word of the ECV missionary seems to have been the determining factor. This role for the missionary helping to select leadership was akin to a New Testament apostolic role in practice, though certainly none of the ECV missionaries would have considered themselves to be a New Testament apostle in the narrow sense of the term.

Haverkamp was particularly sensitive to the sense of those attending a local assembly when prospective elders and deacons were considered. Haverkamp taught the biblical principles for recognizing leaders, and he solicited the insights of the believers as to who should be recognized. Haverkamp reported in a letter to supporters,

> I have been to three of our churches the last couple of months to give a special study on leadership in the church, elders and deacons. I have also given the Christians a letter with explanations in regards to this subject and asked them to send this letter back to me with their thoughts about who the elders and deacons in their churches ought to be. Also mentioning the weak points of these brothers or any other remarks they have.[184]

---

183. H. Gelling, interview, 25 April 2003.
184. R. Haverkamp, letter to supporters, 9 February 1987.

Ecclesiology of the Evangelische Christengemeenten Vlaanderen

Not surprisingly, many of the leaders of the local ECV churches were those in whose home the original evangelistic Bible studies were conducted. This is in line with a number of recent studies which note instances in the New Testament where the leaders of the local church were also the owners of the home in which the local churches gathered. Roger Gehring's study of the workings of the early Church, entitled *House Church and Mission*, in some ways reads like the history of church planting in Flanders associated with the ECV. Gehring writes,

> The private domestic house served as the foundation for the missional outreach and community formation in the primitive church in Jerusalem, just as it did in the ministry of Jesus and his disciples. Because of the small size of house churches, it was possible to maintain a family-like atmosphere and practice brotherly love in a very personal and concrete way. Thus they became very attractive to outsiders . . . [T]he ancient *oikos* served as the source of evangelistic contacts, with its built-in network of relationships reaching far beyond immediate family to servants, friends, clientele, and business associates.[185]

Some scholars think that this practice was the result of socio-economic standing within society, and others, such as Ritva Williams, see this as a natural outgrowth of how the social structures of the day were constructed. In fact, Williams understands the structures of the local church as a challenge to the prevailing paternalistic culture. The structures of the local church replaced the paternalistic societal structure with one in which the church gathered together as brothers and sisters whose only father was their Father in heaven.[186] This has interesting ramifications for the planting of churches in Flanders by Haverkamp and Gelling as they planted churches into a religious milieu which had a very strong paternalistic, top-down structure. This structure was, of course, that seen in the Roman Catholic Church. Even the titling of the local priest as "father" reinforced this paternalistic structure. Williams' perceptions aside, certainly Gehring's observation about the ancient household is quite pertinent to the situation in Flanders such that the household provided a number of evangelistic contacts. Those within and those observing the growth of the ECV remarked that the studies spread "like a strawberry plant," since new groups were formed primarily through personal contacts of people already in the local church or through an evangelistic Bible study.

---

185. Gehring, *House Church and Mission*, 116–17.
186. Williams, *Stewards, Prophets, Keeper of the Word*, 30.

Initially, Haverkamp and Gelling had the goal of recognizing elders as soon as possible. This was in part due to the rapid expansion of the ECV as well as their conviction that elders were the biblical pattern of leadership. Gelling noted, however, that the quickness in recognizing elders was not always the best thing in some cases. They learned to go more slowly as relatively new believers who functioned as elders brought with them unforeseen challenges.[187] That said, many assemblies had a leadership team of sorts as quickly as possible, the *verantwoordelijken*.

The very first elders were recognized as a result of the need for the elders to come and anoint with oil and pray for healing. One of the new believers in the Peer assembly had been diagnosed with breast cancer in 1976. Haverkamp was back in Canada but had promised to return for this lady's funeral. During this time, one of the brothers read James 5:14–15 and wanted to follow what he had read in a very straightforward manner. Since that assembly had no elders, this request could not be met. Elders had to be recognized. Gelling remembered,

> All the elders were less than two years old in the Lord . . . The men met and fasted and prayed, just like the choosing of elders and deacons in the New Testament. Men were thus chosen. Because of this method, there were repercussions. One of the men became a full-time worker; one man had to step down as his wife said, "If you become an elder, I will never come back to the church;" and the last man also stepped down over time . . . Even though you make mistakes, the Lord is gracious and helps you through it. This was the only [assembly] in which a fast choosing of elders was made.[188]

In the ensuing years, the men recognized as elders normally had been Christians for around ten years, though a few were a bit less and at least one had been converted for twenty years.[189] The process became much more deliberate and was not without challenges and, at times, setbacks.

Haverkamp wrote in 1989, "In two churches elders were appointed, which we praise the Lord for. Difficulties arose all at once in a third church where we had hoped to see elders recognized too. The enemy puts up a real fight when it comes to leadership in the churches."[190] He later noted that the assembly in Roeselare split due to "an unwillingness to accept leadership

---

187. H. Gelling, interview, 25 April 2003.

188. Ibid.

189. "Enquêteformulier voor Leiders van de Christengemeenten (ECV)." This average is gleaned from the results of this questionnaire.

190. R. Haverkamp, letter to MSC, 28 November 1989.

Ecclesiology of the Evangelische Christengemeenten Vlaanderen

and authority." Particularly noteworthy is that this was the first split in the then twenty-year history of the ECV.[191] Even everyday events hindered the selection of elders such as when the twenty-nine year old wife and mother of four of an "elder-in-training" was diagnosed with cancer. While the letter announcing this tragedy noted the setback it would cause to the work, the writer clearly looked to God as the One who had this under His control and was acting according to His unknown purposes.[192]

As the ECV matured as an organization, it understood three divisions among the nationwide leadership: evangelists, teachers, and pastoral workers. In one meeting of the full-time workers, the evangelists' work was described primarily to those outside of the local assembly. They would make contacts and lead *Startstudies*. The teachers would preach on Sundays and lead Bible studies during the week. Among the pastoral worker responsibilities was the youth work, but this 1986 meeting also noted that the workers had care for the nine hundred people associated with the ECV.[193]

Even with this understanding of recognized elders and the somewhat broader authority of some of the national leadership, the priesthood of the believer was a continual emphasis among the ECV assemblies from the very start. This could be seen in the lectures on finding and exercising one's gifts as well as the importance placed on the believer being an active part of the local church. The ECV understood that "membership" in a local church was important to the believer, and that the believer was important to the local church. The ECV taught that the believer needed the local church for five things: for fellowship, since a believer was not "healthy" if he was on his own; teaching, even though each believer has the Holy Spirit to teach him; worship, since God desires both individual and corporate worship; service, because the local church is a loving place to begin to learn to serve, and a place where loving correction for mistakes can be made; and for correction since, as the Word was taught, the believer was corrected if he followed what was taught. The ECV taught that the church needs the believer, just as the body needs its members, and every part of the body is important (1 Corinthians 12). "The temple needs her priests" as the believer brought sacrifices of praise in his role which stressed the priesthood of the believer; and the assembly needs all the gifts as exercised by the believers who have them (1 Corinthians 12; Romans 12).[194]

---

191. R. Haverkamp, letter to MSC, 14 January 1992.

192. P. and J. Gifford, letter to MSC, December 1989.

193. H. Gelling, "Werkers vergadering—Berchem," Personal diary, "Werkers Fall 85," 04 September 1986.

194. R. Haverkamp, "Wie der Herr Jesus Christus Gemeinden baut," session 9.

Perhaps one of the most interesting aspects of the study of the ECV is to witness the change of church government from the planting of the initial churches until the beginning of the 1990s. In some ways, these forms of government parallel the experiences found in the first centuries of the Early Church.[195] The ECV churches transitioned from purely organism to visible organization within a span of fifteen years. This was seen in activities such as council meetings, the formal name change of their group, and the seeking of official government recognition and the resultant funding.

INTERACTION OF THE ECV AMONG THE MEMBER ASSEMBLIES: FROM A LOOSE ASSOCIATION TO AN ORGANIZED DENOMINATIONAL STRUCTURE

The ministries of the ECV which developed over the last three decades of the twentieth century in Belgium were remarkable both for their success by any standards and for the rapidity of their change in character. The 1970s saw eight new churches started, the 1980s saw twenty new churches, and the 1990s saw two.[196] What started as an extension of the ideas and convictions related to the autonomous, traditional, Canadian Open Brethren assemblies from which the founders came became more of a denominational, free church quite unknown in the Brethren backgrounds of the ECV founders. While true to the theological ideals and New Testament convictions of the wider Brethren movement, some of the forms and practices would have seemed unusual and even would have received criticism had these same forms and practices been found in a North American Brethren context.

So how did the organization of the ECV come to be? What was the historical path that took the local assemblies planted by the Canadian founders from a loose association to a recognized denomination? At least three phases can be discerned: the church-planting, "apostolic" phase; the pragmatic, organizational phase; and the formal denominational phase.[197]

---

195. For a summary of this process, cf. Hannah, *Our Legacy*, 258ff, esp. the chart on p. 258.

196. While the total number of unique assemblies associated with the ECV ultimately was thirty-one, one of these was an assembly from the Open Brethren whose roots went back to the early twentieth century.

197. Clues to this process are evident even in the change of the name by which these assemblies identified themselves; *christengemeenten* (lowercase "c"), *Christengemeenten*, *Evangelische Christengemeenten Vlaanderen*. Cf. chapter 1, "Overview of the Study and Its Setting," concerning "brethren" versus "Brethren."

Ecclesiology of the Evangelische Christengemeenten Vlaanderen

Phase One: Loose Association

The initial phase of the ECV was a time even before the name *ECV* was used. During this timeframe, Haverkamp, Shindelka, and Gelling were busy with a myriad of home evangelistic Bible studies which they hoped would become local Brethren assemblies. As assemblies were formed, Bible studies also were taught by the ECV founders to help the new converts learn about their faith. The common thread for teaching and preaching generally was the work of one of these three men, and eventually the work of den Boer—though his influence and efforts were much more localized. Once Shindelka left the work in Flanders, the common thread primarily was the work of Haverkamp and Gelling during the early years. Locally, both den Boer and Symons played an active part in the guiding of assemblies in their part of Flanders, den Boer as a full-timer from 1979 forward, and Symons from 1981.[198]

The local churches which eventually comprised the ECV were well aware of one another because of the common source of the founding of those assemblies via the Brethren missionaries from Canada, and because of the continued teaching and preaching ministry of the founders among these assemblies, and because of the radically few numbers of evangelical believers in Flanders. Further, given that all the assemblies of the ECV either were planted by the Canadian founders or were hive-offs from ones which they or another full-time worker of the ECV had planted, a natural relationship existed from the earliest days. In addition, many of the new contacts for evangelistic, home Bible studies which might develop into local churches came though believers already affiliated with the ECV who had a family member or a friend about whose spiritual condition the believer was concerned.

Meetings can be documented as early as 2 October 1982 at which Gelling, Symons, and den Boer met to discuss issues among and planning for the assemblies in Limburg.[199] These meetings for the workers in Limburg would continue through the years. Within a few months of this first recorded meeting, monthly gatherings of the workers or full-timers also are recorded concerning all the ECV assemblies in Flanders. Nevertheless, initially these meetings were more for the practical nature of the exchange of information and general coordination of ministry as opposed to setting overall, long term direction or exercising control. The sense one gets from

---

198. The terms "full-timer" and "worker" are used interchangeably to refer to those people whose primary vocation was the work of the ECV. This designation includes the missionaries as well as those who were recognized as workers by the assemblies of the ECV.

199. H. Gelling, personal diary, "Workers." Records of events from 1982–83.

reading the notes of these meetings is that they were held more because of a practical need to know something about what other workers were doing than for the execution of a master plan. This was seen in notes recorded at an all-Flanders workers' meeting held on 20 October 1982. One can gain such a tone even from the title Gelling put on the notebook which contained some records of these early meetings from 1982: *Dagelijkse dingen* [Daily things].[200] Notes from the workers' meeting of early 1983, which listed the strong points and the weak points of the ECV churches, specifically recorded ideas such as, "Jesus Christ central-no organization" as well as "simplicity." Thus, at this juncture, the workers were happy to see how well the assemblies thrived without any formal national structure. Shortcomings included "lack of teaching" as well as "not enough consistent Bible studies." Nonetheless, no mention was made of the creation of some sort of formal organization to help resolve these identified deficiencies.[201] Particularly noteworthy in the records of all these early meetings was the practice of opening the meeting with a lesson from the Bible. One of the workers would prepare a devotional for each meeting. This practice would continue even as the ECV was organized formally many years later. More than a mere mention of the passage was recorded in the notes of Gelling, and then later in the formal minutes of the ECV. An outline or at least a summary of the main idea was included.

As was commonly practiced within Brethren circles, each assembly had a correspondent as a point of contact. Each printed list of ECV churches from the beginning would have not only the place of meeting, but the name and contact details of the correspondent. This practice continued as the ECV built and displayed a website, though the name of the correspondent changed simply to "contact."[202] This position was not one of decision-making or authority such as that of an elder or a *verantwoordelijke*, but provided a sure way to transmit information from one assembly to another. That said, one of the elders or *verantwoordelijken* might also be the correspondent.[203] Typically, announcements for upcoming events, missionary report letters, and other matters of interest to an individual assembly would come via the

---

200. H. Gelling, personal diary, "Dagelijkse dingen." Gelling also noted that he hated to write things down, but only did so when he had to in order to keep his schedule and memory clear as he worked with five different assemblies. Cf. H. Gelling, interview, 01 May 2003.

201. "Werkers," in H. Gelling, personal diary, "Workers," 03 February 1983.

202. Cf. any of the ECV assemblies listed at the website, "Evangelische Christengemeenten Vlaanderen."

203. E.g.: The listing for the assembly at Lommel has one of the elders as the correspondent, Martijn Symons. "Adressenlijst Christengemeenten," 9.

Ecclesiology of the Evangelische Christengemeenten Vlaanderen

correspondent. In addition, this individual might be the first person contacted by someone outside an individual assembly as the seeker wanted to know more about a particular ECV church.

When disagreements arose during this initial phase with respect to practice or direction, neither Gelling nor Haverkamp exercised a top-down oversight. In one instance in September 1979, for example, den Boer was convinced that a new assembly should be formed from the three new converts he had in Oost-Ham. In response, Gelling wrote a letter to den Boer reasoning from Scripture and from logic. While the advice and challenge to den Boer was straightforward, Gelling's letter was pastoral in nature; the letter did not exhibit the characteristics of a superior writing to a subordinate even though den Boer was a brand new worker.[204] Den Boer came to see the wisdom of Gelling's counsel, and the planting of a new assembly in Ham was delayed until the following year.[205] Gelling's response was typical of the informal structure of the ECV at that time. Gelling and Haverkamp had a very great influence given that most of the members of the ECV either were converted through their ministry or greatly affected by their ministry. Nonetheless, their influence was one based on the respect for their roles as the church planters and the primary teachers among the assemblies; it was not based upon the demands or unbending expectations of either Haverkamp or Gelling.

Haverkamp considered himself as fulfilling the role of an apostle in his work in Flanders. He was careful to emphasize, however, that he did not mean that he was to be numbered with the twelve who also were called the disciples in the Gospels. He used the term apostle in the wider sense used of some others throughout the New Testament; Haverkamp was an apostle in the "secondary sense" as noted in books written about church planting.[206] As Haverkamp would say, "An apostle is a sent one, and I have been sent by God."[207] Consequently, he conducted himself accordingly as he worked tirelessly to plant churches in Flanders. Given his drive and his gifts, the many converts viewed him in much the same way such that he was accorded a very large voice in the direction of the ECV, especially for the first three decades. He took this responsibility seriously and was held in high esteem

---

204. H. Gelling, letter to John den Boer, 14 September 1979. Letter is contained in one of Gelling's personal notebooks with a series of black, white, red, and blue geometric angles on the cover. The first notebook entry is a lecture on "Church Planting" by Haverkamp, dated 20 August 1979.

205. H. Gelling, telephone interview, 02 December 2008.

206. Malphurs, *Planting Growing Churches for the 21st Century*, 89. Cf. Hesselgrave, *Planting Churches Cross-Culturally*, 96.

207. Haverkamp, "Wie der Herr Jesus Christus Gemeinden baut," session 3.

by the men and women within the ECV. This "apostolic role" provided an informal thread which tied together the ECV, especially in the years before formal organization was designed and implemented by De Kegel and others. In fact, De Kegel noted that Haverkamp made all the decisions in the early years of the churches that would become with the ECV.[208] Again, this would have been in line with the commonly understood model of the lone church planter. As one author wrote, "Lone church planters need to be strong, visionary leaders. This proves most helpful in the early stages of starting churches when there is a need for significant direction and numerical growth, and there's a potential for discouragement."[209] This is an apt description of Haverkamp and the times in which he found himself. Nevertheless, the historical record shows that Haverkamp was neither dictatorial nor autocratic in his leadership.

As an "apostle," Haverkamp recognized that he had to have "little bits of all the gifts," but was fully cognizant that he had great lacks in a number of areas such that he was continually looking for men to fill these roles.[210] To Haverkamp's credit, he allowed the ECV assemblies to go in directions with which he would not completely agree, as long as doctrinal orthodoxy was maintained. Still, his strong presence and personality did at times seemingly dampen the desire by some to put forward ideas that would not be in line with his.[211] As the ECV matured in the next phase of its existence, some wanted a greater voice for the full-time workers and elders of the ECV. Den Boer in particular spearheaded efforts to have the visible leadership at the workers' meetings be other than Haverkamp. He thus suggested that each full-timers' meeting be chaired on a rotating basis rather than have Haverkamp lead every meeting.[212] While den Boer respected Haverkamp, "he was not a soldier in Haverkamp's army" in this or other matters.[213]

A Flemish theologian and former teacher among the ECV assemblies noted that the churches which Haverkamp and Gelling planted "had a great success in getting laypeople involved." This would have been in line with the historical understanding of the priesthood of all believers held by the Brethren. Additionally, these churches were Flemish, "much more than

---

208. De Kegel, interview, 13 August 2007. De Kegel clearly stated that this way of decision making was no problem. He merely noted the change in the primary decision makers from Haverkamp, to the fulltime workers, and finally to the structure that included representatives from all the assemblies of the ECV.

209. Malphurs, *Planting Growing Churches for the 21st Century*, 97.

210. R. Haverkamp, "Wie der Herr Jesus Christus Gemeinden baut," session 3.

211. Anonymous, interview by author.

212. De Kegel, interview, 12 August 2007.

213. Anonymous, interview by author.

Ecclesiology of the Evangelische Christengemeenten Vlaanderen

the BEZ with their pastors coming from the Netherlands."[214] Records of the BEZ and VEG back to the beginning of the organizations show a long list of leaders for the local churches originating in the Netherlands. BEZ president Wilfried Goossens clearly saw that the Dutch comprised the vast majority of the leaders and workers of the BEZ, especially during the 1970s and 1980s.[215] In contrast, the vast majority of the workers and the leaders of the ECV assemblies were from Flanders when one looks back at the era of the planting and forming of the ECV. Finally, the ECV assemblies were "much more from the roots . . . they didn't make it a Canadian Brethren movement."[216] As noted earlier, the practices of the ECV might even have aroused opposition had they been tried among the Canadian assemblies. The ECV indeed tried to practice what they did according to how they understood the Bible as distinct from only how the Brethren had practiced since the early nineteenth century.

Phase Two: Organized Association

Beginning in 1984 when he became a worker, De Kegel also became a common thread across the whole of the ECV; he became a well-traveled teacher and preacher within the group full time. Additionally, he brought a conviction that the assemblies planted by Haverkamp and Gelling throughout Flanders needed to be organized with more than just the informal ties they had up until this time. His appointment as a full-timer to the work of the churches planted primarily by Haverkamp and Gelling marked the arrival of the second phase of change from organism to organization. Given the planting of twenty new Flemish churches in the 1980s in addition to the eight from the 1970s, De Kegel saw a need for better organization. As he said, "Structure is a means to help us to work more efficiently."[217] This was in line with his consummate managerial skills as an expediter before he became an ECV worker. Further, the work of the ECV was happening at a frantic pace throughout Flanders, and Haverkamp and members of his family also had a number of serious health problems during the 1980s causing Haverkamp to take increasingly longer furloughs in Canada.[218] Nevertheless, De Kegel did not propose structure for its own sake as that had its own risks—risks which

---

214. Nullens, interview, 10 September 2003.
215. Goossens, interview, 14 November 2006.
216. Nullens, interview, 10 September 2003.
217. De Kegel, interview, 13 August 2007.
218. R. Haverkamp, "Haverkamp History," 2.

he readily acknowledged. "Risk is when structure becomes an end, a goal." He wanted "structure to be a servant."[219]

The first permanent, visible sign across Flanders of something other than an informal arrangement was the publication of a newsletter for all the assemblies which were part of what would become the ECV. The *Nieuwsbrief van de christengemeenten* was begun in 1984 with De Kegel as the first editor, a position he would hold until 1986 when Eric Rutten became the editor.[220] The *Nieuwsbrief* supplied a valuable service by providing a means of making the work of the ECV churches throughout Flanders, Germany, and the Netherlands known to all the assemblies which were part of this movement. Notice was made of planned evangelistic outreach, study days, conferences, missionaries being sent out from the ECV, and eventually the cooperation of the ECV with other Flemish evangelical churches and organizations. In addition, the *Nieuwsbrief* had interviews with the full-timers, leaders from individual assemblies, and testimonies of new converts. As time went on, the *Nieuwsbrief* also contained notices of celebrations for individual assemblies' significant events including five-year, ten-year, or other noteworthy anniversaries and the building of a new place of meeting. In addition, a list of the assemblies which were part of the ECV was published periodically along with a person to contact should one want to communicate with or attend that assembly. This newsletter provided a significant source of information and encouragement to the assemblies which came to be spread across three countries. As the ECV matured as a movement, the *Nieuwsbrief* also was used to communicate teaching in a variety of areas.

Another publication for all those within the ECV was printed from late-1999 until mid-2005 and edited by Anastasi, *De Werkerskrant: nieuws- en gebedsbrief van het binnenlands zendingsteam van de ECV* [The Workers Newspaper: news and prayer requests from the national missions team of the ECV]. As the title indicated, *De Werkerskrant* concerned the life and ministries of the workers of the ECV. The first issue noted that it was a "news and prayer letter, in which you can find all kinds of information concerning our work, our plans, problems, joys, care and more."[221] Each issue focused on one of the workers and provided information such as their background and their present work. Part of the motivation was to make the workers bet-

---

219. De Kegel, interview, 13 August 2007.

220. "Verantwoordelijke uitgever Nieuwsbrief van de Christengemeente," *Nieuwsbrief van de christengemeenten*, ed., Eric Rutten, 1986, no. 1, 7. This same publication also was entitled *Nieuwsbrief van de christengemeentes* (1989, nr. 1–1990, nr. 1), *Nieuwsbrief van de E.C.V.* (1997, nr. 13.4), and *Evangelische Christengemeenten Vlaanderen Nieuwsbrief* (1998, nr. 13.1–to this writing).

221. "Stelt an u voor . . . het binnenlands zendingsteam," 1.

Ecclesiology of the Evangelische Christengemeenten Vlaanderen

ter known throughout the entire group of ECV assemblies as well as to help the reader know specifically how to pray. Additionally, humorous accounts were included, such as a worker's biggest "blunder." This pamphlet ended as a separate publication in mid-2005 as too much work was required to maintain it by itself. At that point, the information it contained became a subset of the *Nieuwsbrief*. An added advantage to this decision was the increased potential readership of those who would learn about the workers since more read the *Nieuwsbrief* than *De Werkerskrant*.[222]

As the workers' meetings continued which had begun during the first phase of the ECV, records indicate that the workers thought more and more about the general makeup of the ECV as well as the practices within each assembly. This was in line with the second phase of the move from organism to organization. For example, at the workers' meeting of 4 September 1986, three activities were identified as those which should be demonstrated by all the ECV assemblies: "toward the outside, evangelism; toward the inside, teaching; toward above, worship."[223] In addition, another threefold list of evangelization, teaching, and shepherding was identified as needful activities in each assembly. Noteworthy was the comment that not all men had the ability to preach. This was significant as many Brethren assemblies traditionally thought that every man should be allowed to preach irrespective of the man's gifting. How often and by whom the evangelism should be undertaken also was discussed: eight to ten young men, once a month or six weeks and sponsored by one assembly. Discussions even included abolishing the usual Dutch name of *avondmaal* to refer to the weekly communion service which was the mark of unity and identity among the Brethren, including the ECV. Instead, the proposal was to use either "the breaking of bread" or "the Lord's supper."[224] As the level of comment and specificity increased pertaining to the ECV assemblies across Flanders, the next step was not surprising—though certainly the founders would not have foreseen this move when they came to Flanders.

Even as the ECV moved toward more organization, however, the voice of Haverkamp was significant due to the respect he had engendered among the members of the ECV. His opinion was solicited, and it held great weight once his ideas were expressed. For example, when Symons wanted to repent and return to the ECV, he began by contacting Haverkamp as opposed to the elders or other ECV workers though he eventually did contact the elders

---

222. J. Gelling, telephone interview, 13 December 2008.
223. H. Gelling, "Werkers vergadering—Berchem," 04 September 1986.
224. Ibid.

and ECV workers.[225] After this, a letter was composed by all the ECV workers asking that Symons be returned to his role as a full-timer.[226]

Attempts at forming the first truly national organization were seen at a meeting in 1990. The purpose of this meeting was to outline the practical points making it possible for the assemblies of the ECV to have some sort of national organization. All the workers were present, and each assembly sent at least one representative. Suggested guidelines were that three quarters of all associated assemblies had to be represented, and that each vote had to be made with ninety percent approval of those present in order for a decision to be taken. Each assembly had two votes, and each worker one. Matters concerning individuals were to be decided by secret ballot, and all other matters were to be decided with a public vote. A national commission of between five and ten members was created from representatives appointed at the two regional meetings. Each region had not less than two and not more than five representatives. The initial members of the national commission were Freddy Mantels, Rosario Anastasi, Jo Bloemen, Gerard Gielen, Rudi Vosters, Jan Swiers, Paul Vanhaelewijn, Wim Pieters, Eric Rutten, and Guido De Kegel.[227]

To participate, the assemblies and full-timers all had to sign a statement which formally associated themselves with the group of assemblies which eventually would be called the ECV. This statement read

> The Assembly at/worker _____ will be part of the association of the *Christengemeenten* and concurs with the above agreements and designates as voters (name, address, telephone number).[228]

Particularly noteworthy was the specificity and formality of this arrangement among each of the assemblies, the workers, and the overall organization. Also particularly noteworthy was that the text of the agreement capitalized the title of what had been a loose association of local churches. Previously, the group of assemblies had referred to themselves with lower case nomenclature, *christengemeenten*, such as in the *Nieuwsbrief*. A few months later, another national meeting proposed and defined the General Commission. The General Commission was formed to coordinate activities

---

225. Gielen and Symons, interview, 14 August 2007.

226. Workers of the ECV, letter to all in the ECV, May 1990. Cf. chapter 3, "Eric Schraepen, 1992–2007."

227. "Praktische afspraken om te kunnen vergaderingen." This list is in the order in which their names appeared on the document.

228. Item 8 in the notes of the Nationale Vergadering, 15 June 1990.

Ecclesiology of the Evangelische Christengemeenten Vlaanderen

related to the *Nieuwsbrief*, conferences, the TCV, youth work, the workers, and contact with other Christian churches and organizations.[229]

The first official National Meeting based upon the proposed agreement which resulted from the meetings in 1990 was held in Genk on 24 June 1991. Mantels was appointed as chairman and Anastasi as secretary, both for a two-year term. A departure from previous meetings was both the authority of the participants as well as the expectations. As De Kegel later wrote,

> In the beginnings or pioneer years there was little or no need for structure: a lot of matters were new, and almost nobody had experience with church planting and mutual cooperation. Thus, the expansion did not progress without increased pains: sometimes everything moved very fast and there was lack of sufficient consultation. But there was much good will and enthusiasm, and that made up for a lot. Over the course of time, people increasingly started to feel the need for a more sound and workable structure.[230]

Nevertheless, this new arrangement did not form as a top-down organization. As the first meeting of 1990 made clear reference,

> The association can never participate or make binding decisions with regard to the specific and internal matters of each local assembly. Thus each affiliated assembly remains sovereign with regard to its own governing board and activities.[231]

This paragraph had to be communicated more than once to allay fears that an episcopal or presbyterian form of ecclesiology would form or had formed. This especially was a concern once the association of assemblies became a government-recognized, non-profit organization with the formal title of the ECV.[232] In addition to this statement of limitations was another which allowed any assembly to withdraw from the association at any time.[233] Still, by the time the assembly at Mariakerke was planted, organization was such that this assembly had to make formal application to become part of the ECV national structure. This was quite a change since it was a hive-off of Gentbrugge and Eeklo as well as a *Startstudies* led by Haverkamp.[234]

---

229. "Algemene verg.," attachment to Nationale Vergadering, 24 September 1990.

230. De Kegel, "Structuur van de ECV."

231. Christengemeenten Vlaanderen, "Verslag Nationale Vergadering DD. 15/06/91." Cf. item 1 of "Nationale Vergadering," 15 June 1990.

232. De Kegel, "Structuur van de ECV."

233. Item 1, "National Vergadering," 15 June 1990.

234. De Kegel, letter to the National Vergadering van christengemeenten, 05

Another significant step in the movement of the ECV from an organized association to an organized denomination was the clear description of the position of the full-timers within the ECV. An attachment to the minutes of the National Meeting of 25 November 1995 formally noted that the worker could be a missionary or someone from within evangelical circles in Flanders. The three categories of workers were identified as a local worker who primarily served one assembly, a regional worker who served two or three assemblies, and a national worker who served throughout Flanders due to his work, such as an evangelist or teacher. Significantly, each worker had to be associated with one local assembly, both for the well-being of that worker overall and to have a group of elders to whom he was responsible. Finally, new workers would be accompanied by a more experienced worker for a trial period of one year with an evaluation made at the end of that time.[235] This indeed was a fundamental change given the roots of the ECV and the free hand that the original Canadian workers exercised.

Finally, at this same meeting of 25 November 1995, the name *Evangelische Christengemeenten Vlaanderen* (ECV) officially was selected as the title by which the assemblies which had associated as the *christengemeenten* would be known. Two proposed logos also were provided to represent these assemblies under this new name. A definitive choice was made by the National Commission at their next meeting.[236]

Phase Three: Organized Denominational Structure

The ECV was incorporated officially as a *v.z.w.* [non-profit organization] on 11 March 1996 with its "headquarters" in Berchem. Eleven men from the ECV signed on behalf of all the ECV assemblies: Rosario Anastasi, Bart Biesbrouck, François Cremers, Guido De Kegel, Henk Gelling, Gerard Gielen, Richard Haverkamp, Eric Rutten, Hubert Welvaert, Jos Willems, and Jos Wagemans.[237] This official incorporation marked the third phase of organizational structure; it formally put the ECV in much the same category as other non-profit groups in the eyes of the Flemish government. The announcement of the official forming of the ECV clearly noted a sampling of

October 1992.

235. "De Werkers," an attachment to minutes of "National Vergadering Christengemeenten," 25 November 1995.

236. De Kegel, letter to the elders and *verantwoordelijken* of the assembly at Overpelt, 10 January 1996.

237. "Oprichtingsaktie van een vereniging zonder winstoogmerk," cf. item 11460. The signatories included eight Belgians, two Canadians, and one Italian. This list is in the order in which their names appeared on the document.

Ecclesiology of the Evangelische Christengemeenten Vlaanderen

pragmatic reasons for this new organization, namely, keeping the assemblies in contact with one another, coordinating the youth work, and representing these assemblies to "third parties." Also vitally important was the necessity for a government-recognized organization so that the full-timers could become part of the health and pension schemes. Prior to this formal organization, the Flemish workers had an uncertain relationship with the Belgian government. In fact, one man did not become a full-timer specifically because his wife did not want him to be considered a part of this uncertain relationship.[238] This man's reluctance was not an isolated incident and, without more workers, the concern was that the ECV would not grow.[239]

Further, the National Meeting of some fifty plus people was deemed not an "efficient way to work."[240] Accordingly, another organizational structure came into existence at the same time as the ECV, the National Commission. This initially was made up of the eleven men above, but the makeup was designated as being a representative of the *Nieuwsbrief*, at least one elder from each of the four regions, three full-timers, and one representative from the youth work. In another pragmatic move, one of the members of the National Commission was Sus Cremers, someone who was familiar with the technicalities of business and legal matters related to the forming of the non-profit.[241] This group was tasked to meet four times per year and to set the agenda for the National Meeting, but organizationally it was under the National Meeting. In a summary of the reasons for the National Commission, the announcement stated, "The steps that we have now enacted have been meant to develop a new, workable structure with the result that each assembly will get many chances to grow and to be equipped in such a way that Christ's Great Commission can be fulfilled."[242] Once again, these actions reflected not only thinking of a practical bent, but also gave evidence of the continued commitment to evangelism for the purpose of church planting.

The initial hope of the founders of the ECV was to plant autonomous churches modeled along the lines of how the more conservative Brethren traditionally interpreted the New Testament. Instead, the churches that were planted became part of a much more integrated grouping, indeed a denomination whose outworking of New Testament principles would not reflect the practices of the more conservative Brethren in North America. European

238. Anonymous, interview by author.
239. De Kegel, interview, 12 August 2007.
240. B. Biesbrouck, "Evangelische Christengemeenten Vlaanderen!?," 1.
241. Ibid., 2.
242. Ibid.

scholar Brian R. Wilson, recognized in academic circles for his work on religious minorities both in Britain and throughout the world, noted about the founding of the Brethren movement, "The early conception of Christian fellowship, based on minimal organization, proved to be inadequate for the maintenance of an integrated separate community in the longer run."[243] While not primarily reacting to an institutional Protestant Church, as did the founders of Brethren in the early nineteenth century, the founders and shapers of the ECV also concluded that more organization was necessary if the assemblies of the ECV were to flourish. As one of the ECV elders wrote in a 2005 training course for elders, "Organization is important throughout the Bible. A good organization makes an assembly strong, and it gives her the basis for growing in depth and size . . . The larger the assembly, the more organization is necessary."[244]

Though committed to the autonomy of the local church, pastoral needs necessitated more oversight. This was especially true during the years that a number of the assemblies had neither elders nor *verantwoordelijken*. At the national meeting of 22 November 1997, a decision was taken to divide the assemblies among the full-time workers for helping these assemblies. The goal was eventually to have one full-time worker for each two assemblies within five years.[245] Further, long-range planning was committed to paper as was a statement of the beliefs and practices of the ECV.[246]

Another indication of the organizational structure of the ECV was the production and distribution of a DVD in 2006 which clearly related the financial needs of the five full-timers supported by the ECV. None of the foreign missionaries nor Anastasi were included as they had other sources of income. (The missionaries primarily from sources outside Flanders and Anastasi his disability pension.) The five workers presented on the DVD were De Kegel, Symons, Julie Gelling, Koen Schelstraete (working 1999–present), and Raymond Hausoul (working 2007–present). Each of the five had his particular work with the ECV and his personal vision presented.

Two particular points of the presentation were especially significant. First, none of the five workers had church planting as their primary vision. The ministries of four involved church building, pastoral care, teaching and management, and youth work. The fifth listed not even a ministry, but

---

243. Wilson, "'The Brethren': A Current Sociological Appraisal."

244. Thomas, "Cursus Oudstenbegeleiding," 72.

245. De Kegel, "Bij Hem is kracht en beleid," 3.

246. "Groei en Toerusting van de Evangelische Christengemeenten: Beleidsnota 2002–2006," 23 November 2002; and "Om U te dienen," Beleidsplan, 2008–2011, November 2007.

Ecclesiology of the Evangelische Christengemeenten Vlaanderen

"to learn as much as possible."[247] This change from evangelism for the purpose of church planting (as was the vision of the founders) to the care and maintenance of the churches already in existence further demonstrated the organizational changes which had happened.

Second, each of the primary ministries of these workers was related to the printed policy document of the ECV, *Beleidsplan 2008–2011*. Given the unplanned nature of the initial works of the founders, and indeed the ECV churches for many years, this type of connection between written, stated goals and the work of the workers was significant. As an aside, making the needs of the workers known in such specificity, such as an €18,000 shortfall, and including an account number for prospective donors, would not have been a common practice among most Brethren churches, since a Georg Müller-style of funding would have been the historical norm.[248] Still, this was a DVD produced for those already a part of the ECV and not as a fundraising tool in the general sense. In keeping with the vision of the ECV and the history of the Brethren, the priesthood of all believers and the necessity of all in the ECV to help with the work was emphasized strongly at the beginning of the presentation.

With all these changes from organism to organization, Haverkamp's view still was that the ECV was not so much a denomination as it was a collection of like-minded churches. "Our churches in Belgium have formed a fellowship. We have started a little bit of an organization. We had to do this because of the government. We also did this because there are some activities we do together."[249] He listed them as six camps, support of full-time workers, having conferences, making newsletters, and various other unspecified activities.[250] "We work tighter, but every church is totally responsible to the Lord. There has to be a balance. We are independent, but in fellowship with others because we are a body of believers."[251] Gelling as well

---

247. "Funding the Workers of the *Evangelische Christengemeenten Vlaanderen*."

248. Georg Müller, or George Muller as he commonly was called, was an early Open Brethren worker who financed a series of orphanages in Bristol, England, as well as many missionaries through "faith alone." Within Brethren circles especially, he is touted as having never asked for money, but only praying that the Lord would provide. This style of never asking and only praying is what was commonly held among the Brethren as how a commended worker should be financed. Cf. Pierson, *George Muller of Bristol and His Life of Prayer and Faith*; Connolly, *Obstacle to Comfort: The Life of George Muller*; Brown, "When God Led His People Back to First Century Practices of Church Truths: A condensed but interesting account of this great Spiritual revival," 4.

249. R. Haverkamp, "Wie der Herr Jesus Christus Gemeinden baut," session 3.

250. Ibid., session 6.

251. Ibid.

was not comfortable with the term denomination given the historical and cultural concepts to which the term was attached.[252]

Though identifiable as a legal entity which functioned as a denomination in the eyes of the Belgian government, the ECV nevertheless continued to present itself as more of an association of autonomous churches committed to performing four practices when they met. These four are described in Acts 2:42: apostles' teaching, fellowship, prayer, and the Breaking of Bread. A video created in 2002 emphasized these four practices, and the same ideas were found on the ECV website well after all of the structures of the ECV and their national associations were made. This same presentation and the website also strongly identified the beliefs and practices of the ECV with the teachings and pattern found in the New Testament for the Church and the local church.[253]

INTERACTION OF THE ECV WITH VARIOUS CHRISTIAN GROUPS IN FLANDERS

The ECV had a diverse interaction with evangelical churches and parachurch organizations which varied from mere acknowledgement to active cooperation with the member churches of the ECV. Additionally, a category of direct opposition was present in their interaction with churches outside of the evangelical orbit. The material below will be presented from a perspective from inside the ECV and thus move from those groups closest to its organic and theological roots to those Christian groups more foreign to these roots. This is consistent with the view of the Brethren, and certainly the initial understanding of the ECV, which thought of itself as closely following the teachings of the New Testament in its form of church government as well as its practices as the local church gathered.[254] Hence, although Flanders was a predominantly Roman Catholic culture during most of the years under study, the relationship with the Roman Catholic Church will be considered last.

---

252. H. Gelling, telephone interview, 02 December 2008.

253. "De ECV voor elkaar." Cf. "Introductie."

254. "The appeal to the norm of the apostolic church functioned as *principium quod* for Brethren ecclesial piety-apostolic practice was the basis upon which contemporary ecclesial existence was structured" (Callahan, *Primitivist Piety*, 59).

Interaction of the ECV with Other Brethren Groups in Flanders and the Netherlands

While the founders were sent out by the Brethren from Canada, and other Brethren workers came from the United States and Scotland over the years, the ECV's relationship with the Brethren in Flanders and the Netherlands was a mixed record. This mixed record has to do with the character and history of the Brethren in Flanders and the Netherlands, the popular perception of the Brethren in Flanders, and the views of the founders and shapers of the ECV.

While the Open Brethren were present in small numbers when the founders arrived in the early 1970s, the insularity of the Open Brethren was much the same as the Exclusive Brethren. Although some among the Flemish and Dutch Continental Brethren would have denied this Exclusive title, given that the much more extreme group of Taylor Brethren or even the Tunbridge Wells Brethren present in Flanders also had this title, the fundamental commitment to "guarding the purity of the Lord's table" and the restricted circles of fellowship meant that these Continental Brethren indeed were Exclusive Brethren.[255] Within Exclusive Brethren groups, a distinction was made between the "table of the Lord" as found in 1 Corinthians 10 and the "Lord's Supper" of 1 Corinthians 11. As one Brethren author wrote,

> The Lord's Supper (the memorial) and the Table of the Lord (the communion) are distinguished in Scripture but are inseparably tied together. To respond to the desire of the Lord (in participating of the Lord's Supper) implies the recognition of His rights over our personal life (1 Corinthians 11: 27–32) and in the assembly (at the Table of the Lord).[256]

Or as Exclusive Brethren author van de Bijl wrote,

> At the Lord's Supper, the emphasis is on the remembrance celebration and each person is individually responsible to judge the body of the Lord (1 Cor. 11). The term "Table of the Lord" signifies the corporate coming together and is the responsibility of the community.[257]

---

255. For a good summary of this need for purity among the Dutch-speaking Continental Brethren, cf. J. van der Bijl, *Met de Heer aan zijn tafel*, 46–47.
256. Müller, "Old Paths."
257. J. van der Bijl, *Met de Heer aan zijn tafel*, 13.

New Brethren in Flanders

Accordingly, one must be a part of the Table of the Lord to be able to celebrate the Lord's Supper.[258]

To prevent any sort of "pollution" of the Table of the Lord, any who wish to become part of an approved Exclusive Brethren assembly first must be questioned, usually by two or three men. Then the results of that examination are offered to the assembly for their approval of this believer coming into fellowship, becoming an active participant at their particular local church.[259] The Dutch-speaking Continental assemblies also exhibited the usual Exclusive practice of "circles of fellowship" such that church discipline pronounced in one local assembly was supposed to be supported by all assemblies in their circle everywhere in the world as well as the concept that one could fellowship only within these circles on any given Sunday morning whether at home or away. In fact, to participate in the celebration of the Lord's Supper when away from one's home assembly, the adherent would need a "letter of commendation" from his home assembly, and that home assembly had to be within the circle of fellowship.[260] While the Open Brethren in Flanders did not have quite as tight an understanding of the circle of fellowship, a visitor still would need a letter in order to participate in the celebration of the Lord's Supper. This practice came from an example seen in the New Testament Church. As one very conservative, Open Brethren writer observed,

> If one in Assembly fellowship visits an Assembly where he is not known, we believe he should if possible have a letter of commendation from his home Assembly showing he is in good standing there (cf. Acts 18:27 and Romans 16:1 and II Corinthians 3:1).[261]

While this need for a letter would have been held and practiced rigidly in the Exclusive assemblies, the Open assemblies might have reflected a bit

---

258. For further explanation of the Table of the Lord from a Dutch and Flemish Continental Brethren viewpoint contemporaneous with the founding of the ECV, cf. the summary in Heijkoop, *De Gemeente van de levende God*, 220–22. For a more complete rehearsal, including Old Testament reasoning, as well as a comparison and connection of the Table of the Lord with the Lord's Supper, cf. Heykoop, *Hoe en waar moeten gelovigen zich vergadering*; Briem, *Daar ben Ik in het midden van hen*, 232–65; Ouweneel, *De Maaltijd des Heren*, 105–30.

259. J. van der Bijl, *Met de Heer aan zijn tafel*, 21–26.

260. This letter is not to be confused with a Letter of Commendation in Brethren circles which announces that a person is a full-time Christian worker. The letter of commendation which allows a person to participate in and celebrate the Lord's Supper vouches for the conversion and character of the one about whom it is written, and it has been signed by the leadership or appropriate brothers from the bearer's home assembly.

261. Reid, *The Chief Meeting of the Church*, 53.

more flexibility. As Alfred P. Gibbs states, "Two extremes are to be avoided: the extreme of ultra exclusivism on one hand, and the extreme of gross carelessness on the other."[262] Gibbs goes on to note commonly understood categories for allowing a person to participate at the Lord's Supper in a Brethren gathering: 1) a believer who has been converted and baptized at the assembly where he is seeking fellowship; 2) a believer "vouched for by a brother or sister in whom the assembly has confidence;" 3) a letter of commendation from the believer's home assembly, signed by "responsible brethren," which "commends this person to the love and care of any company of believers meeting on scriptural lines;" 4) a "well known and respected preacher or teacher of the Word," since "his work has already commended him to the attention of the Lord's people;" and 5) through personal interview by "a few courteous, well taught, and spiritually discerning brethren."[263] These stipulations might seem to be a middle ground, as Gibbs hoped, but in practice the outworking was not always as encouraging. In practice in Flanders among the Open Brethren when Shindelka and Haverkamp arrived, the barrier was such that these founders of the ECV thought it better to start new assemblies rather than have any new believers from their evangelistic Bible studies have to run such a gauntlet in order to celebrate the Lord's Supper. Accordingly, a cordial but not close relationship developed between the Open assemblies and the ECV. Nonetheless, as the numbers of converts grew and as the ECV assemblies multiplied, some from the Open assemblies were drawn to these works. For example, minutes from ECV workers' meetings note the transfer of people from the Waregem assembly to the ECV.[264] At least one well known Brethren family settled in to the ECV assembly in Kuurne.[265] More interestingly, even the grandson of the founder of the first Flemish assembly in the Netherlands left that assembly in Gent to come with his family to the ECV assembly in Gentbrugge in 1993.[266] Also, the assembly in Tienen, planted just after the First World War, became part of the ECV in 1992.[267] Nonetheless, this was not always a smooth relationship as matters relating

---

262. Gibbs, *The Lord's Supper*, 123. Cf. Littleproud, *The Christian Assembly*, 108–10.

263. Gibbs, *The Lord's Supper*, 126–27.

264. H. Gelling, notes from "Samenkomst met à Ouweneel—Medema—Steenhuis—Fijnvandraat," personal diary: orange notebook labeled, "Werkers." [09?] November 1990.

265. De Kegel, "RE: Waregem: Paul Huygens," email, 08 July 2008.

266. Van Der Smissen-Wackenier, interview, 08 September 2004. Other parts of the family left the Brethren assemblies altogether and became liberal Protestants. Cf. Van Der Smissen-Wackenier, "Re: Family Studies," email, 25 July 2005.

267. "Betreft: Toetreding van de gemeente Tienen," attachment 1 to "Verslag Nationale Vergadering," 28 November 1992.

to disputes concerning Tienen's theology and practice often were found on the agenda of full-time workers.

Given the troubled history and insular reputation of the *vergadering van gelovigen* in the Netherlands and Flanders, Haverkamp was careful to say that the ECV were not part of the Brethren, and he said this in many settings. Typical of these statements was the following:

> Our churches in Belgium are not Brethren assemblies. When we came to Belgium, we tried to work with the Brethren assemblies, but we found they were far too closed that it did not work . . . So our churches are just evangelical Christian churches, but we do break bread every Sunday.[268]

When asked for further elaboration, Haverkamp stated,

> The Brethren assemblies we met when coming to Belgium have a negative testimony. In some countries in Europe too. That's why I shy away from them and from being seen as one of them. I want to love and fellowship with all the Lord's people. We are just Christians, evangelical churches.[269]

He was careful to note that he happily ministered among the Brethren in North America. "I love the way they meet, I love to fellowship with them and I continue to minister in their assemblies *as being part of them*, in Canada and the US" [emphasis added].[270] Accordingly, his distancing himself and the ECV assemblies from the title "Brethren" was for the primary goal of planting New Testament churches unhindered by rigid traditions or an unhelpful reputation. That said, the theology and practices of the ECV churches easily would have fallen within the spectrum of Open Brethren worldwide in a left-of-center manner. Haverkamp's public statements of disassociation thus were not a rejection of either the ideas or the identity of the churches in Canada who had sent him out and supported him, but a culturally attuned, needful differentiation within the Belgian context so that the historical problems and contemporaneous reputation of the Brethren in Flanders and the Netherlands would not hinder the work of planting New Testament churches.

The identity of the ECV and the organizational changes by the beginning of the twenty-first century were such that some among the formerly Continental Brethren assemblies in Flanders also did not consider them Brethren assemblies. One worker associated with newly planted Brethren assemblies from what had been the Continental Brethren wrote about the ECV,

268. R. Haverkamp, "Wie der Herr Jesus Christus Gemeinden baut," session 4.
269. R. Haverkamp, interview, 30 April 2008.
270. Ibid.

Ecclesiology of the Evangelische Christengemeenten Vlaanderen

> The blessing of the Lord was with them and a great lot of people came to believe in the Lord Jesus. They started as real assemblies but changed themselves by the time more and more into evangelical churches. Although they hold fast the weekly supper. But in structure and overall organisation they have taken over the evangelical structure. They participate as an [sic] denomination in different governmental organisations.[271]

Further, the fact that this worker came from the Netherlands to plant Brethren assemblies in West Vlaanderen in 1992 gives another clue as to his understanding of the ECV versus the Brethren assemblies. The assemblies he planted were located not far from existing ECV churches, and no record is found among the ECV meetings as to his contact with the ECV assemblies. Another long-time conservative Brethren church planter from a different part of the world noted that Haverkamp planted assemblies which were more "adaptive" in nature, and he thought that Haverkamp was not teaching the people the way they should be taught with respect to "principles of gathering."[272] Still, Gelling stated when asked about the identity of the ECV churches, "We are Brethren assemblies. I mean, what else are we?"[273] He then went on to note the identity of the sending churches of all the missionaries associated with the ECV.

Gelling, indeed, asked the right rhetorical question, as the ECV churches used people from the Dutch assemblies as speakers at conferences and workers' gatherings from an early date. Further, Brethren workers from English-speaking countries were scheduled as conference speakers. Though all conference speakers were not of Brethren origin, the number of Brethren speakers was significant, certainly more than in the years after the beginning of the twenty-first century. Thus, even a cursory view of Gelling's journals and the newsletters of the ECV finds names from the Dutch Continental Brethren as conference teachers, men such as Ouweneel, Fijnvandraat, and Steenhuis. In fact, the first study days sponsored jointly by the ECV and the BEZ in 1984 had these three men as the speakers.[274] Other Brethren speakers over the years included Eric Bermejo, Brethren former missionary to Spain,[275] Northern Ireland's Septuagint scholar David Gooding,[276] and

---

271. Vergouwe, "RE: Vergadering in Woesten," email, 30 Jul 2005.
272. Anonymous, interview by author.
273. H. Gelling, telephone conversation, 22 April 2008.
274. "Studiedagen," 4.
275. "Broederconferentie met Eric Bermejo," 6.
276. "Studieweek gaat door," 4; H. Gelling, notes from a David Gooding Bible conference, blue with yellow stripes notebook labeled "papier5," 9 January 1989.

New Brethren in Flanders

English mathematician John Lennox—who not only held a conference, but taught a Tuesday evening Bible study in Houthalen while in Limburg.[277] In addition, every worker who came from other parts of the world to help with the ministries of the ECV on a long term basis came from Brethren assemblies or were listed by the Brethren missions service agency in the country from which they came.[278] Finally, even contemporaneous studies of Protestantism in Belgium categorized the churches planted by Haverkamp and Gelling in a group with the pre-existing Exclusive and Open Brethren assemblies.[279] More specific studies placed the ECV assemblies among the Open Brethren in contradistinction from the Exclusives given the beliefs and practices of the assemblies which Haverkamp and Gelling planted.[280]

Even with all this contact between the ECV and other Brethren workers from a variety of groups, as well as the continual flow of Brethren missionaries from the English-speaking world, a more open acceptance of the ECV assemblies by the Continental Brethren assemblies in the Netherlands did not happen until the beginnings of the breakaway from the Continental Brethren of most of the Exclusive assemblies in the Netherlands in the 1990s. Even then, this acceptance was not as robust as some might have hoped.[281] This breakaway was part of a worldwide breakup of the Continental Brethren, and ultimately was due to an issue of church discipline in Den Helder, Netherlands. In the end, Den Helder's letter of discipline was rejected by the vast majority of the Continental Brethren assemblies in the Netherlands. As one eyewitness from the Den Helder assembly noted, the situation in the assembly in Den Helder was not one of unrepentant sin on the part of the man being disciplined, but the legalism and desire for power on the part of the leading brother and his family at the Den Helder assembly.[282] An attempt by Continental Brethren in Germany to force acceptance of Den Helder's letter of discipline and refusal by the Dutch assemblies to do so was an important catalyst in the worldwide breakup as well as the breakaway in the Netherlands which had been building for some time.[283]

---

277. H. and B. Gelling, letter to MSC, April 1989.

278. Cf. Appendix 2 for a list of Brethren workers associated with the ECV who came from outside the Dutch-speaking world.

279. For example, Dhooghe, "Het Belgische Protestantisme," 359; Demaerel, "Tachtig jaar pinksterbeweging in Vlaanderen," 381–82.

280. van der Laan, "Gemeentestichtende Evangelisatie in Vlaanderen," 43–44.

281. H. Medema, interview, 18 September 2003.

282. Anonymous, interview by author.

283. "'Keiner kann mir Vorwürfe machen, dass ich mich geändert habe': Interview mit Willem J. Ouweneel," 20–21. Cf. J. Fijnvandraat, "Open brief van JGF mei 1996."

Ecclesiology of the Evangelische Christengemeenten Vlaanderen

As the buildup to this fracture was happening, meetings were held in late 1990 and early 1991 between the leadership of the ECV and five "leading brothers" from the Netherlands: Jaap G. Fijnvandraat (b.1923–d.2012), Johan Ph. Fijnvandraat (b.1925–), Henk Medema (b.1950–), Willem Ouweneel (b.1944–), and Dato Steenhuis (b.1937–). These men would not have had the power to make a final decision on behalf of all the Continental Brethren in the Netherlands and Flanders (such as was accorded to men like J. N. Voorhoeve until his death in 1948); nevertheless, these meetings were of some significance due to the respect given the opinions of these men. Their standing came about as the result of their widely traveled speaking ministries to conferences and assemblies within the Netherlands and Flanders as well as to their copious writings.[284] The purpose of the meetings was to see if better acceptance and some sort of joint ministry could be arranged between the Continental Brethren in the Netherlands and the ECV.[285] Historically, the matter of acceptance was a challenge only for the Continental assemblies in the Netherlands and Flanders since the ECV had no barriers to these Brethren or any other believer who wished to associate with the ECV or celebrate the Lord's Supper as a visitor. Typical of the attitude of the ECV assemblies was the pamphlet given to visitors at the assembly in Houthalen:

> We give you a hearty welcome this Sunday morning. We are happy to be able to celebrate this time of worship with you. We ask you to respect our usual course of events and take part in a worthy manner . . . We ask that you do not take part [in the Lord's Supper] unless you are a born again, child of God.[286]

At least two meetings took place, one in Flanders and another in Breda, Netherlands. At the first meeting, Steenhuis began by saying that the Dutch brothers had noticed that "a work of the Lord has been done in Belgium." This immediately made Gelling uncomfortable as it ignored all the work done previously by the BEZ, and he mentioned this to the Dutch brothers. Issues discussed ranged from the recognition of elders to the choice of Bible translation to the role of women in the local church. One of the more instructive encounters happened when J. Fijnvandraat asked the opinion of the ECV on Tunbridge Wells, a problem associated with a church discipline

---

284. Medema, interview, 18 September 2003; J. Fijnvandraat, "Re: Vergadering in NL en Vlaanderen," email, 22 November 2005.

285. H. Gelling, notes from a meeting at the end of 1990 [November?] between leaders of the ECV and Ouweneel, Medema, Steenhuis, and Fijnvandraat in an orange notebook of meetings from 1989–1991 entitled, "Werkers."

286. "Evangelische Christengemeente Houthalen."

New Brethren in Flanders

case among the Exclusive Brethren in the UK nearly ninety years earlier. After a long silence, Gelling answered,

> Brothers, what you asked, we don't know. Even if we did know, we don't want to bring the history of the Brethren into Belgium so that they have to deal with that, too. We just want to bring them the New Testament, New Testament principles, the Lord start assemblies, and see people saved.[287]

J. Fijnvandraat answered, "I can live with that." Medema noted that he was "quite sympathetic to this answer of not allowing historical difficulties to be imported from elsewhere to Belgium."[288] While nothing was settled definitively at these meetings, an easier relationship was begun between the ECV and a number of the brothers from the Continental assemblies in the Netherlands. Closer contact was not possible initially as the ability of women to participate actively at the ECV's Lord's Supper meetings was an obstacle. This easing of barriers, however, eventually resulted in Haverkamp being asked to preach at the major annual assembly conference at Betteld, Netherlands, even as the Bible study days led by Ouweneel and Steenhuis continued among the ECV churches.[289]

Approximately five years before these meetings between the ECV and the five brothers from the Netherlands, a tension had developed between the ECV and the Continental assembly in Gent. During a short visit of the Gellings to Canada, the son of one of the "leading brothers" from the assembly in Gent moved to Limburg and began to attend the ECV assembly in Houthalen.[290] Eventually, he tried to go back to the Exclusive assembly in Gent, but he was not allowed to participate in or partake of the Lord's Supper since he was in fellowship with a church outside their circles. A meeting was called, and about a dozen men from the Gent assembly and six from Houthalen met to discuss the matter. All seemed to be going well until a Dutch brother, the owner of the Bible bookstore in Gent, asked about the position of the Houthalen assembly on the role of women.[291] Houthalen

287. H. Gelling, interview, 11 September 2002.

288. Medema, interview, 18 September 2003.

289. J. Fijnvandraat, "Re: Vergadering in NL en Vlaanderen," email, 22 November 2005.

290. Exclusive assemblies do not have formally recognized elders, but are led by a meeting of the men in fellowship. This "brothers' meeting" is the manner in which decisions are made. That said, almost all Exclusive assemblies have one or more "leading brothers," and their word at least carries more weight. In many instances, their word is the final decision for any matter under discussion.

291. This was probably John van der Bijl, as he and his son Jacques ran the Christian bookstore in Gent. Medema, interview, 18 September 2003.

Ecclesiology of the Evangelische Christengemeenten Vlaanderen

followed the common Brethren practice of having the women wear a head covering during the Lord's Supper, but the fact that the women could pray aloud or ask for a song to be sung at the Lord's Supper was an obstacle for the Exclusive men. An additional issue was that the Exclusive assemblies did not recognize elders as did the ECV assemblies since the Exclusives believed that only one of the Apostles or his helpers could appoint elders.[292]

While the ECV men were happy to live with the different practices, the Exclusive men were not, and a letter came six weeks later confirming that the young man could not be in fellowship with the assembly in Gent because the ECV positions were "unbiblical." This answer from Gent was particularly troubling to a number of the ECV men since the Exclusive assembly in Gent maintained fellowship with assemblies in France who practiced infant baptism, something practiced among some Exclusive assemblies due to the teachings of J.N. Darby.[293] A decision was taken to leave the matter alone, and for a number of years this young brother could not fellowship at the assembly in which he had grown up.

About a week or so after the second meeting between the five Dutch brothers and the ECV leaders in 1991, a letter came from Gent saying that all now was well.[294] While no certain record of contact between the Gent assembly and the five Dutch brothers is known, most likely one or more of the five men contacted at least John van de Bijl or another man named Jacques van de Elst to ask that this young man be received back into the Gent assembly since the matter had been broached at these meetings.[295] Eventually, one of the leading brothers from the Exclusive assembly in Gent left that assembly and began coming to the ECV assembly in Gent. He then would leave with a group which split off of the ECV assembly and began attending a Vineyard church in the area. After a time at the Vineyard church, he was asked to leave as his views related to the "charismatic gifts" were considered too extreme.[296]

While some measure of fellowship was had between the Flemish Open Brethren and the ECV, and eventually with the leading Bible teachers from the Continental Brethren in the Netherlands as well, the Brethren assemblies or circles of fellowship which existed when the founders arrived never associated with the ECV. While the ECV welcomed any believers from the pre-existent Brethren assemblies, this openness was not reciprocated in the same manner by either the Exclusive or the Open assemblies in Flanders or

---

292. Cf. chapter 2, "Exclusive Brethren Leadership."
293. Darby, letter to [Mrs. Walter] dated 04 November 1869, 47–52.
294. H. Gelling, interview, 11 September 2002.
295. Medema, interview, 18 September 2003.
296. H. Gelling, interview, 11 September 2002.

New Brethren in Flanders

by the Exclusive assemblies in the Netherlands—even after the worldwide breakup of the Continental circles in the mid-1990s and the subsequent breakaway by the Dutch Continental assemblies. While the record indicates that men such as Gelling and De Kegel spoke at conferences of the Brethren in the Netherlands over the course of the years, a close relationship never was built.[297] Additionally, the paper listings and subsequent website maintained by a Dutch Brethren man to notify people of the Brethren assemblies in the Netherlands and Flanders never listed any of the ECV assemblies.[298]

Over the years, some of the historically Open Brethren in the Netherlands also asked the founders of the ECV to come and speak at their annual conferences.[299] That said, no record exists of any significant contact between the Canadian missionaries associated with the ECV and the lone Canadian Open Brethren missionary in the Netherlands also listed with MSC, Lawrence Swaan. Swaan was commended to his work of evangelism and church planting in the Netherlands by Clearbrook Assembly of Christians in Abbotsford, BC, as well as West Richmond Gospel Hall in Richmond, BC, in 1971.[300]

Interaction of the ECV with Other Christian Groups in Flanders

The ECV's interaction with the various Christian groups in Flanders over the years fell into the categories of isolation from them, cooperation with them, or displaying a less accommodating attitude and subsequent action toward them.[301] Over the years, the ECV changed in its attitudes toward and interaction with most of the Christian groups, and certainly with respect to all of the evangelical groups. This especially was evident in the 1990s as the formal organization of the ECV took shape, though a change in attitude and practice was seen even before this time.

Initially, the work of Haverkamp and Shindelka was done very much in isolation from other evangelical groups in Flanders with the exception of the initial six month contact with the Open Brethren and some evangelistic

297. H. and B. Gelling, letter to MSC, January 1989.

298. Conversely, the new assemblies planted by Jaap Vergouwe were included on this list. Cf. Sleijster "Zuid-Nederland."

299. "Landelijke Ontmoetingsdag," 9.

300. "Missionary Prayer Handbook for daily use," 60. For more information on Swaan and his work, cf. Hofman, "3.3: Een derde groep open vergaderingen: Swaan en Bouwman," in "Open broeders in Nederland: Een onderzoek naar de geschiedenis en identiteit van open vergaderingen van gelovigen"; Tatford, *West European Evangel*, 288, 291.

301. In this section's appraisal, "Christian groups" are defined broadly as any group within the world religion of Christianity.

Ecclesiology of the Evangelische Christengemeenten Vlaanderen

contacts gained from Operation Mobilization. Shindelka's and Haverkamp's manner of action was such that some within other evangelical groups initially thought them to be very sectarian in nature. Johan Lukasse, later to become the head of the BEZ, noted that new converts from the work of Shindelka and Haverkamp were surprised that Christians existed outside the ECV as "they thought they were the only Christians in the whole country."[302] As one observer noted,

> The isolation of the ECV was due to Richard's teaching. "I am teaching only what the Bible teaches." He also made the impression that the ECV was the only one that followed what the Bible said . . . Richard never said it in so many words, but the impression was that the ECV was the best, the real."[303]

This was very much in line with both the North American and Flemish Brethren thinking of the era among the more conservatively practicing Open assemblies and certainly among all the Exclusive ones. Unless a Brethren assembly was nearby, a Brethren believer would think that no "testimony of the Lord" existed. Lukasse was familiar with this Brethren attitude toward other evangelical works from personal contact with a Brethren woman who was active in an orphan's ministry in Genk sponsored by the BEZ. Though this city had a BEZ church of nearly eighty believers, this woman would travel to Eindhoven each Sunday "to be part of the Lord's table."[304] Still, the observation above and related perceptions may have been in error as Haverkamp's record before coming to Flanders showed him working amongst a wide variety of evangelical churches. In later years, Haverkamp himself summarized his open attitude when he stated, "I respect anybody's belief and practice as long as they are evangelical."[305]

Nonetheless, the BEZ had direct contact with Haverkamp in the early years of his work. In a 1973 letter to Lukasse, Haverkamp responded to his inquiry about his intentions. After describing twenty-hour work days and his wife's health issues, Haverkamp told Lukasse that he hoped Luesink soon would join the work and maybe live in Turnhout, but that this location was not certain. This information especially was of interest to the BEZ as it had just planted a church in Turnhout that year.[306] Haverkamp also noted, "We will continue quietly with the Bible study in Beerse, but we don't yet have

---

302. Lukasse, interview, 05 December 2003.
303. Anonymous, interview by author.
304. Lukasse, interview, 05 December 2003.
305. R. Haverkamp, "Wie der Herr Jesus Christus Gemeinden baut," session 4.
306. "File: POST GEMLYST 2; Report: BEZ–overzicht."

any intention to plant a church or something like that. We believe that it is not the time for it. We are waiting on the Lord for His leading."[307]

Within just a few years, however, the ECV actively cooperated with various evangelical church and parachurch organizations. Some thought that the cause of this more cooperative attitude was as the result of the new converts of the ECV coming in contact with other believers from other groups in Flanders and thus forcing change on the leadership.[308] Haverkamp's wide background of serving with and alongside of various groups in Canada, however, questions the veracity of this perception of forced change. As early as 1975, Haverkamp's reputation garnered him an invitation to speak at an evangelistic campaign sponsored by the BEZ. Surprisingly, he declined the invitation, reportedly saying, "I am too busy doing a big work. This distracts me." Thus, any isolation normally was of a pragmatic, purpose-driven nature as opposed to a theological conviction such as would have been held in Exclusive Brethren or the more conservative Open Brethren thinking. Within a few years of arrival in Flanders, however, even this hesitation no longer existed.[309] Over the years, he and other teachers from the ECV would be featured as speakers in joint evangelistic efforts and teaching times sponsored by the BEZ and the VEG.[310]

A number of the efforts of cooperative work with other evangelical groups in Flanders came as the result of individuals having contacts with these groups. Much as locations for new *Startstudies* came from personal contacts of people within the ECV, cooperative works often came from similar personal contacts or interests by those who attended one of the ECV assemblies. Thus, a good deal of the cooperative work initially came from the bottom up as opposed to the top down. For example, in the very first issue of the *Nieuwsbrief* which started in 1984, a prayer request is made for the health of Jean-Pierre Borgonjon, "a member of the assembly in Gentbrugge since 1.2.1983 and full-timer serving with the Tear Fund," a Christian relief and development charity.[311] The next issue announced the sponsorship by the assemblies in Gentbrugge and Eeklo of a pancake meal to raise funds for two Tear Fund projects.[312] Even before the beginning of the *Nieuwsbrief*, however, meeting notes of the Houthalen assembly from the late summer of 1982 mention the Tear Fund as well as individuals who were in contact

307. R. Haverkamp, letter to Johan Lukasse, 20 April 1973.
308. Lukasse, interview, 05 December 2003.
309. Ibid.
310. E.g., "Gentse Conferentie '94."
311. "Gezen," 5.
312. "Pannekoeken voor Tear-Fund," 8.

Ecclesiology of the Evangelische Christengemeenten Vlaanderen

with them.[313] The Tear Fund would have a prominent role in the cooperative efforts of the ECV over the years.

Another prominent cooperative work was related to the youth work of the ECV. At least as early as 1982, for example, the assembly in Lanaken was supporting the efforts of *EO Jongerendag*, an event of the evangelical broadcasting association of the Netherlands which held an annual, one-day youth outreach.[314] More important in the cooperative work related to the youth was the relationship of the ECV with the *Evangelisch Jeugdverbond* (EJV), an evangelical youth organization which served the whole of Flanders. So involved was the ECV with this cooperative work that it became one of the two largest groups represented as part of the EJV along with the original groups which founded the EJV in 1936—namely, the BEZ along with the churches of the BEZ and the VEG.[315]

In another area of cooperation, the ECV commonly sent out missionaries to work with evangelical groups outside the Brethren. For example, one Flemish couple with four children were sent out in 1991 as missionaries to Burkina Faso with Wycliffe Bible Translators. Their work was to run a center for the Wycliffe missionaries as opposed to being translators. This couple's work was applauded and well noted in the ECV newsletters and in letters sent by the Canadian missionaries to their supporters. As Haverkamp wrote, "It is great to see a family from Belgium go to another mission field."[316]

By 1995, the ECV cosponsored a one day family conference with the BEZ and the VEG. This conference was reported to have been the largest evangelical conference meeting in the history of Belgium.[317] Nearly 3,500 people attended. Teaching was provided by a speaker from the Netherlands and music by blind British singer Marilyn Baker.[318] Other cooperative works across the entirety of Flanders included involvement with Discipling a Whole Nation (DAWN), a worldwide organization which came to Flanders in 1998 with the goal of organizing efforts across the various evangelical

---

313. H. Gelling, "Broedervergadering in Houthalen," in personal diary: notebook covered with a blue and green geometric design and missing the back cover, entitled "Houthalen Christen Gemeente," 18 September 1982. Cf. the first page of this notebook for an undated list of individuals in contact with the Tear Fund.

314. H. Gelling, "Gemeente vergadering," 10 September 1982, in personal diary: notebook covered with a blue-black-white plaid design, labeled "Christen Gemeente van Lanaken."

315. Presentatie_ejv2006.ppt, a PowerPoint presentation linked to "Evangelisch Jeugdverbond: Wie zijn we?" Evangelisch Jeugdverbond, http://www.ejv.be/index.php?id=41.

316. R. Haverkamp, letter to MSC, 20 March 1991.

317. R. Haverkamp, letter to supporters, 11 October 1995.

318. R. Haverkamp, "Flanders Fields," letter to supporters, January 1997.

denominations to plant evangelical churches. Gelling was the representative from the ECV to this organization.

Over the years, young men and women from the ECV went to the BIB and later the ETF. In fact, for a number of years the ECV helped with the expenses of such an education for those men and women who were members of an ECV assembly.[319] Around a third of the religious education bachelor's degrees granted by the BIB were given to people from the ECV, a total of about fifty people.[320] Additionally, four or five men from the ECV went on for master's studies at the ETF and one for doctoral studies, though he has since left the ECV as a result of living too far away from any of the ECV assemblies.[321]

At the urging of Theo Le Jeune and De Kegel, the ECV became part of the *Evangelische Alliantie Vlaanderen* (EAV). Initially, the EAV had been an organization of which individuals could become a part, so Le Jeune encouraged De Kegel to join the EAV as he had done himself. After joining as individuals, Le Jeune and De Kegel helped to restructure the EAV such that it became an organization of evangelical church denominations and parachurch organizations. The organizational change was made for pragmatic reasons. "The change was made because, as individuals, we did not have substantial influence here in Belgium . . . We could do more as denominations."[322] Subsequently, De Kegel and Le Jeune were the catalyst for the ECV to become part of the EAV. De Kegel went as far as to become the president of the EAV from 1998–99.

A couple of years after the ECV formally became organized, the ECV became part of the *Federale Synode van Protestantse en Evangelische kerken in België* (FS), a national organization of evangelical churches which combined the EAV with the *Fédération Evangélique Francophone de Belgique*. Founded in 1998, the FS was the evangelical response to the older organization, the *Verenigde Protestantse Kerken van België* (VPKB), which was founded in 1978.[323] De Kegel's pragmatism and proclivity for organization once again was seen in the ECV's joining and in the formation of the FS as he was one of its founders.[324] By being a part of this national organization, the ECV could have a voice in governmental policy in religious matters to include

319. Schraepen, interview, 27 June 2007.

320. Boven, interview, 03 September 2008.

321. This man, Jelle Creemers, continued to maintain the ECV website, however, for a number of years after his departure.

322. De Kegel, interview, 13 August 2007.

323. Interdisiplinair Centrum voor Religiestudie en Interlevensbeschouwelijke Dialoog, "Het Protestantisme in België."

324. De Kegel, interview, 13 August 2007.

Ecclesiology of the Evangelische Christengemeenten Vlaanderen

religious education at all levels. De Kegel also was active in the negotiations which led ultimately to the recognition by the Belgian government of the evangelical organizations he had helped to form.

Ultimately, the ECV became part of a nationwide organization, an "administrative unity" of both the FS and the VPKB. This "historic decision" was made at a meeting on 9 November 2002. De Kegel noted, "This was the only way to get official recognition from the authorities. The government would not recognize evangelicals alone."[325] The purpose of this administrative unity was to insure that the evangelical churches of Flanders were not considered a sect by the government, a category which meant they could be asked to cease what they were doing. Even as late as 30 April 1997, the ECV was labeled a cult by a Belgian parliamentary study along with twenty other evangelical groups. The report was vigorously protested by the evangelical churches as well as by the Roman Catholic Church whose Opus Dei also was included on the list of cults. The publication of such a report gave an indication of the state's lack of understanding and their hostility to any churches or organizations outside the officially sanctioned governmental religious associations.[326] Further, by agreeing to the administrative unity of the FS and the VPKB, the evangelical groups, including the ECV, could be involved in all the services financed by the government such as "chaplains in prisons, the army, hospitals and retirement homes, broadcasting on radio and television, Protestant religious education, etc."[327] Thus, after years of discussions between the FS and the VPKB, the *Administratieve Raad van de Protestants-Evangelische Eredienst* (ARPEE) began its work in 1 January 2003.[328]

In 1999, the churches of the ECV, BEZ, and VEG made plans to have joint "regional training."[329] The topic chosen for the year 2000 was a discussion of how the church meets when it comes together. More significantly, the decision was taken at a meeting on 5 October 1999 to create long-term plans for a closer working relationship between the churches of the ECV, VEG, and BEZ. While it was noted that official decisions had to be taken by each of the three groups to make such a move possible, "clearly all want to go in that direction."[330] From this time forward, minutes of the official meetings of the BEZ, VEG, and ECV referred to a work group which involved all three organizations.

325. Ibid.
326. Fautré, "21 Evangelical Denominations Labeled as Cults in Belgium."
327. De Kegel, annual letter to the people of the ECV, 20 December 2002.
328. "Een nieuw christelijk orgaan," 8.
329. "Agenda Vlaamse raad maandag 8 november."
330. Lukasse, "Verslag ontmoeting tussen de V.E.G en B.E.Z te Brussel."

Eventually, overtures were made to combine the ECV with the VEG churches into one new denomination of some fifty churches. Three men were appointed to consider the theological implications of such a merger, and three others to consider the organizational consequences.[331] While some such as De Kegel and Jacque Rommel saw a great advantage for such a merger, other workers and leaders were less sure of the benefits, and some were resistant to such a move. Both Haverkamp and Gelling were not great supporters of the merger, but were willing to let the ECV move in the direction chosen by the national leaders. They continued with their commitment to the churches in Flanders being led by and directed by the Flemish believers in contradistinction to missionaries or other workers from outside.[332]

Perhaps one of the last evangelical groupings with which the ECV had a less-open working relationship would have been the churches and organizations related to Pentecostal Christianity. The record, though not clear, seems to be that a cessationist flavor was found in the early teachings of the ECV. Cessationism means that not all of the gifts of the Holy Spirit, and especially the so-called sign gifts, were active in modern times. Certainly this would have been the viewpoint of the Canadian Brethren at the time when Shindelka, Haverkamp, and Gelling came to Flanders as well as the prevailing viewpoint of the Dutch writers of the Reformed churches and the Brethren. Gelling specifically remembers hearing this viewpoint when he was a new believer at the assembly in Clinton, ON, though he recalled that it was the first teaching he really questioned as he compared what he heard with what he found in the Bible.[333] Nevertheless, whether Haverkamp, Gelling, or De Kegel was teaching in this area, cessationist ideas were present or at least perceived by the listeners. De Kegel noted that during his early years in the ECV, the books he encountered held almost exclusively to a cessationist viewpoint.[334] Nonetheless, Haverkamp said he never held to a cessationist position. He understood that the sign gifts of the Holy Spirit were more active in the Early Church because these were the foundational years. He said they distanced themselves a bit due to the extreme practices and beliefs of some among the Pentecostals.[335] He and other leaders in the ECV also were somewhat taken aback by their perception of the beliefs of the Pentecostal churches. The perception was that the Pentecostals thought they were somehow better. "They had the 'full gospel;' we only had a part

---

331. Schraepen, interview, 27 June 2007.
332. H. Gelling, telephone interview, 02 December 2008.
333. H. Gelling, telephone interview, 15 December 2008.
334. De Kegel, interview, 12 August 2007.
335. R. Haverkamp, telephone interview, 15 December 2008.

Ecclesiology of the Evangelische Christengemeenten Vlaanderen

of the gospel."[336] Further, the ECV thought that the Pentecostal churches put too much emphasis on the sign gifts and conflated the concept of the baptism of the Holy Spirit with the filling of the Holy Spirit. The baptism of the Holy Spirit was understood by the ECV as something that happened at the time of salvation to put a person into the body of Christ (1 Corinthians 12:12–13). The filling was something that could come any number of times, and Haverkamp understood this filling to be directly related to the level of surrender to God by the individual believer.[337] Nonetheless, even during the early years of less than an open attitude between the ECV and the Pentecostal churches, one Pentecostal believer admitted to Shindelka, "We have the Spirit, but you have the blessing."[338]

Another factor which caused the ECV to be wary of some parts of the Pentecostal churches in Flanders was the damage caused by people who championed the views and practices of what commonly was called "the Toronto-blessing."[339] Thirty to forty of the practitioners of this more radical part of the Charismatic Movement left the assembly at Ieper, also causing damage among those who remained. In one instance, a man stood up and asked for prayer for his wife, a woman who had an aggressive form of cancer. He was convinced that if the church would pray in faith along with him, his wife would be healed. When she died shortly afterward, the same man stood up and said that if the church had had faith, he could have prayed for her and she would have been healed. This caused a number of people great hurt as they felt responsible for this woman's death.[340]

Nevertheless, as the years passed, both the Pentecostal churches and the ECV moved toward one another in practice and beliefs. The more extreme views within the Pentecostal circles were moderated more and more from the perspective of the ECV. Additionally, people within the ECV came into contact with Pentecostal viewpoints of a less extreme nature through the reading of evangelical authors outside the Brethren as well as through contact with Pentecostal believers at the BIB. Further, people within the ECV came into contact with Pentecostal believers through joint efforts, such as a national prayer day and a joint evangelistic outreach.[341] When the *Verbond van Vlaamse Pinkstergemeenten* (VVP) became part of the

---

336. De Kegel, interview, 12 August 2007.

337. R. Haverkamp, telephone interview, 15 December 2008.

338. H. Gelling, telephone interview, 15 December 2008.

339. "Recipients [of the Toronto blessing] often begin to quiver, go limp, or fall. Others sob or laugh. Some lay in prolonged states of seeming ecstasy" (Maxwell, "Is Laughing for the Lord Holy?," 79).

340. H. Gelling, telephone interview, 15 December 2008.

341. De Kegel, interview, 12 August 2008.

EAV in 2002, representatives of the ECV then had regular contact with the Pentecostal churches. Together, they tried to further the cause of evangelical Christianity in Flanders.[342]

In contrast with the relationship of the ECV with other Christian groups in Flanders, less accommodating attitudes toward the Roman Catholic Church were seen by a number of comments and interactions throughout the decades under study. The founders and shapers of the ECV most certainly saw the Roman Catholic Church as a Christian group which was not conducting itself or holding beliefs according to the Bible. In particular, the evangelical gospel taught and propagated by the ECV was distinctly different from the soteriology espoused by the Roman Catholic church. This soteriology was not peculiar to the ECV, but was a mainstream evangelical view of the gospel held by groups both inside and outside of Flanders. The ECV taught an imputed grace by faith alone. This imputation was neither sacerdotal nor sacramental in nature. In contrast, Roman Catholic soteriology taught what could be termed an "infused grace," grace through faith via the sacraments properly administered by a priest.[343] Thus, evangelical groups such as the ECV would have understood the mechanism by which soteriology was effected in a very different fashion than the Roman Catholic Church would have. This difference was important enough that special evangelistic efforts noting the difference were made during the Pope's visit to Belgium in 1985.[344] The BEZ authored an eight-page evangelistic pamphlet and spearheaded efforts among the evangelical churches to have this paper distributed along with an invitation for follow-up if any reader was interested.[345] They challenged the evangelicals by writing:

> When the papal visit to Belgium takes place later this year everyone will be talking about it. People's spirits will begin to stir. All of this is a wonderful opportunity to proclaim the Gospel . . . *We must grasp this opportunity*. It is vital for the Christian to be a true witness; to be moved in love to speak and to point to the one and only Mediator and way of salvation. The great crowds who surround the Pope during his visit will not hear the simple proclamation of the way of life. What they most need to know will not be told them on this occasion. This is why it is the Christian's duty to do this—and this is exactly what we want to do.[346]

342. "VVP – Gemeenten sluiten zich aan bij EAV," 4.

343. *Code of Canon Law*, canons 840–42.

344. Lutz, "Evangelicals Give Out 1.2 Million Evangelistic Papers During Pope's visit to Belgium," 53–54.

345. "De Paus in België: een uitdaging," 16.

346. "Pausbezoek België," *Evangeliekoerier*, appendix. This article was in both

Ecclesiology of the Evangelische Christengemeenten Vlaanderen

In addition to soteriological differences, the ECV and Roman Catholic Church had major ecclesiological differences. The ECV held to the autonomy of the local church as a representation of the universal Church and an apostolic succession of doctrine. Membership in the Church—the body of Christ—is through conversion to the evangelical faith. The Roman Catholic Church, in contrast, understood the Church "as a society [which] subsists in the catholic Church, governed by the successor of Peter and the Bishops in communion with him," whose people became members through the sacrament of water baptism properly administered.[347] *Dominus Iesus*, as written by Cardinal Ratzinger, clearly states,

> The Christian faithful are therefore not permitted to imagine that the Church of Christ is nothing more than a collection—divided, yet in some way one—of Churches and ecclesial communities; nor are they free to hold that today the Church of Christ nowhere really exists, and must be considered only as a goal which all Churches and ecclesial communities must strive to reach.[348]

Hence, Volf could note of the Roman Catholics,

> Only those local fellowships "united to their pastors" [i.e., bishops] are, therefore, churches in the full sense of the word. This is why all other Christian fellowships . . . exhibit merely more or less significant ecclesial elements, but do not qualify as churches.[349]

When queried as to the status of "Christian Communities" born out of the Reformation, the *Congregatio Pro Doctrina Fidei* referenced both the documents of Vatican 2 and *Dominus Iesus*:

> According to Catholic doctrine, these Communities do not enjoy apostolic succession in the sacrament of Orders, and are, therefore, deprived of a constitutive element of the Church. These ecclesial Communities which, specifically because of the absence of the sacramental priesthood, have not preserved the genuine and integral substance of the Eucharistic Mystery cannot, according to Catholic doctrine, be called "Churches" in the proper sense.[350]

Dutch and English in the archives of the BEZ. The English translation above is the one found in the archives.

347. *Code of Canon Law*, canons 204, 849.

348. Ratzinger, "Declaration *Dominus Iesus* on the Unicity and Salvific Universality of Jesus Christ and the Church."

349. Volf, "Community Formation," 215. For a further elaboration, cf. Volf, *After Our Likeness*, 259–63.

350. Levada, "Responses to some Questions Regarding Certain Aspects of the

Thus, the Roman Catholic Church consistently held to its unicity. In the areas of soteriology and ecclesiology at the very least and certainly most importantly, the ECV and the Roman Catholic Church held decidedly different views. Accordingly, the goal of those within the ECV was to see Flemish Roman Catholics converted to evangelical Christianity.[351]

In the first decades, for example, Haverkamp used a direct, apologetic approach when confronting Catholic priests. He would say that he and the priest agreed that Matthew 16:18 was the most important verse in the Bible. Haverkamp noted, however, that he put his emphasis on the second part of the verse where the Lord Jesus speaks about the Church He will build, whereas the priest would put his emphasis on the first part concerning Peter, upon whom he thought the Church was built.[352] In another approach, Roman Catholic festivals, such as the annual 15 August Feast of the Assumption of the Blessed Virgin Mary, were viewed early in the history of the ECV and from then forward as particularly good opportunities to present an evangelical witness distinct from what the Roman Catholic Church would have believed.[353] Thus, just as the early Brethren in Flanders used these holidays as a time to hand out gospel tracts and books to any who might be interested, the various assemblies of the ECV would set up book stalls, send out drama and singing groups, or engage in other forms of street evangelism as a way to spread their evangelical faith.

Opposition to the doctrine of the Roman Catholic Church did not mean that the ECV displayed a hostility toward its people or even its priests. During a door-to-door evangelistic effort in Gellik in the early 1980s, Gelling came face to face with the local Roman Catholic priest. Gelling explained the evangelical gospel, and the priest asked if he would like to speak at his parish church. Gelling agreed, and the priest said to come back another time to set the appointment. Just after the new year began, Gelling returned and the priest noted that on only one Sunday per year was an outsider allowed to preach. When he offered Gelling the only possible slot, he was surprised that Gelling immediately agreed without even checking his agenda. Thus, at

---

Doctrine on the Church."

351. For an apologetic from a Roman Catholic perspective aimed especially at "Bible Christians," cf. Keating, *Catholicism and Fundamentalism: The Attack on "Romanism" by "Bible Christians."*

352. R. Haverkamp, "Wie der Herr Jesus Christus Gemeinden baut," session 1.

353. E.g.: Gerard, letter to Eric Rutten, 27 February 1988. In this letter, Gerard describes a 15 August "successful evangelistic outreach" at *De Scoutsrallye*, a park in Neerpelt. Author also notes a 15 August 2007 interview with Gelling at the close of which Gelling was headed to a nearby village to support the assembly's evangelism teams who were at the Feast of the Assumption of the Blessed Virgin Mary festival.

the Sunday eleven o'clock mass on the set date, Gelling spoke from 1 John 5:11–13 on the topic, "We can be sure [that] we can be saved." Hearing his Netherlands accent, the parishioners thought that a Dutch Protestant minister had spoken that morning.

As Gelling later looked back at this event, he noted two reasons why he accepted the invitation. First, he was given a "clean slate," he was allowed to preach anything he wanted. Second, he did not see this as something that would compromise his evangelical beliefs or set a bad example for the younger believers from the assembly. He had not taught anything different than he would have at an ECV church, nor had he served or partaken of the eucharist during the mass and thereby given some sort of affirmation to the Roman Catholic beliefs in this area. He likened this event to the examples of Peter and Paul in the book of Acts who were continually in the synagogues preaching the evangelical gospel.[354]

In contrast to this event, Gelling refused to speak at the Roman Catholic wedding of a young woman who had grown up in the ECV. This woman was to marry a Roman Catholic man, the wedding would be officiated by the local priest, and a mass would be held. Gelling not only opposed the marriage of the young woman to a man who would have been viewed as an unbeliever, he also did not want to participate in the ceremony and thus set a bad example for the any newer converts who might think that the ECV supported marriage to an unconverted person. He was both surprised and saddened to see young people marrying the unconverted as well as to see some younger couples who, though they claimed to be converted, left the ECV and began to attend the local Roman Catholic church.[355]

Opposition to the official teachings of the Roman Catholic Church never changed among the founders or the shapers of the ECV. Indeed, in the official pronouncements of the Roman Catholic Church as noted above, neither did the Roman Catholic Church change in its view toward the ECV as well as others outside the Roman Catholic Church. However, toward the beginning of the twenty-first century, some softening was seen between the local Roman Catholic parish churches and the ECV in Flanders. This softening of attitudes came from both groups. In the mid-seventies, in contrast, the senior priest in Peer wrote articles against the ECV after hearing of a funeral conducted in the home of one of the assembly's members. After a few articles were published, Haverkamp went to visit the priest, and the priest said he was glad that Haverkamp had found the gospel, but now he needed to find the Church. Haverkamp noted that by the twenty-first century,

---

354. H. Gelling, telephone interview, 04 January 2009.
355. Ibid.

however, he no longer preached against the Roman Catholic Church because their adherents really did not know what they believed any longer. The ECV often used the Roman Catholic chapels for funerals and weddings conducted by the ECV. Usually the parish priest was present, and the priest's response often was something like, "You people still believe," often through "tear-filled eyes." In fact, Haverkamp reflected that he believed that some evangelicals were to be found in the Roman Catholic Church by the early twenty-first century.[356]

In 2008, Haverkamp once again preached at a Roman Catholic wedding. He wanted to take advantage of this platform to preach the gospel freely. When questioned by a supporter from Canada whether he was marrying this couple, Haverkamp responded first that this couple was getting married and Haverkamp had no say in the matter. Second, he wanted to preach the gospel. "Why not?" he asked the supporter. The couple had asked him to speak, and the devoted Roman Catholic parents of the bride would be present in addition to many family and friends. Finally, Haverkamp was unsure if either the bride or the groom was a believer, but the bride wanted to come to the assembly as the groom was doing. Haverkamp did not want to create an obstacle and perhaps drive away this young lady. Overall, Haverkamp understood that the believers of the ECV supported his activities and saw this wedding ceremony and similar events as great opportunities for the gospel.[357]

The ECV looked for opportunities to build relationships with the local Roman Catholic leaders for the purpose of preaching the evangelical gospel in a Roman Catholic setting, yet the leaders still saw and maintained their soteriological and ecclesiological differences with the Roman Catholic Church. That said, some among the second generation of those who grew up in the ECV assemblies looked to closer cooperation between evangelicals and Roman Catholics in Flanders as the necessary path of the future. At least one teacher of Bible and theology who grew up in the ECV assemblies held that even soteriological issues separating Flemish evangelicals and Roman Catholics were too much overplayed by the ECV.[358]

---

356. R. Haverkamp, "Heikoops," email, 06 January 2009.

357. R. Haverkamp, telephone interview, 09 January 2009.

358. Creemers, interview, 06 September 2007; Creemers, discussions with author, 02–3 September 2008.

Ecclesiology of the Evangelische Christengemeenten Vlaanderen

ECCLESIOLOGICAL MODELING OF THE ECV

Given the actions and beliefs of the ECV, how might the four traditional marks of the essential Church look? How do the concepts of "one," "holy," "catholic," and "apostolic" apply to the work of the ECV in the decades under consideration?

From the planting of the first assemblies in the early 1970s, the founders of the ECV held to the primacy of the Lord's Supper as the identifying and unifying mark of the Church. As noted earlier, a local manifestation of the Church was not considered as having begun to function until the regular celebration of the Lord's Supper on a Sunday was in place.[359] In the weekly practice of this ordinance, the commitment to the oneness of the Church was evident. The ECV allowed any believer to partake of this central identifying ordinance, the Lord's Supper, the mark of unity in the Church.[360] This was a consistent practice which had gone unchanged from the earliest days to the present, and no evidence was seen of this practice being narrowed. While all were allowed to partake, some change was evident in allowing women to participate in much the same manner as the men in their expression of thanks for the person and work of Christ, through asking for a song to be sung, offering a prayer, or reading a portion of Scripture in the service at which the Lord's Supper was celebrated. Nonetheless, women had not been excluded previously from partaking, but merely from participating in the same manner as the men according to the traditional manner in which the weekly celebration of the Lord's Supper was conducted. Thus, the ECV demonstrated a balanced approach to the oneness of the Church throughout its history. Haverkamp, for example, never hesitated to recognize the one body of Christ, even when he may have differed from the emphases or practices of those who had undergone evangelical conversion.

Within the ECV, the practical aspects of holiness were emphasized as part of the preparation of the believer as he attempted to be part of the Lord's purpose to build His Church. Haverkamp, Thomas, and others repeatedly noted the importance of the "purity of walk" if the believer hoped to be used by God generally or filled by the Holy Spirit specifically. While the ECV emphasized this aspect of preparation significantly more than other contemporary evangelistic or church planting organizations among the Brethren, certainly this emphasis was not an exaggeration of a legitimately defensible position of Scripture related to matters of evangelism. Further, none of the leaders of the ECV would have propounded a practical

---

359. Cf. chapter 4, "The Centrality of the Lord's Supper."
360. Cf. chapter 4, "The Centrality of the Lord's Supper."

holiness akin to a Wesleyan or typically Pentecostal "complete sanctification." All that said, matters of personal holiness which related to preparation for evangelism and service were not ignored, either. Significant efforts both in teaching and counseling were made to help the members of the ECV live lives "pleasing to God." Gifford in particular identified and helped in areas related to marital relationships, as well as issues in the lives of youth, so that they could progress in their life of faith.[361] Similarly, Dryburgh worked with young women so that problems from their youth would not affect their Christian behavior as they matured.[362]

The practice of catholicity saw the greatest change over the life of the ECV. The first years of the ECV saw much less cooperation with evangelical groups throughout Flanders than what transpired toward the end of the twentieth century and into the twenty-first. Pragmatically, Haverkamp and Gelling were "too busy" to stop their work in order to enter into arrangements with other groups.[363] Nonetheless, as the number of ECV assemblies multiplied and the converts increased, the ECV had contact with these other groups. Initially, these contacts were welcomed if they were part of the narrowly focused goal of building the Church. Thus, the practice of benefiting from evangelistic outreach by OM rapidly became cooperating with these same campaigns. Certainly, cooperating with outreach associated with the Billy Graham crusades caused the ECV to be more in contact with and accepting of other evangelical works in Flanders with which they would have had some differences in theology and practice. In the move from organism to organization, the ECV practiced a greater catholicity since they formally joined together with other evangelical groups, first in the EJV and then in the EAV. In fact, a case might be made by some that the ECV became overly generous in their catholicity as they became part of the ARPEE since this group encompassed organizations whose membership included those who had not undergone evangelical conversion. However, this understanding of an overly generous catholicity only could be posited with the strictest of interpretations given the autonomy of the various groups which made up the whole of these organizations. Further, to practice such a strict view probably would have meant that the ECV would have needed to redefine holiness. To hold such a strict view, the ECV would have begun to look more like the Exclusive Brethren in practice.

A number of these memberships would have been for pragmatic reasons. Joining together in a council with the EAV and the ARPEE did

---

361. Cf. chapter 4, "The Emphasis on Pragmatic, Sound Teaching."
362. Cf. chapter 3, "Final New Assembly, Oost-Vlaanderen: Mariakerke."
363. Cf. chapter 4, "Interaction of the ECV with other Christian groups in Flanders."

not mean that the ECV approved all of the beliefs and practices of their partners. Certainly the pneumatological practices and beliefs among some of the churches of the VVP would not have been supported, nor would have the soteriology of the traditional Protestant churches of Flanders, nor would have some aspects of the ecclesiology of the VEG and the BEZ, both in its top-down control and the installation of an ordained minister in each local church. Ultimately, catholicity would have undergone the greatest change as compared with the other three marks of the Church. That said, at least the assembly which joined the ECV from the Flemish Open Brethren never really practiced this more expansive catholicity.

From the beginnings of the church planting up through the time of this writing, the churches of the ECV have been apostolic in nature. As seen in the commitment to pragmatic, sound teaching by many means and at many venues among the churches of the ECV, the importance of biblically based practices and beliefs was taught in the ECV. While certainly a criticism may be made by some concerning whether or not the ECV properly interpreted what they found in the Bible, such criticism should be absent when considering whether or not the ECV truly attempted to conduct itself according to the Bible. When the ECV did make decisions for pragmatic reasons, these would have been in areas where the Bible was silent or no prohibition reasonably could be found such as forming associations, creating schools, using music groups to attract people to a gospel presentation, and so forth.

In summary, even though they were not consciously seeking to balance the traditional four marks, the ECV does appear to have done so over time. The ECV continually recognized the oneness of the body of Christ; it stressed without overstressing the practical outworking of positional holiness; it developed a wider practical demonstration of catholicity; and, in keeping with other Conservative Protestant groups generally, the ECV was keen to emphasize conforming to apostolic doctrine.

# 5

Conclusions

This book has presented the story of new Brethren in Flanders. It has traced the origins and development of the *Evangelische Christengemeenten Vlaanderen* from 1971 to 2008. The ECV grew surprisingly rapidly initially, but then leveled off and developed in ways its founders might not have expected.

In the early days, the assemblies planted primarily by Haverkamp and Gelling were not organized in a denominational manner, even though these churches were very similar in nature. The common connections were the two missionaries themselves and the teaching and practices they propagated. Initially, these assemblies were the result of evangelistic Bible studies held in homes. As these home Bible studies grew in number and became local churches, however, the personal abilities and available time of the founding missionaries was limited, and organizational change was deemed necessary if this movement was to grow or even to continue without significant decline. De Kegel perceived this need and helped to organize this loose association into an organization formally recognized by the Belgian authorities, an organization that functioned in many ways like an official denomination. Subsequently, the gatherings of leaders from the various ECV assemblies took on the semblance of a Presbyterian synod, though the individual churches retained the right to withdraw from the ECV, and this assembly of representatives could not dictate on matters particular to a local church. This change was similar to the Disciples of Christ, another restorationist group founded in the US at the same time as the Brethren in early nineteenth-century Ireland and England. The Disciples of Christ did not adopt a Presbyterian pattern of organization until 1968, but they were

Conclusions

committed to the autonomy of the local church and other New Testament principles so the pattern is remarkable in its similarity to the Brethren.[1]

As the founders came to Flanders, they had a vision to plant churches consistent with the practices of the Open Brethren. They did not foresee either the explosive growth or the recognized denomination that these churches would become. Further, they did not envision a need for a Flanders-wide organization. They instead thought that these newly planted assemblies would be very autonomous and would relate to one another in a family-of-churches fashion. This is quite distinct from what they became: an official, government-recognized organization with by-laws, written long-range plans, and a written statement of faith. They became a new type of Brethren in Flanders.

POSSIBLE REASONS FOR THE RESULTS

While the founders of the ECV envisioned the planting of Brethren assemblies, or what they viewed as "New Testament churches," all over Flanders, none of the founders had any vision to create a new denomination, and none foresaw the explosive growth. Still, the work of the founders and the shapers resulted in the creation of a family of twenty-eight assemblies in Flanders, one in the Roman Catholic province of Limburg in Netherlands, and "three" for a time among the Flemish soldiers stationed in Germany. While this growth of assemblies from 1972 through 1991 was remarkable in nature, a number of factors can be observed which suggest that this type of growth and the subsequent sudden stop of growth should not be viewed as surprising. At least five reasons exist for the way in which the ECV came to be and subsequently developed.

Timing of the Founding and Shaping of the ECV

The founders and shapers of the ECV did their work at a unique time in the modern religious and social history of Flanders. The timing of the founding and shaping of the ECV was such that the explosive growth is not unexpected when viewed through the lens of history. Additionally, comparable rapid growth was evident among similar evangelical groups in Flanders during the same era, such that all had a "season of revival." Certainly this was the view of Haverkamp:

---

1. Mead, "Christian Church (Disciples of Christ)," 75–77.

New Brethren in Flanders

> I have found from my own study of history and from my own personal experience that God works in different areas and in different moments. We saw twenty years ago a real movement in Belgium. Every week, almost every day people were converted. For several years we had a baptism every month with thirty or thirty-five people. I went day and night. I couldn't keep up with these studies and these services, but it's not that way now ... When I was a young man in Canada I prayed very much for revival. We prayed day and night and no revival came. When I came to Belgium, revival came.[2]

The evangelical, free church groups in Flanders during the years under consideration experienced an explosive growth in the numbers of new converts as well as the local churches which ensued. For example, 1944 was the last time the BEZ/VEG planted a church in Flanders prior to 1972 according to records in the BEZ/VEG archives. From 1919 through 1944, the method of church planting was through the work of colporteurs, tent meetings, and open air evangelism.[3] The total number of churches planted during those twenty-five years was fifteen or sixteen, nine of which were planted during the 1920s. While the BEZ records differ from the VEG records by one church, both accountings maintain the gap between 1944 until 1972.[4] From 1972 to 1988, however, thirty new churches were planted. Interestingly, the same records do not reflect any similar thirty-year gap with no new churches planted in either Wallonia or Brussels, nor do they show a similar explosive growth in those regions during the 1970s and 1980s. However, the fastest growing, French-speaking African immigrant church in Brussels did form an administrative association with the BEZ in 1987. This church, which began in 1984 and formally organized on 20 October 1985, formed this administrative union with the BEZ to have "institutional coverage" in the eyes of the Belgian government.[5]

In the same years, the Flemish Pentecostal churches also saw explosive growth. Before 1971, one academic study noted that Flanders had twenty-one churches associated with some kind of Pentecostal gathering; these were categorized in ten identifiable groupings.[6] Using the same identified groupings, the Pentecostal gatherings numbered fifty-six by 1990.[7] Addi-

2. R. Haverkamp, "Wie der Herr Jesus Christus Gemeinden baut," session 3.

3. Lukasse, "Een lijst van posten en gemeenten gesticht door de B.E.Z."

4. Cf. Lukasse's list of fifteen to the sixteen in "File: POST GEMLYST 2; Report: BEZ-overzicht."

5. Way-Way, "The African Christian diaspora in Belgium," 453.

6. Demaerel, "Tachtig jaar pinksterbeweging in Vlaanderen (1909–1989)," 3–8.

7. Ibid., 374.

tionally, the number of Pentecostal devotees had grown by three hundred percent during the same nearly twenty years.[8]

During the same timeframe, no similar growth happened among the Flemish or Wallonian churches associated with the VPKB because they had "no vision for church planting [and] their problem [was] one of decline of membership."[9] Additionally, a serious and accelerating decline was evident in the number of practicing Roman Catholics.[10] As an American priest observed while visiting Antwerpen in the early 1990s, "Antwerp is a city of half a million in a country estimated to be 90 percent Catholic. It bills itself as the 'city of monumental churches.' Its tourist literature, however, does not add that most of them are empty."[11] Similarly, even official Roman Catholic publications noted the paucity of Roman Catholic communicants and priests as well as the hostility toward the Pope himself among Belgians during the Pope's 1995 visit to Belgium. One observer quoted in a Roman Catholic periodical said,

> The fact that the pope will spend less than 48 hours in one of the church's traditionally most loyal and most Catholic nations appears hard to understand, given the warm welcome he received in 1985. At best he's expected to draw 10,000 faithful—out of a population of 9 million Catholics.[12]

The same article then observes, "The clerical model of church in Belgium is fading fast. The average priest is 63, and hundreds of parishes are without a priest."[13] Islam was the only other religious group in Flanders which showed a noteworthy increase in practitioners at the end of the twentieth century. The reason for its increase, however, was due to increased immigration from countries in which Islam was the predominant religion.[14]

Sociological studies from a number of sources note that the time period from the early 1970s until the turn of the twenty-first century marked a paradigm change from modernism to postmodernism. In fact, at least one relatively recent academic study examining the evangelical movement in Flanders and the Netherlands chose the years 1972 to 2002 for examination because of this paradigm change. This study notes that, while

---

8. Ibid., 376.
9. Bos, "Church Planting in Flanders," 12.
10. Cf. chapter 2, "General Religious Milieu."
11. Gilhooley, "The Church in the Low Countries," 430.
12. Lefevere, "Pope to face disgruntled laity in Belgium," 13.
13. Ibid.
14. Kanmaz, "The Recognition and Institutionalization of Islam in Belgium," 100.

these three decades had no unique name in particular, it was a time of significant change.[15] A major part of the sociological change was the rapidly diminishing influence of the Roman Catholic Church in Flanders as well as a concurrent rise in secularization.[16] Additionally, "the conjunction of two phenomena—secularization and individualization—probably were [sic] amplified by the bursting of the traditional social categories."[17] Luc de Fleurquin, a Roman Catholic professor of canon law in Belgium, said that "he feared much more the 'indifference and secularization without limit' that is buffeting Belgian society" than he did the changes within the Roman Catholic Church as it attempted to stay relevant.[18]

Studies sponsored by the European Values Study Foundation (EVSF) confirmed what people sensed: secularism was on the rise and Roman Catholicism was on the decline. Belgium saw respondents' self-identification as "not a religious person" rise from 11.3 percent in 1981 to 24.5 percent by 1999. Convinced atheists were 4.3 percent in 1981 and 7 percent by 1999. Respondents who stated that God was "not at all important" in their lives rose from 9.6 percent in 1981 to 22.2 percent in 1999—nearly a 250 percent increase. As noted in chapter 2, Roman Catholicism was in decline according to a measurement of Roman Catholic practices.

The EVSF also noted the same decline using self-identification. In 1981, 71.7 percent of respondents stated Roman Catholicism as their religion, but by 1999 this had dropped to 56.9 percent. Interestingly, people identifying themselves as free church or non-denominational actually increased from 0.3 percent in 1981 to 1.1 percent by 1999. Belief in no God rose from 11.7 percent in 1981 to 27 percent by 1999.[19] In another study comparing confidence in "the church" for the years 1981 and 1990, affirmative responses dropped from 60 percent to 49 percent.[20] These surveys were in line with the larger picture noted by sociological studies cited earlier, the change sensed by Roman Catholics and evangelicals alike, and contemporary stories in the popular media.[21]

---

15. Boersema, "De Evangelische Beweking in de Samenleving," 137.

16. This is not an isolated phenomenon, but readily seen in studies of other Roman Catholic countries such as Brazil, Chile, and Guatemala. Cf. Ruby, *Spirit and Power*, 72–77.

17. Voyé et al., *Belges Hereux et Satisfaits*, 228.

18. Lefevere, "Pope to face disgruntled laity in Belgium," 13.

19. "European and World Values Surveys Four Wave Integrated Data File, 1981–2004, v.20060423."

20. Voyé et al., *Belges Hereux et Satisfaits*, 202.

21. Cf. Knox, "Religion Takes a back seat in Western Europe." While written at the popular level, this article uses statistics from both the Center for the Study of Global

Conclusions

In a similar vein, Haverkamp noted that people were interested in religion when the founders of the ECV arrived in the early 1970s. As he looked back at the beginning of the twenty-first century, though, Haverkamp noted,

> Twenty years ago when I would start a home Bible study with ten people, the next week would be twelve, and the next fifteen, and then twenty and twenty-five, and it would keep growing. People would bring relatives and friends. Six months ago I began a Bible study with about fourteen. The next week was twelve, and then ten, and now only six. I am doing exactly the same thing, but something strange is going on. Thirty years ago people were open for the truth, especially the Roman Catholics. They were always told "we are the unchanging Church." But in the last fifty years the Roman Catholic Church has changed so much that people don't know what to believe any more. So we came with the Bible, we came with the truth, and they were open for it. But today, people are not interested in truth.[22]

Looking back after two decades in Belgium, Gifford also noted a lack of interest and a change in attitudes. He observed,

> Where there was an openness for the Gospel twenty years ago, there is an overwhelming apathy today. Belgium, a formerly Catholic country has thrown religion overboard and lives in the illusion of self-sufficiency— "I have everything I need. I don't need God."[23]

For Gifford, one of the most obvious examples of this change was the increase in the number of television stations. He realized that this increase may have been minor in the larger scheme, but all kinds of entertainment took up the potential converts' time. "When we came to Belgium, there were three stations, and now there are thirty-three. I remember talking to one man who said, 'Who needs God? We have VTM?'"[24]

In an interview at the beginning of the twenty-first century, the head of the BEZ also noted a similar phenomenon in his work. He said that people had become uninterested in "eternal things:"

> [for] people today, religion has to be relevant in the social impact, whereas in the eighties, religion was relevant in the gospel.

Christianity and the World Values Survey Association.

22. R. Haverkamp, "Wie der Herr Jesus Christus Gemeinden baut," session 1.

23. P. and J. Gifford, letter to supporters, May 2005.

24. P. Gifford, interview, 25 August 2003. VTM is the commercial television station *Vlaamse Televisie Maatschappij*.

> And in the seventies, too. Religion was relevant because of the gospel, because of eternity, because of the message ... You want to bring them to the message, but they have no [felt] need for that message. Their [felt] need is on a different level ... Today if I tell someone they are going to hell, they say, "So what?"[25]

Further, he noted that the two diagnostic questions of Evangelism Explosion, for example, no longer were methodologically relevant by the last decade of the twentieth century.[26] Interestingly, Evangelism Explosion noted the same change and altered their purpose statement in the 1990s to say that their program was for "equipping churches for friendship, evangelism, discipleship and healthy growth." Previously, friendship was not one of the goals. Additionally, the chapter on "friendship and relational evangelism" was moved from the end of their textbook to the second chapter.[27] In one response to these perceived societal changes, the BEZ moved to an issues-related approach in their evangelistic literature. This included printing tracts referencing popular culture, such as the movie *The Passion of the Christ*, or tracts dealing with controversial current events, such as the legalization of euthanasia.[28] Nonetheless, even with the new methods, the BEZ did not see significant growth any more than did the ECV with its continued employment of the *Startstudies* such as it used in its founding decades.

Even church planting groups such as Discipling a Whole Nation (DAWN) saw no results in the late 1990s when they spearheaded efforts to begin a new round of church planting in Flanders. DAWN called for a "prayer offensive for Flanders," forty days of prayer preceding "a church planting congress for church leaders" of the evangelical churches at which they would set goals for church planting.[29] The purpose of the meeting was to coordinate efforts and to state how many new churches each group would attempt to plant by 2015. Their organizing purpose to plant churches was based on twelve clearly stated principles; DAWN was a group that carefully but determinedly aimed to plant churches, and they would thoroughly research an area before proceeding with their work.[30] Thus, DAWN

---

25. Goossens, interview, 14 November 2006.

26. Those two questions were, "Do you know for sure that you are going to be with God in Heaven?," and "If God were to ask you 'Why should I let you into My Heaven?,' what would you say?"

27. Lawton, "Evangelism Explosion Retools Its Approach," 58.

28. Goossens, interview, 14 November 2006.

29. Godert, email to evangelical church leaders in Flanders, 24 March 1998.

30. Scholman and Walsmeer, "DAWN 2015," 10–11. For a summary of the number, locations, and points of contact for the Protestant churches in Flanders in 1998, cf. Appendix 1 on pages 351ff of Scholman and Walsmeer's work as well as Appendix 2 on

thoroughly analyzed Flanders, presented the facts of their sociological and religious research, and then asked the participants to respond with church planting goals based upon this information. The binder containing this 368-page analysis plainly asked on its title page, "How many churches are in Flanders? How many could there be?"[31] One eyewitness to the meeting of 4 April 1998 said that the Pentecostals aimed for 160 new churches; the BEZ 35; the VEG for 50; and Haverkamp, as he represented the ECV, said, "None. We hope to keep what we have."[32] Gelling's simple response at that same meeting was, "Well, brothers, if it is going to pour showers in your families, then I am sure God will drop some drops here."[33] Haverkamp's and Gelling's comments were neither pessimistic nor obstructionist responses, but a realization that the religious and social milieu in Flanders had undergone a transformation. Further, Haverkamp and Gelling wanted to strengthen the existing ECV assemblies by seeing them grow to at least eighty adults.[34] Interestingly, Haverkamp and Gelling were correct in their understanding of the times. The ECV did not plant any new churches, nor did any of the other groups present. All of the evangelical groups struggled to keep the churches they already had planted. That said, the ECV continued via a variety of methods to look for contacts which could be gathered into a new *Startstudies*.

The lack of interest among the listeners was not limited to the unconverted, however. Haverkamp again noted that in the early years of the founding of the ECV assemblies, believers would come to two or three Bible studies a week; this was not true by the end of the 1990s and beyond. As Haverkamp said, "It's like Christians are coming to a smorgasbord and pick here and there. And what suits them, they believe."[35] Sociologists noted the same phenomenon, labeling it *religion á la carte* or *bricolage*, and they associated this with the change to a postmodern paradigm.[36] Additionally, as the newly converted believers matured, their faith became merely one part of their life rather than the all-encompassing center around which all other aspects of life orbited. This is not to say that their conversion meant less or that they were not committed to their faith. It does suggest, however, that the believers moved toward the typically Western view of faith as a

---

page 367, which set DAWN's priorities based upon the number of churches per capita.

31. Scholman and Walsmeer, "DAWN 2015," 1.
32. Lukasse, interview, 05 December 2003. Cf. van der Woude, "DAWN Flanders."
33. H. Gelling, interview, 01 May 2003.
34. van der Woude, "DAWN Flanders."
35. R. Haverkamp, "Wie der Herr Jesus Christus Gemeinden baut," session 1.
36. Dobbelaere and Voyé, "From Pillar to Postmodernity," S4.

small slice of the wheel of life, rather than the hub by which all the spokes were held together.

Thus, the founding and growth of the ECV happened in a time during which all the leading evangelical, free church groups in Flanders grew, and grew at a rapid pace. These same groups all ceased to grow significantly in numbers of new converts and new local churches by the first few years of the 1990s. Neither changes of technique nor the number of personnel working at the task made a difference. Additionally, Haverkamp noted a difference in his own sense of burden for Belgium.

Before coming to Flanders in the early 1970s, he would pray by the hour with another Canadian believer; they would "pray and weep for the needs of Belgium." Many decades later, he was equally concerned, enthusiastic about, and committed to evangelism for the purpose of church planting, but he felt that the times were now different. The situation was different; the urgency was no longer there.[37] Hence, a case can be made that the growth of the ECV was part of a revival—a pneumatological reason for both the beginning and the end of the numbers of evangelical conversions and the amazing years of church planting throughout Flanders. Certainly this was the perspective of the founders and shapers of the ECV; they looked to God as the cause of any success they had seen. As Haverkamp said, "God has to be in it, and God's timing is important."[38]

That said, history records the work of men and women as the revival takes place. What was significant about the workers and works of the ECV during the last decades of the twentieth century?

Character and Gifts of the Founders and Shapers

All of the founders of the ECV were gifted evangelists. They had both the necessary ability and the great desire to communicate the message of the evangelical faith. In fact, this desire to communicate this message for the purpose of conversion with a goal of church planting animated the actions and attitudes of Haverkamp and Gelling. Both were gifted evangelists and endowed with an entrepreneurial character. Both had proven records of starting various enterprises in Canada before coming to Flanders both in the field of business and associated with local church. Additionally, both were hard working, wanting to make the most of every available hour. For example, Beryl Gelling noted that her husband initially worked twelve-hour days, seven days a week because he felt responsible to those who were

---

37. R. Haverkamp, interview, 06 January 2009.
38. R. Haverkamp, "Wie der Herr Jesus Christus Gemeinden baut," session 3.

supporting the work financially.³⁹ As Gelling himself said after nearly three decades of ministry in Flanders, "I have a Calvinistic upbringing, and we have a work ethic. If I stop and read a book, I feel guilty . . . I still struggle that I don't do enough."⁴⁰ Haverkamp's schedule was just as intense, if not more, since he also traveled long distances within Flanders and accepted invitations to speak at conferences outside of Belgium. Both men thus combined skills and gifts with a consistently hard-working manner of conduct.

Nonetheless, neither was hoping to create a denomination or any other sort of association. Organization was informal and done only as the situation necessitated. In the early years, this meant that each man merely made sure that he physically could make it to the many appointments to which he had committed. Haverkamp and Gelling did not coordinate their activities with one another in a formal manner, and Gelling noted that he did not even see very much of Haverkamp after the first eighteen months because they lived at opposites ends of Flanders.⁴¹ When den Boer became a full-time worker, some regular coordination began between him and Gelling. This coordination included Symons as well once he became a full-time worker.⁴² Nevertheless, this rise of coordination was again more of a pragmatic necessity than a pre-planned activity which was part of some overarching scheme when the churches were planted. Also, these three formally did not coordinate their activities in Limburg with Haverkamp's efforts elsewhere in Flanders. Formal organization and written statements of faith neither were desirable nor needed in the opinion of the founders. The "Bible alone" provided both the content of the evangelical faith as well as the subsequent conduct when this faith was practiced individually and in the local church.⁴³ Their focus was singular, and that was both a strength and, in the opinion of some, a weakness. One long-time church planter in Flanders noted,

> Richard Haverkamp is extremely gifted in a narrow stretch. So when he went out to other groups to say how to church plant, he projected his gifts as the way to do it. The typical Haverkamp style is a lot of enthusiasm—and overpowering—using Scripture, of course. He knows his Bible very well . . . The problem is that people are so inspired while he is there and think, "This is

39. B. Gelling, interview, 15 August 2007.
40. H. Gelling, interview, 01 May 2003.
41. H. Gelling, telephone conversation, 12 January 2009.
42. Cf. chapter 4, "Phase One: Loose Association."
43. H. Gelling, interview, 24 April 2003.

going to work!" A month later they realize it is not going to work because I am not as [gifted].[44]

Clearly, audio recordings of Haverkamp's lectures demonstrate an enthusiastic presentation, both in his manner and by his own statements about his work. Equally clear is his constant, singular focus on evangelism for the purpose of church planting. The criticism that he "projected his gifts," however, may be overstated on the whole. Rather than projecting his gifts as such, Haverkamp was communicating his vision, a vision based upon his understanding that the believer is responsible to help build the Church of Jesus Christ. His personality as well as his unshakable conviction made the presentation of his vision strong and dynamic. Haverkamp did not have a goal as a mere motivator, but as one who was committed to the task of the believer as he understood it. He thus taught what he saw as a vital truth for the listening believers to know and to apply. For him personally, this was an apostolic task whose success was left to the work of the Spirit of God. One elder from Haverkamp's commending assembly highlighted this aspect of Haverkamp when he said, "I've known few men that, for thirty or forty years, the fires are still burning . . . But his enthusiasm, convictions have not changed. His theology has not wavered." Going on to appraise the work of Haverkamp overall, he summarized by saying, "He goes to the top of the list."[45]

De Kegel's addition as a full-timer brought a decidedly different, though usually complementary perspective and set of gifts to the mix. He observed the need for coordinated efforts among the workers, the local churches, and indeed the evangelical churches of Flanders and the whole of Belgium. If the founders had gifts and a vision for evangelism for the purpose of church planting, De Kegel had gifts and a vision for administration and teaching for the purpose of nurturing and strengthening the churches that had been planted. De Kegel believed that the chances were better for the survival and growth of the evangelical churches if both the organization and collaboration were strong among the assemblies of the ECV, as well as between the evangelical groups within Flanders. Additionally, he posited that a larger, better organized evangelical group would have a greater voice in the political decisions that would affect its work than would a number of isolated, smaller groups. The resultant effect was the steady movement of the ECV from a loose association of likeminded churches to the establishment of a government-recognized organization, one that worked in concert with other evangelical groups in Flanders, as well as in administrative activities with the other historically Protestant

---

44. Lukasse, interview, 05 December 2003.
45. Former elders of Wallenstein Bible Chapel, interview, 01 September 2006.

groups in Belgium. One of the benefits and reasons accompanying these changes was that the ECV would have an easier time purchasing a building or a piece of land or repairing one of its buildings once it was recognized.[46] Specifically, this meant that the ECV could apply to the local city government to have its property treated in the same way that the local Roman Catholic churches had been treated for generations.[47]

The organizational changes begun and shepherded by De Kegel also had the effect of changing the identity of these assemblies in the eyes of outsiders from "the Haverkamp churches" to an organization named the ECV. By the time the ECV formally was organized as a government-recognized denomination, many if not most outsiders had ceased to refer to these assemblies as "the Haverkamp churches."[48] While Haverkamp remained as one of the chief figures within the ECV, the structure and cooperative works were such that he was no longer the only face known to those outside the ECV. More often, De Kegel was the point of contact in wider Christian circles, as is seen in his role on a number of interdenominational boards. In addition, Anastasi or Julie Gelling, for example, were liaisons along with Haverkamp and Gelling for cooperative works with other evangelical organizations. Thus, no one person remained as the sole identity of these assemblies.

De Kegel was more than an administrator, however; his vision was much more than merely organizing the ECV. He combined his organizational goals with a ministry focus as a Bible teacher as distinct from an evangelist. He wanted to do all he could to ensure that the new believers were well-versed in the evangelical faith to which they had been converted. This theme of creating biblically literate believers was readily evident, both in his personal ministry and as a member of a number of significant, interdenominational boards associated with the various Flemish evangelical groups. He saw a need for solid, biblical teaching within all the Flemish evangelical groups. Hence, his written records of preaching and teaching demonstrate a combination of presenting basic Bible knowledge with specific efforts to create a biblical foundation to treat the needs he perceived among the listeners. Further, he was active organizing and presenting at various cooperative times of systematic teaching. These ranged from annual conferences, to schools aimed primarily at the non-specialist, to places such as *Evangelische Theologische Faculteit* whose primary target was those

46. H. Gelling, interview, 04 January 2009.

47. Haeck, "Aanvraag tot erkenning van een protestantse kerk te Houthalen-Helchteren."

48. Minutes of meetings held by the BEZ and VEG, for example, no longer referred to these assemblies as "the Haverkamp churches."

interested in some form of vocational Christian work. His teaching was not merely the transmission of information, however, as his only published books were aimed more at the pastoral needs of the readers.[49] De Kegel's influence on the character of the ECV really cannot be overstated. Though different in his skills and personality from Haverkamp or Gelling, he nonetheless left his stamp on the ECV.

Other personnel who became the full-time workers after De Kegel's addition also were mostly those with gifts primarily other than evangelism. Workers such as Gifford and Symons, and later Dryburgh, concentrated primarily on pastoral ministries such as counseling and encouragement as they led Bible studies or ministered to the people within the ECV. Gifford, Anastasi, and Julie Gelling also had a driving motivation to see effective youth work associated with the ECV and, indeed, the whole of Flanders. They were convinced that one of the best ways to ensure the healthy growth and continuance of the ECV was to deal with issues in the life of young men and women so that these problems did not later become part of their adult life.[50] As with the founders, these later workers also worked long hours. They used what they understood to be God-given gifts to help build up the converts and relatively immature believers which composed the dozens of churches associated with the ECV.

Methods and Techniques

Methodologically, the rapid planting of churches was the result of the singular focus of the founders on forming and leading evangelistic, home Bible studies composed of the interested people of whom they were made aware. In contrast with an academic or sociological study of a region to ascertain where to plant a church, the founders simply followed up on as many contacts as health and time permitted, contacts from a variety of sources. Gelling noted that unlike some of the other organizations in Flanders, neither he nor Haverkamp would pray over a map as they pondered where to plant a church.[51] This did not mean that the founders of the ECV did not pray; it simply meant that as they planted the assemblies in Flanders, they did their work as it happened and prayed continually "for God's strength and blessing."

---

49. Cf. chapter 4, "The Emphasis on Pragmatic, Sound Teaching Throughout the ECV."

50. P. Gifford, interview, 25 August 2003.

51. H. Gelling, interview, 01 May 2003.

Conclusions

Accordingly, one of the chief avenues by which a new home study was founded was through a contact of a friend or family member of someone associated with an ECV assembly or one of the *Startstudies*. This is in contrast to targeting a specific area after a series of planning meetings. Haverkamp said, "We never go to a place and say we are going to start a church there. Almost all the churches are started because we already have some people living in those places, or for some reason we feel very definitely that God is leading us."[52] Nonetheless, the founders, later workers, and people of the ECV assemblies also did a prodigious amount of door-to-door work in order to create contacts. Again, however, the choice of areas for the efforts was for pragmatic reasons such as in the locale of an existing work or because a handful of contacts already had been made in an area. These pragmatic reasons can be seen in the announcements of the *Nieuwsbrief*. Thus, the popular church growth techniques favored in many circles at the end of the twentieth century were not employed, techniques predicated on carefully researched targets based on factors such as age, social standing, education, and so forth.[53] For example, the nucleus of the assembly in Gentbrugge was a motorcycle club.[54] This had the effect of a somewhat homogenous group, at least in the initial stages of the church plant. The motorcycle club, however, was not a planned target group. This assembly was the result of an initial contact, and then the introduction of one of the founders of the ECV to the personal friends and family of this contact—friends and family who had an interest in motorcycles, as it turned out.

A speaker at the International Brethren Conference on Mission 4 (ICBM 4), a 2007 worldwide gathering of Brethren, compared and contrasted his experience of successful church planting in Nairobi, Kenya, with that of a visitor from America. Oscar Muriu related the observation of a man from the United States who had come to see what was different about the work of Nairobi Bible Chapel. This visitor hoped to learn why this assembly had experienced such explosive growth. When asked what he had learned, the visitor replied to Muriu,

> "There is something different about the way you Africans do ministry," and he gave us the example of someone shooting a rifle and the three steps you take when firing a rifle. "The first

---

52. R. Haverkamp, "Wie der Herr Jesus Christus Gemeinden baut," session 3.

53. E.g., Hesselgrave, "Selecting Target Areas," in *Planting Churches Cross-Culturally*, 62ff, outlines a necessary seven-part study before a church plant should be attempted. The opening of this chapter states, "Before we can get on with the task, we must decide on definite areas and peoples that will become the foci of our immediate attention and labors" (Hesselgrave, "Selecting Target Areas," in *Planting Churches Cross-Culturally*, 62).

54. P. and J. Gifford, conversations with author, 20 August 2008.

is ready, the next is aim, and then fire. You know, in America we say 'Ready. Aim. Aim. Aim. Aim. Aim . . .' and we never fire. You Africans take the gun, 'Ready—fire!' and then look to see if you hit anything."[55]

The ECV in its years of rapid growth looked much more like what Muriu described–fire and see what you hit rather than continually aiming—and it had the same remarkable growth as did Muriu's group in Kenya. Accordingly, widely divergent methods were employed to generate interested people to form new *Startstudies*. Over the years, door-to-door interviews, literature distribution, festivals, open air preaching, drama, film, music, assembly anniversary celebrations, and so forth were employed to find people with whom a home Bible study could be conducted.

Overall Vision

Clearly, the goal of the founders of the ECV was church planting, not merely evangelism, and certainly their goal was not the planting of Brethren assemblies such as had been present in Flanders previously. In a spirit more akin to the founders of the Brethren in the early nineteenth century, the founders of the ECV sought to plant churches based simply on New Testament principles as opposed to Brethren traditions. Where these two worlds overlapped, the traditions were kept. Where they differed, the ECV felt free to follow another course of action.

The ECV was not alone in adopting this attitude, as seen in the writings of Vision Ministries Canada (VMC), a church planting ministry and formal association of churches among the Canadian Open Brethren whose work was contemporaneous with that of the ECV. A 2004 paper by the president of VMC, Gord Martin, noted that modern Brethren churches struggled in six areas: 1) the style and centrality of the Lord's Supper; 2) the role of women in the local church; 3) leadership, decision making processes, governance and pastoral rules; 4) the influence of Brethren history on present behavior; 5) the identity of a local Brethren assembly in answering the question, "What kind of church are you?"; and 6) the level of autonomy and interdependence between Brethren assemblies.[56] These questions were significant as Haverkamp's commending assembly, Wallenstein Bible Chapel, became part of the VMC association of churches. While many of the ECV churches would have had more "liberal" practices than Wallenstein, Wal-

---

55. Muriu, "Let My People Go, Acts 2:42–47."
56. Martin, "What does it mean to be Brethren in a VMC World?"

lenstein followed much the same path as the ECV churches in its approach to ministry. The primary difference between Wallenstein and the ECV assemblies was that Haverkamp and the other founders started new churches. As a result, any changes from traditional Brethren practices could come more quickly than they could at Wallenstein. Nevertheless, both the ECV churches in Belgium and Wallenstein in Canada committed themselves to what they understood as being New Testament churches first, as opposed merely to being identified among the Brethren. This commitment to practices drawn from the New Testament was consistent with the nineteenth century founders of the Brethren.

Another driving force in the vision of the ECV was the consistent faith of the founders of the ECV with respect to their purpose for being in Flanders. The founders of the ECV believed that church planting was a supremely important task and was what God wanted of them.[57] "The Church is like the Jews in the Old Testament; it is like Jerusalem; it is the city of God. Nehemiah left his position to rebuild the city of God. Building the Church is the most important job on earth."[58] While they may not have expected the rapid forming and growth of assemblies in Flanders, they did believe that God would use them to plant churches "all over Flanders." The surprise to their vision would have come with the explosive growth and the organization which later formed. Nevertheless, after more than thirty years of work in Flanders, both Haverkamp and Gelling maintained their singular focus on evangelism for the purpose of church planting as the primary reason for which they believed God called them to Flanders. Their work was as the result of a deep-seated evangelical faith as well as their understanding of the biblical purpose of the evangelical Christian to build the Church of Jesus Christ. Hence, organization was done for pragmatic reasons of furthering this singular purpose, and other reasons for organization were greeted with less enthusiasm by the founders and, at times, even opposed.

The ECV saw obstacles to the church-building task as "Satan's attack" and any success as "God's blessing." An example of this thinking was seen in Haverkamp's story of his auto accident in Canada as he was on the way to see the people and elders of Wallenstein Bible Chapel to announce his decision to go to Belgium. As noted earlier, both the accident and the preservation of Haverkamp and his wife were understood as God's confirming hand on their call to Europe, as well as a message from Satan. "This was an absolute miracle. We felt as if the devil was trying to say, 'If you want to announce

---

57. This conviction that one is doing what God wants him to do has been noted as the "common dynamic" in contemporary articles examining other successful works. Cf. Minnery, "Success in Three Churches: Diversity and Originality," 65.

58. R. Haverkamp, "Wie der Herr Jesus Christus Gemeinden baut," session 1.

this, I am going to give you something.'"[59] This viewpoint of a struggle with Satan also was held by supporters and members of the ECV. In the aftermath of Shindelka's necessary departure from full-time Christian service, a supporter noted the need for people to pray "especially for those in the forefront of Satan's attack," meaning those who served in full-time Christian service.[60] In the events surrounding Martin Symons being placed under church discipline, Gerard Gielen wrote in the *Nieuwsbrief*, "Satan shook our unity."[61]

Haverkamp looked back on the rapid growth of the ECV and accredited the success to God. "God is sovereign. He is the One who does the work."[62] In a series of lectures on church planting in 2002, Haverkamp again emphasized this; he ultimately credited God for any who might undergo evangelical conversion, even in the midst of so few responding. "I believe that God still has His elect here and there."[63] Gelling also was conscious of "God's work" as he wrote to supporters, "On the 8th of March we want to begin a series of start studies in Wellen. Along with that we have meetings (too many it seems sometimes), Bible studies, speaking on Sundays, visitation, evangelism, etc., etc. We are thrilled the Lord allows us to do this."[64] Similarly, Gifford wrote supporters concerning an extended stay in Canada, "It will be good to share with you the way the Lord is working in Belgium both in and through us . . . [W]e continue to preach Christ and trust Him to awaken a need in people's lives."[65]

This type of thinking was not limited only to the work of the ECV, however, as seen in Threadcraft's account of the accreditation of ETF:

> It was truly a work of God that the school became accredited. In order for that to happen, the government had to fall, a new government established and for a new constitution to be written to include the recognition and accreditation of an Evangelical Seminary which would be different from the "Protestant" or Catholic one. All of that came about in one fell swoop.[66]

---

59. R. Haverkamp, interview, 30 April 2003. Cf. chapter 3, "Haverkamp's Call to Belgium."

60. B. Tordoff, letter to author, undated (postmarked 1 February 2008).

61. Gielen, "Overpelt, Hamont, Hamont-Overpelt?," 7.

62. R. Haverkamp, interview, 06 December 2008.

63. R. Haverkamp, "Wie der Herr Jesus Christus Gemeinden baut," session 1.

64. H. and B. Gelling, letter to supporters, 19 February 2002.

65. P. and J. Gifford, letter to supporters, May 2005.

66. Threadcraft, "Re: ECV in Belgium," email, 02 September 2008. Cf. Campbell, *Light for the Night in Europe*, 233.

Threadcraft thus gave credit to God for what he understood as an unlikely series of events which resulted in the accreditation of the school.

The founders also had confidence in the execution of their overall vision because they were convinced that they were doing the will of God. Frequent references to doing God's will especially were seen in the decision-making process for Haverkamp and Gelling before they left Canada as well as once they arrived in Belgium. Hay's book gives a clear connection between faith and the knowledge of God's will.

> True faith is dependent upon a knowledge of God's will. To exercise faith for the carrying out of His purpose we must know what that purpose is . . . Nowhere in God's Word are we given authority to exercise faith for something that is simply our own plan or desire. A believer or church has no right to decide what is to be done and then to have "faith" that it will be done . . . When we know what God's will is, we can have faith that He will accomplish it.[67]

The process which the founders followed to determine the will of God was one of the mainstream evangelical approaches often called the traditional view.[68] In this view as described by Gary Friesen, the Christian trying to determine God's will uses the Bible, circumstances, an inner witness of the Holy Spirit, mature counsel, personal desires, common sense, and perhaps special supernatural guidance such as might come through a vision, a dream, or a miracle. Many if not all of these factors were part of the decision-making process before Haverkamp and Gelling came to Flanders.[69] A similar process was evident over the years throughout their work in Belgium. Further, their certainty that they had done God's will came as these factors agreed, as they prayed about a decision, as they maintained a "close communion" with God, and then as they witnessed the results.[70]

One of the surprises for the founders which was not part of their overall vision was the creation of the ECV as a government-recognized organization. As Haverkamp often noted, they had not come to start an organization but to return to the Bible.[71] Nonetheless, a very well defined organization did result, complete with a carefully enunciated structure, written long-range plans, evaluations of the plans in retrospect, and a statement of faith.

---

67. Hay, *The New Testament Order for Church and Missionary*, 425.

68. For a more complete description of what has been termed "the traditional view" to determine the will of God, cf. Friesen, *Decision Making and the Will of God*, 45–80.

69. Cf. chapter 3, "Haverkamp's Call to Belgium" and "Gelling's Call to Belgium."

70. Friesen, *Decision Making and the Will of God*, 69.

71. R. Haverkamp, interview, 25 April 2003.

All this happened primarily through the vision and efforts of De Kegel as well as the efforts of men such as Le Jeune. Still, even De Kegel and Le Jeune did not help to create a new denomination for its own sake, but as a tool to further the growth and strength of the churches which had been planted.

While this organizational aspect did not turn out as the founders might have expected, the founders' overall vision was achieved by the planting of churches whose leaders had not come from outside of Flanders and the overall control of which was not outside the country. As Gelling noted in the often-repeated statement by Haverkamp, "We came and we knew that God had sent us, and our desire was to see local churches started that were run by local people."[72] Success in this area of local people running the churches is especially evident when a list of ECV workers is compared with that of similar free church groups such as the BEZ or the VEG.[73] Further, this Flemish character was noted by those who had grown up in the ECV. During his studies at ETF, one young man noted as he looked back at his time in the ECV, "I [realize] that the ECV, unlike BEZ and VEG, is probably the only thoroughly evangelical church growth movement in Flanders where the majority of churches are not directly guided by non-Flemish leaders such as Dutchmen or Dutch Canadians."[74]

Formal Theological Training

Before beginning their work in Flanders, Haverkamp's only formal theological training was at the Millar Memorial Bible Institute; Shindelka and Gelling had none; and den Boer was in the midst of undergraduate studies at BIB. Thus, the ECV's founders were characterized as having little, if any, formal theological training. That said, all four had extensive practical experience in evangelism, and the Canadian missionaries had been active in various aspects of their assemblies in Canada before coming to Flanders. Gelling remarked, for example, that he learned most of what he knew about the Bible after coming to Flanders. "My biblical language is Dutch. When I came here I was saved only five years. I can't get into propitiation, but *verzoening*, wow!"[75] He also noted that it was not until he heard the teaching of the ECV's first seminary-educated North American, Hal Threadcraft, that he learned he had been training people to study the Bible through a process

---

72. H. Gelling, interview, 11 September 2003.
73. E.g., "Belgische Vereniging van Vrij Evangelische Gemeenten," 14–16.
74. van Nes, "ECV," email, 20 September 2004.
75. H. Gelling, interview, 01 May 2003.

of 1) observation, 2) interpretation, 3) application. "I was already doing it, but now I learned what I had been doing."[76]

This lack of formal theological education would not have been unique among Brethren missionaries or other full-time workers in North America at the end of the twentieth century. In fact, many Brethren held a certain hostility toward formal theological education; this education was thought to taint those who had it. An often repeated encounter by many with or considering theological education was the false dichotomy between being "taught by the Holy Spirit" and "taught by men."[77] While the founders certainly were not hostile to formal theological education, they did at times display a certain amusement toward it, both in private conversations and in public lectures such as those given by Haverkamp in Germany in 2002.[78] In contrast, De Kegel and those who followed as the shapers placed an open premium on the value of formal theological education. Nevertheless, both the founders and the shapers were quick to sense the need for an efficient, effective method of teaching the newly converted members of the ECV. As a result, scheduled study days were made available to the new converts as taught by the Canadian missionaries, De Kegel, Nullens, or other men who were considered to be qualified.

Initially, no extensive planning had gone into the formal training of the next generation of workers for the ECV. It was expected that the new workers would be discovered in much the same way as the founders had been, as the result of a commission from God. As the ECV matured as a movement, however, the need for a more formal program of training was recognized and designed. In addition, a year of probation for each new full-time worker was instituted along with the pairing of the new worker with an experienced one for this year.[79] Interestingly, all of the Flemish full-timers either already had formal theological education before becoming a worker or completed it while serving the ECV.

The effect of the lack of formal theological education on the work of the ECV is not clear, especially when compared with the trained workers of the BEZ and the VEG. All three groups grew during the same years, all three groups stopped growing at the same time, and all three groups experienced similar challenges in the local churches associated with their organizations.

76. Ibid.

77. MacLeod, review of *Bible Colleges? A Warning Against the Spread of Bible Teaching institutions Among NT Local Assemblies*, 122n43. This extended review article also provides a good summary of the hostility toward formal theological education present in some quarters within the Brethren.

78. R. Haverkamp, "Wie der Herr Jesus Christus Gemeinden baut," session 1.

79. "Zendings werk Binnen de E.C.V.," 4–8.

The ECV did, however, change from a group whose workers had little or no theological training to one whose workers had at least a bachelor's level theological education. This change certainly would have been a surprise to the founders, but likely was a natural outgrowth of the emphasis on the importance of Bible teaching and Bible study noted earlier.[80] That said, perhaps this lack of formal theological training provided some context to an observation about Haverkamp and Gelling made by Haverkamp as he looked back on the work that had been done. He noted that both of them were evangelists, and that as a result they neglected teaching. "The challenge is to keep both evangelism and teaching in balance."[81]

RESEARCH FOR THE FUTURE

While the history of the Brethren in Flanders, and the forming of the new Brethren in particular, is a worthwhile study in church planting in addition to the founding and maturing of a denomination, the story of the ECV is far from complete. This study indicates that profitable research related to missiology, ecclesiology, and Church history should be pursued in the future. Below are some seemingly profitable avenues of study which fell beyond the scope of this research.

Will the ECV continue to change? If so, into what will it change?

One of the most interesting questions at this writing concerns the future identity of the ECV. With the retirement or stepping back of founding missionaries Haverkamp and Gelling, what will the group of assemblies look like that they helped to plant? De Kegel, along with some of the younger workers, began a process whereby they strongly supported a formal union with the churches of the VEG and the BEZ. At the very least, functional ecclesiological issues will need to be worked through, such as the role of a local pastor, the importance and style of a weekly celebration of the Lord's Supper, and the autonomy of the local church, if such a merger is to happen. Even before this, however, the elders and workers of the ECV have to be convinced that this merger is a good idea. Both Haverkamp and Gelling saw no need for such a move, and the same is true of a number of the ECV workers and elders from across Flanders. Once again to their credit, both

---

80. Cf. chapter 4, "The Emphasis on Pragmatic, Sound Teaching Throughout the ECV."

81. R. Haverkamp, interview, 25 April 2003.

Haverkamp and Gelling were willing to let the ECV go in whatever ecclesiological direction the Flemish leaders wanted to take it, as long as doctrinal orthodoxy was maintained.[82]

Related to this potential shift in functional ecclesiology is the character of the full-timers most recently added to the ECV. All of these men have at least a Bachelor of Divinity, and all are graduates of the *Evangelische Theologische Faculteit*. Accordingly, profitable studies may be found in a few years to see how this collection of men with higher theological education from this one educational institution have influenced the ECV. The researcher also should note that three of these four have little or no firsthand knowledge of the practices and beliefs of Roman Catholicism as adherents, and half of these men grew up within the ECV as the children of those who were converted from Roman Catholicism due to the work of the ECV. All have grown up in Flanders or the Netherlands during a time when the culture rapidly secularized. What effect might these factors have on their outlook in the years ahead?

Anecdotal information also was encountered during this research which suggests a discernible difference in character between the assemblies planted by Haverkamp and those planted by Gelling. First, is this an accurate observation? Second, if so, what factors can be attributed to the personalities of the men themselves, and what factors can be attributed to the different parts of Flanders in which they worked? Missiological and sociological studies may prove fruitful.

Will the ECV continue to be identified as a Brethren group in some manner? Will anyone outside the ECV continue to identify it as a Brethren group? Already this Brethren identity seems to be waning, and perhaps only part of the thinking of the founding and serving missionaries. That identity, along with the rest of the six questions put forward by VMC, could provide a fruitful study.

Was the ECV part of a greater time of "revival?" If so, how widespread was this event?

While strongly indicated, will further research confirm that the ECV was not only part of the "Flemish revivals," but also of a larger worldwide "time of blessing?" Similar explosive growth happened during the same years among the Open Brethren in parts of France, Austria, Quebec, and parts of Latin America. Can a model be developed which correlates these events? Why did this growth happen in some places but not others? Further, does

82. H. Gelling, interview, 02 December 2008.

the rapid growth of the Brethren assemblies in the countries mentioned have a parallel among the other evangelical churches? The listed countries were all predominantly Roman Catholic in the early 1970s, or at least the areas of the country that experienced rapid growth. Could this provide an important clue as to a direction of research?

Related to this category would be a socio-religious study which examines the history of the fifteen people whose testimonies comprised the book, *Nieuw: Vijfteen Vlamingen vertellen hoe Jezus hun leven veranderde*.[83] What transpired personally for them in the next three decades after their conversion? The history of one of the fifteen, De Kegel, is known. What about the others? As products of "the Flemish revivals," this could prove a profitable grid through which to examine the work of the ECV as well as its milieu.

How will the ECV adapt to a culture that is less religious, more materialistic, and aging?

In the long run, how will the ECV adapt to the changes in culture very evident by the turn of the twenty-first century? In another few decades, further historical studies may build upon the information already presented in this book to ascertain further reasons for the continued success or failure of the ECV. Related to this is the economic and political crisis prevalent in Flanders at this writing. Economically, times are very uncertain, and politically, Belgium is unable to form a stable government. If these crises grow, what effect might they have on the growth of the ECV? Sociologically, the ECV grew during a time of great religious and cultural change, a time of uncertainty. After a few decades, a study may be made which compares the growth during the 1970s and 1980s with what happens during the next decade. As part of this study, the aging demographics also may provide interesting clues as to the changing audience to which the ECV ministers.[84]

FINAL REMARKS

While much more could have been written about the founding and growth of the ECV, the information contained here presents a remarkable record of the founding and growth of a collection of independent local

---

83. R. Haverkamp, *Nieuw: Vijfttien Vlamingen vertellen hoe Jezus hun leven veranderde*.

84. Debuisson et al., *De bevolkingsevolutie: de bevolking naar leeftijd en geslacht*, 44ff.

Conclusions

churches planted primarily by Haverkamp and Gelling as they developed into the government-recognized organization known as the ECV. While the history shows that the ECV was not in any sense a perfect movement, either in its forms or people, the history does record a remarkable work nonetheless. In summary, the words of one of the people who grew up in the ECV as he looked back at his years in the group seems appropriate. "I have told myself that whatever there may be lacking, the Spirit of God, through the ECV's founders, built up an altogether masterly piece of work right in front of us."[85]

---

85. van Nes, interview, 20 September 2004.

Appendix 1

Thirteen Essential Qualities for a Church Planter[1]

1. VISIONISING CAPACITY

- being a person who projects into the future beyond the present
- developing a theme which highlights the vision and philosophy of ministry persuasively selling the vision to the people
- approaching challenges as opportunities rather than obstacles
- coping effectively with non-visionising elements
- not erecting artificial walls or limits either overtly or subconsciously
- establishing a clear church identity related to the theme and vision
- believing in God's capacity to do great things

2. INTRINSICALLY MOTIVATED

- having a desire to do well and a commitment to excellence

---

1. Ridley, *How to Select Church Planters: A Self-Study Manual for Recruiting, Screening, Interviewing and Evaluating Qualified Church Planters*, 7-11. These thirteen qualities are provided as an explanation of chapter 3, "Analysis of the Founders of the ECV," and its subsequent subsections.

Thirteen Essential Qualities for a Church Planter

- stick-to-itiveness and persistence
- having initiative and aggressiveness without the negative connotations
- having a willingness to work long and hard
- being a self-starter with a willingness to build from nothing
- having a high energy and vitality level; physical stamina

3. CREATES OWNERSHIP OF MINISTRY

- helping people to "buy in" and feel responsible for the growth and success of the church
- gaining commitment of the people to the vision
- establishing a congregational identity
- avoiding stereotyping of congregation by imposing unrealistic goals for which it cannot claim ownership

4. RELATES TO THE UNCHURCHED

- communicating in style that is understood by the unchurched
- understanding the "psychology" or mentality of the unchurched
- moving and functioning in the "personal space" of the unchurched without fear
- quickly getting to know the unchurched on a personal level
- breaking through the barriers erected by the unchurched
- handling crises faced by the unchurched

5. SPOUSAL COOPERATION

- having an explicit agreement regarding each partner's respective role and involvement in ministry
- having explicit rules regarding the use of home as an office
- evaluating the consequences of ministry demands upon the children
- functioning as a team through individual and collective action
- having a strategy for dealing with strangers

- modeling wholesome family life before church and community
- agreeing upon and sharing the ministry vision
- deliberately planning and protecting private family life

6. EFFECTIVELY BUILDS RELATIONSHIPS

- responding with urgency to expressed needs and concerns of people
- displaying Godly love and compassion to people
- getting to know people on a personal basis
- making others feel secure and comfortable in one's presence
- not responding judgmentally or prejudicially to new people
- appreciating and accepting a variety of persons
- spending quality time with present parishioners without overstepping them for new people

7. COMMITTED TO CHURCH GROWTH

- believing in church growth as a theological principle
- appreciating steady and consistent growth without preoccupation with the quick success factor
- committing to numerical growth within the context of spiritual and relational growth (more and better disciples)
- recognizing that non-growth is threatening and self-defeating
- establishing the goal of becoming a financially self-supporting church within a specific period of time
- not prematurely falling into a ministry of maintenance
- seeing the church project within the larger context of God's kingdom

8. RESPONSIVE TO COMMUNITY

- understanding the culture of the community
- identifying and assessing community needs

- responding to community needs on a priority basis such that resources are most efficiently used
- determining successes and failures of other organized religious attempts to respond to community needs
- not confusing what the community needs with what the church wants to offer
- acquiring and understanding of the character and "pulse" of the community
- adapting the philosophy of ministry to the character of the community

9. UTILIZES GIFTEDNESS OF OTHERS

- releasing and equipping people to do the task of ministry
- discerning of spiritual gifts in others
- matching the gifts of people with ministry needs and opportunities
- delegating effectively in areas of personal limitation
- avoiding personal overload by delegating effectively
- not prematurely assigning ministry assignments before people are adequately equipped
- not placing unwarranted restrictions on other's spiritual giftedness

10. FLEXIBLE AND ADAPTABLE

- coping effectively with ambiguity
- coping effectively with constant and abrupt change
- adapting oneself and one's methods to the uniqueness of the particular church planting project
- shifting priorities and emphasis during various stages of church growth
- doing "whatever" is necessary "whenever" necessary

11. BUILDS GROUP COHESIVENESS

- developing a nucleus group or groups as a foundation

- quickly incorporating newcomers into a network of relationships
- engaging others in meaningful church activity
- monitoring the morale of people
- utilizing groups effectively
- dealing with conflict assertively, constructively and tactfully

12. RESILIENCE

- experiencing setbacks without defeat
- riding the ups and downs (i.e., attendance)
- expecting the unexpected
- rebounding from loss, disappointments and failure

13. EXERCISES FAITH

- possessing a conviction regarding one's call to church planting ministry
- believing in God's action
- having expectation and hope
- having a willingness to wait for answers to specific prayer requests

Appendix 2

Fulltime Workers of the *Evangelische Christengemeenten Vlaanderen*

Name	Years of Service	Nationality	Brethren Missions Service Agency
Herb Shindelka	1971–1976	Canadian	MSC
Richard Haverkamp	1971–2009	Canadian	MSC
Martin Luesink	1971–1974	Canadian	MSC
Henk Gelling	1975–	Canadian	MSC
John den Boer	1976–1996	Dutch	
Hal Threadcraft	1979–1983	USA	CMML
Martin Symons	1981–1983; 1990–	Belgian	
David Dunlap	1983–1989	USA	CMML
Guido De Kegel	1984–	Belgian	
Peter Gifford	1984–	Canadian	MSC
Luc Vandevorst	1984–1992	Belgian	
Rosario Anastasi	1990–	Italian[+]	
Eric Rutten	1991–1997	Belgian	
Erik Schraepen	1992–2007	Belgian	
Henry Heikoop	1997-2000	Canadian	
Julie Gelling[*]	1997–2009	Canadian	
Anne Dryburgh	1999–	Scottish	Interlink
Koen Schelstraete	1999–	Belgian	
Raymond Hausoul	2007–	Dutch	
Kristof Vermaut	2008–	Belgian	
Pieter Lenaerts	2008–	Belgian	

[+]Born in Belgium
[*]Part timer worker

Appendix 3

Assemblies of the *Evangelische Christengemeenten Vlaanderen* (see following page)

Assemblies of the Evangelische Christengemeenten Vlaanderen

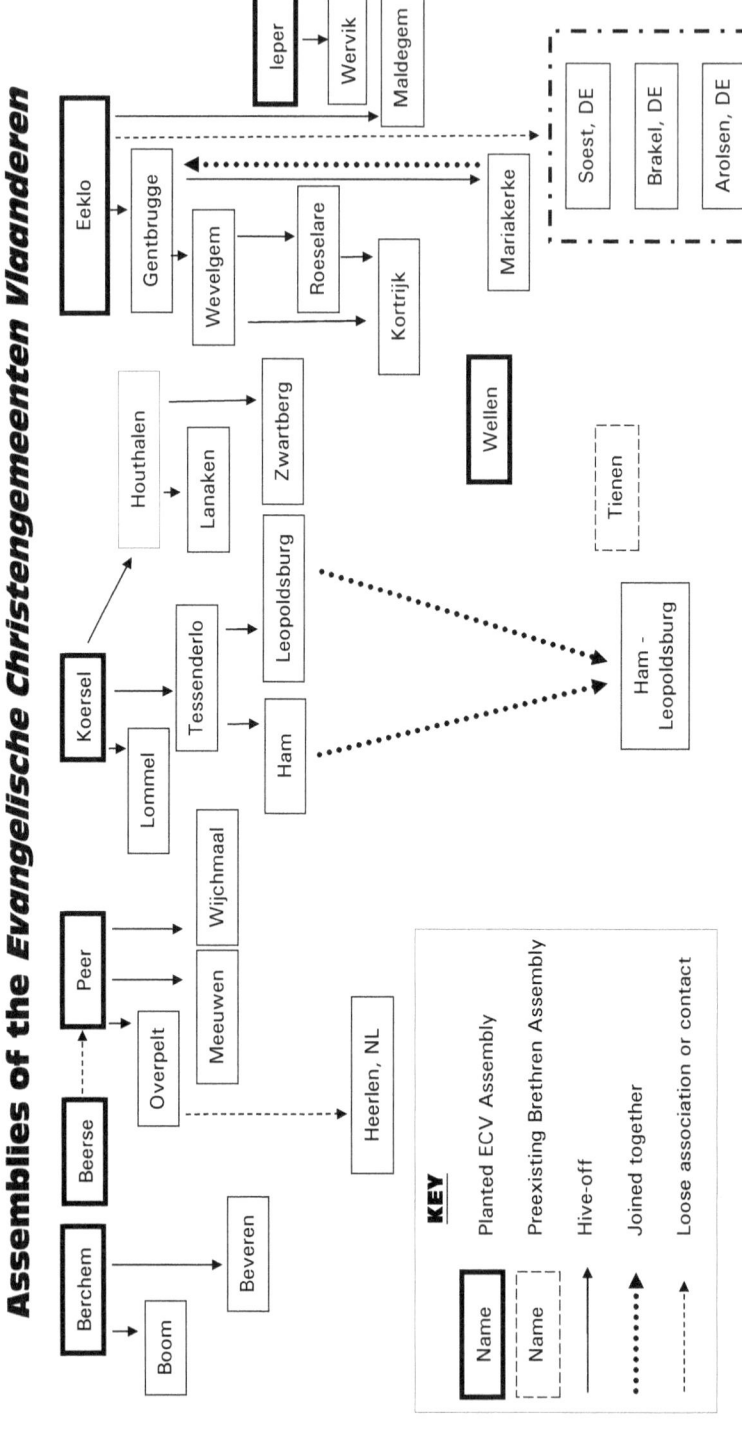

Appendix 4

Locations of the Assemblies of the *Evangelische Christengemeenten Vlaanderen* (see following page)

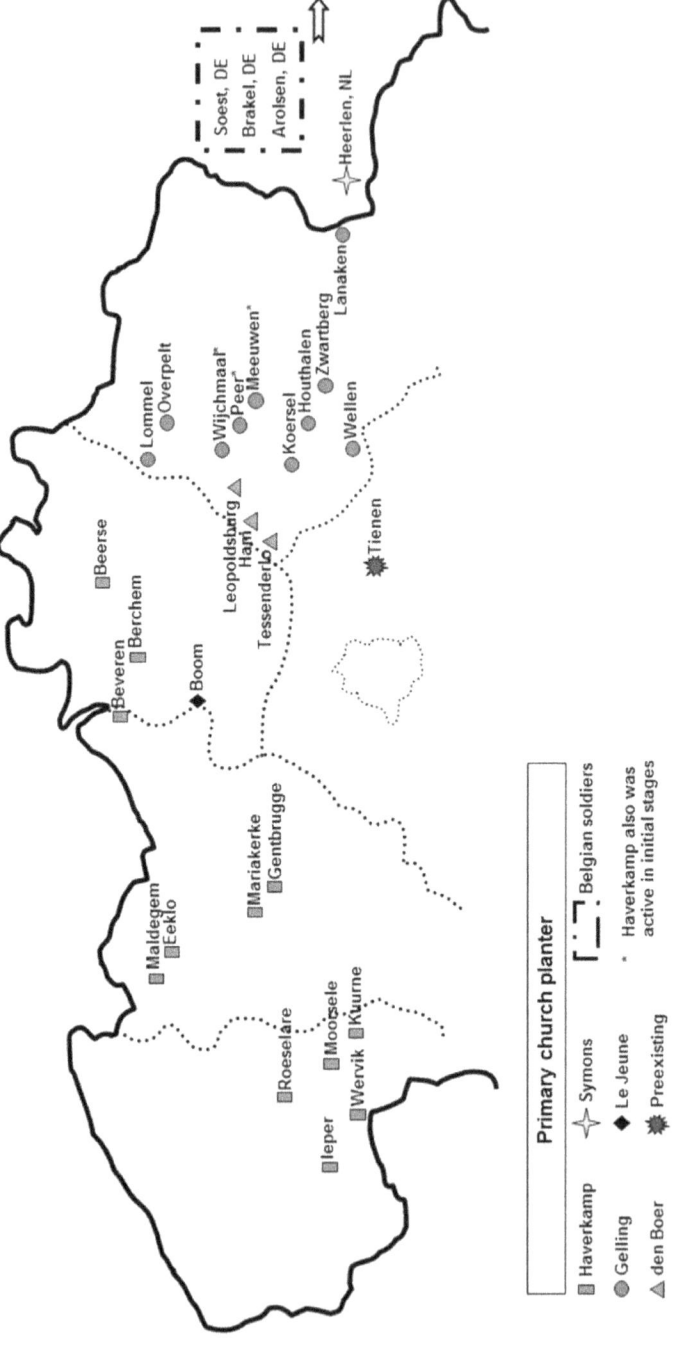

Bibliography

"1 Peer gedeeld door 3=. . . ." *Nieuwsbrief van de christengemeenten*, edited by Guido De Kegel, September-October 1984.

"2. Accession methods for a new assembly." *Nationale Vergadering Christengemeenten*, 30 November 1991.

2006 Address Book of Some Assemblies of Christians in the United States, Canada, and Other Countries. Kansas City: Walterick, 2006.

29 October 1996 BEZ "Aan de leden van de Vlaamse raad." Letter from Leslie Message announcing a meeting of 09 September 1996.

A Few Hymns and Some Spiritual Songs, selected 1856 for the Little Flock. Rev. ed. New York: Loizeaux, 1881.

"A party unlike any other." Vlaams Blok Party. Appendix One: A Short History of Flanders and the Flemish Movement. http://www.vlaamsblock.be/site_engels_11.shtml.

A. C. W. *Thanks for the Interest: A letter to a concerned saint about the support of commended workers*. 1994. Reprint, York, PA: Spread the Word, n.d.

Abbott, Walter M., editor. *The Documents of Vatican II*. Translated by Joseph Gallagher. Piscataway, NJ: New Century, 1966.

"Adreswijzigingen." *Evangelische Christengemeenten Vlaanderen Nieuwsbrief*, edited by Marc Van Den Bogaerde, October 1991.

"Agenda Vlaamse raad maandag 8 november." *Belgische Evangelische Zending*, 11 October 1999.

Ahlstrom, Sydney E. *A Religious History of the American People*. London: Yale, 1973.

"Alberta Population Profile: Sherwood Park." Accessed via Urban Service Areas, dropdown list. http://www.altapop.ca/unincorp.htm.

"Alg. Overzight." VEG archives, Brussels, 12 August 1988, 1. This is a report which lists church planting by the BEZ since 1919 and was printed from a file named "Post Gemlyst 2".

"Algemene verg." Attachment to Nationale Vergadering. Schaffen, Belgium. 24 September 1990.

Anastasi, Rosario. Interview by author. Bergneustadt-Wiedenest, Germany. 30 June 2005.

_____. Interview by author. Bergneustadt-Wiedenest, Germany. 01 July 2005.

Andrews, John S. "Brethren Hymnology." *Evangelical Quarterly* 28/4 (1956) 208–29.

"Arbeiders." *Nieuwsbrief van de christengemeenten*, edited by Guido De Kegel, January-February 1984.

Bibliography

Bain, H. Undated report in "Notes and Comments." *Echoes of Service Magazine*, 1924, n.p.
Baines, T. B. *The Lord's Coming, Israel, and the Church*. 4th ed. N.p.: Broom, 1881. *Mighty Men* CD-ROM. Kent: STEM, 1999.
Barlow, John. "Commendation by the Local Church." In *Global Strategy: The Biblical Plan of Missions*, 2nd ed., 28–37. Toronto: Missionary Service Committee, 1981.
Barrett, David V. *The New Believers: Sects, "Cults," and Alternative Religions*. London: Cassell, 2001.
Baylis, Robert. *My People: The History of those Christians Sometimes Called Plymouth Brethren*. Wheaton, IL: Shaw, 1995.
BC Stats. http://www.bcstats.gov.bc.ca/Files/351b80e7-081c-473c-b494-9d642ed4d5d9/Census2006-ProfilesB-Edmonton-SherwoodParkFED.pdf
Beattie, David J. *Brethren: The Story of a Great Recovery*. Kilmarnock: Ritchie, 1940.
"België." *Mededeelingen omtrent het werk Gods in onze dagen*. Vol. 6. Edited by H.C.V.(oorhoeve). N.p.: n.p., [Summer 1875].
"Belgien: Tienen." Wegsweiser: Ausgabe Herbst 1998. Dillenburg: Christliche Verlagsgellschaft, 1998.
"Belgische Vereniging van Vrij Evangelische Gemeenten." March 1987.
"Beliefs." Christian Reformed Church. http://www.crcna.org/crbe/index.htm (site discontinued).
Bellett, J. G. "The Lord's Supper." *Christian Friend* 5:295 / *Bible Witness and Review* 2. *Mighty Men* CD-ROM. Kent: STEM, 1999.
Berkhof, Hendrikus. *Christian Faith: An Introduction to the Study of the Faith*. Translated by Sierd Woudstra. Grand Rapids: Eerdmans, 1979.
Berkouwer, G. C. *The Church*. Translated by James E. Davison. Studies in Dogmatics. Grand Rapids: Eerdmans, 1976.
Bethel Bible Chapel. Letter of commendation for David Dunlap. 27 June 1983.
"Betreft: Toetreding van de gemeente Tienen." Attachment 1 to "Verslag Nationale Vergadering." 28 November 1992.
Biesbrouck, Antoon. "Een eigen gebouw voor Ieper." *Nieuwsbrief van de christengemeenten*, edited by Marc Van Den Bogaerde, November 1992.
Biesbrouck, Bart. "Evangelische Christengemeenten Vlaanderen!?" *Nieuwsbrief van de christengemeenten*, edited by Eric Rutten, September 1996, 12.3.
Biesbrouck, Hans. "En Ieper bouwde voort." *Evangelische Christengemeenten Vlaanderen Nieuwsbrief*, edited by Marc Ladon, 13/4.
Billy Graham Crusade Statistics: Chronological, June 2005. http://www.billygraham.org/assets/media/pdfs/festivals/BGCrusadeChronology.pdf.
Bloesch, Donald G. *Life, Ministry, and Hope*. Vol. 2 of *Essentials of Evangelical Theology*. 1978. Reprint, Peabody, MA: Prince, 1998.
Blondeel, Robert. "artikel niewsbrief [sic] Ieper." Email to Koen Schelstraete. 12 October 2002.
Boersema, Pieter R. "De Evangelische Beweging in de Samenleving: Een antropologisch onderzoek naar religieuze veranderingen in de Evangelische Beweging in Vlaanderen en Nederland gedurende de periode 1972–2000." PhD diss., Katholieke Universiteit Leuven, 2004.
Borland, Andrew. "The Lord's Supper." In *The Church: A Symposium of Principles and Practice*, edited by J. B. Watson, 66–81. London: Pickering & Inglis, 1949.

Bibliography

Bos, Egbert A. "Church Planting in Flanders." MA thesis, Evangelische Theologische Faculteit, 1988.
Boven, Pim. Interview by author. Heverlee, Belgium. 03 September 2008.
Bredin, Mark. "NBBI's Beginnings: An Early History of the New Brunswick Bible Institute." An edited message delivered for the fiftieth anniversary celebration of NBBI. October 1994. http://personal.nbnet.nb.ca/nbbi/nbbihist.html.
Briem, Christian. *Daar ben Ik in het midden van hen*. Den Helder, Netherlands: Vereniging Verspreiding Bijbelstudies, 1990.
Broadbent, E. H. *The Pilgrim Church*. London: Pickering & Inglis, 1931.
"Broederconferentie met Eric Bermejo." *Nieuwsbrief van de christengemeenten*, edited by Guido De Kegel, July-August 1984.
Brown, Tim. "When God Led His People Back to First Century Practices of Church Truths: A condensed but interesting account of this great Spiritual revival." Waynesboro, GA: Christian Missions, n.d.
Bruce, F. F. *In Retrospect: Remembrance of Things Past*. Grand Rapids: Eerdmans, 1980.
Burness, J. H. "Message from Dr J H Burness, Trustee, Echoes of Service." Email to author. 01 August 2007.
Callahan, James P. *Primitivist Piety: The Ecclesiology of the Early Plymouth Brethren*. London: Scarecrow, 1996.
Campbell, Robert J. *Light for the Night in Europe: Reflections on a Lifetime of Ministry*. N.p. [USA]: printed by the author, 1999.
Cantini Cristiani. 5th ed. East Orange, NJ: La Voce Nel Deserto, 1963.
Carson, Patricia. *Fair Face of Flanders*. Rev. ed. 1974. Reprint, Ghent: E. Story-Scientia, 1978.
Cataford, Lisa C. *"Because of the Angels": A Biblical Look at the Women's Headcovering*. Scarborough, ON: Everyday, 1993.
Célébrons sa Mémoire: Cantiques pour le Repas du Seigneur. Ottawa: Le Van, 1993.
Chafer, Lewis Sperry. "The Dispensations." In *Major Bible Themes: 52 Vital Doctrines of the Scripture Simplified and Explained*, rev. ed, revised by John F. Walvoord, 126–38. Grand Rapids: Zondervan, 1974.
Chester, Tim, and Steve Timmis. *Total Church: A Radical Reshaping around Gospel and Community*. Wheaton, IL: Crossway, 2008.
Christel. "Evangelisatieweek Zwartberg." *Nieuwsbrief van de Christengemeenten* 12/3, edited by Marc Van Den Bogaerde, September 1996.
"Christengemeente Eeklo bestaat 25 jaar!" *Evangelische Christengemeenten Vlaanderen Nieuwsbrief*, edited by Marc Ladon, 18/2.
"Christengemeente Koersel 15 Jaar." *Nieuwsbrief van de christengemeenten*, edited by Marc Van Den Bogaerde, February 1992.
Christengemeenten Vlaanderen. "Verslag Nationale Vergadering DD. 15/06/91," 24 June 1991.
"Chronologische indeling van het Gemeentestichtend werk van de B.E.Z." Gent: *Belgische Evangelische Zending* (BEZ) archives, January 1975, typewritten.
Christian Missions in Many Lands. http://www.cmmlusa.org/.
Christian Missions in Many Lands (Canada) Inc. "Pertinent Information, Necessary to Complete our Records" form. 10 July 1972.
Coad, F. Roy. *A History of the Brethren Movement: Its Origins, its Worldwide Development and its Significance for the Present Day*. Exeter: Paternoster, 1968.
Code of Canon Law: In English Translation. London: Collins Liturgical, 1983.

Bibliography

Coleman, Robert. *The Master Plan of Evangelism.* Old Tappan, NJ: Revell, 1963.

Conard, William W. *Family Matters.* Wheaton, IL: Interest Ministries, 1992.

Connolly, Ken. "Obstacle to Comfort: The Life of George Muller." VHS tape. Orlando: Biblical Heritage Collection Archives, 1994.

Cooper, Ransome W. Letter dated 1913, Echoes of Service Magazine. 1913, n.p.

"Countryside Bible Chapel." http://www.countrysidebiblechapel.org/about/.

Creemers, Jelle. Discussions with author. Heverlee, Belgium. 02-3 September 2008.

———. Interview by author. Heverlee, Belgium. 06 September 2007.

Cronin, Edward. "Note regarding the remembrances of J.G. Bellet on the Early Years of the Brethren." July 1871. http://www.mybrethren.org/history/hy01earl.htm#cronin.

Cronin, John F., editor. *The Encyclicals and Other Messages of John XXIII.* Washington, DC: TPS, 1964.

"Daarbij die molen." *Nieuwsbrief van de christengemeenten,* edited by Guido De Kegel. July-August 1984.

Darby, J. N. "An Appeal to the Conscience of those who take the Title of 'Elders of the Evangelical Church at Geneva'; and a Reply to one of them." In *The Collected Writings of J. N. Darby: Ecclesiastical No. 2,* edited by William Kelly, 4:307-38. N.d. Reprint, Winschoten: Heijkoop, 1972.

———. "Examination of a Few Passages of Scripture, the force of which has been questioned in the discussion on the New Churches; with remarks on Certain Principles Alleged in Support of their Establishment." In *The Collected Writings of J. N. Darby: Ecclesiastical No. 2,* edited by William Kelly, 4:228-70. N.d. Reprint, Winschoten: Heijkoop, 1972.

———. "God's Principle of Unity." In *The Collected Writings of J. N. Darby: Ecclesiastical No. 1,* edited by William Kelly, 1:353-65. N.p. Reprint, Winschoten: Heijkoop, 1972.

———. Letter to [Mrs. Walter] dated 04 November 1869. In *Letters of J. N. Darby, Volume Two: 1868-1879,* 47-52. N.d. Reprint, Winschoten: Heijkoop, 1971.

———. Letter to Prof. Tholuck dated [1855]. In *Letters of J. N. Darby, Volume Three: 1879-1882,* 297-305. N.d. Reprint, Winschoten: H. L. Heijkoop, 1971.

———. "On the Formation of Churches." In *The Collected Writings of J. N. Darby: Ecclesiastical No. 1,* edited by William Kelly, 1:138-55. N.d. Reprint, Winschoten: Heijkoop, 1971.

———. "On Worship." In *The Collected Writings of J. N. Darby: Doctrinal No. 2,* edited by William Kelly, 7:87-126. N.d. Reprint, Winschoten: Heijkoop, 1972.

———. "Principles of Gathering." In *The Collected Writings of J. N. Darby: Doctrinal No. 9,* edited by William Kelly, 31:381-83. N.d. Reprint, Winschoten: Heijkoop, 1972.

———. "Scriptural Views Upon the Subject of Elders, in answer to a tract entitled 'Are Elders to be Established?" In *The Collected Writings of J. N. Darby: Ecclesiastical No. 2,* edited by William Kelly, 4:183-227. N.d. Reprint, Winschoten: Heijkoop, 1972.

———. "The Apostasy of the Successive Dispensations." In *The Collected Writings of J. N. Darby: Ecclesiastical No. 1,* edited by William Kelly, 1:124-30. N.d. Reprint, Winschoten: Heijkoop, 1972.

———. "The Church-What is It?" In *The Collected Writings of J. N. Darby: Evangelic No. 1,* edited by William Kelly, 12:372-84. N.d. Reprint, Winschoten: Heijkoop, 1972.

Bibliography

_____. "The House of God; The Body of Christ; and the Baptism of the Holy Ghost." In *The Collected Writings of J. N. Darby: Ecclesiastical No. 3*, edited by William Kelly, 14:15-75. N.d. Reprint, Winschoten: Heijkoop, 1971.

_____. "What Has Been Acknowledged? or the State of the Controversy about Elders, followed by a Short Answer to an Article of Mons. de Gasparin." In *The Collected Writings of J. N. Darby: Ecclesiastical No. 2*, edited by William Kelly, 4:286-306. N.d. Reprint, Winschoten: Heijkoop, 1972.

"David: een hart voor België." *Nieuwsbrief van de christengemeenten*, edited by Guido De Kegel. March-April 1984.

Davies, J. M. "The Church: Its Formation, Fellowship and Features." In *The Church of God: A Symposium*, edited by R. E. Harlow, 15-26. Toronto: Everyday, 1976.

"Day 8." *Missionary Prayer Handbook*. Wall, NJ: CMML, 1975.

de Clerq, Peter. "Ninove: de oudste, de stoutste en de wijste van de steden." http://users.pandora.be/peter.de.clercq/ninove.html.

"De ECV voor elkaar." Evangelische Christengemeenten Vlaanderen, VHS tape. 2002.

De Kegel, Guido and Marianne. Interview by author. Zwartberg, Belgium. 12 August 2007.

De Kegel, Guido. Annual letter to the people of the ECV. 20 December 2002.

_____. "Bij Hem is kracht en beleid." *Evangelische Christengemeenten Vlaanderen Nieuwsbrief*, edited by Marc Ladon, 14/1, 3.

_____. Email to author. 30 January 2008.

_____. Email to author. 30 June 2009.

_____. "Enkele gegevens over de Christengemeente." *Evangelische Christengemeenten Vlaanderen Nieuwsbrief*, edited by Marc Ladon, 13/2.

_____. "Het doorgeven van een avondmaalsgedachte." Lecture given among the ECV churches. n.d.

_____. Interview by author. Lovendegem, Belgium. 13 August 2007.

_____. "Leiding in de gemeente." *Nieuwsbrief van de christengemeenten*, edited by Marc Van Den Bogaerde, 10/4, 5-6.

_____. Letter to the elders and *verantwoordelijken* of the assembly at Overpelt. 10 January 1996.

_____. Letter to the National Vergadering van christengemeenten. 05 October 1992.

_____. List of sermon topics provided to author. August 2007.

_____. "Nieuwe werkers uit Canada." *Evangelische Christengemeenten Vlaanderen Nieuwsbrief*, edited by Marc Ladon, 13/2.

_____. "RE: Waregem: Paul Huygens." Email to author. 08 July 2008.

_____. *Splinters in je hart*. Ieper, BE: Jered, 1995.

_____. "Structuur van de ECV." Attachment to a letter to the elders and *verantwoordelijken* of the ECV. 18 December 1997.

_____. *Zalf voor je ziel*. Ieper, BE: Jered, 1994.

"De Parel." *Nieuwsbrief van de christengemeenten*, edited by Eric Rutten, 1987, nr. 3.

"De Paus in België: een uitdaging." *Het Zoeklicht* 60/24 (1985) 16.

"De Werkers." Attachment to minutes of "National Vergadering Christengemeenten." Genk, Belgium. 25 November 1995.

Debuisson, M., et al. *De bevolkingsevolutie: de bevolking naar leeftijd en geslacht*. Brussels: Algemene Volks- en Woningtelling, 2001. http://www.statbel.fgov.be/nl/binaries/01_nl[1]_tcm325-57657.pdf.

"Deletions." *Missions*. December 1983.

Bibliography

Demaerel, Ignace. "Tachtig jaar pinksterbeweging in Vlaanderen (1909–1989): Een historisch onderzoek met korte theologische en sociologische analyse." MA thesis, Universitaire Faculteit voor Protestantse Godgeleerdheid te Brussel, 1990.

den Boer, John, and Marga den Boer. Written interview with Koen Schelstraete. 14 August 2001.

den Boer, John. "All-, Old-, en Full-timers." *Nieuwsbrief van de christengemeenten*, edited by Marc Van Den Bogaerde, October 1991.

———. Interview by P.H. van der Laan. Schaffen, Belgium. 26 June 1989.

den Tek, Klaas. "Dutch Sunday shopping: the debate continues." Radio Netherlands. http://www.expatica.com/nl/news/news_focus/Dutch-Sunday-shopping-_-the-debate-continues_61063.html.

Derweduwen, Toon. "Gentbrugge en Mariakerke: de fusie." *Evangelische Christengemeenten Vlaanderen Nieuwsbrief*, edited by Marc Ladon, 15/1.

———. "Officiële Opening Gemeente Gent." *Evangelische Christengemeenten Vlaanderen Nieuwsbrief*, edited by Marc Ladon, 16/3.

"Deur aan deur in Beveren en Berchem." *Nieuwsbrief van de christengemeenten*, edited by Marc Van Den Bogaerde, February 1992.

Dhooghe, Jos. "Het Belgische Protestantisme." In *België en Zijn Goden: Kerken, Religieuze Groeperingen en Lekenbewegingen*, edited by Karel Dobbelaere, 341–64. Leuven: Cabay, 1985.

Dickson, Neil T. R. Review of "The Lord's Supper in Brethren Ecclesiology: the Mark of Identity, Unity, and for some, Purity," by Thomas J. Marinello, in *My Brother's Keeper*, edited by Thomas J. Marinello and H. H. Drake Williams III, 122–39 (Eugene, OR: Wipf & Stock, 2010). *Brethren Historical Review* 7 (2011) 98–100.

Diorio, F. P., and Joseph De Carlo. *La Storia Delle Assemblee Italiane In America*. N.p.: n.p., 1945.

Dixon, Larry E. "The Importance of J. N. Darby and the Brethren Movement in the History of Conservative Theology." *Christian Brethren Review* 41 (1990) 42–55.

Dobbelaere, Karel, and Liliane Voyé. "From Pillar to Postmodernity: The Changing Situation of Religion in Belgium." In "Sociology of Religion: International Perspectives," edited by James A. Beckford, special issue, *Sociological Analysis* 51 (1990) S1–S13.

Dobbelaere, Karel. "Trends in de Katholieke godsdienstigheid eind 20ste eeuw." *Tijdschrift voor Sociologie* 24/1 (2003) 9–36.

Dreese, William. Response to written questions by Koen Schelstraete. 2002.

Dronsfield, W.R. *The "Brethren" Since 1870.* biblecentre.org. http://www.biblecentre.org/topics/wrd_brethren_since_1870.htm#The%20Exclusive%20Brethren%20(so-called).

Dryburgh, Anne. Interview by author. St. Die, France. 25 August 2003.

———. Letter to Echoes of Service. 31 December 2007. *Echoes*, vol. 137, no. 1959.

———. Letter to Richard Haverkamp. 13 January 1998.

———. "Re: Anne or Ann?" Email to author. 24 June 2008.

———. "RE: Letter of Commendation??" Email to author. 24 June 2008.

Dryburgh, Anne; Henk, Beryl, and Julie Gelling; Peter and Joanna Gifford; and Don and Edie Tinder. Netherlands/Belgium roundtable discussion. Brethren European Christian Workers Conference. St. Die, France. 26 August 2002.

Dulles, Avery. "The True Church." In *Models of the Church*, exp. ed., 114–29. London: Image, 2002.

Bibliography

Dunlap, David. Interview by author. Land O' Lakes, FL. 19 September 2006.

———. Personal diary: maroon and silver notebook. Notes from church meeting of 14 June 1986.

———. "Re: Pictures arrived." Email to author. 17 July 2008.

Eadie, John. *Commentary on the Greek Text of the Epistle of Paul to the Philippians.* New York: Carter & Brothers, 1859.

Echoes Daily Prayer Guide 2008. Bath: Echoes of Service, 2008.

"Een nieuw christelijk orgaan" *Evangelische Christengemeenten Vlaanderen Nieuwsbrief*, edited by Marc Landon, December 2002, 18/4.

"Eindelijk wat ik zocht!" In *Nieuwsbrief van de christengemeentes*, edited by Eric Rutten, 1989, nr 2.

Elders of Sherwood Park Bible Chapel, Sherwood, AB. "Letter of Commendation." Letter to Missionary Service Committee. 26 May 1971.

Elders of Wallenstein Bible Chapel, Wallenstein, ON. Haverkamps' Letter of Commendation. 12 September 1970.

Elders of Westminster Gospel Chapel, Burnaby, BC. "Letter of Commendation" as sent to *Letters of Interest* and Missionary Service Committee. 31 July 1984.

"Enquéteformulier voor Leiders van de Christengemeenten (ECV)." March 2006.

"European and World Values Surveys Four Wave Integrated Data File, 1981–2004, v.20060423." The European Values Study Foundation and World Values Survey Association. http://margaux.grandvinum.se/SebTest/wvs/index_data_analysis.

"Evangelische Christengemeente Houthalen." Pamphlet given to visitors to this Limburg assembly. n.d.

"Evangelische Christengemeenten Vlaanderen." Evangelische Christengemeenten Vlaanderen. http://home.scarlet.be/~pin21516/.

Evangelische Christengemeenten Vlaanderen. "geloofsbelijdenis." http://home2.pi.be/pin21516/onze_geloofsbelijdenis.htm (site discontinued).

Eylenstein, Ernst. *Carl Brockhaus: Ein Beitrag zur Geschichte der Entstehung des Darbysmus in Deutschland.* N.p.: bruderbewegung.de, 2004. http://www.bruederbewegung.de/pdf/eylenstein.pdf. Originally published in *Zeitschrift für Kirchengeschichte* 46, NF 9 (1927) S. 275–312.

Fautré, Willy. "21 Evangelical Denominations Labeled as Cults in Belgium." Compass Direct. https://www.strategicnetwork.org/index.php?loc=kb&view=v&id=772&fct=BEL& (site discontinued).

"Feestzaal wordt Christengemeente." *Evangelische Christengemeenten Vlaanderen Nieuwsbrief*, edited by Marc Van Den Bogaerde, 12/2.

Fellowship Bible Chapel, Clinton, ON. "Letter of Commendation." 28 October 1974.

Fijnvandraat, Jaap. "Open brief van JGF mei 1996." Jaap Fijnvandraat. http://www.jaapfijnvandraat.nl/index.php?page=artikel&id=3124.

———. "Re: Vergadering in NL en Vlaanderen." Email to author. 22 November 2005.

"File: POST GEMLYST 2; Report: BEZ-overzicht." Summary report in the BEZ/VEG archives dated 30 December 1988.

Fish, John H., III. "Brethren Tradition or New Testament Truth?" *Emmaus Journal* 2/2 (1993) 111–53.

———. "Women Speaking in the Church: The Relationship of 1 Corinthians 11:5 and 14:34–36." *Emmaus Journal* 1/3 (1992) 214–51.

Fleming, Kenneth C. *Essentials of Missionary Service: Studies in Paul's Missionary Strategy.* Carlisle, UK: OM, 2000.

Bibliography

———. "Leadership in Open Brethren Assemblies of North America." *Emmaus Journal* 5/1 (1996) 57–66.
———. "Missionary Service in the Life of Paul–Part 1." *Emmaus Journal* 1/2 (1993) 109.
Form 122-62, Schedule C. "Resolution of the Board of Directors of Missionary Service Committee, Inc." 17 July 1963.
Former elders of Wallenstein Bible Chapel. Interview by author. Wallenstein, ON, Canada. 01 September 2006.
Fox, Renée C. *In the Belgian Château: The Spirit and Culture of a European Society in an Age of Change*. Chicago: Dee, 1994.
Fraser, Neil M. *The Lord's Supper*. Chicago: Emmaus Correspondence School, 1965.
———. *The Lord's Supper*. Rev. ed. Oak Park, IL: Emmaus Bible School, 1970.
Friesen, Garry. *Decision Making and the Will of God: A Biblical Alternative to the Traditional View*. Portland: Multnomah, 1980.
"Funding the Workers of the *Evangelische Christengemeenten Vlaanderen*." DVD. Evangelische Christengemeenten Vlaanderen. August 2007.
Gaudibert, G. F. Letter dated 27 March 1898, *Echoes of Service Magazine*. 1898, n.p.
———. Letter dated 25 March 1919, *Echoes of Service Magazine*. 1919, n.p.
Geestelijke Liederen. 17th ed. Vaassen: Uitgeveru Medema, 1993.
Geestelijke Liederen. 18th ed. Vaassen: Uitgeverij Medema, 2003.
Gehring, Roger. *House Church and Mission: The Importance of Household Structures in Early Christianity*. Peabody, MA: Hendrickson, 2004. Originally published as *Hausgemeinde und Mission*. Giessen: Brunnen, 2000.
Gelling, Beryl. Interview by author. Houthalen, Belgium. 15 August 2007.
Gelling, Hank and Beryl. "Belgium — A Mission Field!" *Missions*, July/August 2005.
Gelling, Henk and Beryl. "44th." Email to MSC. 15 August 2004.
———. Letter to MSC. Fall 1977.
———. Letter to MSC. May 1985.
———. Letter to MSC. January 1989.
———. Letter to MSC. April 1989.
———. Letter to MSC. 31 January 1991.
———. Letter to MSC. 08 October 1991.
———. Letter to MSC. December 1991.
———. Letter to MSC. 25 September 1995.
———. Letter to MSC. 25 January 1996.
———. Letter to MSC. December 2002.
———. Letter to MSC and supporters, February 1988.
———. Letter to supporters. Fall 1977.
———. Letter to supporters. February 1987.
———. Letter to supporters. January 1989.
———. Letter to supporters. Spring 1992.
———. Letter to supporters. 19 February 2002.
Gelling, Henk. "23rd Belgium." Email to MSC. 14 March 2004.
———. "52nd Belgium." Email to MSC. 17 October 2004.
———. "Broedervergadering in Houthalen." 18 September 1982. In personal diary: notebook covered with a blue and green geometric design and missing the back cover labeled, "Houthalen Christen Gemeente."

Bibliography

_____. "Gemeente vergadering." 10 September 1982. In personal diary: notebook covered with a blue-black-white plaid design labeled, "Christen Gemeente van Lanaken."
_____. "Koersel avondmaal." In personal diary: green Classic Russley Quality labeled, "Koersel eerste helft." 16 January 1977—13 March 1977.
_____. "Koersel Broeder Vergadering, 9 December 1976." In personal diary: orange-brown spiral notebook labeled, "Limburg-gemeente."
_____. "Opinieonderzoek," A survey to make contacts in and around the town of Lanaken.
_____. "RE: Wellen assembly." Email to author. 05 September 2008.
_____. "Verantw. Verg. Hamont Overpelt Gebouw." Personal diary: green denim-colored Clairefontaine notebook labeled, "Overpelt." 1986.
_____. Email to author. 11 December 2007.
_____. Email to author. 26 May 2008.
_____. Email to author. 30 June 2009.
_____. Handwritten letter to MSC on the reverse of a letter to supporters. Spring 1990.
_____. Interview by author. Gentbrugge, Belgium. 25 April 2003.
_____. Interview by author. Heverlee, Belgium. 01 September 2008.
_____. Interview by author. Houthalen, Belgium. 11 September 2002.
_____. Interview by author. Houthalen, Belgium. 01 May 2003.
_____. Interview by author. Houthalen, Belgium. 03 April 2003.
_____. Interview by author. Houthalen, Belgium. 12 August 2007.
_____. Interview by author. Houthalen, Belgium. 15 August 2007.
_____. Interview by P. H. van der Laan. Houthalen, Belgium. 16 May 1989.
_____. Letter to John den Boer. 14 September 1979.
_____. Letter to MSC. 11 June 1979.
_____. Letter to MSC. 12 September 1980.
_____. Letter to MSC. April 1989.
_____. Letter to MSC. January 1993.
_____. Letter to supporters. Fall 1977.
_____. Letter to supporters. Fall 1981.
_____. Letter to supporters. November 1987.
_____. Notes from a David Gooding Bible conference. In notebook: blue with yellow stripes labeled, "papier5." 09 January 1989.
_____. Notes from a meeting at the end of 1990 [November?] between leaders of the ECV and Ouweneel, Medema, Steenhuis, and Fijnvandraat. In personal diary: orange notebook of meetings from 1989–1991 labeled, "Werkers."
_____. Personal diary: blue denim-colored Clairefontaine notebook labeled, "Werkers Fall 85."
_____. Personal diary: green notebook labeled, "Overpelt."
_____. Personal diary: green notebook with color-code list on front.
_____. Personal diary: green notebook with purple geometric designs labeled, "Workers." Records of events from 1982–83.
_____. Personal diary: mottled blue notebook labeled, "Koersel."
_____. Personal diary: orange notebook labeled, "Werkers."
_____. Personal diary: purple Clairefontaine notebook labeled, "→Jan 86→ Lommel."

Bibliography

———. Personal diary: red plaid notebook labeled, "Dagelijkse dingen." Records of planning, preaching, payments, and meetings of workers or assembly meetings from 1982 to 1985.
———. Quarterly Report." Email to MSC. 08 May 2003.
———. Telephone conversation with author. 22 April 2008.
———. Telephone conversation with author. 12 January 2009.
———. Telephone conversation with author. 26 June 2009.
———. Telephone interview by author. 24 April 2003.
———. Telephone interview by author. 02 December 2008.
———. Telephone interview by author. 08 December 2008.
———. Telephone interview by author. 15 December 2008.
———. Telephone interview by author. 04 January 2009.
Gelling, Julie. "RE: Beryl's birthplace?" Email to author. 05 July 2008.
———. Interview by author. Houthalen, Belgium. 12 August 2007.
———. Telephone interview by author. 13 December 2008.
"Gemeentekaantje in Roeselare." *Nieuwsbrief van de christengemeenten*, edited by Guido De Kegel, January-February 1985.
"Gemeentenieuws." *Nieuwsbrief van de christengemeenten*, edited by Eric Rutten, no. 3, 1987.
"Gent, van huisgemeente tot. . . ." *Nieuwsbrief van de christengemeenten*, edited by Guido De Kegel, March-April 1984.
"Gentse Conferentie '94" in "A.V. —VEG—11 March 1995."
Gerard, Gielen. Letter to Eric Rutten. 27 February 1988.
"Gezen." *Nieuwsbrief van de christengemeenten*, edited by Guido De Kegel, January-February 1984.
Gibbs, Alfred P. *Scriptural Principles of Gathering or Why I Meet Among those Known as the Brethren*. Kansas City: Walterick, 1935.
———. *The Lord's Supper*. Kansas City: Walterick, 1963.
Gielen, Gerard, and Martin Symons. Interview by author. Lommel, Belgium. 14 August 2007.
Gielen, Gerard. "10 Jaar Overpelt Geteld." *Evangelische Christengemeenten Vlaanderen Nieuwsbrief*, edited by Marc Van Den Bogaerde, 12/1.
———. "Overpelt, Hamont, Hamont-Overpelt?" *Nieuwsbrief van de christengemeenten*, edited by Guido De Kegel, 2/1.
Gifford, Joanna. Telephone conversation with author. 08 February 2008.
Gifford, Peter and Joanna. "All-, Old-, en Full-timers." *Nieuwsbrief van de christengemeenten*, edited by Marc Van Den Bogaerde, June 1991.
———. "Personal Testimonies of Peter and Joanna Gifford." An attachment to a letter from Peter Gifford to Bill Coffey, Executive Director of Missionary Service Committee. 20 March 1985.
———. Interview by author. St. Joritz, France. 20 August 2008.
———. Letter to MSC. December 1989.
———. Letter to MSC. December 1996.
———. Letter to supporters. May 2005.
Gifford, Peter. "prayer letter." Email to MSC. 06 September 2006.
———. "Tienerkampen." Lecture for 2007 summer camp leaders. File created 30 July 2007.
———. Email to MSC. 21 July 2002.

_____. Interview by author. St. Die, France. 25 August 2003.
Gifford, Stephanie. Conversation with author. Oudorp(NH), Netherlands. 26 August 2007.
Gilhooley, James. "The Church in the Low Countries." *America* 167/17 (1992) 429–31.
Global Strategy: the Biblical Plan of Mission. 3rd ed. Spring Lake, NJ: CMML, 1999.
Godert, Renaat. Email to evangelical church leaders in Flanders. 24 March 1998.
"Gods strijders in de Vlaamse christengemeenten!" *De Werkerskrant: nieuws- en gebedsbrief van het binnenlands zendingsteam van de ECV*, edited by Rosario Anastasi, October 1999,
"Gods wondere wegen van Houthalen over Waterschei naar Zwartberg." *Nieuwsbrief van de christengemeenten*, edited by Guido De Kegel, no. 4, 1985.
Goossens, Wilfried. Interview by author. Brussels, Belgium. 14 November 2006.
Grass, Tim. *Edward Irving: The Lord's Watchman*. Milton Keynes, UK: Paternoster, 2011.
_____. *Gathering to His Name: The Story of the Open Brethren in Britain and Ireland*. Bletchley, UK: Paternoster, 2006.
"Groei en Toerusting van de Evangelische Christengemeenten: Beleidsnota 2002–2006." 23 November 2002.
"Groeten uit Canada." *Nieuwsbrief van de christengemeenten*, edited by Guido De Kegel, March-April 1984.
Groves, Anthony Norris. Letter to John Nelson Darby, 10 March 1836. In F. Roy Coad, *A History of the Brethren Movement: Its Origins, its Worldwide Development and its Significance for the Present Day*. Exeter, UK: Paternoster, 1968.
_____. *Memoir of the Late Anthony Norris Groves*. Edited by Sentinel Kulp. 1856; Reprint, Sumneytown, PA: Sentinel, 2002.
Haeck, R. "Aanvraag tot erkenning van een protestantse kerk te Houthalen-Helchteren." In "Bekendamaking: Gemeenteraadsvergadering van 17 Maart 2005." Genk, Belgium.
"Hallo, wie geht es ihnen." *Nieuwsbrief van de christengemeenten*, edited by Eric Rutten, no. 1, 1988.
Hampton, Ron. Email message to author. 24 January 2008. A forward from Sid Tordoff. Email message to Ron Hampton. 24 January 2008.
Hannah, John. "The Church in America." Dallas Theological Seminary: unpublished class notes, 1985.
_____. *Our Legacy: The History of Christian Doctrine*. Colorado Springs: NavPress, 2001.
Hanssens, Marc-Eric. "Re: Brussels assembly." Email to author. 24 June 2006.
_____. Email to author. 13 December 2005.
Haverkamp, Marina. Interview by author. St. Martens Latem, Belgium. 30 April 2003.
_____. Written response to questions from Koen Schelstraete. n.d. (file dated 09 September 1999).
Haverkamp, Richard and Marina. "The Haverkamp News." Letter to supporters. Spring 1986.
_____. Letter to MSC. 13 February 1990.
_____. Letter to MSC. 20 March 1991.
_____. Letter to supporters. November 1977.
_____. Letter to supporters. March 1979.
_____. Letter to supporters. Spring 1980.

Bibliography

———. Letter to supporters. February 1982.
———. Letter to supporters. Spring 1982.
———. Letter to supporters. Spring 1986.
———. Letter to supporters. Fall 1987.
———. Letter to supporters. December 1988.
———. Letter to supporters. June 1990.
———. Letter to supporters. January 1992.
———. Letter to supporters. March 2004.
———. Newsletter to supporters. May 1972.
———. Newsletter to supporters. Fall 1975.
———. Newsletter to supporters. Winter 1977.
Haverkamp, Richard, editor. *Nieuw: Vijftien Vlamingen vertellen hoe Jezus hun leven veranderde*. Leuven: OM Benelux, 1980.
Haverkamp, Richard. "Belgium-the Land." *Echoes*. August 2001.
———. "Church Planting." European Christian Workers Conference France, 20–24 August 1979.
———. "Flanders Fields." Letter to Supporters. January 1997.
———. "God is at Work in Belgium." *Missions* 17/6, June 1988.
———. "Haverkamp History." Informal record of the ministry and house moves of the Haverkamps from 1972–2002.
———. "Heikoops." Email to author. 06 January 2009.
———. "Het avondmaal—de samenkomst van de gemeente." Lecture given in a number of places throughout Flanders, n.d.
———. "Mijn weg naar de realiteit." Gospel tract. circa 1973.
———. "Re: Question on the Brethren." Email to author. 30 April 2008.
———. "RE: Song Ttile [sic], please?" Email to author. 16 July 2007.
———. "*Startstudies*: 10 Evangelische Bibjbelstudies vanuit Johannes 1–3," (1979?).
———. "Wie der Herr Jesus Christus Gemeinden baut." 8 lectures & 1 question and answer period. Deutsche Gemeinde-Mission, KfG Ostdeutschland, 2002.
———. Email to supporters. 22 April 2000.
———. Interview by author, St. Martens Latem, Belgium. 25 April 2003.
———. Interview by author. St. Martens Latem, Belgium. 30 April 2003.
———. Interview by P.H. van der Laan. 02 September 1988.
———. Letter to Johan Lukasse. 20 April 1973.
———. Letter to John H. McKechnie of MSC. 30 August 1971.
———. Letter to John H. McKechnie, Secretary of MSC. 26 August 1971.
———. Letter to MSC. 08 September 1970.
———. Letter to MSC. March 1981.
———. Letter to MSC. 12 July 1987.
———. Letter to MSC. 4 August 1988.
———. Letter to MSC. 28 November 1989.
———. Letter to MSC. 14 January 1992.
———. Letter to MSC. 20 March 1991.
———. Letter to supporters. May-June 1977.
———. Letter to supporters. September-October 1977.
———. Letter to supporters. February 1982.
———. Letter to supporters. April 1983.
———. Letter to supporters. Spring 1986.

———. Letter to supporters. 9 February 1987.
———. Letter to supporters. 11 October 1995.
———. New Year's letter to supporters. [21] January 1992.
———. Newsletter to Canadian supporters. May 1972.
———. Telephone interview by author. 29 July 2005.
———. Telephone interview by author. 06 December 2008.
———. Telephone interview by author. 15 December 2008.
———. Telephone interview by author. 06 January 2009.
———. Written response to questions from Koen Schelstraete. n.d. (file dated 06 November 2000).
Hawthorne, Gerald. *Philippians*. Word Biblical Commentary 43. Waco: Word, 1983.
Hay, Alexander R. *The New Testament Order for Church and Missionary*. 2nd ed. Welland, ON: New Testament Missionary Union, 1947.
Heijkoop, H. L. *De Gemeente van de levende God*. Winschoten, Netherlands: Uit het Woord der Waarheid, 1975.
Hesselgrave, David. *Planting Churches Cross-Culturally: North America and Beyond*. 2nd ed. Grand Rapids: Baker, 2000.
Heykoop, H. L. *Hoe en waar moeten gelovigen zich vergadering*. Winschoten, Netherlands: Heykoop, n.d.
Heyman, Herman. "Verslag van de vergadering." Vlaams Evangelisatie Comité, BEZ. Heverlee, Belgium. 08 May 1984.
Hindmarsh, D. Bruce. "The Winnipeg Fundamentalist Network, 1910–1940: The Roots of Transdenominational Evangelicalism in Manitoba and Saskatchewan." *Didaskalia* 10/1 (1998). http:/prov.ca/Didaskalia/Articles/fall1998.asp.
"History of Global Literature Outreach." GLO Europe. http://www.glo-europe.org/history.html.
Hitchman, Henry. *Some Scriptural Principles of the Christian Assembly or things which are most surely believed among us*. Kilmarnock, Scotland: Ritchie, 1929.
"Hoe het begon in Leopoldsburg." *Nieuwsbrief van de christengemeenten*, edited by Eric Rutten, no. 2, 1988.
Hofman, Mirjam. "3.3: Een derde groep open vergaderingen: Swaan en Bouwman." In "Open broeders in Nederland: Een onderzoek naar de geschiedenis en identiteit van open vergaderingen van gelovigen." Bachelor's thesis, Universiteit Leiden, 2008.
Holthaus, Stephen. "Die Gründer der Bibelschule: A. John Parschauer." In *Gott ist Treu: Die Geschichte der Bibelschule Brake*. http://www.bibelschule-brake.de/gesch5.htm (site discontinued).
"How Did MSC Canada Begin?" *MSC Canada*. http://msccanada.org/history.html.
Hymns of Worship and Remembrance. Fort Dodge, IA: Gospel Perpetuating Fund, 1950.
"Identiteit en Werking van de Evangelische Christengemeenten." Evangelische Christengemeenten Vlaanderen. http://home2.pi.be/pin21516/onze_geloofsbelijdenis.htm (site discontinued).
"In Koersel ann de toog." *Nieuwsbrief van de christengemeenten*, edited by Guido De Kegel, September-October 1984.
Inrig, Gary. *Life in His Body: Discovering Purpose, From, and Freedom in His Church*. Wheaton, IL: Shaw, 1975.

Bibliography

Interdisiplinair Centrum voor Religiestudie en Interlevensbeschouwelijke Dialoog. "Het Protestantisme in België." Katholieke Universiteit Leuven. http://theo.kuleuven.be/icrid/icrid_religies/icrid_religies_christendom/protestantisme/.

"Introductie." Evangelische Christengemeenten Vlaanderen. http://home.scarlet.be (site discontinued).

Ironside, H. A. *Expository Notes on the Gospel of Matthew*. New York: Loizeaux, 1948.

"Jaarsverslag Vlaams Evangelisatie-Komitee vor de BEZ Konferentie van 19 November 1977." Report. P. Sevaas, secretary.

Johnson, Paul. *A History of the American People*. New York: HarperCollins, 1997.

Johnstone, Philip. *Operation World*. 4th ed. Kent: STL, 1986.

Kanmaz, Meryem. "The Recognition and Institutionalization of Islam in Belgium." *Muslim World* 92/1-2 (2002) 99–113.

"Karrewegel 47." *Evangelische Christengemeenten Vlaanderen Nieuwsbrief*, edited by Marc Van Den Bogaerde, June 1992.

Keating, Karl. *Catholicism and Fundamentalism: The Attack on "Romanism" by "Bible Christians."* San Francisco: Ignatius, 1988.

"'Keiner kann mir Vorwürfe machen, dass ich mich geändert habe': Interview mit Willem J. Ouweneel." Interview by Michael Schneider. N.p.: brueder*bewegung*.de, 2004. http://www.bruederbewegung.de/pdf/ouweneelinterview.pdf.

Kelly, William. "Letters on the Lord's Supper." *The Kelly Collection CD*. Kent: STEM, 1998.

Knott, Carl. "Additional Reading on Evangelism." Insert attached to Sanny's work which was used as the basis of evangelistic training. Lubbock Bible Chapel, TX. January 1978.

Knox, Noelle. "Religion Takes a back seat in Western Europe." *USA Today*, 11 August 2005.

Kolde, T. "Catholic Apostolic Church." In *The New Schaff-Herzog Encyclopedia of Religious Knowledge, Vol. II: Basilica–Chambers*, edited by Philip Schaff. http://www.ccel.org/s/schaff/encyc/encyc02/htm/iv.vi.cxcix.htm#iv.vi.cxcix.

Kopp, Herb, and Gordon Zerbe. "Bibliographic Essay on Church Leadership." *Direction Journal* 8/2 (1979). http://www.directionjournal.org/article/?308.

"Kortrijk: 'We zijn benieuwd.'" *Evangelische Christengemeenten Vlaanderen Nieuwsbrief*, edited by Marc Van Den Bogaerde, 11/1.

Krayenhoff, Jack. "Changing of the Guard at Oaklands Chapel." canadianchristianity.com: A ministry of Christian Ministry Info. http://www.canadianchristianity.com/cgi-bin/bc.cgi?bc/bccn/1006/i03guard (site discontinued).

Küng, Hans. "The Dimensions of the Church: The Church is Catholic." In *The Church*, translated by Ray Ockenden and Rosalein Ockenden, 296–318. New York: Sheed & Ward, 1967.

La Voce Nel Deserto, edited by Michael Rannelli. 45/1, October 1965.

"Landelijke Ontmoetingsdag." *Nieuwsbrief van de Christengemeenten*, edited by Guido De Kegel, nr.3, 1985.

Laügt, Etienne. *Région de Bruxelles*. In "Historie des assemblées en Belgique francophone." http://fileo.free.fr/Histoire/Belgique/belgique.htm.

Lawton, Kim A. "Evangelism Explosion Retools Its Approach." *Christianity Today*, 03 March 1997.

Le Jeune, Theo. "Boom: flink op weg." *Nieuwsbrief van de christengemeenten*, edited by Guido De Kegel, May-June 1984.

Bibliography

Lefevere, Patricia. "Pope to face disgruntled laity in Belgium." *National Catholic Reporter* 31 (1995) 13.

"Legerdienst." *Nieuwsbrief van de christengemeenten*, edited by Guido De Kegel, January–February 1985.

Leslie, L. M. "Is the Church of God an Organization or an Organism?" *STEM Publishing*: *The Writings of L. M. Grant*: *Is the Church of God an Organization or an Organism?* http://www.stempublishing.com/authors/grantlm/ORGANISM.html.

Levada, William. "Responses to some Questions Regarding Certain Aspects of the Doctrine on the Church." Congregation for the Doctrine of the Faith. http://www.vatican.va/roman_curia/congregations/cfaith/documents/rc_con_cfaith_doc_20070629_responsa-quaestiones_en.html.

Liagre, Roldolphe L. P. "Re: History of the Brethren in Flanders." Email to author. 31 July 2003.

Liberek, Samuel. *Belgische Vereniging Van Vrij Evangelische Gemeenten*. N.p.: n.p., 1987.

Liefeld, Walter L. "Suggestions for Defining Some Identifying Characteristics of the Brethren." Paper presented at a special summer course, "The Christian Brethren Movement: Its Past History, Present Status and Future Prospects," Regent College, Vancouver, BC, 29 June—3 July 1990.

Lindsay, Hal. *De planeet die aarde heette*. Laren, Netherlands: Novapress, 1972.

Linsted, Leonard E. *The Womens' Head Covering: Fact or Fallacy*. Waynesboro, GA: Christian Missions, n.d.

Little, Paul. *Geloven: Waarom eigenlijk?* Translated by Richard Haverkamp. Apeldoorn: Uitgave Medema, [1975?]).

———. *How to Give Away your Faith*. Downers Grove, IL: InterVarsity, 1966.

Littleproud, J. R. *The Christian Assembly*. Grand Rapids: Gospel Folio, [1955?].

Lobb, Bruce and Diane. Interview by author. Seaforth, ON, Canada. 02 September 2006.

"Luc en Nicole 'fulltime.'" *Nieuwsbrief van de christengemeenten*, edited by Guido De Kegel, July–August 1984.

Lukasse, Johan. "Een lijst van posten en gemeenten gesticht door de B.E.Z." Brussels, Belgium. Summary report by the VEG dated 29 June 1988.

———. "Verslag ontmoeting tussen de V.E.G en B.E.Z te Brussel." 05 October 1999.

———. Interview by author. Badhoevedorp, Netherlands. 05 December 2003.

Lutz, Lorry. "Evangelicals Give Out 1.2 Million Evangelistic Papers During Pope's visit to Belgium." *Christianity Today*, 14 June 1985.

MacDonald, William. *Christ Loved the Church*. Chicago: Emmaus Correspondence School, 1956.

Mackintosh, C. H. "The Assembly of God." In *The Assembly of God: Miscellaneous Writings of C.H. Mackintosh*, vol. 3. New York: Loizeaux, 1898.

———. "Thoughts on the Lord's Supper: Designed for the Help of Christians in the Day of Difficulty." In *The Assembly of God: Miscellaneous Writings of C.H. Mackintosh*, vol. 3. New York: Loizeaux, 1898.

MacLeod, David J. "The Primacy of Scripture and the Church." In *Understanding the Church: the Biblical Ideal for the 21st Century*, edited by Joseph M. Vogl and John H. Fish, 11–64. Neptune, NJ: Loizeaux, 1999.

———. Review of *Bible Colleges? A Warning Against the Spread of Bible Teaching institutions Among NT Local Assemblies*, by Michael Browne. *Emmaus Journal* 7/1 (1998) 117–28.

Bibliography

"Maldegem, twee jaar op eigen benen." *Nieuwsbrief van de christengemeenten*, edited by Guido De Kegel, March-April 1984.

Malphurs, Aubrey. *Planting Growing Churches for the 21st Century: A Comprehensive Guide for New Churches and Those Desiring Renewal*. Grand Rapids: Baker, 1992.

"Manifesto of the Vlaams Belang, The." http://www.flemishrepublic.org/manifesto.htm (site discontinued).

Martin, Gord. "What does it mean to be Brethren in a VMC World?" Vision Ministries Canada, August 2004.

Martin, John. *Saved to Serve: The Treasure in Earthen Vessels*. Grand Rapids: Gospel Folio, 1994.

Martin, John and Melissa. Interview by author. Tavistock, ON, Canada. 01 September 2006.

Masuello, Edith. Email to author. 13 August 2007.

Matthews, Donald G. "The Second Great Awakening as an Organizing Process." In *Religion in American History: Interpretive Essays*, edited by John M. Mulder and John F. Wilson, 199–217. Englewood Cliffs, NJ: Prentice-Hall, 1978.

"May we introduce... David Dunlap." *Missions*, December 1983.

"May we introduce... Hal and Marion Threadcraft." *Missions*, September 1981.

Maxwell, Joe. "Is Laughing for the Lord Holy?" *Christianity Today*, 24 October 1994.

McClure, William J. *The Tabernacle: Its Types and Teachings*. Kilmarnock, Scotland: Ritchie, [1914?].

McDowell, Josh. *Meer dan een timmerman*. Noordwijkerhout: Internationale bijbelbond, 1978.

McLaren, Ross. "Triple Tradition: The Origin and Development of the Open Brethren in North America." MA thesis, Vanderbilt University, 1982.

Mead, Frank S. *Handbook of Denominations in the United States*. 7th ed. Nashville: Abingdon, 1980.

Mededeelingen omtrent het werk Gods in onze dagen. Vol. 13. Edited by H.C.V.(oorhoeve). N.p.: n.p., [Spring 1876].

Mededeelingen omtrent het werk Gods in onze dagen. Vol. 58. Edited by H.C.V.(oorhoeve). N.p.: n.p., [Winter 1887].

Medema, Henk. Interview by author. Vaassen, Netherlands. 18 September 2003.

Meschkat, Edwin. Conversation with author. South Plains Bible Chapel, Lubbock, TX. Spring 1978.

"Met zijn allen naar de film." *Nieuwsbrief van de christengemeenten*, edited by Guido De Kegel, November-December 1984.

"Millar College of the Bible." http://www.millarcollege.ca/history.html.

Minnery, Thomas. "Success in Three Churches: Diversity and Originality." *Leadership* 2/1 (1981) 57–65.

Missionary Orientation Program. CMML and MSC Canada. Greenwood Hills, PA.

Missionary Prayer Handbook. Wall, NJ: CMML, 1975.

Missionary Prayer Handbook for daily use: Listing many missionaries commended by United States and Canadian assemblies, 2009. N.p. [USA]: Christian Missions in Many Lands, 2009.

Moloney, Francis J. "Vatican II: The Word in the Church Tradition." Catalyst for Renewal: Seeking Renewal Through Conversation. http://www.catalyst-for-renewal.com.au/index.php?option=com_content&view=article&id=193&catid=44:archive-vatican-ii-the-mix-esssays&Itemid=102.

Bibliography

"More than a Carpenter." Amazon.com. http://www.amazon.com/More-Than-Carpenter-Josh-McDowell/dp/0842345523.
"More than a Carpenter." Campus Crusade for Christ. http://www.campuscrusade.com/Josh_McDowell/more_than_a_carpenter.htm.
MSC: Local Church Driven Missions. http://www.msc.on.ca/.
Mudditt, B. Howard. *The New Fellowship*. Exeter: Paternoster, 1975.
Müller, Jean. "Old Paths." Translated by Richard K Gorgas. *le messager évangélique*, 1994. http://www.stempublishing.com/authors/various/OLDPATHS.html.
Munnings, Fred and Hilda. Interview by author. Seaforth, ON, Canada. 02 September 2006.
Munnings, Hilda Mae, compiler. *A History of Fellowship Bible Chapel*. N.p.: n.p., 1988.
Muriu, Oscar. "Let My People Go, Acts 2:42–47." Lecture, International Brethren Conference on Mission 4. Bergneustadt-Wiedenest, Germany. 30 June 2007.
Murray, Iain H. *Revival and Revivalism: The Making and Marring of American Evangelicalism 1750–1858*. Carlisle, PA: Banner of Truth Trust, 1994.
Murray, Stuart. *Post-Christendom: Church and Mission in a Strange New World*. Bletchley, UK: Paternoster, 2004.
Naismith, James. "Christ the Centre." In *The Church of God: A Symposium*, edited by R. E. Harlow, 7–14. Toronto: Everyday, 1976.
"Nationale Commissie Agenda." 15 December 1997.
Neatby, William B. *A History of the Plymouth Brethren*. London: Hodder & Stoughton, 1902.
"Nieuw initiatief voor de christengemeentes." *Nieuwsbrief van de christengemeentes*, edited by Eric Rutten, 1990, nr. 1.
"Nieuwe aanpak voor Maldegem." *Nieuwsbrief van de christengemeenten*, edited by Eric Rutten, 1988, nr. 1.
"Nieuwe christengemeentes." *Evangelische Christengemeenten Vlaanderen Nieuwsbrief*, edited by Marc Van Den Bogaerde, October 1991.
"Nieuwe gemeente in Guigoven." *Evangelische Christengemeenten Vlaanderen Nieuwsbrief*, edited by Marc Van Den Bogaerde, October 1991.
"Nieuws uit . . . Meeuwen." *Nieuwsbrief van de christengemeenten*, edited by Eric Rutten, no. 2, 1988.
"Nieuws van het oostelijk front." *Nieuwsbrief van de christengemeenten*, edited by Guido De Kegel, November-December 1984.
Nicholson, J. Boyd. "Divine Ordinances." In *The Church of God: A Symposium*, edited by R. E. Harlow, 58–72. Toronto: Everyday, 1976.
Nock, William J. Letter dated 20 August 1896, *Echoes of Service Magazine*. 1896, n.p.
_____. Letter dated 5 January 1898, *Echoes of Service Magazine*. 1898, n.p.
_____. Letter dated 27 February 1899, *Echoes of Service Magazine*. 1899, n.p.
_____. Letter dated 12 September 1902, *Echoes of Service Magazine*. 1902, n.p.
_____. Letter dated 23 October 1906, *Echoes of Service Magazine*. 1906, n.p.
_____. Letter dated 6 August 1920, *Echoes of Service Magazine*. 1920, n.p.
_____. Letter dated 21 June 1920 from Ghent, *Echoes of Service Magazine*. 1920, n.p.
Noel, Napoleon. *The History of the Brethren*. Edited by William Knapp. 2 vols. Denver: Knapp, 1936.
Norbie, Donald L. *New Testament Church Organization: Defined and compared with the major ecclesiastical systems*. Chicago: Interest, 1955.

Bibliography

———. *The Early Church: Rediscovering Truth for the Churches.* Waynesboro, GA: Christian Mission, 1983.

Norman, J. G. G. "Moravian Brethren." In *The New International Dictionary of the Christian Church*, 2nd ed., edited by J. D. Douglas, 676. Grand Rapids: Zondervan, 1978.

Novak, George. " Sociology and historical Materialism." Marxists Internet Archive. http://www.marxists.org/archive/novack/works/history/ch10.htm.

Nullens, Patrick. Interview by author. Heverlee, Belgium. 10 September 2003.

"Nuttige inlichtingen." *Nieuwsbrief van de christengemeenten*, edited by Guido De Kegel, November-December 1984.

"'Om U te dienen:' Beleidsplan, 2008–2011." *Evangelische Christengemeenten Vlaanderen*, November 2007.

"Onstwedde." http://www.onstwedde.nl/ (site discontinued).

"Op de koffie bij . . . Julie Gelling." *De Werkerskrant: nieuws- en gebedsbrief van het binnenlands zendingsteam van de ECV*, edited by Rosario Anastasi, December 2003.

"Op de koffie bij . . . Martin en Lydia Symonds [sic]." *De Werkerskrant: nieuws- en gebedsbrief van het binnenlands zendingsteam van de ECV*, edited by Rosario Anastasi, September 2003.

"Op de koffie bij . . . Martin en Lydia." *De Werkerskrant: nieuws- en gebedsbrief van het binnenlands zendingsteam van de ECV*, edited by Rosario Anastasi, March 2001.

"Op de koffie bij . . . Ann [sic]." *De Werkerskrant: nieuws- en gebedsbrief van het binnenlands zendingsteam van de ECV*, edited by Rosario Anastasi, February 2003.

"Op de koffie met . . . Rosario en Anita." *De Werkerskrant: nieuws- en gebedsbrief van het binnenlands zendingsteam van de ECV*, edited by Rosario Anastasi, December 2001.

"Op de koffie . . . interview Pete en Joanna." *De Werkerskrant: nieuws- en gebedsbrief van het binnenlands zendingsteam van de ECV*, edited by Rosario Anastasi, December 2000.

"Op de koffie." *De Werkerskrant: nieuws- en gebedsbrief van het binnenlands zendingsteam van de ECV*, edited by Rosario Anastasi, December 1999.

"Op de koffie." *De Werkerskrant: nieuws- en gebedsbrief van het binnenlands zendingsteam van de ECV*, edited by Rosario Anastasi, February 2000.

"Op de koffie." *De Werkerskrant: nieuws- en gebedsbrief van het binnenlands zendingsteam van de ECV*, edited by Rosario Anastasi, September 2002.

Opp, James W. "'Culture of the Soul': Fundamentalism and Evangelism in Canada, 1921–1940." MA thesis, University of Calgary, 1994.

———. "Fwd: Attn: Dr. James Opp." Email to author. 30 July 2003.

"Oprichtingsaktie van een vereniging zonder winstoogmerk." 11 March 1996. Appendix to *Belgisch Standard*, 23 May 1996.

"Our History." Scripture Union Scotland. http://www.suscotland.org.uk/about_us/about_us.html (site discontinued).

Ouweneel, Willem. *"Gij zijt allen broeders": Het Nederlands Reveil en de "Vergaderingen" van "De Broeders."* Vaassen: Uitgeverij Medema, 1980.

———. *De Maaltijd des Heren.* Vaassen: Uitgeverij H. Medema, n.d.

———. *Het verhaal van de "Broeders": 150 jaar falen genade*, deel II (1890–1978). Winschoten: Uit het Woord der Waarheid, 1978.

Paisley, Harold S. *The Believers Hymn Book Companion.* Glasgow: Gospel Tract, 1989.

Bibliography

"Pannekoeken voor Tear-Fund" *Nieuwsbrief van de christengemeenten*, edited by Guido De Kegel, March-April 1984.
"Pausbezoek België." Appendix, *Evangeliekoerier* 17/1, February 1985.
Pelikan, Jaroslav. "The Predicament of the Christian Historian." Lecture, Center of Theological Inquiry, Princeton, April 1997.
Peters, George W. "The Missionary of the Seventies." *Bibliotheca Sacra* 128/509 (1971) 50–61.
Peterson, Jim. *Evangelism as a Lifestyle*. Colorado Springs: Navpress, 1980.
Peterson, Robert L. "A History of Some Assemblies of Christians in the United States and Canada." Emmaus Bible College. http://www.emmaus.edu/files/Documents/History%20of%20Brethren%20Mvt/history_0.htm.
Peterson, Robert L., and Alexander Strauch. *Agape Leadership: Lessons in Spiritual Leadership from the Life of R.C. Chapman*. Littleton, CO: Lewis & Roth, 1991.
Petrovic, John E. "Balkanization, bilingualism, and comparisons of language situations at home and abroad." *Bilingual Research Journal* 21/2–3 (1997) 233–54. http://brj.asu.edu/articlesv2/petrovic.html (site discontinued).
Phalet, Karen, and Marc Swyngedouw. "Measuring immigrant integration: the case of Belgium." *Studi Emigrazione / Migration Studies* 40/152 (2003) 773–803. http://business.bilgi.edu.tr/pdf/Immigrant_Integration_SE.pdf.
Piepkorn, Arthur Carl. "Plymouth Brethren (Christian Brethren)." *Concordia Theological Monthly* 41 (1970) 165–71.
Piérard, Mme. Letter of 1922 in "Notes and Comments," *Echoes of Service Magazine*, 1922, n.p.
———. Letter of 1924 in "Notes and Comments," *Echoes of Service Magazine*, 1924, n.p.
———. Letter of Easter, 1921 in "Brief Notes," *Echoes of Service Magazine*, 1921, n.p.
Pierson, Arthur T. *George Muller of Bristol and His Life of Prayer and Faith*. London: Revell, 1900.
"Plano Bible Chapel." http://www.planobiblechapel.org/index.php.
Plomp, Martien. "Re: Geschiedenis van de vergadering en Eindhoven." Email to author. 10 July 2008.
Pope John XXIII. "The Roman Synod And The Priest." Lecture, Rome, 24 November 1960. http://www.catholicculture.org/culture/library/view.cfm?RecNum=3227.
Porter, Mark. *Commendation: Answers to Key Questions*. Wheaton, IL: Interest Ministries, 1991.
"Praktische afspraken om te kunnen vergaderingen." Nationale Vergadering. 15 June 1990.
Presentatie_ejv2006.ppt. A PowerPoint presentation linked to "Evangelisch Jeugdverbond: Wie zijn we?" Evangelisch Jeugdverbond. http://www.ejv.be/index.php?id=41.
"Programma." Evangelische Toerustingschool Vlaanderen. http://www.ets-vlaanderen.be/index.php?id=27.
Protestants-Evangelisch Archief-en Documentatiecentrum (EVADOC). http://www.evadoc.be.
Pulleng, A. *"Go Ye Therefore . . ." Missionary Service in a Changing World*. 1958. Reprint, Spring Lake, NJ: CMML, 1984.
Ratzinger, Joseph Cardinal. "Declaration *Dominus Iesus* on the Unicity and Salvific Universality of Jesus Christ and the Church." Vatican. http://212.77.1.247/roman_

curia/congregations/cfaith/documents/rc_con_cfaith_doc_20000806_dominus-iesus_en.html.

Rauert, Matthias H. and Annelie Kümpers-Greve. *Van Der Smissen: Eine mennonitische Familie vor dem Hintergrund der Geschichte Altonas und Schleswig-Holsteins: Texte und Dokumente*. Hamburg: Nord Magazin, 1992.

"Regarding: The Accession of the Assembly in Tienen." *Nationale Vergadering Christengemeenten*, Appendix 1, 28 November 1992.

Reid, John. *F.W. Grant: His Life, Ministry and Legacy*. Plainfield, NJ: John Reid Book Fund, 1995.

_____. *The Chief Meeting of the Church*. 5th ed. N.p.[Waynesboro, GA]: Christian Missions, 1993.

_____. *The Chief Meeting of the Church: ". . . in remembrance of Me."* Plainfield, NJ: Christian Mission, 1978.

Ridley, Charles R. *How to Select Church Planters: A Self-Study Manual for Recruiting, Screening, Interviewing and Evaluating Qualified Church Planters*. Pasadena, CA: Fuller Evangelistic Association, 1988.

Rossier, H. L. "What is a Meeting of the Assembly?" *Mighty Men* CD-ROM. Kent: STEM, 1999.

Rowdon, Harold H. *The Origins of the Brethren: 1825–1850*. London: Pickering & Inglis, 1967.

_____. *Who are the Brethren and Does It Matter?* Exeter: Paternoster, 1986.

Ruby, Robert, ed. *Spirit and Power: A 10-Country Survey of Pentecostals*. Washington, DC: Pew Forum on Religion & Public Life, 2006.

Ryrie, Charles C. *Dispensationalism Today*. Chicago: Moody, 1965.

"Samenkomst van de gemeente." In minutes of the "Werkersvergadering," Berchem. 28 June 1991.

Sanny, Lorne. *The Art of Personal Witnessing*. Chicago: Moody, 1957.

Saucy, Robert L. *The Church in God's Program*. Chicago: Moody, 1972.

Schakelaar, Gerrit, Assistant Treasurer MSC. Email to author. 13 May 2008.

Schelstraete, Koen and Esther. Interview by author. Borgerhout, Belgium. 03 September 2007.

Schelstraete, Koen. "Handelingen (1)." *De Werkerskrant: nieuws- en gebedsbrief van het binnenlands zendingsteam van de ECV*, edited by Rosario Anastasi et al., December 1999.

_____. "Handelingen (3)." *De Werkerskrant: nieuws- en gebedsbrief van het binnenlands zendingsteam van de ECV*, edited by Rosario Anastasi et al., May 2000.

_____. "Handelingen (4)," *De Werkerskrant: nieuws- en gebedsbrief van het binnenlands zendingsteam van de ECV*, edited by Rosario Anastasi et al., November 2000.

_____. "Handelingen (6)." *De Werkerskrant: nieuws- en gebedsbrief van het binnenlands zendingsteam van de ECV*, edited by Rosario Anastasi et al., March 2001.

_____. "Handelingen (7)." *De Werkerskrant: nieuws- en gebedsbrief van het binnenlands zendingsteam van de ECV*, edited by Rosario Anastasi et al., June 2001.

_____. "Handelingen (10)." *De Werkerskrant: nieuws- en gebedsbrief van het binnenlands zendingsteam van de ECV*, edited by Rosario Anastasi et al., December 2001.

_____. "Handelingen (14)." *De Werkerskrant: nieuws- en gebedsbrief van het binnenlands zendingsteam van de ECV*, edited by Rosario Anastasi et al., February 2003.

———. "Handelingen (16)." *De Werkerskrant: nieuws- en gebedsbrief van het binnenlands zendingsteam van de ECV*, edited by Rosario Anastasi et al., September 2003.

———. "Handelingen (17)." *De Werkerskrant: nieuws- en gebedsbrief van het binnenlands zendingsteam van de ECV*, edited by Rosario Anastasi et al., December 2003.

———. "Handelingen (18)." *De Werkerskrant: nieuws- en gebedsbrief van het binnenlands zendingsteam van de ECV*, edited by Rosario Anastasi et al., March 2004.

———. "Handelingen (19)." *De Werkerskrant: nieuws- en gebedsbrief van het binnenlands zendingsteam van de ECV*, edited by Rosario Anastasi et al., June 2004.

———. "Handelingen (21)." *De Werkerskrant: nieuws- en gebedsbrief van het binnenlands zendingsteam van de ECV*, edited by Rosario Anastasi et al., January 2005.

———. "Handelingen (22)." *De Werkerskrant: nieuws- en gebedsbrief van het binnenlands zendingsteam van de ECV*, edited by Rosario Anastasi et al., March 2004.

Schneider, Floyd. *Evangelism for the Faint-hearted*. Portland: Earl C., 1991.

Scholman, Patrick, and Albert Walsmeer. "DAWN 2015, Visie voor Gemeentestichting in Vlaanderen: Kerken en Gemeenten in Vlaanderen 1998." N.p.: n.p., 1998.

Schraepen, Eric. Interview by author. Bergneustadt-Wiedenest, Germany. 27 June 2007.

Scofield, C. I., editor. *Scofield Reference Bible*. New York: Oxford, 1909.

Shuff, Roger N. "Open to Closed: the growth of exclusivism among the Brethren in Britain, 1848–1953." *Brethren Archivists & Historians Network Review* 1/1(1997) 10–23.

Sleijster, Harry. "Vergadering.nu." http://www.vergadering.nu/.

———. "Zuid-Nederland." Vergadering.nu. http://vergadering.nu/kaartzuid.htm (site discontinued).

Smith, Nathan D. *Roots, Renewal, and the Brethren*. Pasadena, CA: Hope, 1986.

Spong, John Shelby. "A Bishop Speaks—European Christianity: A Bleak Picture." Beliefnet. Onine: http://www.beliefnet.com/story/80/story_8099.html.

Stahr, James A. personal letter to Ross McLaren concerning Lloyd Walterick and his publishing company, 8 October 1975. Quoted in Ross McLaren, "Triple Tradition: The Origin and Development of the Open Brethren in North America." MA thesis, Vanderbilt University, 1982.

Stallard, Mike. Paper presented at the annual Pre-Trib Study group, 8–9 January 1997, Tyndale Theological Seminary, Ft. Worth, TX. http://www.conservativeonline.org/journals/01_01_journal/1997v1n1_id03.htm#_ftn17 (site discontinued).

Stanford, Miles J. "Plymouth Brethren Emulators." *withChrist.org* http://www.withchrist.org/MJS/pbemulators.htm (site discontinued).

"Stap voor stap verder in Vlaanderen." *Evangelische Christengemeenten Vlaanderen Nieuwsbrief*, edited by Marc Van Den Bogaerde, 12/3.

"Stelt an u voor . . . het binnenlands zendingsteam." *De Werkerskrant: nieuws- en gebedsbrief van het binnenlands zendingsteam van de ECV*, edited by Rosario Anastasi, October 1999, 1.

Strauch, Alexander. *Biblical Eldership: An Urgent Call to Restore Biblical Church Leadership*. Littleton, CO: Lewis & Roth, 1986.

Bibliography

"Studiedagen." *Nieuwsbrief van de christengemeenten*, edited by Guido De Kegel, May-June 1984.

"Studieweek gaat door." *Nieuwsbrief van de christengemeenten*, edited by Guido De Kegel, November-December 1984.

Swatos, William H. "The Comparative Method and the Special Vocation of the Sociology of Religion." *Sociological Analysis* 38/2 (1977) 106-14.

Taffijn, Edmond. "1883-1988: Geschiedenis van het ontstaan en verdere ontwikkeling van de vergadering van gelovigen te Ninove." Ninove: n.p., 1988.

Tatford, Fredk. A. *West European Evangel*. Vol. 8 of *That the World May Know*. Bath: Echoes of Service, 1985.

Thomas, Yvan, and Richard Haverkamp. *10 startstudies, handleiding voor het doorgeven van geloofsprincipes*. Ieper, Belgium: Jered, 1995.

Thomas, Yvan. "Cursus Oudstenbegeleiding." Flanders: n.p., [2005(?)].

_____. *En jij gelooft dat?!!* Brussels: Het Goed Boek, 1990.

_____. *Evangelisatie? Wat doet u eraan?* Ieper: Jered, 1993.

Thompkins, Al. "Guidelines for Interviewing Confidential Sources: Who, When, and Why?" The Poynter Institute. http://www.poynter.org/content/content_view.asp?id=4361.

Thränhardt, Dietrich, editor. *Europe—A New Immigration Continent: Policies and Politics in Comparative Perspective*. 2nd ed. Munster: Transaction, 1996.

Threadcraft, Hal. "Re: ECV in Belgium." Email to author. 02 September 2008.

_____. Email to author. 11 January 2009.

_____. Letter to David Dunlap. 14 April 1982.

Tinder, Donald G. "The Brethren Movement in the World Today." Lecture delivered to Granville Chapel, Vancouver, BC: December 1971.

_____. "Christian Brethren." In *Religions of the World: A Comprehensive Encyclopedia of Beliefs and Practices*, edited by J. Gordon Melton and Martin Bauman, 1:268-69. Oxford: ABC-CLIO, 2002.

Tordoff, Betty. Letter to author. Undated (postmarked 01 February 2008).

Tordoff, Sidney. Email to author. 13 February 2008.

_____. Letter to author. Undated (postmarked 01 February 2008).

_____. Letter to Missionary Service Committee. 10 July 1976.

V.(oorhoeve), H. C., editor. *Mededeelingen omtrent het werk Gods in onze dagen*. Vol. 13. N.p.: n.p., [Spring 1876].

_____. *Mededeelingen omtrent het werk Gods in onze dagen*. Vol. 53. N.p.: n.p., [Summer 1885].

Valkenburg, Rik. *België: kent u het zo . . . ?* Turnhout: Het Goede Boek, [1975].

van der Bijl, J. *Met de Heer aan zijn tafel*. Apeldoorn: Uitgeverij Medema: [1975?].

van der Bijl, Jacques. "Re: Vergadering in Vlaanderen." Email to author. 23 June 2007.

Van Der Elst, J. Letter to author. 20 August 2005.

van der Laan, P.H. "Gemeentestichtende Evangelisatie in Vlaanderen." Doctoraal thesis, Theologische Universiteit van de Gereformeerde Kerken (Broederweg) in Kampen, 1991.

Van Der Smissen, Family. Ninove, to Samuel Van Der Smissen, Kwaremont, 12 February 1943. Printed death notice for Lodewijk Van Der Smissen.

Van Der Smissen, Pitou. *Genealogie de la Famille Van Der Smissen, 1570-1970*. Wavre: n.p., 1977.

Van Der Smissen, S. *Genealogie Van Der Smissen, 1600-1983*. Gent: n.p., 1983.

Van Der Smissen-Wackenier, Sara. "Re: Family Studies." Email to author. 29 June 2005.
_____. "Re: Family Studies." Email to author. 25 July 2005.
_____. Interview by author. Heverlee, Belgium. 08 September 2004.
van der Woude, Marc. "DAWN Flanders: At least 245 new churches before the year 2015." Joel News 186-81. 09 April 1998. http://www.joelnews.nl/news-en/jn186.htm (site discontinued).
van Isacker, Karel. *Ontwijding*. Leuven: Davidsfond, 1989. Quoted in C. Mennen, *De Eucharistie als Mysterieviering*. http://www.latijnseliturgie.nl/nieuws/050515_lezing_pastoor_mennen.html (site discontinued).
van Nes (*née* den Boer), Christel. Email message to author. 26 October 2007.
van Nes, Hans. "ECV." Email to author. 20 September 2004.
Van Wijngaarden, Wout. "Rooms Katholieke Gebruiken Onze Houding?" *Evangelische Christengemeenten Vlaanderen Nieuwsbrief*, edited by Koen Schelstraete, 21/2-4; 22/1-3.
Vandelannoote, Dominique. "Bei uns in Deutschland." *Nieuwsbrief van de christengemeenten*, edited by Guido De Kegel, May-June 1984.
_____. Email to Richard Haverkamp. 18 August 2008.
Vandereyken, Eddy. "Afschied en intrede." *Evangelische Christengemeenten Vlaanderen Nieuwsbrief*, edited by Marc Ladon, 13/2.
Vanhecke, Frank. "Today we were executed, but we rise." Vlaams Blok Party. http://www.vlaamsblok.be/site_engels_index.shtml (site discontinued).
"Verantwoordelijke uitgever Nieuwsbrief van de Christengemeente." *Nieuwsbrief van de christengemeenten*, edited by Eric Rutten, 1986, no. 1.
Vergouwe, Jaap. "RE: Vergadering in Woesten." Email to author. 30 Jul 2005.
"Verslag Nationale Commissie. " 21 April 1997.
"Verslag Nationale Vergadering." 22 November 1997, Punt 14: Ontbinding Christengemeente Beveren.
Vleugels, Gie. Interview by author. Heverlee, Belgium. 14 August 2007.
Volf, Miroslav. "Community Formation as an Image of the Triune God." In *Community Formation in the Early Church and in the Church Today*, edited by Richard Longenecker, 213-37. Peabody, MA: Hendrickson, 2002.
_____. *After Our Likeness: The Church as the Image of the Trinity*. Cambridge: Eerdmans, 1998.
Voorhoeve, J. N. *Gelovigen vergaderd in de Naam van Jezus*. Den Haag: n.p., n.d.
Voorhoeve, J. N., editor. *Mededeelingen omtrent het werk Gods in onze dagen*. Vol. 186. N.p.: 's-Gravenhage, July 1919.
Voyé, Liliane, et al. *Belges Hereux et Satisfaits: Les Valeurs des Belges dan les annees 90*. Brussels: De Boeck-Wesmael, 1992.
"VVP—Gemeenten sluiten zich aan bij EAV." *EAV-nieuws*, edited by Don Zeeman, March-April 2002, 4.
"Waar naar toe?" *Evangelische Christengemeenten Vlaanderen Nieuwsbrief*, edited by Koen Schelstraete 22/2.
Wagner, C. Peter. "Homogenous Unit Principle." *The Evangelical Dictionary of World Missions*, edited by A. Scott Moreau et al., 455. Grand Rapids: Baker, 2000.
"Wallenstein Bible Chapel: The first thirty years, 1968-1998." N.p: n.p., n.d.
Ware, James. *The Mission of the Church in Paul's Letter to the Philippians in the context of Ancient Judaism*. Leiden: Brill, 2005.

Bibliography

Way-Way, Dibudi. "The African Christian diaspora in Belgium with special reference to the International Church of Brussels." *International Review of Missions* 89 (2000) 451–96.

"Weeral een nieuwe gemeente? Ja, te Kortrijk." *Nieuwsbrief van de christengemeenten*, edited by Eric Rutten, no. 1.

"Welkom bij de Protestantse Kerk in Nederland." De Protestantse Kerk in Nederland. http://www.pkn.nl/.

"Welkom." Evangelische Toerustingschool Vlaanderen. http://www.ets-vlaanderen.be/index.php?id=21.

Weremchuk, Max S. *John Nelson Darby*. Neptune, NJ: Loizeaux, 1992.

West, Gerald. "Worship and the Lord's Supper." *Christian Brethren Review* 39 (1988) 53–62.

"Wijziginen:" *Nieuwsbrief van de christengemeenten*, edited by Marc Ladon, 13/3.

Wilkerson, David. *The Cross and the Switchblade*. New York: Berkley, 1976.

Williams, Ritva. *Stewards, Prophets, Keeper of the Word: Leadership in the Early Church*. Peabody, MA: Hendrickson, 2006.

Willis, Chuck. *What Am I Living For?* Words and music by Fred Jay and Art Harris. Atlantic Recording Corporation, 1958.

Wilson, Bryan R. "'The Brethren': A Current Sociological Appraisal." Cult Awareness and Information Center. http://www.caic.org.au/biblebase/brethren/soc%20appraisal.htm.

Wolston, W. T. P. "Another Comforter." In *Thirteen Lectures on the Operation of the Holy Ghost*, 4th ed. N.p.: n.p., 1945. *Mighty Men* CD-ROM. Kent: STEM, 1999.

———. "King David's New Cart." In *The Church: What is It? Mighty Men* CD-ROM. Kent: STEM, 1999.

Workers of the ECV. Letter to all in the ECV, May 1990.

Worship. Windsor, ON: Turner Road Chapel, 1995.

Yuille, William. "Commendation." In *Global Strategy: The Biblical Plan of Mission*, rev. ed., 37–48. N.p.: CMML/MSC, 1999.

"Zendings werk Binnen de E.C.V." 23 November 2002.

Index of Names

ECV Fulltime Workers in bold

Allaert, Johan, 129
Anastasi, Rosario, 122, 131–32, 135, 165, 173, 194, 196–198, 200, 239–40, 258

Bloemen, Jo, 196
Blondeel, Robert, 125
Biesbrouck, Antoon, 125
Biesbrouck, Bart, 198
Brockhaus, Carl, 31–32

Crana, Carmen, 102, 124
Cremers, François (Sus), 198–99

Darby, J. N., 23–24, 31, 38, 45, 47, 50, 145–47, 182, 211
de Bock, Hugo, 129
De Kegel, Guido, 97–99, 141, 171, 173, 176–79, 192–94, 196–98, 200, 212, 216–18, 228, 238–40, 246–48, 250, 258
den Boer, John, 83–86, 88, 111, 113, 116–20, 126, 150, 158, 164, 172–73, 177, 189, 191–92, 237, 246, 258
Denville, Pierre, 141
Dryburgh, Anne, 138–40, 226, 240, 258
Dunlap, David, 133–36, 171, 258

Fijnvandraat, Jaap G., 207, 209–10
Fijnvandraat, Johan Ph., 209
Fleming, Kenneth, 51–53, 163

Frey, Ezra, 174

Gaudibert, Georges F., 34
Gelling, Beryl (Mrs. Gelling), 72, 75–82, 88, 90, 92, 96, 122, 236
Gelling, Henk, 59, 63, 72, 74–83, 85–96, 99–100, 111–16, 120–22, 125, 130–32, 135–37, 149, 151, 155–58, 160, 164–66, 168, 172–76, 183–86, 189–93, 198, 201, 207–10, 212, 216, 218, 222–23, 226, 228, 235–37, 239–40, 243–46, 248–49, 251, 258
Gelling, Julie, 122–23, 149, 200, 239–40, 258
Gielen, Gerard, 196, 198, 244,
Gifford, Peter, 99–103, 124, 129, 138, 151, 179, 226, 233, 240, 244, 258
Gooding, David, 176, 178, 207
Goossens, Wilfried, 193
Graham, Billy, 75, 85, 158, 226,
Groen, Joanna (Mrs. Gifford), 100–101, 124, 129

Hanssens, Guillaume, 26–27, 29
Hanssens, Jacques, 27
Hanssens, Jean-Baptiste, 27
Hausoul, Raymond, 200, 258
Haverkamp, Marina (Mrs. Haverkamp), 64, 66–67, 69–71, 73, 88, 90, 124, 151, 161, 167

Index of Names

Haverkamp, Richard, 59, 61–74, 76, 80–82, 85–96, 98–102, 104–10, 114–15, 119, 121, 123–28, 134–35, 138, 144, 146–47, 149–51, 153–76, 180, 183–86, 189, 191–93, 195, 197–98, 201, 205–8, 210, 212–15, 218–19, 222–26, 228–29, 233, 235–49, 251, 258
Heikoop, Henry, 108, 258
Hengeveld, Gerard-Jan, 28, 31
Hoffman, Israel, 69
Hutchkins, Erich, 84

Kunst, Theo, 128

Le Jeune, Theo, 126–127, 216, 246
Lenaerts, Pieter, 258
Lennox, John, 208
Lindsay, Hal, 106, 159
Little, Paul, 159, 162
Luesink, Martin, 107, 213, 258
Lukasse, Johan, 84, 154n47, 213

MacLeod, David, 143–44
Mackintosh, C. H., 110
Maeyens, Luc, 141
Mantels, Freddy, 141, 196–97
Martin, Gord, 242
Martin, John, 68–69, 81, 147
Medema, Henk, 208, 210
Message, Leslie, 84
Müller, Georg, 85, 201, 201n248

Nock, William, 33–36
Nullens, Patrick, vii, 177–78, 247

Ouweneel, Willem, 110, 207, 209–10

Palau, Louis, 158
Pieper, Rinus, 126–27
Piérard, Ghislain, 34–35, 141
Piérard, Mme. Ghislain, 36
Pieters, Wim, 196

Roan, Winston, 60
Rommel, Jacque, 218
Rutten, Eric, 86, 125–26, 125, 194, 196, 198, 258

Schelstraete, Koen, 200, 258
Schraepen, Erik, 118–20, 168, 258
Shindelka, Herb, 59–63, 74, 81, 86–91, 93–95, 104–6, 157, 164–66, 189, 205, 212–13, 218–19, 244, 246, 258
Steenhuis, Dato, 207, 209–10
Stephenson, Bob and Carole, 79
Swaan, Lawrence, 212
Swiers, Jan, 196
Symons, Martin, 109–13, 125, 173, 176, 189, 195–96, 200, 237, 240, 244, 258

Tapernoux, Marc, 27
Thomas, Yvan, 146, 158–59, 161–62, 182, 225
Threadcraft, Hal, 101, 127–29, 135, 179, 244–46, 258
Tinder, Donald, vii, 55

van de Berk, Adri and Petra, 121
Van Der Smissen, Piérre, 28–29
Van Der Smissen, Aloysius (also Louis or Lodewijk), 6, 28–30
Vandelannoote, Dominique, 129, 141
Vandevorst, Luc, 137, 258
Vanhaelewijn, Paul, 196
Vermaut, Kristof, 258
Vleugels, Gie, 84
Voorhoeve, H. C., 26, 30–31
Voorhoeve, J. N., 30–31, 209
Voskamp, Marian, 102, 124
Vosters, Rudi, 196

Wagemans, Jos, 198
Welvaert, Hubert, 198
Willems, Jos, 198

Index of Places

All locations are in Belgium unless otherwise indicated

Antwerp, 14, 31, 32–34, 61, 231
Arolsen, DE, 129–30
Avelgem, 136

Baarel-Nassau/Hertog, 117
Beerse, 83, 104, 106–8, 114–15, 213
Berchem, 34, 81, 95, 104–5, 114, 126, 152, 167, 198
Beveren, 104–5, 124
Blizen, 137
Boom, 126–127, 141
Brakel, DE, 129–30
Brussels, 6, 15–16, 19, 26–31, 34–36, 230

Edegem, 74, 104–105
Eeklo, 99, 107, 123–24, 127, 129, 138, 197, 214

Geel, 120–121
Gent, 28, 32, 57, 98–99, 107, 138, 152, 167, 205, 210–11
Gentbrugge, 123–24, 127, 138–39, 197, 205, 214, 241
Guigoven, 137

Hasselt, 122
Ham, 86, 108, 116–17, 191
Hamont, 109, 111–12
Heerlen, NL, 64, 108, 111–12
Houthalen, 114, 116, 120–21, 130, 152, 208–10, 214

Ieper, 32, 123–26, 219
Izegem, 124

Koersel, 107–8, 114–17, 120, 151, 168, 172
Kortrijk, 98, 136
Koudekerk aan de Rijn, NL, 73
Kuurne, 126, 136, 205

Lanaken, 121, 215
Lommel, 116, 120, 169, 171
Lovendegem, 99, 123, 127
Leopoldsburg, 86, 108, 117–18, 126

Maldegem, 127, 138, 152
Mariakerke, 124, 137–38, 197
Mechelen (Malines), 36
Meeuwen, 114
Menen, 32, 36, 57
Moorsele, 124–26

Neerpelt, 109
Nieuwpoort, 32
Ninove, 28–32

Oudenaarde, 98, 127
Overpelt, 108–9, 111–13, 116

Peer, 108–109, 111–15, 126, 151, 156, 186, 223

Reet, 126

Index of Places

Riksingen, 137
Roeselare, 123–26, 136, 186

Sittard, 112
Soest, DE, 129–30

Tessenderlo, 108, 117–21
Tienen (Tirlemont), 36, 103, 141, 205–6

Veldegem, 32
Vliermaal, 137

Waregem, 36, 205
Waterschei, 130
Wellen, 137, 244
Wervik, 124–26
Wevelgem, 123–25, 136
Wijchmaal, 114
Wijshagen, 114
Winterslag, 130
Woesten, 32

Zutendaal, 121
Zwartberg, 130–33

www.ingramcontent.com/pod-product-compliance
Lightning Source LLC
Chambersburg PA
CBHW071236230426
43668CB00011B/1468